# PUBLIC RELATIONS IN HYPER-GLOBALIZATION

Public relations is the essential skill top leaders need to inspire and motivate globalized stakeholders, survive crisis, and take advantage of rapid technological and social change in today's hyper-globalization. Embedding this book's ethics-based "self-correction model" assures governance to navigate a rapidly changing global environment. The book's unique strategic PR Life-Cycle Model brings the power of PR to achieve goals fast, economically, and consistently.

**Takashi Inoue** is CEO of Inoue Public Relations and Visiting Professor at Kyoto University's Graduate School of Management, Akita International University, and Communication University of China. He has over 45 years in public relations, and has published three PR books. He has presented numerous speeches on public relations, and is also creator of the "PR Life-Cycle" and "PR Self-Correction" models.

T0393968

# PUBLIC RELATIONS IN HYPER-GLOBALIZATION

## Essential Relationship Management – A Japan Perspective

*Takashi Inoue*

Routledge
Taylor & Francis Group

LONDON AND NEW YORK

First published 2018
by Routledge
2 Park Square, Milton Park, Abingdon, Oxon OX14 4RN

and by Routledge
711 Third Avenue, New York, NY 10017

*Routledge is an imprint of the Taylor & Francis Group, an informa business*

*British Library Cataloguing-in-Publication Data*
A catalogue record for this book is available from the British Library

*Library of Congress Cataloging-in-Publication Data*
Names: Inoue, Takashi, 1944- author.
Title: Public relations in hyper-globalization : essential relationship management : a Japan perspective / by Takashi Inoue.
Description: First Edition. | New York : Routledge, 2018. | Includes bibliographical references and index.
Identifiers: LCCN 2017047485| ISBN 9781138054950 (hardback) | ISBN 9781138054967 (pbk.) | ISBN 9781315166315 (ebook)
Subjects: LCSH: Public relations. | Public relations—Japan. | Leadership. | Crisis management.
Classification: LCC HD59 .I556 2018 | DDC 659.20952—dc23
LC record available at https://lccn.loc.gov/2017047485

ISBN: 978-1-138-05495-0 (hbk)
ISBN: 978-1-138-05496-7 (pbk)
ISBN: 978-1-315-16631-5 (ebk)

Typeset in Bembo
by Apex CoVantage, LLC

MIX
Paper from
responsible sources
FSC
www.fsc.org    FSC™ C013985

Printed in the United Kingdom
by Henry Ling Limited

# CONTENTS

# FIGURES

# INTRODUCTION

Here at the start of the 21st century, almost every aspect of business is being globalized, the third-world country that was China is now the second largest economy, social media has rapidly become a major form of instantaneous global communication, and a number of new technologies, such as the Internet of Things (IoT), big data analytics, and artificial intelligence (AI) are all bringing even more far-reaching change. This dramatic transformation is continuing to accelerate, and where it will ultimately lead is not clear. Although, for Ray Kurzweil, who is a futurist, it seems clear that we are moving toward a world of "Singularity," where Man will become a "hybrid of biological and non-biological thinking" (Del Prado, 2015) with little difference between Man and machine. While these changes might point to a bright future, the top news stories in any given week speak of a dangerous and unstable world with many deep-seated problems. England has voted for Brexit, which casts a shadow over the future of the European Union. The U.S. has withdrawn from both the 2015 Paris Agreement on climate change, and the Trans-Pacific Partnership (TPP) negotiations. We have gone from a unipolar world at the end of the Cold War to a multi-polar world, where the U.S. is being challenged by other global powers. Global terrorism is now threatening the lives of ordinary citizens throughout the world. And yet, as a public relations professional for over 45 years, I am convinced and confident that no matter how many problems surround us, public relations, which is stakeholder relationship management, can teach leaders of organizations, businesses, governments, and nations an essential skill needed to survive and prosper in these difficult times.

Unfolding before our eyes is a radically new environment, which I call hyper-globalization, where people and cultures are undergoing deep sociological transformation, for which the pace of change is continuing to accelerate. It is being driven by the three forces of an expansive growth in global trade volumes along with extensive economic integration, by digital communications of the Internet and social media, and by all those disruptive technologies in Kurzweil's future world of Singularity. Your employees are not just citizens of one country, they are citizens of numerous countries with widely differing cultures, languages, and levels of economic development. The same is true for the other types of stakeholders, such as investors, suppliers, dealers, customers, and government regulators. In this new hyper-globalized environment, where stakeholders have become multi-dimensional and communications has become global and instantaneous, and where technologies such as AI will redefine the very word "labor," you as a leader must learn, master, and use public relations.

In the late 1990s the International Public Relations Association (IPRA) assembled various experts, practitioners and scholars to study the role of PR in globalization, and as a board member I was the chairman of that special project. This resulted in the publishing of *The Evolution of Public Relations Education and the Influence of Globalisation* in which I wrote: "In global institutions and companies it is acknowledged that public relations specialists need to be included in the decision making process for important management strategies" (Inoue, 1997, p. 7). This remains true, but today the world is far more complex. It is no longer enough to just include public relations specialists in the development and implementation of major strategies. The leader of an organization must also have a degree of fluency in public relations in order to carry out stakeholder relationship management that will achieve the organization's goals in this new environment. In short, public relations has gone from being something that can add great value to any organization to being something it cannot survive or thrive without.

Why is this true? Effective public relations today is essentially relationship management, where two-way communications is used to maintain a dialogue with the various relevant stakeholders to accomplish an organization's goals, while at the same time satisfying needs of those same stakeholders. Public relations is not just about finding the best way to communicate your message. It is not propaganda, where one-way communications is used as a tool to control people. Although it is used in public relations, it is also not advertising, which tries to persuade people about the value of a product or a point of view. There is no one public nor one type of stakeholder, and therefore there cannot be only one message. Moreover, central to this two-way communications process used in relationship management is the need to listen to stakeholders so that changes and corrections can be made to messages being sent and to the very products, services, and benefits that an organization provides.

When he returned in 1997 to transform Apple from a failing company into the largest and most successful corporation of today, Steve Jobs had to win over stakeholders, such as the application development community. To engage them in a two-way communications process, Apple held a Worldwide Developers Conference, where a skeptical developer asked in a hostile voice why a certain application was being dropped. Up until then, Steve Jobs had been walking around the stage of this conference very much in control and very self-confident. Jobs suddenly sat down, looked at the floor in silence, and made no immediate response to the question. There is always risk in any honest dialogue, but he was willing to take that risk, and understood the importance of such two-way communications with stakeholders and the importance of listening and self-correction, all of which are core skills of public relations. Steve Jobs stood up and carefully began his reply: "One of the things that I have always found is that you have to start with the customer experience and work backwards to the technology" (Cane, 1997). Customers, he explained, will buy technology that creates the most value for them, rather than technology that is most valued by developers. After Jobs finished his reply, this critical stakeholder group applauded with great enthusiasm.

This book is based on my book *Public Relations*, which was first published in Japanese in 2006, and which was revised in a second edition in 2015, published as *Public Relations: Relationship Management*. However, this international version in English has been updated with new case studies, and reoriented for global executives and leaders, who will need public relations skills in the new environment of today. And my Self-Correction Model has been given a more central focus in this book, because of the growing occurrence in Japan and other major countries of scandals, caused by a failure to embed an ethics-based process of self-correction that ensures success in times of crisis management and allows you to more assuredly take advantage of challenges and major external changes to achieve your goals.

It is also a Japanese perspective based on my experience of running my own public relations firm in Tokyo, and from my teaching effective stakeholder relationship management at Waseda University to the next generation of leaders. In recent years I have been teaching public relations at the Graduate School of Management of Kyoto University, including at its Asia Business Leadership Program. And there I have had the pleasure to work with colleagues from the top MBA schools of Asia and from whom I have often heard the words: "Japan is our model."

This appreciation for Japan is surprising, when I think of what Japan did to people in these countries in World War II. But, talking to these colleagues in more detail, I have found that most have grown up in the post-war period with happy memories as children watching Japanese animation (anime) and other enjoyable encounters with Japanese culture. When they visit Tokyo and Kyoto, they look at a rebuilt post-war Japan that has made it to the top level of the industrialized world and at the same time has maintained a rich traditional culture. More importantly, in Japan of today these scholars from Asia appear to see what they hope will be the future of their own countries.

However, public relations in Asia and throughout the developing world is not as well advanced and appreciated as needed. Their race to economic development is somewhat reminiscent of Japan's own history of development from a feudal society to becoming a major force in the modern world. And, like Japan of the past, these developing countries have been so focused on catching up economically that public relations has not been a priority. After the war, Japanese companies primarily used advertising agencies, which provided what they called public relations, but which was no more than publicity. Adding to this is a culture in Japan that values humility and avoids expressing things directly and in great detail. In this "high-context culture" that approach works, but it does not translate globally outside the country. This has unfortunate consequences. In the case of Japan, the lack of public relations has shown itself in various ways, but most notably in the surprisingly low standing that even the most global Japanese companies have among the top 100 globally recognized brands. To succeed globally today requires creating and maintaining global brands, which requires public relations skills. For leaders in the rapidly developing world, lack of public relations is a mistake that needs to be avoided through a full understanding and utilization of public relations.

While Japan has created a unique social system and culture formed in large part by the fact that it is an island nation, it transformed itself into a modern industrial state through a repeated process of trial and error. Excluding the Soviet Union, by 1970 Japan's GDP made it the second largest economy in the free world. Japan was no longer a "developing nation." In 1975 the first global summit of the richest industrial countries, the so-called G6 at the time, which would grow to the G8, met in Rambouillet, France, and joining them was Japan's Prime Minister Takeo Miki as the only non-Western head of state. By 1980 Japanese automakers were number one in the world, and were even producing more passenger cars than their U.S. competitors. But, with the collapse of Japan's bubble economy in the 1990s, until the present day, it has become clear that every aspect of Japanese society, whether politics, the economy, or culture is suffering from structural fatigue and dysfunction. Japan has been trying to move toward a new social system, but with only limited success. Indeed, when viewed from an international viewpoint, particularly in terms of addressing such global problems as the environment, famine, over-population, and ethnic conflicts, Japan is finding it difficult to play a role in keeping with its stature as a leading nation, which I believe strongly is another consequence of a general lack of public relations skills. For leaders looking for a good understanding of public relations in the 21st century, a study of public relations from the perspective of Japan will provide deep insights that are applicable to all nations, but especially to those in Asia and in other non-English speaking countries.

Writing about an earlier age, some two centuries ago in a time of great change, Charles Dickens began *A Tale of Two Cities*: "It was the best of times, it was the worst of times, it was the age of wisdom, it was the age of foolishness ..." As this book is being written there are also many global problems characterizing our times. Although PR is used extensively in all levels of government, its full potential is still not fully appreciated. Public relations is centered on identifying publics within the overall public and then identifying those publics which are the organization's stakeholders. To achieve organization goals, the type of public relations described in this book involves establishing two-way communications with those stakeholders and creating mutual understanding. Public relations is not used to help the organization persuade stakeholders in terms only favorable to the organization. Thus, true PR for the 21st century is aimed at creating win-win outcomes for both parties, and this means also making self-corrections in what the organization seeks. If nations, and their diplomats, obtain a full understanding of public relations, which this book provides, they will be able to apply the power of PR as an "instrument of peace" that greatly reduces conflict between nations through two-way communications and self-correction aimed at producing a wide benefit for all stakeholders, rather than simply pursuing narrowly the national interest.

A new century is well underway filled with both promise and challenge. The future is ours to make, and if we are to leave a world truly worth living in to future generations, then we must do a better job at creating peace and sustainability. And it is critical that we ensure that all the many far-reaching technological advances, which are rapidly developing all around us, are governed by ethics. In the final chapter of this book I detail my ethics-based Self-Correction Model (Inoue, 2002, pp. 24–27), explain the theory, show actual examples, and discuss the need to embed it into every organization. My hope in writing this book is for you to become a global leader who can apply the discipline of ethics-centered public relations in this most challenging time of hyper-globalization to realize a better world.

August 15, 2017, Tokyo
Takashi Inoue, Ph.D.

## References

Cane, M. (1997). "Steve Jobs Insult Response (Steve Jobs at the 1997 WWDC)." *YouTube*. [Online] Available at: https://www.youtube.com/watch?v=FF-tKLISfPE.

Del Prado, G. M. (2015). "Google Futurist Ray Kurzweil Thinks We'll All Be Cyborgs by 2030." *Business Insider*, June 6, 2015. [Online] Available at: http://www.businessinsider.com/ray-kurzweil-thinks-well-all-be-cyborgs-by-2030-2015-6 [Accessed November 8, 2017]

Inoue, T. (1997). "Evolution of Public Relations Education and the Influence of Globalisation, Survey of Eight Countries." *IPRA – Gold Paper No. 12*.

Inoue, T. (2002). "The Need for Two-Way Communications and Self-Correction (erratum, March 2003)." *IPRA Frontline*.

# 1

# PUBLIC RELATIONS FOR TOP MANAGEMENT IN AN AGE OF HYPER-GLOBALIZATION

## 1 2011 Great East Japan Earthquake and Fukushima Nuclear Plant disaster

Earthquakes and typhoons are a normal recurring part of life in Japan, but the combined earthquake, tsunami, and related nuclear mega-disaster event, known as the "Great East Japan Earthquake," surpassed all past natural catastrophes in the long history of the island nation of Japan. Yet, its significance for Japan and for the world goes far beyond just the extensive damage and disruption to life and property. It dramatically made clear just how globalized and integrated we on planet earth have become in both our economic and social activities.

The magnitude-9 earthquake that hit eastern Japan on March 11, 2011 and the subsequent tsunami that hit the northeastern coast killed some 18,000 persons and caused property damage to buildings and infrastructure of some USD $156 billion. The recovery cost has been estimated at over USD $250 billion (Prime Minister of Japan, 2012). It also triggered a nuclear plant accident that threatened the lives of nations around the Pacific Rim. Although there have been similar disasters in the past that have had a greater toll on human life, such as the 2004 earthquake and tsunami that hit Sumatra and killed over 230,000 people, the 2011 disaster in Japan stands out as more consequential, because:

- Use of social media during and after the event demonstrated the extent and meaning of the words the "the global village,"
- Disruption of the global supply chain showed just how vast globalization of manufacturing has become,
- Lack of crisis management skills by the Japanese government and Tokyo Electric Power Company (TEPCO), which operates the Fukushima Nuclear Plant, and more consequentially, the failure by TEPCO to follow an ethics-based Self-Correction Model, all showed dramatically the importance of public relations.

## Role of social media

While traditional mass media immediately made known to the world the disaster as it was occurring on March 11, it was social media, in particular Twitter and Facebook, that connected people globally with the event in ways never before experienced, allowing millions around the world to almost simultaneously hold their breath as they waited for the approach of an enormous wall of water, which would reached as high as 38.9 meters in Iwate Prefecture (NOAA (National Oceanic and Atmospheric Administration), n.d.), to hit the coastline of northeast Japan. And again, after the tsunami, social media, far more than traditional news media, brought people around the world the details of the unfolding drama of a nuclear plant meltdown. This was made more shocking by the plant's location in a country with one of the world's highest population densities, and, because of the meltdown, there was a possibility of radiation spreading globally through the air, the seas, and the global food chain.

Although Facebook became available to the public only in 2006, by 2011 it already had 800 million active participants. Similarly, Twitter, with its limited character messaging, also started in 2006 and by 2011 had 200 million users (Peary *et al.*, 2012). Between the years 2006 and 2011 there were several major disasters, such as the California wildfires in 2007, Tropical Storm Ondoy in the Philippines in 2009, and the Haiti earthquake in 2010. In each of these events, these two Internet platforms proved that social media has become a vital communications tool for rescue efforts. But, in the case of Japan's 2011 earthquake and tsunami, for the first time social media allowed ordinary persons to participate in actual reporting and commenting on a global news event, and doing so in near real-time as it was happening. This was unique and it set the stage for the reporting of all future global events.

Social media allowed ordinary individuals to create, share, and discuss news content as events were happening. A number of people living on the coast of northeast Japan on March 11 actually took the time as they made their way in desperation to the safety of higher ground to pause and take dramatic photos and video with their cellphones of the approaching tsunami. These pictures were eventually broadcast to the world by both social media and by traditional news media.

Japan is densely populated, but the northeast, especially Fukushima Prefecture, is actually a historically under-populated part of the nation, and there was simply no time or way by which journalists in the more populated areas in and around Tokyo could reach the affected area in time to capture scenes to the same extent as the social media participants that were already on the scene.

During and after the initial dramatic events of March 11, people in and outside of Japan used social media to contact friends and family. Social media was also effective in providing a lifeline to those directly affected by the disaster, raising donations online and providing information to volunteers inside and outside Japan.

## Global supply chain disruption

Globalization of trade is no longer simply exporting goods made in one country to another. The supply chain of material inputs to the manufacturing process from raw materials to finished components is now globalized. This became suddenly very visible with the East Japan Earthquake, because Japan as the world's third largest economy is a global supplier of materials and component parts, especially in the automotive, semiconductor, and consumer electronics industries.

Just as Toyota was impacted in Japan, General Motors in America and Peugeot Citroën in France also had to halt some vehicle production lines, because of a dependence on Japanese part suppliers. Furthermore, the global supply chain is complex with multiple tiers of suppliers. It is not just a matter of Japanese part supplier "A" failing to deliver to company "B." In an April 15, 2011 report in *MIT News Office*, Jennifer Chu explained how the East Japan disaster could reduce production and global distribution of Apple's iPad 2, because Mitsubishi in Japan makes an epoxy resin that is used by a Taiwan semiconductor producer for parts that are shipped to the China assembler (Chu, 2011).

In addition to this complexity of multi-tier interdependence in the global supply chain, it is even more vulnerable to disruption because of the common practice of keeping inventories of parts at a minimum as part of "just-in-time" production.

## Public relations failure

The Japanese government, from the office of the Prime Minister, Naoto Kan, to the many government agencies involved with oversight of the nuclear power plant, and the plant operator, TEPCO, displayed a complete lack of coordination, cooperation, and competent crisis management, giving the world and the Japanese public the sense that the situation was out of control. Writing in Japan's *Yomiuri Shimbun* about PR and the Fukushima nuclear disaster, the author explained that,

> the Japanese government's lack of PR skill in the disaster made citizens fear a worst-case scenario. And it also resulted in overseas reporting that tended to further exaggerate the situation. Moreover, the Japanese government did not adequately disclose facts to the local governments, and this lack of two-way communications added to the sense of danger
>
> *(Inoue, 2011, p. 11).*

Contributing to this, the prime minister made himself the person announcing the size of the evacuation zone around the nuclear plant, and as information about the situation changed, he kept changing the size from 3 to 10 and then to a 20 kilometer radius, without explaining the reasons behind the changes (Wharton School of the University of Pennsylvania, 2013). The public became distrustful of the government and an impression was created that the government was lying or hiding the true gravity of the situation. As this author explained to *The New York Times*, the government also failed to consolidate all the various reports coming from numerous government and private sources. The parties involved, TEPCO, the nuclear regulatory agency, and the office of the prime mister, each held news conferences, but they presented a blizzard of facts and numbers. On top of that, they almost never made broader statements about the extent of the crisis (Bradsher & Tabuchi, 2011). TEPCO also added to the problem by not adequately communicating with the government and the public.

Crisis communications by these parties could and should have been better at transmitting accurate information to the public, but one needs to also remember that public relations is not just effective communication of information. Modern public relations is not one-way communications. It is two-way communications that provide an organization with needed feedback from all their various stakeholders so that it can change and improve its own activities. To that end, a self-correction process based on ethics and two-way communication, which is fundamental to public relations, must be functioning within the organization.

The failure of TEPCO in handling the aftermath of the tsunami is not a case of a well-run and ethical enterprise simply being overrun by a once-in-1,000-years natural disaster. Rather it is the case of an enterprise with a long and consistent record of ethical failings in the years leading up to March 2011. Mistakes happen, but the point of a self-correction system is to learn from past failings. A company like TEPCO seems to be unable to learn from past mistakes, when we examine the companies past scandals:

- 2002 admission of falsifying safety test results on Fukushima Unit 1 reactor's containment vessel,
- 2003 refusal to allow regulators in to inspect reactors, and later admitting to systematic cover-up of data showing reactor cracks,
- 2007 cover-up of hundreds of gallons of radioactive water leakage, after a fire following a minor earthquake (Ferris & Solis, 2013).

We often hear the slogan: "stronger together." A company like TEPCO certainly does have many good and ethical individual employees, some of whom selflessly and heroically risked their lives in the hours and days after the nuclear accident, but as an organization TEPCO, lacking ethics and self-correction, almost seemed to be following a theme of "weaker together."

In contrast, the JX Nippon Oil and Energy Corporation had learned from the earlier Kobe earthquake in 1995, and although their Sendai refinery was devastated in March 2011, it was successful in getting emergency energy supplies where they were most critically needed by working with both government and competitors (Wharton School of the University of Pennsylvania, 2013, p. 8).

As will be discussed further on in this book, while organizations can and do achieve many wonderful things, creating new value that benefits society, the actions of organizations are, in the end, the collective actions of individuals. As the individual members are not perfect, an organization must implement a process of continual self-correction based on ethics, and on an understanding of human free-will, which allows us to choose to act or not act ethically. As Kiyoshi Kurokawa, who was the chairman of the National Diet of Japan Fukushima Nuclear Accident Independent Investigation Commission, expressed so well: "It was a profoundly man-made disaster that could and should have been foreseen and prevented" (Wharton School of the University of Pennsylvania, 2013, p. 4). Unfortunately, the importance of self-correction is generally absent in organizations like TEPCO, which can be said to be the true underlying cause of the nuclear accident of 2011.

The Great East Japan disaster of 2011 brought to the forefront the reality that without a true commitment to ethics and self-correction embedded into the very DNA of an organization, when a crisis of great magnitude occurs, a company will react to events without the aid of ethics to guide it, and therefore, greatly reduce its ability to bring about a successful conclusion that would allow it to smoothly begin the process of rebuilding and recovering.

Poor public relations skills in a crisis have devastating consequences for any organization. Japan's Prime Minister, Naoto Kan resigned on August 26, 2011 over criticism of his handling of the March 11 disaster, and his Democratic Party of Japan (DPJ) lost the election that followed in 2012. TEPCO, which had been considered one of the pillars of corporate Japan, with around 750,000 employees and with its corporate debt accounting for some 8% of the entire domestic debt market, saw its stock price decline 80% from JPY 2,121 to 420. As of December 29, 2016 the price was still only at JPY 472. At TEPCO's June 2011 shareholder's meeting one investor reportedly yelled out: "Throw yourself into a nuclear reactor and die!" (The Economist, 2011).

## 2  What is hyper-globalization?

In this book you may be seeing the word "hyper-globalization" for the first time, although you will undoubtedly have continually come across the word "globalization." And the word seems to explain so well the direction the world is headed. Much of what we all buy is imported. So many of our businesses operate across national boundaries. More people travel the globe than ever before. Our communications, thanks to the Internet, have become instant and global. Yet, does the word "globalization" explain enough about the forces so dramatically shaping our lives and surrounding world with challenges, such as global terror, climate change, and both over-population and depopulation, that seem to threaten the very existence of mankind? The word hyper-globalization as used here is an attempt to more broadly explain the changes taking place in the 21st century that go beyond just the economic factors that are usually associated with "globalization."

Jagdish Bhagwati describes what he calls "economic globalization" as a positive force that results in the "integration of national economies into the international economy through trade, direct foreign investment by corporations and multinationals, short-term capital flows, international flows of workers and humanity generally, and flows of technology" (Bhagwati, 2004).

Pankaj Ghemawat of the Harvard Business School, writes that the term "global" came into use at the end of the 19th century to mean "world scale" and then in the 1940s the word "globalize" started to appear, but not until 1951 did the term "globalization" first appear. Looking at the U.S. Library of Congress catalog listings, Ghemawat found that in the 1990s the library "listed less than 50 publications per year related to globalization" but that "from 2002 to 2008 there were more than 1100 every year" (Ghemawat, n.d.).

In 2013 the term "hyper-globalization" appeared in the work of economists Arvind Subramanian and Martin Kessler of the Peterson Institute for International Economics to describe the "deep economic integration" of international trade that has occurred since the 1990s: "The world is now in a fourth era—of hyperglobalization—in which world trade has soared much more rapidly than world GDP" (Subramanian & Kessler, 2013, p. 4). They describe four stages of globalization as follows:

- Stage 1, Golden Age of international trade starting with the Industrial Revolution, between 1870 and 1914, where world trade as a share of GDP jumped from 9% to 16%.
- Stage 2, 1914 through the end of the Second World War, where GDP share of world trade actually plunged to 5.5%, as the world entered a prolonged period of protectionism and world war.
- Stage 3, after the Second World War, where by the 1970s trade levels finally returned to what they had been in the Golden Age.
- Stage 4, Hyper-globalization begins suddenly in the 1990s and international flow of goods and services dramatically increased to 33%.

In 2016 Professor Dani Rodrik, an economist at the John F. Kennedy School of Government at Harvard University wrote an opinion piece in *The New York Times* that he titled "Put Globalization to Work for Democracies" in which he explains: "Simply put, we have pushed economic globalization too far – toward an impractical version that we might call 'hyperglobalization'…" (Rodrik, 2016).

However, while economists understandably see hyper-globalization in terms of international trade, there are also two additional forces, which are global communications of the Internet and social media, and the disruptive new technologies, such as big data, IoT, and AI. Together these three forces as shown in Figure 1.1 are creating a very challenging new environment.

Back in the 1960s, some 30 years before the explosive growth of international trade and the widespread use of the Internet and social media, Marshall McLuhan famously coined the term "the global village" (McLuhan, 1962, p. 40). The central insight embodied in the global village is that the technologies of electronic media,

| The three forces of hyper-globalization |
|---|
| ① **Economic force:** Expansive growth in global trade, and cross-border economic integration |
| ② **Human communications via the Internet force:** Instant nature of global communication via social media and the Internet are changing norms of human communication, blurring sociocultural barriers |
| ③ **Technological disruptive force:** New innovations in technology driven by IoT, big data, and AI are bringing massive economic and rapid social change, leading to the coming world of Singularity |

FIGURE 1.1 Takashi Inoue's three forces of hyper-globalization

which back then were primarily radio and television, were creating a new environment that changes how people see and experience and behave. In many ways, today's social media is vastly expanding that global village, creating a new global village.

The rise of social media occurred as a 21st century phenomenon, as can be seen in the growth of Facebook from 2006 when it first went public. In terms of monthly active users, Facebook reached 500 million in 2010, 800 million in 2011, and by the end of 2016 1.86 billion (Statista.com, n.d.). In this era, children are growing up experiencing instant global communications and social media just as naturally as they experience feeling the warmth of sunlight and breathing air.

We are now surrounded by new disruptive technologies related to the Internet. In particular, AI and big data are reshaping society and possibly even moving us rapidly into a world of Singularity, where the lines between Man and machine become blurred. It is also a world with over 21 million refugees and over 65 million "forcibly displaced persons" (UN Refugee Agency, 2015, p. 2). And, while the economic integration of hyper-globalization has helped hundreds of millions in the third world enter the middle-class, it has also created economic decline in the developed world, issues of climate change and sustainability. Global terror has become common and it is being fostered by technologies such as social media.

While Subramanian and Kessler set the 1990s as the start of hyper-globalization as a purely economic phenomenon, Facebook and Twitter began publicly in 2006 and reached global dominance with 800 hundred million active users by 2011 as mentioned previously, and in that same year Apple released for the iPhone its AI voice recognition application, SIRI. Kurzweil forecasts that Singularity will occur by 2045. This new environment of hyper-globalization, which is still in the process of being created by the three forces, can be said to have begun in 2011, which interestingly is also the year of the Great East Japan Earthquake. The great challenge of the 21st century is to see and understand clearly this very challenging new environment, for which the skill of strategic relationship management of public relations provides a tool of critical importance for the success of organizations.

## 3 Difference between public relations as communications management and public relations as stakeholder relationship management

Many scholars and practitioners have typically thought of public relations as communications management. In fact, public relations within corporations is often called the "communications department." James E. Grunig and Todd Hunt have described public relations as "the management of communications between an organization and its publics," but they also have described the two-way symmetrical process that gives publics a voice in management, in which "Citizens speak up, often forcing organizations to make changes the citizens demand" (Grunig & Hunt, 1984, pp. 8–10). And, writing about the role that communication management plays in public relations, Grunig wrote about "the nature of effective organizational communication, excellent public relations departments, and the contribution that effective communication makes to successful organizations" (Grunig & Dozier, 1992, p. 2).

Publics speak up because they are stakeholders that are impacted for better or worse by the actions of organizations. In the case of communications management, as the function for managing the communications of an organization, the focus is on the "messages being sent to publics" and the "means of sending them." In contrast, in the case of relationship management, the focus of public relations is on establishing an ongoing dialogue with specific stakeholders as the most efficient and effective way to achieve goals, through two-way communications to create a win–win for both sides. Public relations does involve managing communications, but to best achieve the goals of an organization, building positive relationships with stakeholders is required.

Stakeholder relations have become far more complex and vital, and public relations has in turn been transformed from communications with various publics into stakeholder relationship management, where now "stakeholders" are: [(Stakeholders) x (Cultures) x (Language) x (Level of Economic Development)]. While China is exporting half of all the goods and services that it produces to customers around the world, transnational companies, such as Nestle, Coca Cola, IBM, and Ikea, for example, are not just manufacturing and then exporting from a single country, or setting up manufacturing in multiple countries, they are splitting up manufacturing processes and locating design, development, and manufacturing across the globe. Customers, employees, business partners, shareholders, and government regulators are located globally and with different characteristics, desires, and goals that need to be reached, engaged, motivated, inspired, and persuaded through relationship management. Therefore, in this age of hyper-globalization public relations is more important than ever before.

## 4 Self-Correction Model: the key to achieving goals along the shortest path

Public relations should be defined as: relationship building activities based on "two-way communications" and "self-correction" that are supported by "ethics" to achieve the targets and objectives of individuals and organizations along the shortest path. As we discussed above, TEPCO management seemed to have believed that bypassing ethics was a shortcut to building and operating nuclear power plants in an environment in which the public was strongly anti-nuclear power, but in reality, it was only a shortcut for losing 80% of the company's net worth.

Public relations that is highly ethical and includes two-way communications with a self-correction function seeks to communicate information to "publics," such as markets, taxpayers, citizens, foreign governments, and international organizations, and will continuously analyze the feedback received and other relevant conditions, so that any communications error can be quickly corrected. Then, after planning new policies based on feedback, public relations will once again communicate and implement its message back to stakeholders. By continuously repeating these actions, it becomes possible to quickly respond to changing conditions and to achieve objectives. To say this in another way, it is simply impossible to guide all the related parties in the right "win–win" direction without being highly ethical, nor is it possible to continuously create the optimum environment to achieve objectives without an approach of receiving feedback on the information communicated and then applying better methods and correcting errors.

There are three keywords supporting the definition of public relations: "ethics," "two-way communication," and "self-correction." These concepts, although unfamiliar to Japanese society and other non-Western cultures, are vital elements to guide public relations activities to success, and can be said to be at the very heart of public relations. To deepen your understanding of the above definition, these concepts will be discussed one by one.

## Ethics

While animals simply react to their surrounding environment, human beings have always reflected on the great cosmic questions in search of truths that transcend time and space. It is a difficult task, but a uniquely human endeavor. Explained simply, ethics is an understanding that human activity is either good or evil, and that human beings will find happiness by pursuing that which is good rather than that which is evil.

Human beings need to work with others in society to survive and thrive, which is why public relations as stakeholder relationship management is so important. And stakeholders, which include customers, employees, and investors, not only seek behavior that is aligned to their own beneficial interests from businesses and other organizations, they also demand ethical behavior. While it is a deep philosophical subject that can be debated without-end as to what it means to be ethical, stakeholders have no trouble quickly judging and holding organizations accountable to what they believe is ethical. And, for that reason, "reputation management" is a special discipline within public relations.

The beginnings of ethics as a study go back to the time of the ancient Greek philosophers, Plato, Socrates, and Aristotle, who began to ask the great questions about the right way for a human being to live, and thereby started the study of "ethics." Aristotle (384–322 B.C.) wrote in his *Nicomachean Ethics* that "… moral virtue comes about as the result of habit …" (Cahn & Markie, 2002, p. 140) and was concerned that human beings should pursue a life filled with the habitual practice of virtues. The word "ethics" is derived from the ancient Greek word "ethos," meaning custom or character (Inoue, 2006, p. 4).

Aristotle considered ethics to be those habits or virtues that give human beings goodness and happiness. He applied it to the three human behaviors of "see," "do," and "make" and then divided philosophy into "theoretical science," "practical science," and "productive science." Within them he classified and determined ethics as belonging to "practical science." Today, based on Aristotle's classification, philosophy is broadly divided into "theoretical philosophy" and "practical philosophy" and ethics is positioned within practical philosophy (Inoue, 2006).

Subsequently, our thinking about ethics has changed alongside the changes of history from ethics as viewed from medieval Christianity by St. Augustine and St. Thomas Aquinas to early modern ethical thought. Modern English ethical thought is centered on the works of Thomas Hobbes and J. S. Mill, whilst the modern French view on ethics is dominated by Rousseau, and for the Germans,

Kant and Hegel did much to shape modern ethical thought. Ethics in present-day public relations is considered to have been built from the complementary relationship between the utilitarianism of Jeremy Bentham (Crimmins, 2017), who wrote of "the greatest happiness of the greatest number," and from the deontology, which means "duty" in Greek, of Immanuel Kant (Johnson, 2017), who argued that we must reach out from a sense of duty to help the minority, especially the poor and the weak.

Ethics can be said to be at the core of what it means to be human. In other words, that voice in our heads that tells us what is right and what is wrong is not a burden, it is what makes us human. Human beings are social creatures and human existence can be defined in terms of relationships. Therefore, our deepest experience as human beings comes when we create our own self through our relationship with others. This is also true for organizations as collections of individuals. If we were to ask why ethics is essential for public relations, both for individuals and organizations, the answer is we are moral creatures that desire and demand ethical behavior to find happiness.

If an organization does not have a deep commitment to ethics, it will narrowly pursue its goals and objectives, thinking it is taking the fastest route, but a time will come when stakeholders will hold it accountable for unethical behavior and its very survival will then come into question.

## Two-way communications

Public relations has undergone a historical development in the United States that was classified by Grunig into four models: one-way communication and two-way communication, which he further classified into asymmetrical and symmetrical types (Grunig & Hunt, 1984). The flow of information can be from one-way or two-way communications. As the term suggests, one-way signifies that the information sender communicates information to the other party (the receiver), while two-way indicates that information is sent in both directions between the original information sender and the information receiver. The two-way concept is frequently used in fields such as IT and telecommunications.

According to Grunig, asymmetrical two-way communications is a method for an organization (the information sender) to convince the public (the target) and to obtain its agreement, and it can use the feedback from the public to measure the effects of the information it communicated. Conversely, symmetrical two-way communications between the information sender and the public, in which both sides are the information sender and receiver, provides feedback that promotes mutual understanding.

The distribution of information is two-way in both the asymmetrical model and the symmetrical model, but the major difference between them is that in the former, the information sender affects and transforms the information receiver in a manner only advantageous to the sender, but in the latter, both parties affect and transform each other. It is often the case that the asymmetrical model is used when a company is trying to implement a belief held by the organization that is so strongly held that it could be said to be an "-ism" in a way like a religious belief, only it typically represents the thought pattern of an organization's charismatic founder. The method best suited to public relations is the latter: namely, symmetrical two-way communications that achieve a balance.

It is important to note that a suitable environment is vital to achieve symmetrical two-way communications. Due to the influence of Christianity, the societies of Western Europe have cultures that go beyond hierarchies, such as those in organizations and in which people can freely exchange opinions as individuals. But the awareness of hierarchies is strong within Japanese organizations and this becomes an obstacle to two-way communications. If the awareness of individuals is not in a flat state, or in other words, if information and opinions cannot be exchanged in an equal relationship, then the two-way communications described by Grunig will not be established. Achieving this requires the creation of an environment in which an awareness of hierarchies has been removed and in which people may freely speak their opinions to each other.

Public relations can best be used as a method of achieving objectives and goals along the shortest path, because building and maintaining good relations with the public, which is composed of different stakeholders, ultimately makes it possible to achieve them more smoothly. In other words, the key to guiding an organization to success is for it and stakeholders to come to know each other through symmetrical two-way communications. Ethics acts as the foundation that supports the organization in making the necessary corrections and compromises based on that communications process, and thereby allows it to cultivate a relationship that is beneficial for both sides.

## Self-correction

The "self-correction" concept is one more element that makes it possible to harvest the benefits of symmetrical two-way communications. When the "self-correction" function is part of the mutual transformation of both parties, through symmetrical two-way communication, truly meaningful 21st century-type public relations can be realized. This is because, for different individuals and organizations to maintain good relationships with each other, they must naturally accept the differences between them and make adjustments and corrections.

Public relations experts in the United States consider that in many cases, based on the results of the feedback from two-way communications, "change" and "adjustment" are to be carried out when it is deemed necessary. In contrast, in this book, "self-correction" signifies changing, because of a commitment to ethics, even when it is not made necessary by outside forces. At times, self-corrections will be small adjustments, and at other times it will require making a fundamental change to yourself, and not because of being forced to change, but because of a desire to correct yourself by free-will to follow the ethical path.

For self-correction to function, in addition to understanding your own situation, it is important to fully understand the situation of the other party. Toward this, it is necessary to establish two-way communication, obtain feedback in the form of the reactions and responses from the target, and then use this feedback as the basis for the self-correction.

Moreover, the self-correction required by public relations must be supported by ethics. For example, in the case of an organization, even if it breaks no laws, if it recklessly disrupts the market, the social environment, or willfully seeks its own gain to the detriment of stakeholders, even supposing that doing so enables it to achieve in the short term its objectives, in the long term it will not be sustainable, because stakeholders demand ethical behavior. Being ethical as an organization and utilizing the self-correction function as required enables the organization to protect its reputation, its dignity as a company, and to maintain a highly regarded corporate brand.

Going forward, companies will increasingly have to conduct activities based on flexible, two-way communications with self-correction, which is the essence of public relations that is supported by a high level of ethics.

## Self-Correction Model

When we look at international society in this hyper-globalized world, we can see that the economic supremacy that Japan and Western-developed countries pursued in the last century has stalled, and instead of only following an "economic development model" based on material wealth, we now require a "new model" that emphasizes a high sense of ethics and spirituality. Our collective efforts need to be reoriented to giving priority to living in harmony with our fellow humans, with nature, and also to solving diverse global problems. To that end, presented here in this book is the author's Self-Correction Model, which provides a structure for organizations to achieve goals in ways that seek to maximize the mutual benefit of a world of globalized stakeholders.

This new model, was originally first advanced in the author's writing of "Two-way communication alongside an adjustment function" within "United States public relations in transition: Analysis of evolution and proposal for a new model" published in the *Journal of the Japan Information-Culturology Society* (Inoue, 2002), and then further developed in a research paper for the Japan Society for Corporate Communication Studies (Inoue, 2005).

This "Self-Correction Model" (SCM) is not limited to mere economic efficiency and profit; at the heart of the model is the concept that an organization's activity must be highly ethical and must deepen our humanity. And a public relations that includes this SCM will be a vital key to organizations trying to succeed in an age of hyper-globalization, by providing the essential management resource for reducing and managing a crisis in real-time as events rapidly unfold on the global stage. Chapter 6 covers the author's own practical implementation of the SCM for public relations, which is called the "Public Relations Life-Cycle Model." It is a practical implementation of the SCM for successful and efficient strategic public relations to achieve an organization's goals. Chapter 4, which covers branding and reputation management, describes "Creating Shared Value," which can be thought of as the corporate social responsibility implementation of the SCM by directing organizations to achieve their own goals through solving the needs of stakeholders in ways that create value for both. Chapter 10 provides a comprehensive explanation of the Self-Correction Model.

## 5  Public relations as the fifth management resource

Organizations accomplish goals using four basic resources: "people," "things," "money," and "information." Public relations allows an organization to maximize effectively these four basic resources by acting as an additional fifth "management" resource that provides clear direction and integration of the other resources. In other words, applying public relations increases the value of the four basic organizational resources that have been accumulated inside a company by providing clear direction for effective utilization of resources to the greatest possible extent.

For "people," public relations can help to recruit talented employees by enhancing the reputation of the company, and then as employees it can deepen their understanding of the company, strengthen them as individuals through ethics education, and build loyalty through good employee relations. For "things," public relations makes more effective risk management, branding, and logistics management to name just a few areas. For "money," public relations can help to soundly secure financing and strengthen the company's market capitalization through Investor Relations (IR). For "information," public relations enables the accumulated findings, knowledge, and information to be managed to allow them to be more effectively utilized through two-way communications in an Internet-dominated society. In other words, as the fifth management resource, public relations integrates these four resources that it has strengthened individually, allowing them to function organically and to leverage synergies to the greatest possible extent, thereby making possible the achievement of objectives, targets, and goals along the shortest path. This will become clear in the chapters that follow.

Moreover, even when setting objectives, targets or even principles, an understanding of public relations enables these to be set more effectively and consistently, and by polishing the rough diamonds buried within a company and putting in a sense of soul, a vitality and a strategic direction can be given to company's management. In the case of crisis management, both offensive and defensive management strategies will be strengthened. In this sense, the alignment of management resources through public relations, as the fifth "management" resource, completes and forms the ultimate management system.

The reason why Japan has been unable to clearly take a more significant role internationally is that it has not sufficiently built and integrated a strategy through the techniques of public relations and, as a result, leadership and the activities of individuals in an organization are insufficient to achieve desired outcomes, creating what might be described almost as an overall "power shortage."

The effective utilization of the four management resources has a major impact on the "people" involved in organizations. By introducing and applying the various techniques of public relations as the fifth management resource, the management system is given certainty in these uncertain times in its ability to reliably achieve results in any circumstance, such as in a time of a crisis to defend the organization, or when carrying out a vital competitive strategy.

Finally, the effectiveness of public relations, as a critically important element of successful organizations, can be seen by its widespread use in the United States, as documented in the *2013 Public Relations Generally Accepted Practices (GAP VIII) Study* (Annenberg School for Communications and Journalism, 2013). Among the thousands of people responsible for public relations in companies' public relations departments and other organizations that they surveyed, approximately 40% answered that their communications department had been actively involved in the development of their organization's management strategy. In addition, around 60% answered that management gave importance to the advice given by their department and approximately 45% responded that management considered that public relations and other communications activities contributed significantly to the performance numbers of their company. These answers suggest that public relations is built into the management function in the United States.

## 6 Leaders in today's age of hyper-globalization need to be shrewd and knowledgeable about public relations

If you read about the characteristics of the leaders of the most successful global companies, such as Steve Jobs of Apple, or Carlos Ghosn of Renault-Nissan, you will likely not find public relations described as a key skill-set. But, if you look through the lens of public relations at what these leaders have done, you will see in action the very principles and skills that make up public relations today.

In the July 2014 issue of Stanford Graduate School of Business's *Insights by Stanford*, Carlos Ghosn (Snyder, 2014) explained how he had to take actions in direct contradiction to the conventional Japanese business practices, doing things that "can't be done in Japan," such as closing factories or breaking ties with suppliers. He said that as a leader one must explain and convince stakeholders about taking non-conventional actions. And he remarks: "As long as you can make a company with different cultures working together, you're going to get the best out of every single culture." So success for him is neither ignoring culture differences, nor trying to create a single global business culture, but rather his success comes from sound business strategy executed through relationship management that convinces, inspires, and utilizes the strengths of stakeholders with different cultures. Public relations is the very skill of successfully engaging and persuading global stakeholders.

Steve Jobs, Carlos Ghosn, and many other successful global leaders, typically do not talk about public relations, but they succeed by practicing it. Public relations is no longer a skill only for public relations professionals to use in a time of crisis or when launching a new product, rather it is required skill by which top managers succeed in stakeholder relationship management. This takes on new meaning in our new environment of hyper-globalization where Futurists see that "time" is speeding up to the point where "we won't experience 100 years of progress in the 21st century — it will be more like 20,000 years of progress (at today's rate)" (Kurzweil, 2001). Public relations is the essential management resource that current and future top managers must effectively utilize for organizations to survive and also to efficiently and effectively achieve goals in a world of hyper-globalization; a world where the time frame in which critical decisions must be made is dramatically shrinking.

## References

Annenberg School for Communications and Journalism (2013). *GAP VIII: Eighth Communication and Public Relations Generally Accepted Practices Study (Q4 2013 data)*, California: Strategic Communications and Public Relations Center, USC Annenberg.

Bhagwati, J. N. (2004). *In Defense of Globalization.* New York: Oxford University Press.

Bradsher, K. & Tabuchi, H. (2011). "Lack of Data Heightens Japan's Nuclear Crisis." *The New York Times,* November 16, 2011.

Cahn, S. M. & Markie, P. (2002). *Ethics: History, Theory, and Contemporary Issues.* 2nd ed. New York: Oxford University Press.

Chu, J. (2011). "Japan's Supply Chain Ripple Effects." *MIT News Office,* April 15, 2011.

Crimmins, J. E. (2017). "Jeremy Bentham." *The Stanford Encyclopedia of Philosophy,* Spring Edition.

The Economist (2011). "The Troubles of TEPCO: The Fallout from the Fukushima Nuclear Disaster is Spreading Throughout Japan's Energy Industry." *The Economist,* June 30, 2011.

Ferris, E. & Solis, M. (2013). *Earthquake, Tsunami, Meltdown – The Triple Disaster's Impact on Japan, Impact on the World.* Washington D.C.: Brookings Institute, UPFRONT.

Ghemawat, P. (n.d.) "Globalization of Markets." *Globalization Note Series.*

Grunig, J. E. & Dozier, D. M. (1992). *Excellence in Public Relations and Communication Management.* New York; London: Routledge.

Grunig, J. E. & Hunt, T. (1984). *Managing Public Relations.* New York: Holt, Rinehart, & Winston.

Inoue, T. (2002). "Beikoku ni okeru paburikku rirēshonzu no hatten no bunseki kōsatsu to atarashī moderu no teia" (United States Public Relations in Transition: Analysis of Evolution and Proposal for a New Model) *Joho Bunka Gakkai Magazine (Japan Information Culturology Society),* 9(1).

Inoue, T. (2005). "Nihon ni okeru paburikku rirēshonzu hatten no tame no kōsatsu - shin moderu no jitsugen to kyōiku shisutemu no kōchiku ni mukete" (Toward Consideration of a New Model for Public Relations Development in Japan) *Japan Society for Corporate Communication Studies,* "KOHOKENKYU", Issue 9.

Inoue, T. (2006). *Paburikku rirēshonzu (Public Relations),* Tokyo: Nippon Hyoron Sha.

Inoue, T. (2011). "Anshin ataeru 'Senryaku koho o'" (PR Strategy for Giving Peace of Mind for the Nuclear Disaster). *Yomiuri Shimbun,* August 20, 2011, p. 11.

Johnson, R. (2017). "Kant's Moral Philosophy." *Stanford Encyclopedia of Philosophy,* Spring Edition.

Kurzweil, R. (2001). "The Law of Accelerating Returns." [Online] Available at: http://www.kurzweilai.net/the-law-of-accelerating-returns.

McLuhan, M. (1962). *The Gutenberg Galaxy: The Making of Typographic Man.* Toronto: University of Toronto Press.

NOAA (National Oceanic and Atmospheric Administration) (n.d.) "National Environmental Satellite and Information Service (NESDIS)." [Online] Available at: https://www.ngdc.

noaa.gov/nndc/struts/results?EQ_0=5413&t=101650&s=9&d=101,91,95,93&nd=display [Accessed May 24, 2017]

Peary, B. D., Shaw, R., & Takeuchi, Y. (2012). "Utilization of Social Media in the East Japan Earthquake and Tsunami and its Effectiveness." *Journal of Natural Disaster Science*, 34(1), pp. 3–18.

Prime Minister of Japan and his Cabinet (2012). "Road to Recover." Tokyo: Japanese Government.

Rodrik, D. (2016). "Put Globalization to Work for Democracies." *The New York Times, Sunday Review*, September 17, 2016.

Snyder, B. (2014). "Carlos Ghosn: Five Percent of the Challenge Is the Strategy. Ninety-five Percent is the Execution." *Insights by Stanford Business*, July 9, 2014.

Statista.com (n.d.). "Number of Monthly Active Facebook Users Worldwide as of 2nd Quarter 2017 (in Millions)." [Online] Available at: https://www.statista.com/statistics/264810/number-of-monthly-active-facebook-users-worldwide/ [Accessed April 21, 2017]

Subramanian, A. & Kessler, M. (2013). *The Hyperglobalization of Trade and Its Future*. Washington D.C.: Peterson Institute of International Economics.

UN Refugee Agency (2015). "Global Trends Forced Displacement in 2015." [Online] Available at: http://www.unhcr.org/576408cd7.pdf#zoom=95 [Accessed May 24, 2017]

Wharton School of the University of Pennsylvania (2013). "Disasters, Leadership and Rebuilding – Tough Lessons from Japan and the U.S." *Knowledge@Wharton Special Report*, October 3, 2013.

# 2

# EFFECTIVE STAKEHOLDER RELATIONSHIP MANAGEMENT

## Fostering successful global leaders

### 1 Public relations seen at work: Nissan Motor and Mitsubishi Motors 2016 historic press conference

On May 12, 2016 at 4 p.m. in the city of Yokohama, Japan, Carlos Ghosn, CEO of Nissan Motor Co., Ltd. (NMC) along with Osamu Masuko, CEO of Mitsubishi Motors Corporation (MMC) faced over a hundred members of the press to announce and explain a decision to allow Nissan Motor to purchase a 34% controlling interest in Mitsubishi Motors for USD $2.2 billion (¥237 billion) (Greimel, 2016). Only less than a month before in a press conference on April 20, President Tetsuro Aikawa revealed that MMC had falsified fuel economy ratings of the mini-cars it manufactures and jointly sells under both the Mitsubishi and Nissan brands, and then apologized and announced his resignation. On April 26 MMC further revealed that the falsification was much wider, extending across other MMC vehicles and dating back 25 years. The stock price of MMC in 2016, which had been ¥864 on April 19 began to rapidly decline, reaching a low of ¥434 at the April 26 closing.

At the start of 2016, MMC was Japan's sixth largest and the world's sixteenth largest car manufacturer in terms of number of vehicles produced annually. It was also a proud member of the Mitsubishi Group, which dates back to 1870, and which includes Mitsubishi Heavy Industries Ltd., Mitsubishi Corp., and the Bank of Tokyo-Mitsubishi UFJ Ltd. The Mitsubishi Group was MMC's largest and controlling shareholder, and when MMC's capital tie-up with DaimlerChrysler AG in 2000 was dissolved in 2004, the group came to MMC's rescue by buying ¥600 billion in preferred stock of the automaker. The tie-up in 2000 had a bad start, with MMC being forced that same year to admit to systematically hiding customer complaints and product defects for some two decades. Even with the 2004 bailout, MMC faced a steep uphill struggle to rebuild its brand in the eyes of consumers, because of the recalls and quality issues.

Yet, by 2010 MMC had succeeded in finally rebuilding its image and its financial stability, and had recovered to the point that it bought the preferred stock back from the Mitsubishi Group which had been issued in 2004. And by the end of 2015 it seemed that MMC's strategy of rebranding itself as a leader in electrified vehicles, crossovers, and sport utility vehicles was succeeding, and its stock price at the close of November 10, 2015 was ¥1,090.

Nissan had faced its own existential crisis in 1999, making it seek a tie-up with Renault, which became its major shareholder. At that time, Carlos Ghosn came to Japan to begin the Nissan Revival Plan (NRP), which was successfully completed in 2001, one year ahead of schedule. This success was not without challenges, given that "43 of the 46 products Nissan sold in Japan were unprofitable," and given the nature of Japanese corporate culture to resist change (Nissan Newsroom, 2009). The NRP made Nissan profitable, but also earned Carlos Ghosn the nickname of "Le Cost Killer" as Nissan was forced to close factories and reduce the workforce. However, in January 2002 its all new Altima model won the "North American Car and Truck of the Year" award.

In 2011 Nissan signed a joint venture agreement with Mitsubishi Motors for the manufacture of mini-cars. This NMC and MMC business arrangement was successful, but while working together on the next generation mini-car, Nissan engineers began to question the fuel efficiency ratings, which eventually led to the April 20 MMC press conference (Mitsubishi Motors, 2015).

The auto industry is an integral part of the global economy, very competitive, and very technologically and capital intensive. In addition, the industry is facing competition from formidable new players from Silicon Valley, bringing in new disruptive technologies such as Tesla Motors' innovative electric cars and Google's self-driving car (Lien, 2016).

If NMC and MMC could create a successful alliance, it would allow them to join the ranks of the largest car makers, such as Toyota, GM, and Volkswagen. It would also allow them to develop vital new technologies and new vehicle platforms together, without which they could not survive, and allow them to do so at lower cost measured in billions of dollars.

This was the background for the May 12 press conference in Yokohama. Before walking into this press conference the two CEOs would each be wanting and very much needing to project a positive image of the economic advantages to be gained for their respective companies, and to project a sense of optimism that this capital tie-up would succeed unlike MMC's earlier tie-up with DaimlerChrysler AG some 15 years before, which ended in failure. Both CEOs would also certainly have been aware that for the new alliance to become a reality and to have even a chance of succeeding in the highly competitive auto market, the two executives would need to win, through this press conference, the enthusiastic support of employees, investors, government regulators, suppliers, dealers, stock analysts, and the media, to name just a few of the stakeholders. And, in this world of hyper-globalization, they would be very aware that the full details of this day's press conference would be made available instantly in English to stakeholders around the world via social media and the Internet.

The first indication of success or failure would be in how favorably the press reported the joint announcement, and the second indication would be the resulting change in MMC's stock price. Neither company could afford to see another dramatic fall in stock price like that on April 20. For both leaders, there was much to be either won or lost in this press conference.

With the cameras of the press clicking frantically, creating a sound like the splashing rain of a midsummer storm, the two CEOs stepped into the press conference, and speaking first, Carlos Ghosn, explained about his company's USD $2.2 billion investment that would give it a 34% controlling interest in MMC, summarized the economic benefits, and detailed the reasons why the two companies would effectively work together in a win-win alliance of mutual strengths.

Carlos Ghosn's words were well-prepared and aimed carefully at various stakeholders. Yet, those prepared words would also have been the work of many individuals in both companies, and would have been discussed in depth over a period of several weeks. When you hear his unscripted answers to the questions from the press, Mr. Ghosn's public relations skills become most obvious. In response to the question from a reporter at *Toyo Keizai*, a leading Japanese weekly magazine, asking why the tie-up was being announced before an investigation into the fuel rating scandal had been completed, Carlos Ghosn gave the following remarks:

> Top management has sized the problem and shared this with us. On top of this, there are other considerations, there are business considerations, we believe in the potential of Mitsubishi Motors as a competitor. We think the company can be more profitable, and we think the company can grow faster with our support. That is number one. So, when we become the main shareholder of Mitsubishi, supporting Mitsubishi, supporting Nissan in a certain way, by growing Mitsubishi and making Mitsubishi more profitable, obviously there is a direct benefit for Nissan, so we are in a win-win transaction. That is number one
>
> *(Nissan Motor Corporation Global Newsroom Video, 2016).*

These words were seemed specifically directed at the concerns of shareholders and financial analysts who wanted to hear and to believe that the new alliance would result in greater profits in the near term, and in the long term create higher growth. And one needs to keep in mind that, in this global economy, the shareholders are not only Japanese investors, but also French investors of Renault, which includes the French government's approximately 20% ownership in Renault, and other institutional investors around the globe.

Continuing his answer, Ghosn then addressed all the hard-working MMC employees, especially the dedicated and talented engineers, who needed to be encouraged, motivated, and inspired to maintain quality and create innovation:

> No. 2, there are direct synergies for Nissan, on top of the benefits for Mitsubishi, which we think are going to be enormous, but there are also benefits for Nissan. For example, the performance of Mitsubishi in some regions is

better than the performance of Nissan, particularly in the Southeast of Asia, where Mitsubishi is doing a great job. When you look at their results in SUVs and pickup trucks they are doing a very good job taking into consideration the limited resources they have. So, we have direct synergies for Nissan

*(Nissan Motor Corporation Global Newsroom, 2016).*

Carlos Ghosn then went on to address the wider set of "publics" making up the wider set of stakeholders, as he continued his answer:

Then, there is a 3rd consideration that we understand particularly that we have been in trouble not a very long time ago, so we understand the anxieties of the employees, we understand the anxiety of communities, we understand the anxiety of suppliers, we understand the anxiety of the dealers of Mitsubishi

*(Nissan Motor Corporation Global Newsroom, 2016).*

Although Nissan would be taking control of MMC as the largest shareholder and would appoint several board members, including a new chairman of the board appointed by Nissan, Mr. Ghosn would understand, as an executive skilled in public relations, that ownership by itself means little if many of the different stakeholders are not enthusiastic supporters. This was particularly the case with the employees of MMC who had to be inspired more than just commanded to bring about far-reaching changes, especially changes in corporate governance.

It is also certain that Carlos Ghosn, as "Le Cost Killer," had to be aware of the deep feeling of pride of MMC's senior management and career professionals in the vital areas of engineering and product development. Ownership can be obtained by making a USD $2.2 billion payment, but winning the hearts of stakeholders, such as employees, suppliers, and dealers required the skill of public relations, and with that in mind, his following response can best be understood:

And, frankly, as a Japanese company, working with another Japanese company, extending a hand when they need it, because we think there is a potential to solve this issue, and to overcome the issue very fast, to cut into this unnecessary anxiety and stress is a good thing to do. So, there are considerations of this sort, there are financial considerations, we think it is a good investment, and there is also the trust that exists with top management, and I want to highlight the importance of Masuko-san in making this deal, because we trust him, when he says this is the size of the problem, we trust him, obviously there is the due diligence that will take place …

*(Nissan Motor Corporation Global Newsroom, 2016).*

In contrast, the prepared remarks of MMC CEO, Osamu Masuko, although specifically mentioning "stakeholders," came across as rather blind to the full reality of multiple stakeholders, and blind to the need to speak heart-to-heart to stakeholders as if one is speaking to each separately. His remarks talk about his personal mission "to find a pathway leading to the stability of management." And as for stakeholders, he said: "This capital collaboration will be something that will be very much pleasing to all the stakeholders, including customers who are worried, our dealers, shareholders and employees." Yes, but these words are said as if that fact alone can address all the concerns of these stakeholders. He noticeably does not talk about making MMC more profitable, nor does he give any indication of understanding the need to win the enthusiastic support of employees when he says: "… and I am sure that we will be able to try and promote the change and reform of the corporate culture and awareness of the people concerned in the development and engineering departments" (Nissan Motor Corporation Global Newsroom, 2016).

In the end, because Nissan could overcome the lack of PR skills of Mitsubishi Motors, the press conference was a success as reflected by the stock price of MMC, which had reached ¥495 the day before, and by the end of the May 12 press conference had jumped to ¥575. And, on May 25 the board of MMC approved the alliance with Nissan.

### Lessons learned

Of course, in a literal sense, at a press conference one talks to members of the press. But, viewed from public relations, one is not talking to the press, one is talking "through the press" to the market and the various stakeholders in it, and more importantly talking to achieve successful stakeholder relationship management.

Globalization means that these stakeholders are not only those in your country, but are persons, companies, institutions, and governments located throughout the world. While over 50% of shareholders of Mitsubishi Motors were the companies of the Mitsubishi Group, it was the remaining investors, many of whom are not Japanese, that actively trade the stock and therefore determine the rise and fall of MMC's share price. Employees are likewise not just Japanese workers, but workers in places like Thailand, the Philippines, North America, and Europe. The same can be said for MMC's suppliers, dealers, and customers located throughout the world.

Hyper-globalization means that the May 12 press conference was instantly reported via the Internet, and discussed on social media, reaching the global stakeholders in every region of the world. Carlos Ghosn, who is not a native English speaker, spoke English to global stakeholders. While, of course, it is perfectly natural for Osamu Masuko to speak Japanese in Japan, one cannot help feeling he spoke primarily to the Japanese. This can also be sensed in his words which expressed a feeling, which might be summed up as: "I had no choice; we cannot survive without a partner." And, moreover his words had a tone of a "cup-half-empty, which required doing something radical for that cup not to become completely empty." Such a tone is more fitting for a Japanese audience. In contrast, Mr. Ghosn spoke in a positive tone that expressed the feeling of a "cup-half-full that can now become a full cup." Such a tone is more fitting for relationship management in a hyper-globalized world.

Watching and listening to Carlos Ghosn one can easily appreciate his unique gifts as a speaker and as a global executive. Not every executive will have the advantage of having Mr. Ghosn's background, which is that of a person born in Brazil of Lebanese heritage, who grew up in Lebanon, completed college and post-college studies in France and, as an employee of the global tire company Michelin, began a career turning around failing manufacturing operations throughout the world. But, one also needs to recognize that his skills are less "natural gifts of a unique human being" and more skills acquired through experience and through study, which others can also acquire.

This chapter will begin helping you learn those skills, which are public relations skills, by first replacing the idea of a single, monolithic "public," with the understanding of a diverse world of multiple "publics" that are located throughout the globe and linked together by the power and speed of the Internet. And it will then explain about the basic types of public relations that are generally practiced.

Although this May 12 press conference was a success, going forward would still be a long road ahead for the expanded alliance, with many "bumps" and "detours." But, public relations as the fifth management resource, can be used to inspire employees and executives to reform MMC's culture and replace "fear and despair" with "hope and confidence" through "employee relations" strategies and programs. In the end, however, results count the most, and by July 2017 the half year global vehicle totals were 5,155,600 for Volkswagen, and 5,129,000 for Toyota, but the world's largest automaker with production of 5,268,079 vehicles was Renault-Nissan (Schmitt, 2017).

As important as employee relations are, especially for MMC to motivate employees, something else is needed to stop the disastrous cycle that results in one corporate scandal being resolved only for another scandal to appear several years later. All countries experience these kinds of problems from time to time, and no organization is immune from willful wrong-doing, but it is especially a problem in non-Western countries like Japan, where public relations is not so well established, and where the concept of "ethics" was imported along with Western technology and culture, without a complete understanding. We see this with MMC's defects cover-up in 2000 and the 2016 fuel rating falsification. In 2015, we saw it with the Japanese company Toshiba's USD $1.9 billion profit overstatement over seven years, mainly connected to a USD $1.3 billion impairment charge for the nuclear business it purchased from Westinghouse Electric Company (Fukase, 2015). This will be covered in detail in Chapter 5 of this book. To avoid repeating scandals like those of MMC and Toshiba, the public relations model of self-correction introduced in Chapter 1 and discussed in more detail in the last chapter of this book needs to be implemented by all companies.

The good news of this chapter is that every leader, especially Japanese, Asian, and other leaders in the non-English speaking world, can learn through the study and practice of the skill of public relations how to successfully achieve goals for their organization along the shortest path, just as we have seen with Carlos Ghosn in the above May 12 press conference.

## 2 What is public relations?

### *Who are the public and publics?*

The "public" signifies the many different groups that can be found in society, where each individual person can be said to be in numerous different groups or "publics" at the same time. However, the groups that a company is involved with when conducting its business are its "stakeholders" (including employees), which are those publics related to specific business activities. For example, when a company is looking to increase its capital, its stakeholders will be investors, shareholders, security companies, and the regulatory authorities, but in contrast, when it is launching a new product, its stakeholders will include general consumers, and distributors as well as suppliers. Therefore, even for the same information sender, the message and the method of sending the message will be tailored to its objectives and themes and they will be different for each of the stakeholders it is targeting.

The depth and breadth of public relations is highly complex, because there is not one single monolithic "public." As in the Nissan-Mitsubushi press conference above, one reason for success was this understanding by Mr. Ghosn of the simple and seemingly obvious, and yet often overlooked, fact that there are multiple publics, containing multiple stakeholders.

As an example, looking at Figure 2.1 from the standpoint of a company, the public is made up of a variety of target stakeholders, including general consumers, employees, distributors, shareholders, investors, local communities, and the international community. Furthermore, these target audiences will vary depending on the public relations objectives set by the organization; for example, in investor relations (IR), the target audience will be investors, when the objective is to list the company on the stock market; in community relations (CR) it will be building relations with the local community; and in government relations (GR), the target audience will be the government, such as when lobbying for deregulation. In these ways, the target audience changes as the objectives change, and the related strategies that will be fostered and the approach and techniques that should be focused on will also be different. Figure 2.2 shows the public relations activities between an organization and the public.

Just like target audiences, public relations activities can vary depending on the objectives set by the organization. In such ways, public relations entails targeting specific publics that have been selected from among the various publics, and public relations is the collective name given for the various relations with them.

An understanding of the concept of "public" is vital when practicing public relations, which uses communications as a means of relationship management. And public relations can be thought of as a system like the cardiovascular system of the body

**FIGURE 2.1** Publics (general public) for an organization (company)

*Source:* Takashi Inoue (2015), *Public Relations: Relationship Management*, 2nd edition, p. 17

in which blood vessels carry nutrients and oxygen needed by the various organs of the body, as well as hormones produced by organs needed by the rest of the body. In the case of public relations, "communications" functions to connect in a systematic way an organization and its stakeholders by delivering "information and returning feedback." Based on the feedback from stakeholders the organization will send out new information. But, if the information sender does not understand the information receiver, the information will not flow smoothly, or in other words, the sender will not be able to communicate accurately and effectively. This is because the information receiver is merely one member of the public, so the information sender will not be able to accurately set the target audience (the information receiver), if an understanding of the targeted public is lacking.

In addition, the information sender must also know that the "flow" of information can reverse directions and the information receiver can at any time become the information sender. Being aware of this leads to an understanding of two-way communication and also an understanding of how the original intended information

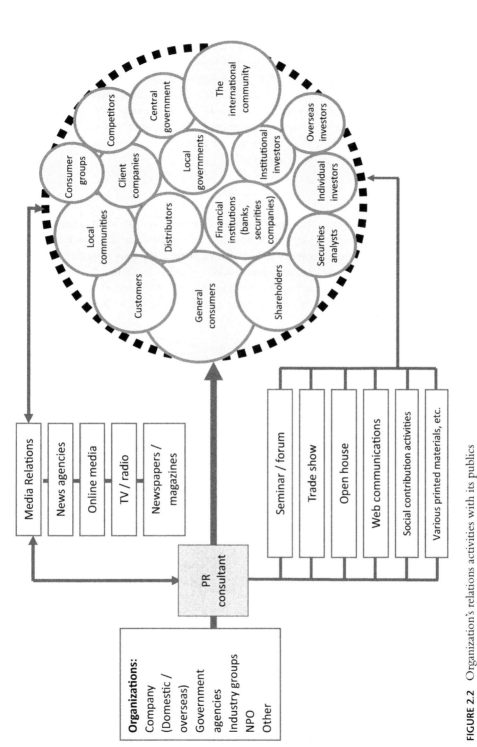

**FIGURE 2.2** Organization's relations activities with its publics

*Source:* Takashi Inoue (2015), *Public Relations: Relationship Management*, 2nd edition, p. 18

receiver in turn reverses the information flow by sending information to their own targeted audiences, and thus becomes the new information sender.

To send information effectively, it is also necessary to understand from both a macro and micro viewpoint, starting with an understanding of the public, and then the separate stakeholders that constitute the public and all the other specific groups that will become the target audiences. Additionally, it is necessary to go beyond a static understanding of the public and to realize that over time that same public is dynamically undergoing gradual change.

## 1) Static publics

Looking at Figure 2.3 (the public surrounding a company), we can see that the public exists all around the company, which is located where the vertical and horizontal axes intersect in the center. As previously explained, here the public is used to mean "the public." But when we consider the existence of cyber space that has emerged through the digitization of society and the spread of the Internet, we can see that there are parts that the word "public" cannot explain. There is also the problem of

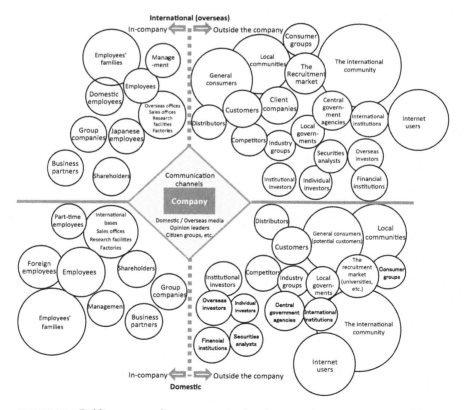

**FIGURE 2.3** Publics surrounding an organization (company)

*Source:* Takashi Inoue (2015), *Public Relations: Relationship Management*, 2nd edition, p. 19

when to conduct a static analysis. Therefore, we will use the word "public" here to incorporate every type of possibility. Determining what these possibilities are, how they develop, and how they change requires carrying out a dynamic analysis, but to do such a dynamic analysis requires first having a static understanding.

So let's assume there is a company that is an information sender, targeting the public. First, we distinguish the communication routes used for communicating with audiences inside and outside of the company. When this route is placed on the horizontal axis, the route on the right is for communicating outside of the company and the route on the left is for communicating inside the company. In addition, in terms of the places where the management activities take place, we can distinguish communication routes that travel domestically and internationally (overseas). When we place this route on the vertical axis, going up the axis shows the international route and going down the axis shows the domestic route. In this way, we can divide the public as seen by the company into the four groups in the four quadrants of the graph.

First, the bottom left quadrant shows the publics within the company and within the company's home country. The sub-groups considered to be within this internal/domestic grouping include potential new recruits, employees including labor unions, and even some organizations that are outside of the company, such as business partners. The shareholder sub-group is also included in this group in the case of a group of companies, resulting from the cross-holding of shares, which is typical in large Japanese companies. Also, looking at the employee sub-group, there are different sub-groups depending on whether from a marketing viewpoint or from a labor union issue, but in some cases these members will overlap. Therefore, the circles of the respective groups shown in Figure 2.3 overlap.

Next, the upper left quadrant shows the publics within the company that are located overseas. The sub-groups within this grouping are employees stationed overseas and their families, employees recruited locally overseas, the overseas sales offices and factories, and local communities to represent various cultural issues.

The bottom right quadrant shows the publics outside the company, but within the company's home country. The sub-groups in this grouping include business partners and competitors, domestic national and local governments, general consumers and consumer groups, local communities that include consumers, general investors, as well as industry organizations.

Finally, the upper right quadrant shows the overseas public external to the company. The sub-groups within this grouping include overseas business partners and competitors, foreign governments and related overseas consumers, and overseas investors. Also, although somewhat vague, the international community can be a large sub-group within this quadrant.

Notice, as we can see from Figure 2.3, there are white spaces that are not included in any of the groups. These are the persons that cannot be recognized as members of a target audience of public relations at the current time. They might be organizations or persons that do not need to be recognized as target audiences, but rather they are persons that are currently beyond the ability of the information sender to recognize. But even if such persons cannot be recognized, it is not the case that they are unrelated, but rather that it is impossible to predict when and in what form the relations with such persons will occur and to what effect. For example, a white space might come to be recognized as a new target audience when a company launches a new business. So, in this sense, these white spaces can be described as potential target audiences.

There are various communication channels between the respective groups in the public that surrounds the company. Starting with the media, these include the academics and critics that influence public opinion (influencers) and various civil constituency groups. Companies aim to indirectly communicate with the public via these channels. But today, they can also communicate directly with the public thanks to the spread of the Internet and social media.

Up to this point, we have grouped the public into distinct target audiences. While there are various groups that become the target of public relations at one moment, there are also other groups that are not a target audience, but which may become one in the future. Also, some of these have not yet been recognized. Making the situation even more complex is the fact that although these groups, which are represented by the white spaces, may not realistically become target audiences as stakeholders, in some form or another they have influence and they surround the information sender and their interests intertwine in a complex manner. In this way all the groups combine to form the public. Viewed like this, identifying stakeholders in public relations is unexpectedly complex and not a simple task.

Further adding to this complexity is that, while we have used the term information sender up to this point, we must not forget that when viewed from the perspective of another information sender, senders too simply constitute one more group or factor within the overall public. For example, let's consider a company as the information sender and a "university" as one of its publics. For the company, the university's teaching staff and students are its clients (including potential clients), but at the same time, the university can be positioned as a recruitment market. Figure 2.4 shows the publics surrounding the university. When we see the university as the information sender, we understand that the situation changes and that the company becomes just one group or one factor within the public. There is the mistaken tendency to always position the information sender at the center of the public, but when viewed from the perspective of another public, we see that the sender is nothing more than one part of the public.

Recognizing that the information sender is both the center of the public and at the same time is also no more than one factor within it, we can understand that the information sender is also the information receiver. This also becomes the basic attitude for practicing relationship management based on two-way communication from multiple perspectives.

Figure 2.5 shows that one person, who is the information receiver, has several "faces" and becomes a member of various "target audiences." The individual, who is the smallest unit within the public, further expands his or her nodes of information, for example at home or in the workplace. From this chain, a single piece of information proliferates endlessly to various publics that are related to that individual,

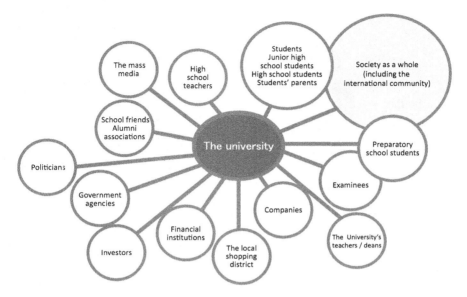

**FIGURE 2.4**  Publics surrounding universities

*Source:* Takashi Inoue (2015), *Public Relations: Relationship Management*, 2nd edition, p. 22

especially in today's Internet environment. Also, as was previously mentioned, this information receiver may also become the information sender.

## 2) Dynamic view of publics

A static understanding only of the public cannot be said to be a true understanding. It is also necessary to understand how the public, or the respective stakeholder groups in the public that become the target for relationship management and for audiences that you are communicating with, are dynamically changing, have already changed, and may change again. In the context of the gradual external environmental change, we can understand that there are no publics that do not change. Even if they don't change within one year, they will change over three years or over five years. Also, groups and targets that do not currently exist will suddenly appear, or oppositely those that currently exist will disappear. For example, 30 years ago there was no cyber space formed by the Internet or the mobile communications network, yet today it is an indispensable part of every-day life. Only capturing a static view of the public from limited research will result in public relations failures in the long term.

There are various approaches to capturing change. Initially, the sociological approach starts with analyzing changes in the public, but there is also the research method of limiting the subject of study to a certain group, like an age group, gender, or actual users. The method will change, and indeed must change, depending on the objectives of the individual public relations activities. So as not to lose sight of the changing public, it is necessary to ceaselessly collect and analyze information from a long-term perspective.

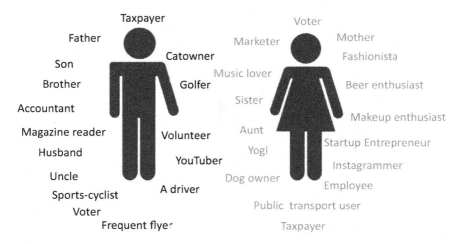

**FIGURE 2.5** Our many roles in the public

What we must be aware of is that when the factor behind a change to a target audience is caused by external factors, we must look very carefully at changes in the surrounding environment. However, for each change within the environment, the change will often bring about other changes, creating a complex chain-reaction of changes. Moreover, the information sender is also changing. So it seems reasonable that the means of analyzing changes in the external environment, both in terms of effects and scope, should be determined by the objectives of the public relations activities and the required time frame, and the budget.

When the complexity of dynamic change is added to the complexity of the static public, then it becomes extremely difficult to accurately understand fully the various stakeholders that are to be the object of public relations activities. How can we be sensitive to change? What kind of "antennas" can we erect to detect it? And how should we respond to it? Answering these questions is the key to making possible effective public relations and conversely, why effective public relations can be thought of like real-time software that is responding to continuous change.

## *What is the meaning of relations?*

As was explained in Chapter 1, "public relations" is relationship management in which organizations, such as companies and governments, build various relations with various stakeholders within the (general) public by becoming information senders to achieve their respective goals and objectives. When Nissan and Mitsubishi "spoke through" the press on May 12 to reach targeted stakeholders to win support for their new capital tie-up and expanded automaker alliance, they succeeded, because objectives were accurately set and the relevant stakeholders were targeted.

The information sender sets the public relations' objectives and sends the appropriate information to targeted publics. In the case of companies, the target audience that they prioritize and the relations that they seek to build will vary depending on their management and marketing strategies. For example, the target audience will be the market, if it takes a marketing perspective.

If a mistake is made in setting the right public relations objectives and/or targeting the right publics, the information analysis needed for successful public relations will be inaccurate. Accordingly, the accuracy and outcome of the public relations program that is subsequently implemented will be reduced and in some circumstances, could result in its failure.

While the most successful global leaders will have a good sense of public relations, they also will need to make effective use of public relations practitioners working for them. A public relations practitioner as one member of an organization or, alternatively, as an external consultant from a PR firm plays the role of the intermediary between the information sender and the public. However, in each case they are positioned on the information sender side.

The following sections of this chapter introduce the characteristics and roles of the major types of public relations that are necessary for organizations to carry out precise relations with a specific stakeholder: "media relations (MR)," "influencer relations," "investor relations (IR)," "government relations (GR)," "employee relations (ER)," and "community relations (CR)."

## 1) Media relations (MR)

### Media relations as a core competence

Media relations is a core competence of public relations that is a distinct activity that functions as a tool for accomplishing the objectives of the various types of public relations, such as employee relations and government relations. By building favorable relations with the media, organizations get access to a communication channel to reach various target audiences in the same way that a press conference is an opportunity to talk through the media to reach stakeholders. Media relations therefore plays a critical role in relationship management as shown in Figure 2.6, in which the information sender is a university.

When looking at the mass media according to the type of medium, we see that there are newspapers (including national newspapers, block newspapers, local newspapers, economic newspapers, industrial newspapers, and community newspapers), magazines (quarterly, monthly, weekly, as well as other economic magazines, trade journals, and women's magazines), TV (nationwide networks, from local stations through to cable television), radio, and communication companies. Moreover, recently online media and social networking services (SNS) delivered via the Internet have rapidly risen to prominence, utilizing their function of immediacy as a weapon which can be very effective. Online media and SNS will be dealt with in detail in Chapter 9, "Essential changes in corporate communication in a digital age."

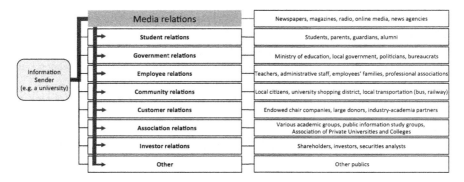

**FIGURE 2.6** Main target audiences for the various relations.

*Source:* Takashi Inoue (2015), *Public Relations: Relationship Management*, 2nd edition, p. 26

Even when viewed globally, Japan is an advanced leading nation in terms of information density and economy. Although readership has declined in the past ten years, Japan's five national newspapers, *Asahi, Yomiuri, Mainichi, Nikkei,* and *Sankei* still boast having a daily circulation as of 2016 of 45 million copies (Nihon Shimbun Kyokai, 2009), and for television networks, NHK and the five commercial broadcasters, cover the whole country, communicating major news instantaneously throughout the nation. In Japan, the reporting by the leading media is said to be highly reliable and effective in shaping public opinion. At the same time, they are concentrated in Tokyo, where more than 90% of media organizations have their head offices, making it an extremely efficient environment in which to conduct media relations. Also, the Foreign Correspondents' Club of Japan (FCCJ) is located on the 20th floor of the Yurakucho Denki Building in Tokyo, from where correspondents from the world's major media send information from Japan to the world.

An organization's relations with the media are critical in its public relations activities, and if the information it provides them with is highly newsworthy and topical, it will be immediately reported. If it first appears in the mainstream print and TV media, it will likely then be picked up and reported on again in digital and online video media, such as on YouTube. This not only shares information on a society-wide scale and promotes the formation of public opinion, it also affects politics, the government, and company activities. In the short term, the public image of the government and of companies will be greatly affected by the tone and content of the media coverage on them.

The information sender utilizes the influence of the media, when it sends its message to its final target audience through the media, because the media has credibility as an objective and professional third party. Therefore, using the media can be far more effective in building public opinion than paid advertising. In this sense, media relations possess different characteristics than the other types of public relations.

Figure 2.7 graphically shows the flow of professional public relations based on a public relations strategy and two-way communications to achieve the objectives of the various types of public relations, such as customer relations, government relations, investor relations, employee relations, and community relations. Media relations can be thought of as a tool used by the other types of public relations,

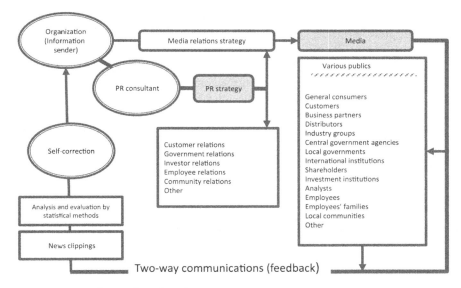

**FIGURE 2.7**   Professional media relations

*Source:* Takashi Inoue (2015), *Public Relations: Relationship Management*, 2nd edition, p. 28

therefore media relations strategy depends on the specific types of public relations that are necessary to achieve goals of an organization. Media relations strategy is positioned as one part of an integrated public relations strategy that aims to realize two-way communication based on the feedback on the information that was originally sent, and so has a self-correction function.

## Publicity and advertising within public relations

It is important to note that "publicity activities" are different from the activities of media relations. These two PR terms tend to be mistakenly used interchangeably. Basically, "publicity" is a one-way communications process, in which the organization supplies information as one part of media relations. For example, in the case of print media the objective is to try and have that information published as an article. Conversely, media relations involve an organization using a two-way communications process to build relations of mutual understanding and trust with the media through the exchange of information, which can be expected to be effective in having it publish articles. In media relations, the organization is required to send precise information to the media it is targeting, after fully understanding the media's reporting viewpoint and the information needs of its journalists and editors.

Publicity also differs from advertising. Although they are both the same in the sense of using the mass media to widely disseminate a message, they are completely different in terms of their formats and backgrounds. Publicity is one part of media relations, while advertising is a general technique used in various types of public relations. While public relations will use advertising to send messages to stakeholders about a corporation, product advertising is a marketing-communications activity and not a part of public relations.

Publicity as one part of media relations entails a program that can include distributing press releases, holding press conferences and individual interviews, and providing product information with the ultimate objective of having information published in the media, such as in the form of news or a feature article (or program). Whether the information provided is turned into an article as well as the timing of the exposure (whether in print or on air) is left up to the decisions of the editors on the media side. Conversely, in advertising, the advertiser (a company, organization, or individual) pays to purchase print space or broadcast time for a CM spot (commercial message) or a program ad (advertisement) slot, has its message published or broadcast, and can choose when this message will appear and in which media.

## Characteristics and roles of the media

As was previously described, there are various types of media and there are two cases when information is sent through them, when the information sender side pays, such as for advertising, and when it does not pay.

The former is advertising publicity, in which, for example, a certain number of pages in a newspaper or broadcast time on television are purchased, and if it is within the standards for the publishing of advertising set by the media and the code of ethics of the advertiser's association, the information sender can freely specify what is published and when it will be published or broadcast. In contrast, for the latter, the media independently selects the information and publishes and broadcasts it in the form of articles or programs. In this case, the media side has the editing rights over content and the information sender does not have the power to determine what is published or broadcast.

Within these two types, media relations target the latter. Although the information sender does not have the power to determine what is published or when it is published, for example as an article, readers trust it more than paid advertising. Moreover, the more reliable the reader considers the media it is published in, the more reliable they will consider the article containing the sender's information, thereby increasing the communication effects. The objective of media relations is not simply to obtain publicity, but instead, through exchanging information with the media, to communicate information that the information sender wants to send to an unspecified number of information receivers accurately, fairly, and as favorably as possible through uninterrupted communication with the media. To achieve this, it is vital that media relations managers (practitioners) build favorable relations with the media daily by actively calling on journalists and deepening their understanding of the organization's philosophy, management-related matters, products, and services.

Good media relations can be said to be the result of an accumulation of efforts by the information sender and the media relations manager. However, sufficient time must be taken to build trust and friendly relations with the media, including by fully understanding elements such as the media's characteristics and attitude to reporting.

If media relations results in incomplete or incorrect information being reported, this information instantaneously forms an impression in society and, depending on its content, can do considerable damage to the relevant parties. Based on this alone, we must be aware of the major role played by media relations.

## Role of the public relations professional as a media relations manager

Organizations, such as businesses, central governments, Not for profit organizations (NPOs) and Non-governmental organizations (NGOs), and local governments, will employ a PR professional or a professional from a PR firm to be their media relations manager. The parties that the media relations manager is involved with can broadly be divided into the following three groups:

* Organization that the media relations manager represents,
* Media (especially journalists),
* Stakeholders of the organization that organizations are trying to influence through the information being sent by the media.

Media relations managers are constantly aware of these three groups as they carry out their work, because the manager's role is to satisfy the demands of these groups.

As a result, an organization's media relations manager must be very knowledgeable about the organization they represent, about the surrounding environment in which the organization must operate, about the media, and about stakeholders. Of these requirements, the key to conducting successful media relations is the ability to grasp changes and trends, and a sense of timing as to when to take advantage of trends to maximize the impact of the information the media relations manager wants to send out to stakeholders.

Being knowledgeable about the following points about the media are of critical importance.

a) Taking the viewpoint of the media   When contacting the media, first, the manager must be very familiar with the news. This does not simply mean being familiar with the news in terms of the information that is reported, but also understanding the value of news from the media's perspective and the characteristics of the media.

For example, even if an organization carries out restructuring, that is not news if many other organizations are also carrying out restructuring. For the restructuring of that organization alone to be reported as news, it must take the media's perspective to think of how to present this information so it has value to the media as news. Also, the manager must be very familiar with analyzing information to understand what sort of news the reader or listener will find interesting and what will create a favorable impression of their company, or alternatively, what will minimize any bad feelings toward their organization.

In addition, it is important for the media relations manager to understand how the common sense that forms the basis for the media's reporting is unique to that profession. While one cannot make sweeping generalizations that one or the other is correct, sometimes conditions in society change and so common sense changes, and it is difficult to make a judgment. Furthermore, there will be cases when the reporting of information is not favorable. When this sort of reporting occurs, it may be necessary to sincerely accept the contents of the reporting and to perform a self-analysis, and if necessary, self-correction. Today, we are in an era in which organizations cannot operate by thinking only from the perspective of the limited world they belong to.

### b) Building appropriate relationships with members of the media

In general, the members of the media such as journalists, editors, and freelancers look harshly upon PR media relations managers who don't understand the meaning and significance of the news. An organization's lack of skill in dealing with the media affects the content of the media's reporting on it. Once information has been reported, it is already too late to criticize the media for essentially inaccurate reporting. Conversely, only commenting on the critical attitude of the media leaves the impression that there is a lack of recognition of and reflection on the problems that were initially reported on, and this type of criticism results in the failure of media relations. For media relations managers, understanding the media and building appropriate relations with it enables them to avoid any extra problems and minimizes the risk of failure.

### c) Maintaining personal relationships with members of the media

Many of the journalists in the news media and other media organizations have a fiercely competitive attitude about seeking news stories. While on the one hand, if a media relations manager can provide information that results in a "news scoop," the journalist receiving the scoop will be very grateful. On the other hand, all those journalists that did not get that information, and whom the media relations manager has built personal relations with, may have bad feelings at not having received the same information. Therefore, the media relations manager needs to be conscious of the negative side to providing one journalist with a "scoop" and weigh the trade-offs between what is gained and what is lost in terms of maintaining good relations with members of the media.

Interviews are generally one-on-one and the media relations manager, before arranging an interview, must contact the media, after first becoming familiar with aspects like the nature of the news media, the personality and characteristics of the journalists, and their behavior patterns.

Another basic requirement is that the media relations manager knows the details of the organization they represent, because members of the media will request a wide range of general information and specific details, before they agree to give news coverage. At these times, the manager must have acquired the ability to explain the relevant information clearly and simply, so that journalists can then write a favorable article that explains to their audience in terms that are readily understandable by the average person (audience).

But despite all the media relations manager's efforts, there will be only a few cases in which the information provided is reported on exactly as was hoped for. Moreover, except for major news stories, the media relations manager will rarely be approached by the media side. The manager takes the initiative, and must consider, based on the public relations program that has been formulated, what information to provide to which media to generate the desired press coverage.

d) Understanding media deadlines for providing information   The biggest
pitfall in building relations with the media is the problem of meeting their deadlines. Whether information is provided in time for the deadline will determine
whether that information is reported on, so the cardinal rule for PR managers
is to obey the deadlines or agreed-on delivery dates. The deadlines in the print
media are particularly strict. In contrast, the electronic media, such as television,
radio, and the Internet, frequently have deadlines for the provision of information of between 5 to 10 minutes before the start of the broadcast (or even instantaneously in the case of the Internet). If there is breaking news, for example
the occurrence of some sort of incident, accident, or political events, it will be
reported as it occurs during the time that the program is being broadcast.

## Media relations programs

Media relations managers utilize various "media programs," such as a press conference or a press release. There are various methods of implementing a media
program but, generally speaking, to implement a program of effective activities it is
essential to always prepare a media list and press kit. Figure 2.8 introduces the main
media relations programs.

Selecting the appropriate media program will depend on the nature of the topic
and the news material. Also, we must not forget that what is shared among all these
activities is the communication of the key message based on type of public relations
being carried out, such as marketing public relations (marketing PR) and corporate
public relations (corporate PR).

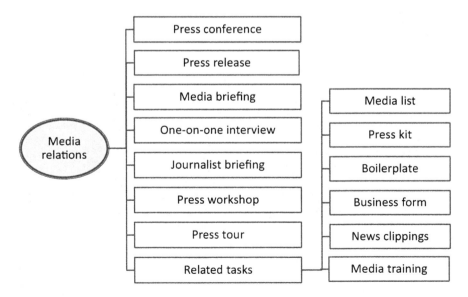

**FIGURE 2.8**   Major examples of media relations

*Source:* Takashi Inoue (2015), *Public Relations: Relationship Management*, 2nd edition, p. 33

a) Press conferences    Press conferences are held based on the attendance of media journalists and editors on topics that have high value as news, so naturally coverage of their content in articles and in other ways is high. Press conferences normally last one hour, although they can be longer depending on the topic. In the first 30 minutes, the organization holding the press conference will give a speech or presentation, while the remaining 30 minutes is allocated to questions and answers. Because press conferences are held for such things as the official announcements of an organization's management changes, business strategies, or innovative new technology or products, it is necessary that responsible heads of the organization, such as the head of product development, head of finance, or top executives attend. Also, in the questions and answers session it is necessary to anticipate questions from various viewpoints and to be able to answer them there and then.

In terms of the layouts of the venues, press conferences usually have a classroom-like layout with the organizers facing the journalists (Figure 2.9), while press briefings tend to be held in a more sociable space, such as with a U-shaped or a square-shaped layout (Figure 2.10).

b) Press briefings    Press briefings are held to provide opportunities for top management to brief the media on its management strategy and global or local business strategy, even on topics where the value as news is not that high. Press

FIGURE 2.9    Press conference venue layout

*Source:* Takashi Inoue (2015), *Public Relations: Relationship Management*, 2nd edition, p. 34

**FIGURE 2.10**   Press briefing venue layout

*Source:* Takashi Inoue (2015), *Public Relations: Relationship Management*, 2nd edition, p. 34

briefings are carried out in a comparatively friendly atmosphere, and sometimes accompanied with lunch or dinner.

In press briefings, the various media being targeted are provided with individual briefings on the information the organization wants to send and the background to it. The objective is not just for the information to be turned into an article, but also to ensure a correct understanding of information that could be easily misunderstood is obtained. As this entails talking directly with the journalists responsible, press briefings also have the purpose of exploring the information needs of the media side. When PR operations have been outsourced to a PR firm, normally press briefings will be carried out by the PR firm's AE (account executive or client manager). Depending on the objective, briefings will also be carried out along with the representatives from the client, such as the PR managers, marketing managers, and technical manager.

c) **Press releases (news releases)**   Press releases are announcements in a pre-scribed format to communicate materials, such as management information, mar-keting information, and technical information about an organization to be reported on by the news media. They are the general format for providing information to the news media and are sent in various ways, including by fax, email, postal mail or simply posted in journalist clubs as is the case in Japan.

There are various types of press releases, including releases to provide topical information with the objective of it being turned into an article, to provide back-ground information, or to provide a reminder to the media about something. When the objective is for the information to be turned into an article, in many cases it is effective to contact and pitch to the journalist in advance of releasing it, including to individually brief journalists on the article you hope they will publish.

**d) One-on-one interviews (individual interviews)**   In this format, a specific media is selected and it is provided with information by setting up an opportunity for it to interview top management and executives. Unlike the previously described press release, in which the same information is sent simultaneously to many media, here the target is narrowed down to a specific media and it alone is provided with information. As a result, it is highly possible that the information provided will be used for an article. The following points should be kept in mind in order to obtain coverage from these opportunities as effectively as possible:

* Confirm in advance such things as the objectives of the interview, the questions, how the interview will be handled, where the contents of the interview will be placed in the media,
* Find out to the greatest possible extent, such things about the journalist as their positions on issues, their track record, preferences and special interests in the field being reported on,
* Provide the journalist with background information materials, such as a company summary, financial data, summary of the business departments, materials on specific topics, and biographies of the people who will be interviewed.

## Japan's journalist clubs system

"Journalist clubs," which are known as "kisha clubs," are a system unique to Japan and there has been much discussion on their advantages and disadvantages. When contacting the media, one possible method is to approach journalists individually, but another method is to approach them via journalist or press clubs. Frequently in Japan it is a mixture of both these approaches.

Currently, journalist clubs rent offices within the facilities of central government ministries and agencies, major political party headquarters, local governments, in various industry groups, and in the main economic organizations. Nationwide, there are journalist clubs in more than 200 locations. These organizations are strongly exclusionary and they tend to be allied to organizations like major newspapers, the main regional media, TV stations, or news agencies, and they almost exclusively receive information from the organization in which they are situated and write articles based on that information. In response to the outcry against them from foreign journalists in the 1990s, because of their exclusivity, they have recently been moving in the direction of becoming more open.

Journalist clubs began in Japan in 1890 on the opening of the Imperial Diet, according to the *Nihon Shimbun Nenkan* (A year book containing extensive information on newspapers, broadcasters, and news agencies) (Nihon Shimbun Kyokai, 2005), when journalists requesting interviews formed the "Group of Journalists Visiting the Diet" (subsequently, Alliance of Journalists Club). Following World War II, in 1949 the Japan Newspaper Publishers and Editors Association expressed its view that journalist clubs were "Voluntary gatherings of journalists who have been assigned to the various public institutions that are organizations for socialization and are not in any way to intervene in matters related to reporting." Subsequently, in 1978 it updated its view and described them as "Organizations that aim to achieve the enlightenment and fellowship of journalists through their daily reporting activities," and then in its opinion expressed in 1997, positioned them as being "bases for reporting."

In 2002, the *Nihon Shimbun Kyokai* (The Japan Newspaper Publishers & Editors Association) issued a new opinion on journalist clubs, stating that they were "Independent organizations for coverage and reporting" (Nihon Shimbun Kyokai, 2002) that were formed from the list of journalists that continually report on public institutions and other organizations. Also, within the major changes to the environment surrounding the media, including media diversification alongside the spread of the Internet and the enforcement of laws on disclosing information, it is recognized that journalist clubs are becoming more open.

Following the establishment of the Yukio Hatoyama Cabinet in September 2009, progress has been made in opening up the press conferences, for example, of the Ministry of Foreign Affairs to those journalists who do not belong to journalist clubs. Journalists on lists of magazines and Internet media separate from journalist clubs and freelancers became able to attend press conferences and ask questions. As of August 2013, the organizations whose press conferences allow freelance journalists and other parties to participate, after completing certain procedures, had expanded to include many government offices and ministries, such as the Cabinet Office, the Ministry of Finance, the Financial Services Agency, the Japan Fair Trade Commission, the Consumer Affairs Agency, the Ministry of Internal Affairs and Communications, the Ministry of Justice, the Ministry of Foreign Affairs, and the Ministry of Education (Inoue, 2015, pp. 36–37).

However, in the journalist club system, the organization provides the same releases and briefings to all the affiliated media, so it weakens the potential for scoops. This environment seems to favor the affiliated press, but if seen from the viewpoint of the sides sending out the information, it can also be understood as enabling them to control the media more easily.

## Case study: Apple's Macintosh campaign for a global product launch

Although personal computers today are so much more advanced then in 1984, at that time Apple's Macintosh (Mac) system was something of a revolutionary breakthrough (Inoue, 2015, pp. 37–39). Much of what we take for granted as standard, such as the use of a "mouse" and a "graphic user interface," first became known from the launch of the Mac. And, although this took place over 40 years ago, and today there are smartphones with full Internet access that have an almost endless variety of "apps," and voice recognition has become common, this case study remains a classic example from which to understand media relations and how it can be used to successfully launch a product based on innovative technology. Through this public relations campaign, which made an extensive focus on media relations, the Mac's user-friendly functions proved to be an enormous hit in 1984 with the Japanese, who up to that time had been relatively unfamiliar with using a keyboard.

Within the gradually increasing market shares of domestic PC manufacturers in the Japanese market, Apple Computer Inc., whose own market share had been growing relatively sluggishly, set a goal to position the Mac as a strategic product to restore its fortunes and set the following three PR objectives:

- Give the impression that Apple remains an innovator in the PC market,
- Obtain the awareness as quickly as possible and among as many people as possible of the existence of the Mac and its superior functionality,
- Spread the product concept advocated by Apple that "the personal computer is a tool to expand the abilities and creativity of individuals."

In its media relations for these targets, the most critical target was the second target of widely obtaining awareness as quickly as possible of the Mac and its superior functionality. Furthermore, Apple conceived of a strategy toward realizing its targets in a highly cost-effective manner by starting with the press conference to announce the Mac, implementing Apple's campaign centered on one-on-one interviews with top management from its head office and on workshops to obtain the understanding of the press on the superior functionality and usability of the Mac.

A press conference was held at Hotel Okura in Tokyo, which is one of the most prestigious hotels in Japan, in front of more than 180 invited journalists. Apple's new product, "the Macintosh," had been attracting a lot of interest and attention since its development stage, but due to the time difference at this press conference, it was to be released onto the Japanese market ahead of the rest of the world.

The press conference is well described in *Ringo no Kinoshitade* (*Under the Apple Tree*) (Saito, 2003) by Yutaka Saito, who reported in detail on the history of the entry of Apple Computers into the Japanese market. From it, we get a clear picture of the atmosphere at that time in terms of the interest that the launch of the Mac generated.

> On January 24, the curtain was raised first in Japan due to the time difference in the press conference for the global simultaneous launch of Apple's new model. On that day, the Macintosh press announcement in Japan, which was to be the first in the world for this product, took place in Tokyo on the second floor of the annex building of Hotel Okura in the exhibition hall. The hall that would serve as the venue for the announcement to the journalists was crowded with hundreds of (press related) visitors. Nearly all the visitors were people from the computer industry. The moderator and facilitator on that day, from Inoue Public Relations, tried to be seen by everyone. In addition to Apple Computers Japan President Fukushima, attending the conference were Head of Sales Kinugawa and Schoenfeld, and Takashi Inoue

(Inoue Public Relations) a representative of a leading public relations agency in Japan

*(Saito, 2003, p. 177).*

Immediately after the press conference, other events were actively held, including key media being given one-on-one interviews with Masaya Fukushima, who was Apple Japan's president at the time, and many journalists and editors being invited to attend workshops arranged according to media category. Mr. Fukushima was a third-generation American of Japanese descent, and his unique Japanese exquisitely matched his sharp wit, which proved very popular among the media.

To provide information that was easy to understand for the media's final audience (readers or viewers), it was first necessary to obtain the complete understanding of journalists, who would be writing about the superior functionality and usability of the Mac. Therefore, participant-type workshops were held centered on demonstrations of the Mac system, the actual software was run, and the participants could experience the functionality through using the keyboard and mouse.

In addition, contacts with the media were strengthened, including by implementing a program to lend Mac systems to the editorial departments of publishers for a certain period of time.

These sorts of media relations could achieve publicity effects greater than anticipated in terms of the column inches published in newspapers and magazines in a wide range of genres, as well as the coverage of the product on television news. If these effects were converted into advertising costs, the monetary amount would be well into the hundreds of millions of yen, and furthermore if converted into PR value, which is three to five times the value of advertising, this amount would be greater still.

## 2) Influencer relations

We are all familiar with seeing celebrities endorsing brands from toothpaste to luxury goods on television, and seeing academics appearing on news programs as experts on topics such as politics, business, and social issues. Traditionally, public relations seeks out eminent journalists as influencers, as discussed in the media relations (MR) section previously. In similar ways, just as with selling products through celebrity endorsements or through the reporting of journalists, people are influenced by other people whom they trust.

In this age of hyper-globalization influencer relations take on a new meaning. Because of the Internet and social media, the number, variety, and effectiveness of influencers is greatly expanded. Social media-based influencers potentially can allow for greater precision in targeting of particular audiences, and allow for two-way communications between influencers and their followers.

Influencer relations can be effective for all the various aspects of public relations. For example, persons with specific knowledge and reputation in their field are often used in government relations and lobbying. Even for things like crisis management and reputation management, influencers can reach and persuade their followers. Influencers not only drive awareness, but also drive actions. And, that action is not limited to purchases of products and brands, but it can include support of a political candidate, legislation, causes, and acceptance of new ideas.

In this Internet age, influencers not only provide you with an ability to reach their followers, but potentially to reach the networks of those followers, when they share content from an influencer with their friends and family.

Just as with media relations, influencers must be identified and relationships with them must be developed. They can be used for a specific PR campaign, but it is better to seek out a long-term relationship with them.

Because people are flooded by advertisements all day long, and because the Internet allows them to more selectively seek out information when they need it and from almost unlimited sources, influencer relations is increasingly become a key tool for public relations.

## 3) Investor relations (IR)

### Objectives and functions of investor relations

When investors decide to invest in a company, naturally its past and present performance is important for that decision, but the most important decision criteria involve the company's future growth potential.

Investor relations are the public relations activities that effectively provide investors with information that serves as investment decision criteria. For listed companies, IR is one part of their public relations activities and its goal is to build and maintain mutually favorable relationships with shareholders, investors, and the financial community. Therefore, the following groups of publics are the target audiences in investor relations:

- Existing shareholders and potential shareholders
- Investors (institutional investors/private investors)
- Securities analysts
- Fund managers and investment advisors
- Regulators, and in Japan that would include the Ministry of Finance, the Financial Services Agency, the Securities and Exchange Commission, and the stock exchanges where the company is listed.

Competition between international companies has been intensifying with globalization, but recently the environment surrounding companies has also been changing dramatically. For example, there has been a dramatic increase in the number of individual investors using the Internet as a source of investor information. In recent years, there was the introduction in Japan of mark-to-market accounting for investments, and cash flow accounting requirements. Also in Japan there has also been an increase in corporate M&A (mergers and acquisitions) activity, a trend to eliminate cross-shareholdings between companies, and the rise of foreign investors. Within these developments, investor relations has been rapidly attracting attention and its importance has increased tremendously.

While in the U.S. investor relations are an internal function in which the CEO and CFO play the leading role, in Japan that is not the normal case. As a result, IR in Japan and other non-Western countries may likely be offered as a service by public relations firms and specialized IR firms that are subsidiaries of brokerage companies such as Nomura Securities and SMBC Nikko Securities.

Compared to other types of relations, investor relations activities are highly specialized and are thought to hold a special position within corporate public relations. *Effective Public Relations* defined IR as "another specialized part of public relations in publicly held corporations" and defined the specialist role of IR as working "… to enhance the value of a company's stock. This reduces the cost of capital by increasing shareholder confidence and by making the stock attractive to individual investors, financial analysts, and institutional investors." It describes investor relations as a "specialized part of corporate public relations that builds and maintains mutually beneficial relationships with shareholders and others in the financial community to maximize market value" (Cutlip *et al.*, 2006, p. 20).

And, that explanation of IR is a good example of one of the key themes of this book, which is that public relations acts as the fifth management resource that reinforces the four types of fundamental resources that corporations utilize to build, maintain, and advance their organizations.

## Effects of IR on company management

So what kinds of effects does the introduction of IR have on company management? Let's consider this by looking at a hypothetical example:

We will assume (listed) Company A issued 10 million shares in its IPO. If its current share price is USD $20, then its market capitalization (share price x outstanding shares) will be USD $200 million. Supposing that groups like institutional investors, securities analysts, and individual investors obtained IR information on Company A and its management team, or on other elements such as its business plan, and decided that it was an appealing investment. Then, when as a result its share price rises to USD $25, its market capitalization will be USD $250 million.

Company A is planning to construct a R&D center to strengthen its research and development capabilities and intends to raise the necessary funds of USD $200 million by newly issuing shares. In this case, when one share is worth USD $25, issuing 800,000 shares would be sufficient, but if one share was worth only USD $20, it would need to newly issue one million shares.

Even in the case of a corporate merger from within M&A, which has been attracting much attention recently, the stock market capitalizations of both companies will form the grounds for calculating the merger ratio. In such ways, when corporate value is improved by IR, it does not merely increase the value of the shares held by investors, it also makes it possible to carry out the relevant company financing through issuing fewer shares, M&A, and obtaining additional financing from financial institutions. This can be said to be exactly "the effects of IR." What is vitally important here is that the share price does not wildly fluctuate and, therefore, does not become a target for speculative investment.

## Roles played by PR and IR practitioners

In the area of investor relations to improve corporate value, maintain an appropriate share price, and deepen investors' understanding, the parts played by the PR and IR practitioners that undertake these tasks are extremely large. Depending on the abilities of the practitioner, especially in the case of a major company, they can increase their own company's corporate value by hundreds of millions of dollars, as well as cause the opposite situation to occur.

The mission of IR experts is to communicate to the target audiences, such as investors and shareholders, a company's specific management vision and the program to achieve it. To achieve this mission, IR experts must be very knowledgeable about a great many aspects, not just about the performance of the corporation, but also such things as corporate finance, requirements and trends of the main stock exchanges both domestically and internationally, international commerce, financial reporting standards imposed by securities trading regulations, and about the securities analysts that follow the corporation's stock price.

Furthermore, in today's age of hyper-globalization, in addition to this knowledge they must have English skills, powers of insight and comprehension for the international economy and international politics, and be able to take advantage of social media. Moreover, a share price is like a living thing that is each day affected by external and internal factors and is constantly changing. So, because companies must respond sensitively to business trends and the direction that will be taken, it is vital that these consultants determine the timing for sending IR messages.

In the finance and securities industries, on the one hand, the fact is that in Japan there are still only a few PR specialists with the required expert IR knowledge and abundant experience, but on the other hand the IR professionals lack communication experience and knowledge. Therefore, to respond to the rapidly increasing demand for IR, for the time being a wise and effective approach is for PR practitioners to carry out IR operations in cooperation with companies' CFOs and IR practitioners. In addition, there is a need to actively develop activities including corporate PR, crisis communication that will be described later, and seminars and related targeting of investors and securities analysts. It would also be preferable for practitioners to demonstrate sufficient ability for the creation of the IR tools listed below.

- Annual reports
- Business reports
- Fact sheets
- Financial statements
- Supplementary materials

- Materials introducing the company, its business activities, technologies, and products

  - Newsletters
  - Online video content, social media
  - Homepages/email newsletters/social media (Facebook, Twitter).

## Case study: SAG (M&A case)

In 2008 the international technology company SAG, based in the city of Mainz in Germany conducted a tender offer bid (TOB) to acquire the majority of the shares of Company M, which had its head office in Tokyo, and was listed on the Tokyo Stock Exchange (TSE).

Company M was a major domestic company in the field of lighting systems, with products based on light-emitting diodes (LED) and optical fiber products, including an optical system for industrial image processing. It had around 450 employees and sales of more than €100 million (fiscal year ended March 2008: approximately ¥16.1 billion).

Conversely, SAG was the world's largest manufacturer of optical fiber transmission cables and image guides. The company's only business department was its Fiber Optics Business Department and it had manufacturing bases in the United States, Mexico, the Czech Republic, and Germany, while its Tokyo sales office employed around 730 staff. The company provided customized, hi-tech solutions based on its fiber optics and LED technologies and had expanded into automotive, lighting, medical, and industrial products, as well as the construction market.

**a) Conducting research and setting targets**   In the context of the intensification of competition in the international market in the fields of optical image processing and lighting systems, and furthermore, the progress in switching from optical fiber systems to LED-based solutions, SAG set the following three targets to make it possible for it and Company M to strengthen their alliance toward increasing their international competitiveness and achieving steady growth:

- Utilize the respective sales networks of Company M, a leading company in Japan, and utilize SAG, a leading company in Europe and North America, to mutually realize sales of their major products in all three markets,
- Specify the products that they could supply to each other and thereby reduce purchasing costs,
- Integrate both companies' development efforts toward developing new products.

**b) Planning**   In this TOB, SAG aimed for a non-hostile acquisition of a majority of the shares (more than 50%) of Company M. Therefore toward implementing the TOB, SAG first selected securities Company S to be its independent financial advisor and asked it to calculate the value of Company M's shares. Based on this calculation, SAG set a purchase price of ¥740 per common share.

c) Implementation    The tender offer period was set as September 25 to October 23, 2008 (20 business days) with the start date for the settlement as October 30, and the "Notification of the Commencement of a Tender Offer for the shares of Company M," was issued through a security-related network and media relations.

d) Evaluation    The results of the TOB exceeded expectations and SAG acquired 70.8% of the shares of Company M. In addition, Company M maintained its listing on the first section of the TSE.

In this way, the business partnership between the two companies was further strengthened, which had been the initial target, and the success of the two companies' partnership was shown to the markets and their customers. During that period, it goes without saying that a lot of attention was paid to communicating with the employees of Company M.

## 4) Government relations (GR)

### Objectives and functions of government relations

It goes without saying that the actions and decisions of central government and local governments have an enormous impact on company management and people's lives. Political trends can greatly affect company management, especially in the era of hyper-globalization.

Professor Yoshihiro Tsurumi an economist and professor of international business at Baruch College of the City University of New York, speaking at a 2012 lecture given at the Society of Global Business in Tokyo, said: "Japan's company managers are required to have an awareness of an information strategy in which politics is inseparable from economics and of lobbying in public relations" (Tsurumi, 2012). Today, in a time of fierce global competition more than ever before companies and organizations are demanding from the government and the regulators more economic deregulation and revisions of laws in order to keep up with other countries.

Government relations is the wide range of activities for organizations to achieve their objectives and targets for their businesses and organizational activities through their relationships with the government and regulatory agencies. These activities include collecting information and holding meetings, seminars and debates, and media relations. The information sender builds persuasive communication with government and regulatory-related parties, related industry groups, and other publics that are its target audiences.

Sometimes in the United States, government relations have the same definition as government affairs.

## Government relations in Japan

Government relations in the United States is actively deployed through lobbying and other activities. But in Japan, for a long time, the relationship between companies and regulatory agencies has had the strong aspect of a convoy system that was mutually beneficial to both sides through lobbying and support in elections under the umbrella of regulations and subsidies. In some cases, a financial institution will employ a Ministry of Finance relations head, who was formerly a high-ranking official of the Ministry of Finance, which is the agency responsible for regulating financial institutions. This practice, has continued as a uniquely Japanese type of close relationship in which business and government lean on each other, and is called by the Japanese name of "Amakudari," which means "descent from heaven."

In other words, transparent government relations in Japan has only been carried out to a certain extent within the context of the demands from foreign companies and their organizations to open up the protected market of Japan. But within the flow of globalization, various international economic agreements have been negotiated, such as the Trans-Pacific Partnership Agreement (TPP) and the Economic Partnership Agreement (EPA), and in this environment, progress in Japan is expected to be made in structural reforms, deregulation, and the expansion of competitive markets. Although the U.S. pulled out of the TPP at the start of 2017, Japan and the U.S. will likely agree on something similar only on a bilateral basis. Government relations as practiced in public relations will continue to be an important part of businesses' efforts to gain access to foreign markets.

For the successful practice of government relations, it is necessary to understand how policy of each country is discussed and decided by the various parties involved, which would include politicians, government bureaucracies, businesses and business associations, and the media.

This can be best understood by seeing this relationship as a structure. Each country will have its own structure. In the case of Japan, it has been described as an "iron triangle" and this is shown graphically in Figure 2.11. While Japan's power structure has been changing little by little since the 1990s, for a long time in the post-war period the structure has involved three groups from the worlds of politics (politicians), bureaucracy (bureaucrats), and business (managers) that have maintained a power balance through their relations with each other.

This arrangement has changed and is now formed by four groups, as the mass media has clearly come to participate as the fourth group, particularly after the Lockheed scandal of 1976. In 1993 the mass media demonstrated its influence in ways that led to the collapse of the Liberal Democratic Party, which had held power continuously from 1955, and to the start of the Hosokawa Administration. This rise of the mass media as the fourth pillar of power has resulted in it taking the position of representing public opinion, while at the same time it also has considerable influence on the formation of public opinion.

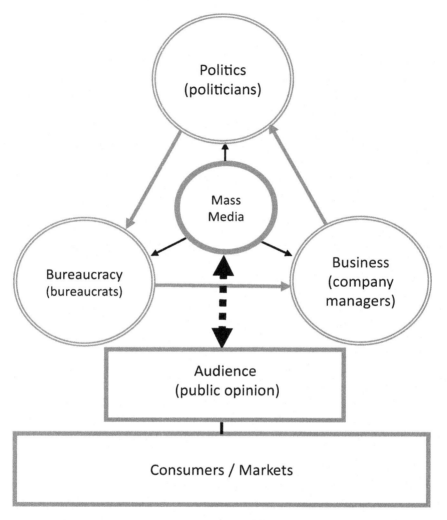

**FIGURE 2.11** Relations between politics, business, bureaucracy, and the mass media in Japan

*Source:* Takashi Inoue (2006), *Public Relations*, p. 43

## Setting clear targets and building a strategy

So what are the points to consider for a company to effectively carry out government relations? First, as with other types of public relations, it is necessary to envisage the objectives to be achieved. Then, it is necessary to determine the period required to bring about results, and the form, such as deregulation, regulatory enforcement, or receiving a subsidy.

In addition, a market analysis is needed, and the PR professional must ascertain the laws and regulations that apply to the objectives. For example, when the objective is deregulation, conventionally it is appropriate to have a program with a period of from a minimum of two years to around five years, starting from the preparation stage.

Like the "public," "government" is very broad and it is necessary to specifically determine the exact target audiences: for example, the government agency that regulates computers and related information equipment, or the agency regulating health care when the government relations objectives are for a drug manufacturer. However, in the matters related to deregulation as the ultimate objective, in many cases, the relevant government bodies will straddle many government ministries and agencies, so usually there will be multiple target audiences.

After setting the objectives and target audiences, it is next vital to build a strategy to steadily achieve the objectives. Unlike normal public relations activities, in most cases an organization conducts government relations in areas where its own power does not extend, such as in changing regulations or passing new laws. Therefore, based on two-way communication, in addition to having high-level information analysis capabilities, an organization must be able to respond sensitively to information coming from the government parties, and if necessary, carry out self-correction and react flexibly to changes in the situation.

Also, for an organization to achieve its objectives, it is important that it takes the viewpoint of how to make consumers and other stakeholders happy. In other words, while it will depend on the program content, the key to guiding a program to success is determining how to create a win-win situation in which as well as your own organization, all the other stakeholders, such as industry, customers, and end-users will benefit.

A strategy should be built with considerable attention to detail based on a survey and analysis conducted in advance, and then after building the program, the creation of the entire scenario is completed.

## Important role of lobbying

"Lobbying" is a core activity of government relations. In a pluralistic society, such as the United States, lobbying is deployed as part of the democratic system. It reflects the voices of the people and businesses that are affected by the laws and regulations that the government plans to enact.

The objective of lobbying is to influence the government's decisions on laws and regulations and involves directly lobbying the targeted institutions through relationship management activities, such as contacting, explaining, and exchanging ideas, collecting information, attending sessions and hearings held by the institutions of government, and gaining access to government officials and influential lawmakers.

Therefore, lobbying requires that the practitioner be knowledgeable about elements of government, such as the procedures for enacting legislation, policy, and the formation of public opinion. These activities will also be directed at publics other than the government and must be closely coordinated and integrated with other public relations techniques. This is the essence of relationship management.

Normally, lobbying is carried out by practitioners known as lobbyists who possess special abilities. In the United States, in addition to specialist public relations practitioners, the task of lobbying is delegated to lawyers and professional lobbyists who have deep relations with lawmakers and government officials, including former lawmakers and members of political parties. In accordance with the Lobbying Act of 1946, in the U.S. these lobbyists must be registered and they are legally required to disclose all the details of their activities, including submitting a report on their income and expenditure.

In Japan, the image of the lobbyist among some people is still of a mastermind pulling the strings behind the curtain, such as Yoshio Kodama who was a central figure in the Lockheed scandal, or of dubious "fixers acting in the shadows." But in the United States, many different types of companies and organizations, including state governments and foreign governments, have a lobbying function in Washington D.C.

According to data published in February 2015 by the Senate Office of Public Relations, there were 11,78_ registered lobbyists in the United States in 2014, which was below the number of the previous year total of 12,128. Also, it estimated that their total cost was USD $323 billion (Senate Office of Public Relations, 2015).

But according to experts, _t is not the case that lobbying is shrinking. Professor James Thurber of American University, who for more than 30 years has studied the activities of lobbyists to the United States Congress, stated that most of the activities taking place in Washington are not covered, and in his latest advice to the American Bar Association's Task Force on Lobbying Law Reform, said that there are nearly 100,000 active lobbyists (Thurber, 2010).

Lobbying is a specialist field of public relations to build and maintain relations with government and mainly has the objective of influencing the passing of laws and regulations. Despite the abuse of their responsibilities that lobbyists are from time to time guilty of and the resulting criticism from citizens, lobbying is a legal and tolerated method in a civil society whereby various organizations, such as trade unions, companies, cr other special groups, try to influence government decision-making.

To deepen your understanding of government relations, please refer to the Tenneco Automotive case study that resulted in deregulation, which is introduced in Chapter 6. It provides a practical example of a PR strategy for deregulation in automotive negotiations between Japan and the United States.

## 5) Employee relations (ER)

### Objectives and meaning of employee relations

The types of public relations described up to this point have mainly been between an organization, or group, and its external target audiences or stakeholders. But employee relations, which are also commonly called "employee communications," are the activities within relationship management to build relationships inside companies and organizations, primarily through communications. Although the word "employee" may sometimes not include top executives, board members, part-time workers, or non-salaried "contract" workers, in this discussion the term is used more broadly to mean any member of an organization.

In Japan, in many cases information or instructions flow in one direction, from the people at the top of the organization toward those at the bottom. But when considered from the viewpoint of communications, it is important that the public relations professional, doing employee relations, cooperates not only with top management, but also closely works with HR. There are many aspects of employee relations that clearly can only be handled by HR, but it is the public relations professional who is better positioned for the kind of strategic communications needed to fully establish a relationship between employees and top management that motivates, inspires, and guides employees in successful completion of the organization's goals. It is essential to understand that the PR professional needs to work in close collaboration with HR to achieve the ultimate objective of building relationships of mutual trust between an organization and its members through effective two-way communications.

Employee relations adds to the value of employees, which are a key resource of any organization, by establishing an environment in which new concepts and innovative ideas are created and employees work for the growth of their organization. In other words, employees' motivation can be improved by creating a public relations program that seeks to encourage people to ask: "What can be done?" and "What can be obtained?" Also, providing a pleasant workplace environment further promotes the kind of communications between an organization and its members that are vital for achieving organizational goals.

To give an example, imagine the case of a company described as having one-man management, where the president rules almost as a dictator, making all key decisions without regard to others in the company. This signifies a critical lack of employee relationships in which trust has been established throughout the members of the company. In this sort of situation, in the event of a M&A or a scandal, this company will be unable to obtain the understanding and cooperation of its employees and will suffer major damage. Employee relations need to be built through a long-term, continuous, and strategic effort, and cannot be created instantly when suddenly needed due to unexpected events.

## Employees are changing

Recently, employee relations have been attracting much attention, because today communication failure is more likely to occur within an organization, especially with all the changes occurring in society, and in every industry.

In the case of Japan, which is an island nation with a unique and homogeneous culture, and where businesses enjoyed similar characteristics that were fostered by the policy of "lifetime employment," this change has been felt very strongly. As a country that was positioned to become "number one" in the 1970s, Japan began to lose competitive advantage to other countries in the global market place and its companies have had to close factories, lay off workers, and begin to employ a mixture of many part-time and full-time employees.

Increasingly the workforce now includes employees from other countries. And, throughout the world, entire industries are having to also make changes in the types of employees that they hire. For example, the transformation in commerce driven by the Internet requires different types of employees that are more suitable for such changes, particularly as stores are being replaced by online shopping, and as entirely new business models are built around Internet and smartphone technologies. As already mentioned, even the car manufacturing industry is having to make similar personnel changes as new types of competitors, such as Google and Tesla, introduce revolutionary changes with self-driving and electric-powered cars. This change in the types of people employed not only transforms the culture of organizations, but also affects various aspects of the working environment, personnel appraisals, and the salary system.

All these changes make it more important that public relations for employee relations be used to shape or reshape the culture of organizations, to reduce tension between different types of employees, as well as between employees and management, and to create the right environment for an organization to survive and prosper in a time of fluid change.

## Systematic communication

Employee relations is mainly public relations within an organization using systematic and symmetrical two-way communications. Systematic communications entails providing a channel to send and receive information with employees utilizing every type of tool and technology. There are a variety of tools currently available and it is highly likely that new ones will appear through the advance in technology. Until recently, a leading method was to print newsletters and booklets; however, the speed and low cost of digital solutions are popular, especially using social media, such as Twitter, Facebook, YouTube, Instagram, and LINE, which can be updated frequently and allow for photos and videos. Moreover, these Internet solutions also allow for two-way communications through such things as online chat and allowing uploading of content by employees.

But simply preparing tools is not in itself sufficient as it is also necessary to understand how to use them effectively, including by investigating the communication process. For example, levels of employee satisfaction can be improved by establishing within the company an awards system, a study abroad program, or an Employee Appreciation Day, and by distributing employee profiles. This is one part of systematic communications that acts like a lubricant within the company.

Because of the recent increase in online information accessed by both employees as internal stakeholders and all the external stakeholders, accelerating the back-and-forth of information within the company and externally, it is necessary to have speedy decision-making to conduct both employee communications and communications with external stakeholders. Rather than rely on a single tool, in many cases it is more effective to use many tools simultaneously.

Going forward, the demands for even greater volumes of more diverse information, and the explosive growth of real-time data created by the Internet will result in the use of AI and big data to analyze employee dissatisfaction and to improve effective communication.

## Symmetrical two-way communication

Symmetrical two-way communication referred to here is where the flow of information is not just going up and down following the typical hierarchal organization structure, but flows across the organization following the non-hierarchal structure of a "flat" organization structure. This is also explained in the context of the four public relations models of Grunig that are detailed in the beginning of the next chapter. Basically, communications that follow along a hierarchal path are one-way instructions of orders or collecting of information in an up-down direction only. In contrast, with symmetrical two-way communications information flows more in a flat direction of mutual discussions and exchanges of documents.

For example, one effective method of communication is establishing opportunities for the leaders of the company and employees to exchange opinions face-to-face while having lunch at the same table. Furthermore, a typical example of taking a step further is the focus groups formed by companies as a technique adopted from the conventional approach to create opportunities to understand actual conditions. In a focus group, the theme is decided on, the participants recruited, and the opinions they express in a free-discussion format without the participation of the organizers or other related parties are then aggregated. Therefore, in this technique, it is left up to the organizers who will participate and what they will do and their aggregated opinions are then reported to the heads of the company and used as materials to determine whether to correct a new strategy. Their effects are extremely large as focus groups create an environment in which the participants can freely express their opinions, and an increasing number of companies are using them.

## Employee dissatisfaction and effective communication

One of the dissatisfactions felt by many company employees is that in a lot of cases, they come to find out information about their own company not via internal communications, but via external communications, such as newspapers or other media. When trying to find out the facts, it is often the case that externally provided information is faster and more detailed than the information that companies are providing employees. Particularly in the case of Japanese companies, from time to time external communications via the press are carried out for important company announcements, so there are cases where employees have lost trust in their company as they are the last to find out the details.

It is preferable not to create this wide gap in timing and content between internal and external information, and important to not build an information wall – namely, information known in detail externally that cannot be confirmed internally.

In the West, particularly in the United States, increasingly companies are preparing annual reports not just for shareholders, but also for employees and moreover notifying them if something is happening from a financial aspect. What is required of the information sent within employee relations is that it has "value," "consistency," and "quality." Effective employee relations cannot be realized unless the information that employees want to know is sent to them as necessary, or regularly with sufficient content. Also, when a scandal occurs in a company, it goes without saying that it must ensure transparency and the appropriate timing of its information disclosure.

## Points to remember to effectively send information

The best way to increase employees' confidence in the company is to tell them the facts honestly and frankly. This makes it possible to reduce any distrust they may feel toward the company.

Most employees will to a certain extent trust their company and will accept information received from it, especially when the information is important to them as the basis for their relationship with the company. It is unavoidable that providing employees with negative information about their company will cause them to feel anxious and upset, but on the other hand communicating this information is also useful in building trust with them. In this case, what is important is to directly communicate the message to employees while anticipating how they will react to it.

What should also be paid attention to is that in today's Internet era, it is highly possible that any type of company-provided information will be easily communicated to external audiences. The causes of this can be carelessness or a deliberate leak and maliciousness. In a company in which a scandal is occurring or that is reducing employee numbers, a situation can arise in which the employees involved and their colleagues are warned internally and the information then leaks externally. But even saying this, to restrict the information provided to employees would be to destroy the foundations on which employee relations are based. It is important to always be careful of what is internally communicated, knowing that the information might be leaked. The best method would seem to be to pay careful attention when writing documents so that no great harm would be caused even if in-company communication documents or files are leaked externally.

## Internal communications for a corporate merger and building a new corporate culture

As was previously stated, the ultimate objective of employee relations is "to build relations of trust between a company and its employees." But, a corporate merger is a classic example of an event that can create a crisis in employees' feelings of trust. For example, there was a case of certain banks merging, in which it took nearly 10 years for personnel departments to become integrated. When companies that were previously competitors become a single organization, various problems exist below the surface of what in name has become a single company.

Fortunately, there are also examples of successful employee relations, in which the disadvantages of a corporate merger were kept to the minimum and the advantages were quickly made real to employees. One such example is the enormous merger involving the major United States aerospace companies of Boeing and McDonnell Douglas.

Both companies announced the merger at practically the same time and, following a survey on the potential problems for the merger, within a week they had recognized that the most important issue was that "a lack of communication with the employees of both companies would produce a bottleneck for the merger." They therefore concluded that "it was critically important for the employees of both companies to have a unified vision" of the merger and toward this they launched a full-fledged employee relations program.

The key message was set as "One Company, One Vision" and various tools were used and a system established so that they could constantly share the latest information with employees. The total number of employees in both companies was around 220,000, but even their families were set as the target audience for communication.

After the merger took effect and the new company was launched, a proactive employee relations program was deployed, including delivering an information package to the homes of every single employee, and having the two CEOs directly visiting related facilities in 14 cities around the world.

In the employee questionnaire on the merger many of the respondents confirmed that they thought "the merger was a good idea," from which we can see that the systematic and symmetrical two-way communication was the key to success.

The employee relations program for this enormous merger between Boeing and McDonnell Douglas is summarized below.

## Case study: Boeing and McDonnell Douglas, employee relations for a merger

In August 1997, the largest and second largest manufacturers of commercial aircraft in the United States, Boeing and McDonnell Douglas, merged to create an enormous company with forecast total sales of USD $48 billion and around a 70% share of the global market (Inoue, 2006, pp. 239–243). Both companies announced the merger in December 1996 and carried out the migration work over a period of approximately 7 months. During that time, they conducted a survey to extract the potential problems for this merger of two major companies, created a plan with the objective of solving the problems identified in the survey, and implemented a program to ensure that the merger made a successful start (Inoue, 2006, pp. 239–243).

### a) Implementing the survey and setting targets
Before giving a press conference on the merger plan, Boeing and McDonnell Douglas surveyed 21 employee focus groups with a view to targeting employees ranging from regular employees up to senior executive officers to ascertain their level of understanding about the merger and to improve the current state of communication and the vision and awareness of the relevant parties toward the merger. Three points were clarified

from the results of the focus groups and the third point was a potential obstacle to achieving the merger.

The first point was the importance of communication and they recognized it was necessary not merely to communicate the facts and other information that they knew, but also to reply honestly that "we don't know the answer yet" if they were unable to find an answer to some pending matter or question. The second point was the need to position the merger not as the "funeral" of both companies, but rather as a cause for celebration on the birth of the new company. The third point was that the preparations were not in place for the two companies to work as a single team and at that point in time the attitude among employees was that the merger was not wanted.

Both companies also identified other companies that had experienced a large-scale merger in recent years, selected people who had experienced being in the same position as their employees, and carried out a fact-finding survey through face-to-face interviews. From this, they understood that in these previous cases, the company side had paid only the slightest attention to their employees at each stage of the merger.

In the initial stage of the migration period, both companies ascertained what would be the biggest obstacle to the merger. In fact, the responsible managers in both companies had agreed to the merger 5 days before the press conference and had launched the survey and finished setting the targets before the announcement, so immediately after the press conference on December 15, 1996, they were able to start the program they had planned.

The three targets set by both companies were:

- Achieve a successful merger,
- Prepare for successful operations as a single company from the first day of the merger,
- Solidify the foundations of the new Boeing.

With the focus placed on employees, they prioritized a strategy of "fostering a culture as a single company."

To achieve a successful merger, it is generally considered important to build and maintain the support of important target stakeholders within the respective companies, both domestically and overseas. Boeing implemented a range of plans to ascertain the actual conditions of regulations in Western countries and of its various stakeholders, such as investors, shareholders, financial analysts, employees, customers, and the media. But what particularly stands out as the biggest characteristic of this case study was the priority given to employees and setting clear employee-related targets in the public relations program that was developed.

b) Planning   Boeing created a strategic plan in which communication with employees was set as the top priority. First, it set the basic target of improving their understanding of the merger by constantly communicating the latest information to all employees and sharing information with them at every stage. In this way, it obtained the employees' passionate support for the new company. The target stakeholders for the communication were primarily the more than 220,000 who would become the employees of the new Boeing company and their families, and the scope was employees throughout the world, including in the United States, Canada, and Australia. Communications activities were deployed by using the existing sales and marketing services departments that mainly supported their customers.

To achieve the targets, it was necessary to secure communication channels, so they planned a large-scale information kit for managers, the publication of an in-house newspaper, a website, a telephone service, an internal television program, and regular meetings with employees across 11 fields. They also actively explained the background of the merger to the media and arranged interviews and tours for journalists at their main production bases. This was because they had prioritized having employees receive a lot of information on the companies from the general media. The responsible persons in both companies' management enthusiastically supported the communication program.

c) Implementation   The plan was implemented on schedule, divided between the migration period of January to July 1997 and then from the first day of the merger of August 1.

On the day after the press conference (December 16), 11 communication teams divided according to field were established and information materials to share with the group's employees were distributed to the desks of every manager. The in-house newspaper was published every week and delivered to all the departments in both companies, and it contained many articles on the merger. Videos and the in-house television program were repeatedly and continuously broadcast. Both companies' websites were updated with the latest information daily and the coverage of the merger by the world's media was summarized and sent to key employees. To symbolically express the message of "One Company, One Vision" and to show graphically what Boeing was inheriting through the merger, Boeing's logo was changed, during the transition period, by adding to the name "Boeing" the image of a rocket circling the globe and the image of a jet flying, which were used in the logo of McDonnell Douglas. Also, they attempted to appeal and obtain a positive response internally through media tours.

On the first day of the merger, constructive events relating to all employees were held. On August 1, the day the merger formally came into effect, complete information packages were delivered to the homes of all 220,000 employees. This package included a videotape of the key responsible members of management discussing the vision for and the importance of the merger; a brochure that explained the products, programs, and capabilities of the new Boeing; and commemorative gifts with the new company logo. These packages were even sent to overseas employees.

On the same day, the 176,000 employees in the factories across the United States and Canada watched a television broadcast that took place in the factory from Washington D.C. to hear messages from Boeing's CEO Phil Condit and McDonnell Douglas' CEO Harry Stonecipher, (who were the members of management responsible for the merger), about important information on the new Boeing prior to the official announcement.

Also, through a satellite broadcast of the global news conference on enormous screens installed at the factories, the employees were able to participate in it. In addition, employees selected from across the United States and Canada were invited to Washington D.C. and participated in a meeting with top management. This meeting was one of the few modifications from the planning stage and was announced three weeks before the merger.

The management responsible for the merger in both companies constantly strove to act in a unified manner. The two men did not simply make the announcement together; for 5 days after the merger, side by side they visited factories in 14 cities, toured the production lines, shook hands with employees, posed for photographs, gave autographs, and attended question-and-answer sessions. This tour, which was billed as "Phil and Harry's Excellent Adventure," proved to be an excellent performance that dramatically conveyed the "single company" image.

d) Evaluation   Both companies had a competitive relationship up to the final agreement for the merger, but despite this hardly any problems occurred. Even the preparations for the events for the 220,000 employees were complete as planned within a very tight schedule. The coordinated program that climaxed with the factory visits on the "Phil and Harry" tour was received extremely positively and was a great success.

Using the factory visits as an example, even though the production lines were stopped for one hour, on the day of the visits these factories still achieved records for daily production output. Almost entirely the employees answered on the questionnaire that "the merger itself was a good idea," and the measures for the merger that focused on the employees were also a success. It is important to point out that the public relations program did not end there. The successful public relations program contains a self-correction function based on two-way communications, ethics, and self-correction, and this Boeing case was no exception to this rule. Even though it reached the targets that were set, after the merger, an evaluation was conducted of the communications program, using a questionnaire survey by email, and holding focus groups, which covered 18 stakeholder categories, such as employees, communities, governments, regulators, locations, and suppliers.

## 6)  Community relations (CR)

It is thought that companies in Japan, which is one of the most industrialized nations, became more aware of local communities in the 1970s in the wake of the rise of citizen movements in response to pollution and other problems.

In Japan, from around the 1960s, pollution caused by industrial activities became a social problem and at the start of the 1970s, environment-related regulatory laws began to be enacted. On entering the 1980s, the focus of environmental problems expanded from on the scale of local communities to a global scale, becoming transformed into problems that threaten the very survival of humanity, such as what is called global climate change and the destruction of the ozone layer. In terms of policy, Japan's Ministry of Economy, Trade and Industry created legal regulations for industrial activities in harmony with environmental regulations, provided support for "Town Planning in Harmony with the Environment" in coordination with local governments, and promoted the voluntary initiatives of industry.

With this as the background, to increase their presence and value, companies began placing importance not simply on their business performance, but also on building good relations with local communities and the wider public through Corporate Social Responsibility (CSR) programs, which are a part of public relations.

## Points to remember when formulating a community relations program

### a) Disclosing information to the public
As was previously mentioned, in the wake of the pollution problems in Japan, residents' distrust of companies increased, and in response, companies began to place greater importance on community relations, which meant that above all they had to actively disclose information to the public. When companies hide information, it only exacerbates the distrust that residents feel toward them.

### b) Establishing a reception desk to receive the complaints and opinions of residents
Fundamentally, public relations involve two-way communication activities with a self-correction function. Therefore, even when "disclosing information to the public," information should not flow in one direction only, from the company side to local communities. Instead, to realize two-way communication, it is necessary to establish a section and an email account within the public relations department in the company to receive the complaints and opinions of residents. More recently, however, there is a trend to use social media, particularly, such as Twitter, Facebook, Pinterest, and Instagram, for handling complaints and recommendations.

## Program for reconciling with the local community

A two-way communications process is the fundamental concept in this type of program. One approach is to invite members of local communities and other residents in surrounding areas to visit the company's facilities, such as by having an open house (tours of company facilities including factories and R&D centers), and deepening their understanding of the company's activities, its products, and services. In other words, this program takes the direction of inviting these people to company facilities. One more way of reversing the normal flow is to have members of the company side join the local community side. This can take the form of participating in local events (for example, in Japan this would include such events as the Obon dance festival and other traditional festivals) and supporting local education facilities or participating in local organizations (including chambers of commerce and industry, store associations, and Rotary clubs). Various programs can be envisaged as case studies of companies' contributions to local communities.

Depending on the program's objectives, it can cover a range from as small as a local shopping district to as large as a municipality or region.

## 3 Abilities required for relationship management

Looking back at the various types of relationship management categories that have been introduced so far in this chapter, you should be able to now see a pattern forming in your mind that explains public relations. At its core, public relations is a professional discipline in which a two-way communications process is used to build relationships with targeted stakeholders for achieving the goals of an organization. Much time was devoted to media relations, because it is a core competency to communicate effectively with each type of stakeholder, such as employees, investors, and regulatory bodies, by "talking" to each through the media.

Basically, there are five basic general conditions required by PR practitioners: ethics, positive thinking, scenarios creation for alternative possible solutions, strong IT skills, and increasingly in hyper-globalization, a degree of fluency in English. And, to become proficient in public relations persons must also then develop 10 qualities and skills, such as creativity, curiosity, and leadership, which are covered in Chapter 4 of this book.

Like any profession, public relations covers a broad range of topics, and for that reason it is useful to see it graphically as shown in Figure 2.12.

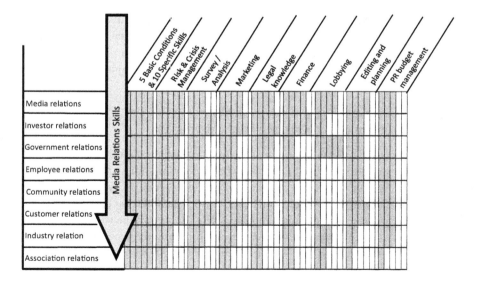

**FIGURE 2.12** Skills required for relationship management

*Source:* Takashi Inoue (2015), *Public Relations: Relationship Management*, 2nd edition, p. 61

The left-most column in Figure 2.12 is a partial listing of the various types of public relations. Floating to the right of that is a downward pointing arrow representing "Media relations skills," which provides an effective means of communicating with each type of stakeholder. And, to the right of that arrow is a column representing the five basic conditions and 10 qualities and skills required by the PR specialist, and the other columns to the right represent various areas of expertise that must be developed to be successful in the profession. These conditions, qualities and skills are used for all the types of stakeholder relationship management; however, the degree of importance will vary for each based on the type of public relations, for example, "marketing" skills are more extensively used for customer relations than for employee relations. Also, the degree of required skills will also vary with the specific objectives to be achieved for each type of public relations. The shading in the boxes is only an indication of the degree of skills and qualities that may be required, but it will vary based on the specific objectives to be achieved.

## References

Cutlip, S. M., Center, A. H., & Broom, G. M. (2006). *Effective Public Relations.* 9th ed. Upper Saddle River, NJ: Pearson Prentice Hall.

Fukase, A. (2015). "Toshiba Accounting Scandal Draws Record Fine from Regulators." *The Wall Street Journal*, December 7, 2015.

Greimel, H. (2016). "Nissan Will Take 34% Controlling Stake in Mitsubishi Motors." *Automotive News*, May 12, 2016, p. 1.

Inoue, T. (2006). *Paburikku rirēshonzu (Public Relations).* 1st ed. Tokyo: Nippon Hyoron Sha.

Inoue, T. (2015). *Paburikku rirēshonzu (Public Relations: Relationship Management).* 2nd ed. Tokyo: Nippon Hyoron Sha.

Kageyama, Y. (2016). "Nissan Takes 34 pct Stake in Scandal-hit Mitsubishi Motors." *Science X Network*, May 12, 2016, p. 1.

Lien, T. (2016). "Tesla and Google Are Both Driving Toward Autonomous Vehicles. Which is Taking the Better Route?" *Los Angeles Times*, July 3, 2016.

Mitsubishi Motors Corporate (2015). "Press Release: Nissan, Mitsubishi Motors and NMKV Reach Agreement on Planning and Development of Next-Generation Minicars." *Mitsubishi Motors,* October 16, 2015. [Online] Available at: http://www.mitsubishi-motors.com/publish/pressrelease_en/corporate/2015/news/detailfa16.html [Accessed November 7, 2016]

Nihon Shimbun Kyokai (2002). *Independent Organizations for Coverage and Reporting.* Tokyo: Nihon Shimbun Kyokai.

Nihon Shimbun Kyokai (2005). *Nihon-Shimbun Nenkan* (A year book containing extensive information on newspapers, broadcasters and news agencies). Tokyo: Nihon Shimbun Kyokai.

Nihon Shimbun Kyokai (2009). "Kisha Club Guidelines." *Nihon Shimbun Kyokai.* [Online] Available at: http://www.pressnet.or.jp/english/about/guideline/ [Accessed August 10, 2017]

Nissan Motor Corporation Global Newsroom (2016). "Full Archive of Nissan and Mitsubishi Motors Joint Press Conference on 16:00JST May 12, 2016." [Online] Available at: http://newsroom.nissan-global.com/videos/video-8b7e1a33d53e6748b65db3e72700cf2f-160512-nissan-mmc [Accessed November 7, 2017]

Nissan Newsroom, Nissan Motor Corporation – Global (2009). "The Renault-Nissan Alliance: Ten years of a Successful Cooperation." [Online] Available at: http://www.

nissan-global.com/EN/DOCUMENT/PDF/ALLIANCE/HANDBOOK/2008/AllianceFigureAndFacts2008.pdf [Accessed November 7, 2017]

Saito, Y. (2003). *Ringo no Kinoshitade (Under the Apple Tree)*. 2nd ed. Japan: Mainichi Communications.

Schmitt, B. (2017). "Nissan-Renault Officially World's Largest Automaker at Halftime." *Forbes*, July 28, 2017.

Senate Office of Public Relations, (2015). [Online] Available at: https://www.whitehouse.gov/sites/default/files/omb/budget/fy2015/assets/objclass.pdf [Accessed 2017]

Thurber, J.A. (2010). "Changing the Way Washington Works? President Obama's Battle with Lobbyists." *Presidential Studies Quarterly*, 41(2), pp. 358–374.

Tsurumi, Y. (2012). *The New Phase of the Third Industrial Revolution in the 21st Century and International Corporate Strategy*. Tokyo: Society of Global Business (First Special Lecture, July 3, 2012 at Hotel New Otani).

# 3

# HISTORICAL GROWTH OF PUBLIC RELATIONS AND ITS DEVELOPMENT IN JAPAN

## 1 Japan and WWII – as seen from the eyes of public relations

After a long period of self-imposed isolation under feudalism, Japan reopened up to the world in the second half of the 19th century, following the twin slogans of "promotion of industry" and "rich country, powerful army." Japan succeeded in industrialization and becoming rich, but the goal of a "powerful army" ended with the dropping of atomic bombs on Hiroshima and Nagasaki. And, given the horrors caused by Hitler and the Nazis, why did the United States choose to drop atomic bombs on Japan and not Germany?

There were various factors, but when considering Japan's surprise attack on Pearl Harbor, which President Roosevelt described as "a date which will live in infamy," it is not hard to understand. The attack fixed in the minds of the American people an image of the Japanese as the "sneaky Japs." The U.S. public, where opinion remained at boiling point from the attack on Pearl Harbor, was emotionally supportive of dropping the bombs, because they had come to see the Japanese as people whose values and culture placed them outside the civilized world.

The Japanese Embassy in Washington D.C. was supposed to deliver the declaration of war to the U.S. government before the attack on Pearl Harbor, but failed, and this diplomatic error created a negative image of the Japanese, which even 70 years after World War II has left an impression in many people's minds of a deceitful Japan and has formed the foundation of a distrust that continues in some American minds. At the point in time that the Japanese government realized that there had been an internal error that caused a delay in notifying the U.S. government of the declaration of war, it should have immediately revealed this fact to the international community. However, it did not admit the error. This is tragic because the atomic bombs might not have been used if Japan had made known to the international community the truth about the diplomatic error involved in the attack on Pearl Harbor. Also, the scorched earth policy of indiscriminate bombing against Tokyo and 65 other Japanese cities might not have been carried out to the same devastating extent, if the truth had been revealed.

From the viewpoint of public relations, the dropping of atomic bombs is the most dramatic illustration imaginable of the consequences of trying to achieve goals by ignoring ethical considerations and not utilizing self-correction to build win-win outcomes with stakeholders. To avoid repeating past mistakes it is worth stopping to learn from Japan.

According to the United States cultural anthropologist Edward Hall, Japanese society is a typical "high-context" society, in which a high degree of cultural code is shared implicitly, and this alone can save on the "quantity of information" that is exchanged when communicating (Hall, 1976). On the other hand, a multi-ethnic society like the United States is a "low-context" society and because only a small amount of cultural code is shared, communication will not go smoothly unless a large amount of clearly coded information is conveyed between the communicating parties. In particular, over the past 2,000 years, Japan has practiced communal living as a single ethnic group that valued *wa* (harmony). This means that rather than achieving objectives while competing based on the abilities of individuals, the Japanese are good at achieving objectives as a group through cooperation. In addition, due to the introduction of Confucianism into Japan, when a mistake is made self-re-examination does not take place and accountability is weakened. Moreover, the Japanese are poor at providing clear arguments and expressions to other parties affected. As a result, foreigners and people from different cultures are sometimes misled, which can cause friction.

The Japanese also are characterized by deep feelings of *haji* (shame) at failure and have a tendency for *amae* (over-dependency), which together encourage a tendency for the intra-organizational hierarchy to submit to authority and to value domestic interests or the interests of one's own organization, such as protecting one's own comrades above those of outside groups (Sriramesh & Takasaki, 1999, pp. 337–351). Consequentially, these Japanese cultural traits work against the openness and speediness that is part of the preferred environment of the public relations profession. This can be seen in the fact that, after the defeat in the war, two diplomats involved at the time of the declaration of war error were promoted to the top bureaucratic positions of permanent secretaries. These cultural characteristics can be said to be deeply related to many of Japan's diplomatic failings.

For cooperation among nations, special attention must be given to understanding those cultural and sociological factors that need to be confronted for public relations to be used as a tool for achieving goals through successful stakeholder relationship management grounded in ethics, two-way communications, and self-correction.

## 2 Development of public relations

### *Historical roots of public relations in the United States*

Public relations is thought to have first appeared in the U.S., although it is not possible to determine precisely the origins of public relations in terms of when this term first came to be used. According to a group of historians in the United States, the third president of the United States, Thomas Jefferson, was the first to combine the words "public" and "relations" to create the term "public relations" in his 1807 presidential election campaign (InfoRefuge, n.d.).

However, another group of academics argue that the first time the term was used was by the lawyer Dorman Eaton in a lecture in 1882 at the Yale Law School entitled "The Public Relations and Duties of the Legal Profession," in which he described the role of public relations as being the welfare and prosperity of the public (Goldman, 1965).

Regardless of which is correct, the term public relations was not used officially until it appeared in 1897 in the *Year Book of Railway Literature*.

In 1908, AT&T President Theodore Vail entitled his company's annual report that year "Public Relations," using the term with the same meaning as it was used by Eaton. But up to that time, there was no fixed definition of public relations, despite the fact that the various definitions in use shared a basic concept. With the passage of time "public relations" developed as an established term and became an integral part of the country's business and government activities, and an important driving forces behind elevating the United States to the status of superpower within modern history.

## Grunig's four models

Dr. James E. Grunig classified the historical evolution of public relations in the United States into the following four main historical eras of the development, along with the associated public relations models (Figure 3.1).

**1850s**

| | |
|---|---|
| Characteristics | Press agentry, publicity |
| Objective | Propaganda |
| Type of communication (form) | One-way, not completely based on facts  Sender → receiver |
| The most notable practitioners in history | P.T. Barnum |
| Application fields | Sports, movies, theater; various types of product promotion |

**1900s**

| | |
|---|---|
| Characteristics | Public information |
| Objective | To distribute information |
| Type of communication (form) | One-way, aims to be factual. Sender → receiver |
| The most notable practitioners in history | Ivy Lee |
| Application fields | Government, NPO, business |

**1920s**

| | |
|---|---|
| Characteristics | Asymmetrical two-way communication |
| Objective | Scientific persuasion |
| Type of communication (form) | Two-way, but unbalanced effects. Sender ← → receiver |
| The most notable practitioners in history | Edward Bernays |
| Application fields | Fiercely competing businesses |

**1960s**

| | |
|---|---|
| Characteristics | Symmetrical two -way communication |
| Objective | Mutual understanding |
| Type of communication (form) | Both ways, balanced effects. Group ← → group |
| The most notable practitioners in history | Bernays, educators, experts, industry pioneers |
| Application fields | PR consultants, stable businesses |

**FIGURE 3.1**   Grunig's four models of public relations

*Source:* Takashi Inoue (2006), *Public Relations*, p. 59

## 1) The press agentry/publicity era (from around 1850)

This model shows public relations' initial historical characteristics, in which the objective was to publicize organizations and products and services (advertising publicity). It is a propaganda-type approach using one-way communication to help the organization, which is the information sender, control the public that it is targeting. During this period the information being sent out was not always completely factual.

*Webster's Dictionary 2nd Edition* did not at that time have a description of public relations, instead explaining publicity as: "Relations with the general public formed through publicity. Its aim is to form public opinion convenient to an organization, particularly companies."

## 2) Public information era (from around 1900)

This was the second historical stage of public relations and its leading proponent was Ivy Lee, who was called "the father of PR" after his activities at the start of the 20th century. This is a public information-type model using one-way communication and was a technique mainly used by government and municipal offices and also non-profit organizations and groups that would employ a so-called "journalist in residence" within their company or organization as a journalist not belonging to the media. They worked for the benefit of both their organization and the public and disseminated information to the public that was as factual and accurate as possible. Lee proclaimed his "Declaration of Principles" in 1906, in which he stated:

> In brief, our plan is frankly, and openly, on behalf of business concerns and public institutions, to supply the press and public of the United States prompt and accurate information concerning subjects which it is of value and interest to the public to know about.

## 3) The asymmetrical two-way communication era (from around 1920)

As this model is established from the company side, it is a technique to persuade and obtain the agreement of the public from the standpoint and perspective of the company or organization sending the information. Its leading proponent was Edward Bernays. It entails ascertaining how the public views the organization and then using this feedback to manipulate the public with the goal of in some way changing its viewpoint so it becomes aligned with the position of the organization. It is a form of communication lacking in symmetry and this model tends to be practiced by companies in fiercely competitive markets.

The definition of public relations after World War II became centered on the concept of two-way communication and for the first time in 1949, "public relations" appeared in *Webster's New International Dictionary 6th Edition*, where it was defined as:

> The activities of an industry, union, corporation, profession, government or other organization in building and maintaining sound and productive relations with special publics such as customers, employees and shareholders, and the public at large, so as to adapt itself to its environment and interpret itself to society.

## 4) The symmetrical two-way communication era (from the 1960s)

In this model, an organization attempts to achieve a state that is acceptable to all its target audiences. This objective entails an approach that recognizes that in order to develop a mutual understanding between an organization's managers and the publics that affect their organization, their relationship should not simply be that the organization is the information sender and the public is the receiver, but rather should be a relation of mutual transactions (exchanges) between both groups.

In the *Webster's New International Dictionary*, public relations was defined as "The art or science of developing reciprocal understanding and goodwill," a definition that has absorbed and reflected the two-way concept.

## Rex F. Harlow's definition of public relations

Stanford University Professor Rex F. Harlow was a public relations researcher and expert in the United States who collected and analyzed various definitions since the start of the 1900s. In 1976, he defined public relations as follows:

> A distinctive management function which helps establish and maintain mutual lines of communication, understanding, acceptance, and cooperation between an organization and its publics; involves the management of problems or issues; helps management keep informed on and responsive to public opinion; defines and emphasizes the responsibility of management to serve the public interest; helps management keep abreast of an effectively utilized change, serving as an early warning system to help anticipate trends; and uses research and sound ethical communication techniques as its principal tools
>
> *(Harlow, 1976).*

What is important in this definition is that public relations incorporates "ethics," which had not been paid much attention to previously. This can be said to reflect that, in the wake of the Watergate scandal (1972) and high economic growth, companies were being urged to become more aware of their social mission in their public relations by fulfilling their social responsibilities in their activities.

## Excellence in public relations and communications management – Grunig

In a study funded by the International Association of Business Communicators (IABC) Research Foundation, James E. Grunig directed a team of researchers in a project called the "excellence project." It sought to understand the best public relations practices of over 300 corporate, non-profit, government agencies and associations.

Some of the findings about the most "excellent" public relations practices were:

- Use of two-way symmetrical communications,
- Senior public relations persons have managerial roles,
- Equal opportunities for both men and women,
- Practitioners have academic training in public relations,
- Have an organizational culture that is participative rather than authoritarian,
- Programs meet communication objectives,
- Reduces the cost of regulations,
- Employees have high job satisfaction

*(Grunig, 1992, p. 28).*

## Dialogue theory of public relations

The theory of dialogue is one in which communications is a give-and-take exchange aimed at understanding the other party and concluding on some common ground that both can agree on and where both can find some mutual satisfaction from that exchange of information. Dialogue theory of public relations tries to understand how dialogue can be used to build relationships that mutually serve an organization and stakeholders.

Historically "dialogue" has been considered communications that is ethical, because it is centered on an attempt to find truth, and because it does not focus on persuasion, but on understanding. Dialogue goes back to ancient Greece and the Socratic dialogue method.

Kent and Taylor point out the challenge of incorporating dialogue into the practice of public relations, but suggest that organizations can use "dialogue and foster more interaction with publics by using mass mediated channels to communicate with publics" (Kent & Taylor 2002, pp. 21–28).

## Rhetorical theory of public relations – Robert Heath

The rhetorical theory approach is one focused on the public relations objective of persuading targeted publics about the truth of an argument. Rhetoric dates back to fifth century B.C. in ancient Greece and when "sophists" were trained intensively in the art of speaking to persuade the public and to persuade judges. Rhetorical training went out of fashion in the mid 19th century, but began to be studied again in the mid 20th century.

In contrast to dialogue theory in which the goal is mutual understanding, rhetorical theory is aimed at convincing. Under rhetorical theory of public relations, an organization seeks to make the most convincing argument that will persuade publics to agree with them. Heath's view is that societies come to understand what is true and what is false through the process of public debate where the best arguments will convince publics: "A theme that runs throughout rhetoric, and by extension public relations, is that it rests on the ability to influence what people think and why they act as they do" (Heath & Toth, 2009, p. 39).

## Sociocultural theory of public relations

While Grunig's theory focused primarily on understanding the value that public relations brings to an organization, especially in achieving its goals, the sociocultural theory of public relations examines how public relations activities are part of the creation of culture. Edwards and Hodges understand "public relations as a locus of transactions that produce emergent meanings, implicates the profession as itself an articulation of the different movements of the circuit of culture." In other words, public relations is not independent of culture and in fact it acts as a means of cultural transmission, and scholars need to analyze the sociocultural context of public relations (Edwards & Hodges, 2011, p. 6).

## Differences between public information, propaganda, and public relations

The term public relations is frequently used in Japan half-synonymously with "public information" and "publicity," for which the Japanese word "*koho*" is commonly used. Also, that which is seen as propaganda from the information receiver side may be considered to be "public relations" by the side sending the information. "Public information" and "publicity" that form a conventional "public-hearing" type of communication forum are merely one part of a program in a public relations strategy and do not constitute public relations itself (Ikari, 1998).

Among Japanese companies, there have appeared those that are actively engaging in communication activities by placing a liaison officer in their PR and public information department, as well as managers responsible for consumers and recently for IR (investor relations). But these companies are still in the minority. Also, propaganda is one-way information sent by information senders with the objective of having their opinion expressed and legitimized as "correct," and it does not necessarily connect to individual and public interest. At times, activities become confused with self-interest and there is a side to them that would be difficult to call public relations. These activities are closely linked to how public relations evolved after it was introduced into Japan and how this evolution was greatly affected by the growth process of the Japanese economy.

Taking companies as the example, they noticeably tend to have a defensive attitude when the information they send is strongly one-way, particularly when the information could easily lead to a negative image of that company if not handled carefully. The same tendency can generally be seen in central and local governments as well as the related administrative agencies, and while they will send certain information, such as through lectures at journalist clubs or elsewhere, they tend to be hesitant about disclosing negative information and will sometimes actively hide it.

## Difference between press agentry and publicity

Press agentry refers to activities to create stories and events that are newsworthy to attract the attention of the media and thereby increase recognition among the public. Press agentry has the qualities of propaganda as exaggerated or false information. In contrast, publicity refers to activities to send information that is of value to the media as news, so that it will be reported on by it. Unlike advertising, publicity is not paid for and therefore the media side has the right to determine whether the information will be published and also what will be published.

## 3 Definitions from public relations associations

### IPRA

The definition of public relations adopted by the International Public Relations Association (IPRA) in 1978 stressed the need for mutual understanding through two-way communication, and required that its practitioners counsel organization leaders and play the role of adjusting policy in order to contribute to the adjustment concept on the corporate side.

This was not limited to one-way communication, because for the first time recognizing the potential harm from this type of communication, resulted in clearly defining the role of public relations as being to carry out two-way communication, in which the information sender not only sends information, but also consciously and voluntarily pays attention to the influence and effects of this information.

### PRSA

Also, the Official Statement of the Public Relations Society of America (PRSA) in 1982 stated that: "Public relations helps our complex, pluralistic society to reach decisions and function more effectively by contributing to mutual understanding among groups and institutions. It serves to bring private and public policies into harmony."

> Public relations serves a wide variety of institutions in society such as businesses, trade unions, government agencies, voluntary associations, foundations, hospitals, schools, colleges and religious institutions. To achieve their goals, these institutions must develop effective relationships with many different audiences or publics such as employees, members, customers, local communities, shareholders and other institutions, and with society at large.

Furthermore, in 2012 the PRSA revised this 1982 definition and announced a new, simplified definition of PR: "Public relations is a strategic communication process that builds mutually beneficial relationships between organizations and their publics."

## 4 Towards a new definition of public relations in hyper-globalization

From Grunig's classic four models and his excellency theory, Harlow's inclusion of "ethics," the more recent dialogue and rhetorical theories, and the IPRA and PRSA definitions we can obtain a very comprehensive understanding of the profession and discipline of public relations. Yet, as explained earlier, the combination of a dramatic globalization of trade, business, and digital communications of the Internet has created a new environment of hyper-globalization, which makes public relations both more demanding and more vital. In today's digital age of rapid dissemination of information, news, and increasingly "fake-news," by a multitude of different sources from traditional media, alternative news media, and social media, organizations and stakeholders are continuously being bombarded; and for public relations to be effective, the more passive communications management carried out in the past needs to be replaced with an aggressive, continuous, focused communications process of stakeholder relationship management.

Back in 2002 this author first started to discuss in IPRA's *Frontline* about redefining the meaning and purpose of public relations by incorporating symmetrical two-way communications and self-correction (Inoue, 2002). From that came the author's development of the Self-Correction Model of public relations. However, given the phenomenon of hyper-globalization, it is proposed to update the definition here as: "public relations is the activity to achieve an individual's and organization's goals and objectives along the shortest path through a continuous strategic stakeholder relationships management process of symmetrical two-way communications, self-correction, and ethics, which seeks wide mutual benefit" (Inoue, 2009).

"Strategic" is used in the definition, because effective public relations is more than communication management, and consists of planning and executing a PR program of specific stakeholder relationship management activities that will quickly, efficiently, and effectively accomplish the goals of the organization. It uses symmetrical two-way communications and the accompanying information feedback to continually adjust the public relations activities in a self-correction process. And, this has been put into practical application in the author's unique "PR Life-Cycle Model" that is at the center of a professional delivery of strategic public relations, and which is the subject of Chapter 6.

"Wide mutual benefit" is part of the definition, because in the global village of today, organizations are asked to positively contribute in ways, big or small, to the mutual benefit of all mankind as well as to stakeholders. This requires a public relations based on ethics that actively seeks to guide the organization along the path of "doing good," to understand stakeholders through a two-way communications process, and to use feedback and self-correction to adjust its practices, products and services for wide mutual benefit. Because human beings have free-will and can choose to act for good or act for narrow self-interest, organizations must actively look to direct their activities and goals through a managed process of self-correction.

It needs to be added that true public relations functions best in democratic organizations, societies, and nations, where the free flow of information is available for the self-correction process. In other words, in an environment where freedom of speech is guaranteed, public relations achieves objectives by precisely targeting stakeholders and sending information, then analyzing the results through feedback to understand the current state of stakeholders and to make needed corrections without delay. In this way, public relations is continuous relationship management that builds trust and friendly relations.

For an organization facing fierce global competition, in which it must respond with speed, public relations that is a continuous, strategic stakeholder relationship management based on ethics and self-correction will help it secure a competitive position.

## 5 The number of public relations practitioners and the market scale

While there is no single definitive source to measure the market size of public relations in terms of fee revenue and number of PR professionals, the Holmes Report is one useful source that is often cited. The report is produced by the Holmes Group, which was founded in 2000, and which attempts to provide the "most sophisticated reporting and analysis on public relations trends and issues, along with an extensive global footprint of events and awards" (Holmes Report, 2016). As we can see in Figure 3.2, which is a summary of the details provided in the Holmes Report's 2016 rankings of the world's top 250 PR firms, the scale of the global PR

| Region | Number of PR Firms | | PR Revenues ($USD) 2015 | | Number of PR Staff | |
|---|---|---|---|---|---|---|
| N. America | 114 | 45.6% | $ 6,951,545,365 | 65.4% | 14,654 | 51.9% |
| Europe | 108 | 43.2% | $ 2,882,115,670 | 27.1% | 9,477 | 33.6% |
| Asia | 17 | 6.8% | $ 669,666,891 | 6.3% | 2,695 | 9.6% |
| Middle East | 4 | 1.6% | $ 38,180,000 | 0.4% | 224 | 0.8% |
| S. America | 5 | 2.0% | $ 85,115,292 | 0.8% | 1,089 | 3.9% |
| Africa | 2 | 0.8% | $ 9,300,000 | 0.1% | 80 | 0.3% |
| Total | 250 | 100% | $ 10,635,923,218 | 100% | 28,219 | 100% |
| | | | | | | |
| USA | 110 | 44.0% | $ 6,863,345,365 | 64.5% | 14,472 | 51.3% |
| UK | 53 | 21.2% | $ 1,257,895,099 | 11.8% | 3,764 | 13.3% |
| Japan | 4 | 1.6% | $ 270,000,000 | 2.5% | 1,092 | 3.9% |
| China | 3 | 1.2% | $ 259,630,843 | 2.4% | 190 | 0.7% |

FIGURE 3.2 "Global Top 250 PR Agency Ranking 2016"

*Source:* based on "The Holmes Report" 2016.

business in 2015 was USD $10.6 billion for just these top firms. The 2015 numbers are presented in this table rather than the 2016 numbers, because there are gaps in the 2016 numbers. The number of staff for the United States alone, according to Holmes, was 14,472 or 51% of the top 250 firms. The large concentration of PR professionals, firms, and revenues in the United States seems reflective of the historic development of public relations in that country. The second largest concentration can be seen in Europe with 33.6% of the total, while Asia has less than 10%. The low number for Asia is particularly startling when we consider that China has the second largest GDP and Japan the third largest.

Another source is the U.S. government's Department of Labor, which puts the number of PR Jobs in the U.S. as of 2014 at 225,000. It also estimates the growth in new jobs at 9%. These much larger numbers are not surprising, since it is an attempt to describe the entire labor pool of PR jobs, rather than reporting on just the top 250 PR agency firms (U.S. Department of Labor, 2014).

## 6 Why has public relations lagged behind in Japan?

### The historical development of public relations in Japan

This section describes the evolution and current state of public relations in Japan, and considers the historical, social, and cultural reasons why it has lagged behind, in order to discover what is necessary for Japan and other nations to catch up.

After Japan's long period of seclusion spanning 260 years in the Edo period, the path it has taken in its modern history of rapid Westernization from the Meiji Restoration onwards has not been without diversions. Because development was done quickly, it required frequent and repeated trial and error, and sometimes Japan's ambition caused incalculable suffering not only to its own people, but also to neighboring countries. After World War II, militarism was replaced with democracy and under the one-party rule of the Liberal Democratic Party (LDP), the collaborative framework of the government, bureaucracy, and business, assisted by the diligence of the Japanese people, saw Japan rise to be a modern industrial society that, by the start of the 1980s, was at the pinnacle of the world, thanks to the results of its economic activities of high-quality mass production. The Plaza Accord agreement reached at the G-7 Finance Ministers' Meeting in New York in 1985 accelerated the appreciation of the yen and added momentum to the globalization of Japanese companies. This signified that instead of the "lifetime employment system" and "the collective decision-making process" that had been formed in Japan up until that time within its unique culture and system, these companies had to acquire the management techniques that they traditionally did not possess, of "openness," "fairness," and "speed."

Since its founding, the island nation of Japan has been influenced by its ethnically homogeneous structure and Confucianism. Unlike Western culture's low-context form of communication employed in countries with contiguous borders and many opportunities to encounter people of different ethnicities, Japan developed a unique, high-context form of communications. In contrast, public relations involves communications activities that are usable worldwide in today's global era. In this sense, it is this area that has been the biggest weakness for Japan up to the present time.

Religion in Japan is centered on Shinto and Buddhism, while in terms of thought, Confucianism was systematically introduced into Japan from the sixth century and penetrated deeply into Japanese society up until World War II. The Confucian way of thinking, which requires strict superior-subordinate relations and reticence, is different to Western culture's Christian way of thinking on many points and in that sense, it is the polar opposite of public relations-type behavior.

The scandals that have repeatedly occurred in the business, bureaucratic, and political worlds in Japan show that the public relations function and its utilization have not taken sufficient root in this country. Moreover, currently Japan's economy stands at a major turning point and there are calls for a review of the social system that has supported its economic growth up to the present time and calls for sweeping structural reforms.

## The important role of social and historical factors in the evolution of PR in Japan

Japan is located in Northeast Asia, has an area roughly the same size as the state of California in the United States, has a population of 126.9 million people (according to the "Population Estimates' of the Ministry of Internal Affairs and Communications, 2016), and is enclosed by the sea on all four sides. In the olden times, its main industries were agricultural and fishing, but then during the Edo period it experienced unique economic, social, and cultural developments based on its relatively stable governance in a self-sufficient economy founded on a policy of seclusion and a feudal society. It developed artisan industries, the manufacture of textiles and pottery, and established a money-based economy.

With the arrival of Commodore Perry's "Black Ships" in the late 19th century Japan opened up to the world, and subsequently, after passing through the Meiji Restoration, Japan hurried to actively introduce Western scientific technologies and systems. Aiming to build a strong and modern nation, Japan decided to walk along the path of imperialism (Shiba, 1996).

This path led Japan into World War II and ultimate defeat. But after the war, it made a fresh start as a nation state based on the separation of judicial, administrative, and legislative powers and it built its own systems, including keeping the economic system of bureaucratic control that had been built before the war (Masamura & Yamada, 2002). A unique collaboration framework of government, bureaucracy, and business continued along with the systems of "seniority" and "lifetime employment," which were formed after the war, but have their origins from around the 1920s. Post-war Japan, characterized by the diligence of its people, reached a high point of being the second largest GDP in the world, only behind the United States.

Looking at the political process, we see that in the 30-year period from Prime Minister Yasuhiro Nakasone in 1982 to Prime Minister Shinzō Abe in 2012 (second Cabinet), Japan has actually had 18 prime ministers. It might be argued that the short terms of office of Japan's prime ministers, which average less than two years, is conversely a testimony to the country's strong social system that does not rely upon the abilities of individuals. The government acted to counter political instability by reinforcing its robust, bureaucracy-led social system, and for a while at the start of the 1980s Japan was the second largest economy and continuing to grow larger. But on entering the 1990s, its bubble economy collapsed. Faced on the one hand with accelerating globalization, on the other hand Japan experienced systemic fatigue in its bureaucratic system that was unable to respond to new changes, and its delay in carrying out structural reforms resulted in a state of deadlock.

## History of public relations in Japan

The history of public relations in Japan is short. Its origins can be seen in the occupation policy of General Headquarters (GHQ) from 1945, following Japan's defeat in World War II. Public relations was introduced to encourage a growth process founded on democracy and a free-thinking culture, but it was introduced without the concomitant growth of democracy and free speech seen in the West. That said, we can see the seeds from which public relations grew even in the pre-war period.

While there are no materials from which we can confirm that public relations was systematically introduced by pre-war companies, Kikuo Shibasaki described that in the South Manchuria Railway Company at that time, a Public Information Office was established under the direct control of the President's Office in 1923 (Shibasaki, 1984). What we should pay attention to here is that the idea for the South Manchuria Railway Company Public Information Office was clearly distinguished from propaganda and it was created to be independent while under the direct control of the president. Also, Kisaku Ikeda, representative of a PR research group, considers that an in-company magazine was published by Kanebo for its female factory workers in 1903 and, based on its popularity, in the following year of 1904 it officially published a company-wide magazine as the first such magazine in Japan (Ikeda, 1997). There are various theories about which was the first PR magazine published in Japan, but we know that they were published by Maruzen in 1897 and by Mitsui Gofukuten (Mitsui Kimono Store; currently, Mitsukoshi) in 1899. The Mitsui Gofukuten PR magazine was a substantial work spanning 350 pages and included sales guidance and features on new and popular patterns, and even stories, such as by Kōyō Ozaki, a well-known writer at that time. As the management teams of both these companies during this period had experience of travelling in the United States, it seems that the publication of company PR magazines in Japan resulted from the success of such magazines in the United States, where they appeared from the second half of the 1880s (Ikari, 1998).

It is said that the Japanese government and military authorities began to recognize the importance of their own publicity after World War I. In addition, the

Manchurian Incident in 1931, which became the trigger for the invasion of the Chinese mainland, provided an opportunity for them to change their understanding of publicity during wartime. The actions of the Japanese military drew criticism from international public opinion, and government and military officials felt they had suffered "a disastrous defeat in the publicity war." This placed under the spotlight the need to develop a system to manipulate international public opinion. Against this background, in 1932 the Information Committee was established in the Ministry of Foreign Affairs, creating an organization that would plan publicity policies for internal and external audiences in accordance with national policy. The structure subsequently passed through a number of transformations, and the information publicity work that, up to that time had been carried out separately by each ministry and agency, was unified in 1940 with the launch of the Information Bureau as an institution under the direct control of the Cabinet (Tokyo Metropolitan Government, 1995). The government began to interfere with and crack down on various institutions and groups related to speech, culture, and thought under the auspices of providing them with guidance. This can be seen to be similar to the strengthening of the PR function in the United States in World War I and World War II. But the decisive difference between the two was that Japan at that time was not a democracy and used propaganda to manipulate the masses to realize its slogan of "rich country, strong army" and to single-mindedly lead its people into war.

The PR that had appeared and evolved in the United States at the start of the 20th century was introduced into Japan starting at the end of the war as part of the democratization policy of the GHQ led by Commander-in-Chief Douglas MacArthur. But already at the start of the 1930s it had been introduced in Japan, albeit in an extremely simple way, in a number of advertising-related books. Also, Tetsuhiko Tozawa's *Publicity Compendium*, published in 1942, cited two books by Edward Bernays as references, *Crystallizing Public Opinion* and *Propaganda*.

The Japanese Constitution was promulgated on May 3, 1947, laying one of the central pillars for democracy in Japan. In the same year, GHQ suggested public relations offices be established in central and local governments through the Military Government. The authority of GHQ was even above that of the Emperor at that time, so its implementation of occupation policy, including the Constitution of 1947, was not really a matter of a suggestion or proposal, but in actuality was equivalent to an instruction or order by GHQ.

In order for GHQ to widely promote the democratization policy described above, it brought two communication techniques to Japan. The first was public relations and the second was public information. Ryoichi Hikami noted that they were informative activities to facilitate understanding, or in other words, public information (Hikami, 1952).

In 1949, when PR departments were being established in administrative agencies nationwide, the GHQ Civilian Information and Education Section held a PR seminar for the employees of the central government. While it included an explanation of public relations, its main content was firmly focused on public information, specifically the topic of "How should government communicate its policies to the people in order to create healthy public opinion?" However, the difference between "public information" and "public relations" became confused, since some of these GHQ officers had titles of "public information officer," while others had the title of "public relations officer." In addition, democracy was only still conceptually understood by Japanese, and had not yet taken root. In such an environment, "public relations" and "public information" came to be incorrectly thought of as being synonymous terms (Ikari, 1998).

There are considered to be four sequences of events in the fully fledged introduction of public relations into Japan: (1) the GHQ sequence, (2) the Dentsu sequence, (3) the democratization of securities sequence, and (4) the economic organizations sequence. But it is natural to assume that the introduction of public relations by the experts in GHQ in 1947 influenced the organizations in the other three sequences.

In this way, public relations was introduced into Japan starting in the public sector and then later into the private sector of the advertising and securities industries. In contrast to the pre-war propaganda that at times was used as a means of thought control to serve the dominant power, modern "PR" involves a way of thinking and activities based on a respect for public opinion and an awareness of social responsibility. It grows best in the soil of an open free society, and it rapidly grew within the storm of fierce social and economic change in the United States.

In July 1949, Japan Telegraphic Communication Company (currently Dentsu) held a summer advertising seminar entitled "About Public Relations" as Japan's first ever PR course for the private sector. In it, PR was positioned as a management function, a management policy issue, and a management philosophy, and it was argued that PR, which starts from the importance of announcements, must be part of management itself (Ogura, 1990).

However, subsequently PR was interpreted as being synonymous with advertising publicity as a method for selling products. An underlying factor that led to PR being misunderstood in this way was the establishment of a new PR department in Dentsu in 1950. While Dentsu had actively introduced PR theory into Japan in the post-war period, as an advertising company it aimed to improve the image of advertising and to expand its business by bringing advertising closer to the center of companies. Because of this, unfortunately PR and publicity became confused, resulting in the mistaken understanding that PR equals advertising publicity, despite PR essentially involving a wider range of business functions.

1951 proved to be a breakthrough year for PR in Japan. In this year, Nikkeiren (the Japan Federation of Employers' Association) dispatched the first "management delegation" after World War II to the United States, where it studied human relations and public relations (based on this visit, Nikkeiren launched a public relations study group in May 1953). In addition, during the same year nine educational books on public relations were published, which was a high point for the dissemination of PR. However, this boom would suddenly deflate at the end of 1952. According to the "30 Year History of Government Public Information":

When the 1951 San Francisco Peace Treaty came into effect and GHQ left Japan, due to the momentum for a reconsideration of occupation policy and the lack of financial resources, public information activities were required for the simplification of the administrative structure and the reduction of the budget

*(Cabinet Secretariat Public Relations, 1990).*

Unfortunately, although GHQ had planted the seeds of public relations in Japan's soil, it did not also introduce the techniques to practice it. A major factor was GHQ leaving Japan following the enforcement of the San Francisco Peace Treaty (1951) and the Japan-U.S. Security Treaty (1960) before such techniques could be introduced. The adverse effects clearly appeared later during the period of high economic growth.

The *Dentsu Advertising Yearbook* (1956 edition) states that with regards to the publication of information through PR: "We have encountered many companies that think that our PR merely consists of them spending money to have us make them a wonderful business report or to place so-called PR advertising in a newspaper" (Dentsu Advertising Cc., Ltd., 1956, p. 450). This clearly indicates that public relations at that time was not being appropriately utilized.

## Japan's corporate PR and media reporting in the 1950s and 1960s

Riding the wave of democratization, administration-related PR activities penetrated throughout local government. Today, there is probably no government agency without a public information section or an equivalent section. But even though these sections were established, their activities have been stagnant. But in contrast, corporate PR activities have developed, for which the background to this being the rise of newspapers, magazines, and the broadcast media.

Commercial radio stations were established with the abolition of newspaper regulations in 1951, and then from 1952 until 1959, a number of magazines were launched one after another, particularly women's weekly magazines, heralding the arrival of the weekly magazine era. In 1953, commercial television stations were established and began broadcasting. It can be argued that the rise of these mass media outlets prepared the ground for the spread of PR in Japan. A similar situation seems to have occurred in the United States, in which the rise of the media in the 1890s prompted the appearance of PR at the start of the 1900s.

Also, from around 1950, the democratization of securities was implemented and securities companies solicited shareholders through newspaper PR advertising. This was the embodiment of corporate PR. According to *Corporate Development and Public Information Strategy,* Tsunao Okumura, the chairman of Nomura Securities and a central figure in securities-related PR, summarized this strategy as follows in an interview with a newspaper at that time:

Even when talking of the democratization of securities, shares are a target of speculative investment and investors' interest in the content of financial assets and of management is low. But in truth, what is required is the opposite; they must become familiar with what goes on within a company and of companies and obtain the awareness and understanding of the shareholders. A PR exercise with regards to shareholders is to try to create a sense of connection between them and the company

*(Cabinet Secretariat Public Relations, 1990).*

On entering the 1950s, companies like Showa Shell Sekiyu, Japan Airlines, Matsushita Electric Industrial, Tokyo Gas, and Mitsubishi Electric took the initiative in establishing public information departments, and from the 1960s to the 1970s, many more large companies followed suit (Ikari, 1998).

PR advertising by advertising companies became the mainstream in the 1950s. In November 1957, the arrival of the Dentsu era was heralded by the one-page advertisement for Matsushita Electric Industrial of "The wife who you selected from among the 1.4 billion women in the world," which became a topic of conversation. In April 1959, Sony published "The transistor story" advertisement in a weekly magazine; then in 1960, Asahi Breweries released the "Three generations brewing beer" advertisement on the theme of a grandfather, father, and son working for its company, and then "Hard working Mr. Kato" on the theme of a husband that delivered beer. These advertisements captured the public's attention and the reputation of PR advertising itself improved. These PR advertisements that were mainly developed by advertising companies can be seen as the result of the growing recognition of the importance of developing a company image, which occurred in the context of the advance of the research and development on marketing techniques.

In this way, while companies continued to generalize PR on the surface, they become more strongly aware of their corporate social responsibilities. The "Awareness and Practice of Social Responsibility by Managers," which was issued by the Japan Committee for Economic Development in 1956, clearly states the social responsibilities of companies and managers includes: (1) the company is one part of the social system and its management must be trusted by all of society, not just by the providers of capital, and (2) management has the responsibility to prioritize harmony with the economy and society, not just the pursuit of their company's interests. In addition, according to a survey by the same organization in 1964 on management philosophy and company activities, more than 90% of company managers considered that management must consciously create harmony and think of the welfare of society as a whole by each company being aware of and meeting its social responsibilities in its actions.

But the fundamental problem is the content of social responsibilities and that it is not clear how they connect to public relations activities. In a survey by the same organization, it was found that the respondents thought the pursuit of profit was absolutely essential to fulfill social responsibilities and that securing profit for their company was a prerequisite to fulfilling social responsibilities.

## Japan's high economic growth and publicity

The Korean War, which broke out in 1950, created special demand for Japanese products and services, resulting in rapid economic recovery, which restored the country's economic strength to the same level as before World War II. This was the start of the Japanese economy's period of high growth. Also under the long-term control of one-party, the LDF – the Iron Triangle of government, bureaucracy, and business – led Japan on a path to high economic growth (Ozawa, 1993).

The 1956 Economic White Paper declared that "it was no longer post-war" and emphasized the success of the reconstruction of the new Japanese economy and its strength. The high economic growth that started in the second half of the 1950s began an era of mass production and mass consumption, and various marketing techniques, such as PR advertising, sales promotions, and publicity were introduced from the viewpoint of increasing demand in order to match the large increase in industrial output. Despite the fact that marketing is related to public relations and should be introduced as one part of it, at that time publicity was accepted as PR itself and the trend that developed was that PR also equaled marketing. Particularly in actual workplaces, publicity was seen as an auxiliary method of advertising and was positioned as a (free) service for advertising products, which caused major damage toward instilling in society an understanding of the inherent meaning and role of PR. It is clear that PR in Japan deviated from its true meaning over the course of the high economic growth period.

In the 1960s, Japan experienced an era of rapid growth with an economic growth rate exceeding 10% per year. The Tokyo Olympics were held in 1964, and in terms of the real conditions of the economy, it was an era of the mass movement of people into large cities, in addition to mass production and mass consumption. As the scale of PR advertising increased relentlessly, it attracted a lot of interest and PR campaigns were taken up by the mass media. The publicity era of providing news material to the media had arrived. Unlike advertising, publicity is subject to the decisions of the reporting side on whether or not to utilize it for news and also what content to select, so it was conceived to be an effective strategy tied to marketing and various ideas emerged. However, just as it is necessary to launch specific prescriptions in order to introduce and establish a new medicine, in this period it was necessary to also introduce specific public relations techniques. The effects of not doing so would subsequently manifest themselves in harmful ways.

In the second half of the 1960s, the automotive industry grew and became the principal proponent of PR campaigns. In January 1966, Nissan carried out a mass advertising campaign in newspapers and on television asking the public to choose the name for its new car. The venue for its announcement was packed with journalists and was given blanket coverage by television and newspapers. This was the birth of the "Sunny" model. Amidst the tide of motorization, automotive-industry publicity became society-wide news and in the two weeks of the Tokyo Motor Show in October 1967, there were approximately 1.4 million visitors.

Ironically, the spectacular achievements of these publicity campaigns further spread the misunderstanding that "PR is publicity."

## Japan's shift from blind pursuit of profit to respect for humanity

PR, advertising, and publicity activities developed greatly at the same pace as the high economic growth. But they reached a major turning point in 1969 with an incident relating to defective vehicles.

The starting point was the morning edition of the *Asahi Shimbun* newspaper on June 1, 1969, which introduced an article from *The New York Times* criticizing Japanese vehicles. According to the report, an article in *The New York Times* on May 12 noted that the custom in the United States was that when a structural defect that constituted a safety problem for the vehicle was found, the manufacturer would voluntarily announce this to the news media and recall the vehicles and repair the defect. But it reported that among the foreign cars being sold within the United States, there were auto manufacturers that did not observe this custom, including Japanese ones. In order to eliminate this problem in Japan, the Department of Transportation and the manufacturers responded that "safety standards are different," that "there was no danger to life," and that a recall "would cause additional anxiety." This prompted an outpouring of distrust in and criticism of the Japanese automotive industry. In Japan at that time, manufacturers were not legally required to announce defects to vehicles. However, while to a certain extent differences in customs cannot be avoided, it was noted that in this instance, which "involved the safety of human lives," these sorts of excuses should not be given and they pointed to "the industry's lack of social responsibility."

This is an example of the fundamental disparity that emerged between publicity activities and public relations activities due to the critical reporting by the media and the passive responses of the government and industry (Ikari, 1998).

Also, the second half of the 1960s was a period when companies' pursuit of profits through mass production and mass consumption, became a social problem, particularly in terms of the problem of pollution. In regards to exhaust gases, in the 1960s the main problem was carbon monoxide, but in the 1970s the severity of the photochemical smog problem increased. Moreover, the rapid growth of the economy had resulted in social anxiety in the form of concerns over inflation.

There were some noticeable developments by government, including the enactment in 1967 of the Environmental Pollution Prevention Act and the establishment in 1971 of the Environment Agency. In the business world, in its 1969 New Year opinion the Japan Committee for Economic Development emphasized "the formation of a society with a respect for humanity" (Ikari, 1998), and in such ways by the start of the 1970s, "restoring humanity" became part of the social consensus. Prior to the legal regulations establishing an environmental standard for sulfurous acid gas by a Cabinet resolution in February 1969, Tokyo Gas and the Tokyo Metropolitan Government voluntarily entered into a "pollution prevention agreement," so there were signs of praiseworthy socially responsible behavior. But at the same time, there was increasing reflection on how a production-first principle and a society that put priority on "creation of things" was creating a loss-of-humanity crisis, and as a result, opposition to corporate activities appeared in the form of civil movements, like anti-pollution movements.

In the 1960s, companies such as Nissan, Toray, and Suntory newly established public information departments. Within them, Nippon Gakki (currently Yamaha) prioritized PR as the driver to corporate growth and development, and from the beginning it established a PR headquarters. On entering the 1970s, a series of Japanese companies, including Tokyo Electric Power Company, Ajinomoto, Nippon Steel, Bridgestone, Dai-Ichi Kangyo Bank, and ANA all established new public information departments or offices. However, in many cases, in the background to this seemingly responsible activity the pollution problem continued, as well as other social problems, and establishing these offices was the "bill" to be paid for high growth by these companies, which were the ringleaders behind these problems. These companies wanted PR to play a stopgap role and obtain a pardon from public opinion. It has been noted that this was the same situation as during the Great Depression in the 1930s in the United States, when large companies and their managers were criticized by society, and major companies like GE and Ford responded by establishing PR departments.

## Effect of stable growth and changes to awareness within Japanese companies

In 1973, exactly when Japan was dealing with a variety of problems, like social anxiety arising from the issues of pollution and inflation and the search for a new economic order in the shadow cast by economic growth, it was hit by the oil crisis. In addition to the abnormal price hikes, which were called "a price frenzy," rumors abounded of a shortage of products, symbolized by the rumor that toilet paper was running out, which led to it being hoarded by housewives. The responsibility for serious inflation was considered to lay not only with the government, but also with companies, and images of top company management being questioned on their responsibilities in the Diet appeared in newspapers and on television. Based on this situation, in the spring of 1974 voices could be heard saying that unless companies changed their awareness and fulfilled their social role and responsibilities, the free enterprise system itself was not sustainable.

In this context, companies' public relations activities could be seen to expand to not just PR advertising and publicity, but also to fields not directly connected to the short-term pursuit of profit, like education and culture.

## Collapse of Japan's bubble economy

One of the clear goals in the hearts of the Japanese people was for their nation to rise up from the post-war devastation and achieve "recovery and development." Japan succeeded in becoming a modern industrial society modeled on the advanced

Western nations to the extent that, by the start of the 1980s, it seemed Japan's economic growth would continue at its rapid pace, becoming ever larger.

In the wake of the 1985 Plaza Accord, when Prime Minister Nakasone converted the austerity policy that had been in place up to that time to a policy of expanding public works, with the intention of expanding domestic demand. The low interest rate policy taken to correct the recession related to the strong yen was removed, which induced the appreciation of the yen.

Due to the monetary easing policy taken by the government in the second half of the 1980s, real estate prices soared and the economy became overheated. During this period, it was common to hear people say that Japan's land prices rose to the extent that it was calculated that for the same price of the land inside the Yamanote Line that circles central Tokyo all the land in the United States could be purchased. The Nikkei Average in the final session of December 1989 reached a record high of ¥38,957.44, and in such ways an asset price bubble was created that came to be known throughout the world as the "bubble economy."

In response to this situation, the Bank of Japan carried out significant monetary tightening, but as a result of this, the bubble collapsed and some financial institutions were forced into bankruptcy. The fall in share prices at the start of the 1990s was called a "triple decline," as it occurred in conjunction with declines in bonds and the yen. Also, with the domestic political instability overlapping the blows from the Japan–U.S. Structural Impediments Initiative talks, the rising interest rate, and the outbreak of the Gulf War, the bubble economy collapsed.

In addition, in parallel to the process of the expansion and collapse of the bubble economy, the development of the Internet society, which would come to have a decisive impact on communication techniques, had begun. The commercial use of the Internet in the United States started from around 1988, while the first browser was completed in 1990. The launch of Windows 95 meant that from 1995 onwards, the Internet became widely known among the general public. The oldest data on the Internet penetration rate is from December 1995, when the worldwide rate was only 0.4%. But from around 2007 the penetration rate grew rapidly, reaching 20% by the end of 2010, and it came to have a major and multifaceted impact on the global economy, politics, and culture. According to the Survey on Communication Usage Trends by the Ministry of Internal Affairs and Communications, Internet use in Japan rapidly increased from the end of the 20th century until, entering the 21st century and by the end of 2005, it exceeded 70%. While the growth rate has slowed since then, the Internet population penetration rate in Japan continues to steadily rise, and as of July 2016, it had reached 91.1%, with the number of users exceeding 115 million people (Internet Live Stats, 2016).

## Japan turns to overseas public relations in response to economic friction

One of the pillars of economic recovery for Japan after its defeat in World War II was becoming a "trading nation," and Japan launched PR activities overseas from the 1950s. In 1958, the Japan External Trade Organization (JETRO) was established. The European Economic Community (EEC) was launched in the same year and competition in the international arena intensified. Japanese companies established overseas sales networks to promote exports and conducted marketing to establish awareness of their brands among overseas consumers, and in conjunction with these efforts, interest in overseas PR activities grew. From the second half of the 1960s to the 1970s, Japan's total export volume expanded rapidly, and after surviving two oil shocks, it continued to grow its exports to the extent that they were critically described as being like "a torrential downpour." Japan continued to record a trade surplus from 1981 until 2010, inviting international criticism that Japan "was not trying to import." This was the source of the so-called economic friction.

From the 1970s, a movement began in Western countries, particularly the United States, to regulate the import of Japanese products. In the 1970s, friction occurred between the United States and Japan over textiles; in the 1980s over communications, automotive, and semiconductors; and subsequently in the 1990s over the issue of Japan's import of agricultural produce (Ikari, 1998).

The Japanese government and companies began to focus their energies into overseas PR activities. They considered differences such as in culture and customs and took positive action, including disclosing a wealth of statistical data, and approached the news media in order to appeal to public opinion overseas. They also recruited local experts to carry out lobbying. However, apart from notable exceptions, in most cases top management did not themselves make personal appearances in which they explained the company's position on issues, or its philosophy and values, and so missed the opportunity to show a human face that would more effectively appeal to stakeholders.

On entering the 1980s, alongside the strengthening of the Japanese economy due to its enormous trade surplus, JETRO shifted its focus to providing business support for foreign companies trying to enter into the Japanese market.

### Birth of public relations firms in Japan

In Japan during the period of high economic growth from the second half of the 1950s to the 1970s, PR firms were established one after another, as if heralding the arrival of the public relations era. The companies established in the 1950s included Chisei Idea Center, International PR, and Cosmo PR, and from the 1960s Dentsu PR Center, Sun Creative Publicity, Ozma PR, Kyodo PR, Prap Japan, and Inoue Public Relations. But up to the 1980s, apart from a few PR firms, in many cases the services they provided were primarily marketing PR, centered on publicity that targeted the media.

What is extremely interesting is that, currently, these PR firms are polarized into two groups. On the one hand there are domestic companies providing services to clients in limited fields, and on the other hand there are mainly overseas companies that cover a wide range of areas through bilingual staff and that primarily provide consultation services. In terms of numbers, the percentage of the former is overwhelmingly higher, but the percentage of the latter is increasing alongside the advance of globalization.

Also, in the context of international competition that has intensified since the second half of the 1970s, foreign companies demanding the opening-up of the Japanese market have strengthened their offensive against Japan, with international PR firms as their vanguard. These are practically always U.S. PR firms, like Burson Marsteller, Hill & Knowlton, Ketchum, and Edelman. These companies were targeting Japan as the world's second largest market and actively developing their businesses there, including by establishing local subsidiaries and partnering with Japanese PR firms. Their practical PR techniques were transferring a lot of theory and techniques to Japanese PR firms and contributing significantly to improving the level of public relations in Japan. Currently, there are more than ten foreign PR firms that have directly started operations in Japan, and around the same number that have formed partnerships with Japanese firms (Public Relations Society of Japan, 2017).

Looking to the future of the PR industry in Japan, due to government deregulation, the series of scandals, and changes to the accounting standards adopted by Japanese companies, demand is rapidly rising in PR fields such as crisis management, investor relations, brand management, and CSR (corporate social responsibility). These are fields to which Japanese companies have not previously paid much attention. Therefore, the outlook is extremely bright. As was previously explained, above all public relations will become more important as a common foundation, when based on ethics in an increasingly heterogeneous and diverse global society.

### *Increasing interest in PR by Japanese leaders of organizations*

In 1979, *Japan as Number One*, published by United States sociologist Ezra Vogel, became a record-breaking bestseller. In 1980 Japan was prospering, with the number of vehicles it produced exceeding 11.04 million units and it was ranking first among capitalist countries in the production of crude steel (Vogel, 1979).

The difficulty in conducting PR activities during a period of economic friction is that political negotiations are carried out separately from the efforts of companies. Also, media reporting in each respective country is prone to being emotional and can become overheated. Even when trying to disseminate the facts, the eyes of the receiving side can become clouded in an inflammatory atmosphere, and in such a situation often PR activities become unable to function effectively. However, there are examples of a successful outcome to calm negotiations through obtaining the backup of PR experts who anticipate this sort of situation.

It seems that top management started to become aware of PR around the middle of the 1980s during the time of the Nakasone Cabinet (December 1983 to November 1987). The impetus for this was the revelation in 1987 that Toshiba Machine had violated the export regulations of the Coordinating Committee for Multilateral Export Controls (COCOM). At that time, the criticism from overseas was that "the true face of Japan cannot be seen," and so following this incident: Keidanren (Japan

Business Federation) dispatched a mission to the United States, headed by its then chairman, Mr. Eishiro Saito, who commented that "Japan's business people should also actively speak" (Saito, 2002). It was after this incident that the leaders of Japanese companies truly started to become aware of the importance of PR. Subsequently also, the new chairman of Keidanren, Mr. Gaishi Hiraiwa, stated that "top management must communicate" (Special Project for Corporate Communications Study, 2001). However, at that stage this was still only one-way communication.

The economic friction between Japan and the United States intensified even after the conclusion of the U.S.-Japan Semiconductor Agreement in 1986 and the establishment of a joint-venture company, New United Motor Manufacturing (NUMMI) by Toyota and GM in Fremont in California during the same period. But even this California joint-venture company was carried out through pressure from the United States side, with GM absorbing Toyota's just-in-time method and "Japan bashing" by the United States reached its peak in the second half of the 1980s.

However, on the collapse of the bubble economy in 1991, the Japanese economy fell into a state of self-doubt. It was during the prolonged economic recession that, coincidentally, the Japan Society for Corporate Communication Studies was launched in 1995. Its activities were centered on corporate communication.

With introduction of the new consolidated accounting standards by Japanese companies in the fiscal year ending March 2000, and the subsequent transition to the mark-to-market valuation system for shares, top management was encouraged to convert to a policy of prioritizing its share price. As a result, while the compliance-based response of reinforcing the PR and communications department grew stronger, it has also been noted that recently there have been compliance problems in which the absence of ethics is apparent.

## Problems facing Japanese organizations

Supporting the above point is that when we look at the actual situation, we see a never-ending stream of corporate scandals, one of the causes of which is the lack of public relations, especially as ethics focused stakeholder relationship management. It is undeniable that at the very least, the constantly repeating scandals arising from the lack of ethics and the absence of two-way communications and self-correction abilities are inviting additional harm.

In the case of the scandals involving Snow Brand Milk Products that started in 2000, there were two scandals in two years (a manufacturing problem that caused food poisoning and a BSE-related scandal involving the mislabeling of meat) and the subsidiary Snow Brand Food that was at the center of the BSE scandal was forced into voluntary closure, while the Snow Brand Group, with sales approaching 1 trillion yen, was brought to the brink of collapse.

Even now, many Japanese are aware that they are poor communicators, and company managers are also aware of the need to strengthen communication abilities. At present, Japanese companies are actively utilizing the PR function, for example to get advice from external PR consultants as a third-party viewpoint during a crisis, but in many cases the day-to-day activities are left up to the in-company PR department. However, an increasing number of companies are outsourcing work to PR firms that requires special expertise.

Japan's problem is that even though managers feel the need for PR and have begun to take on the role of standing at the forefront of their company as spokespersons, even now there are still only a few executives that understand the essential importance of this. Another problem is the lack of practitioners within organizations who have received a specialist PR education and who have an abundance of experience. Moreover, many of them are moved between departments every two to four years due to the practice of job rotation, so the situation is that employees cannot give high-level advice to management due to the unique personnel practices within Japanese companies. In terms of ethical problems also, as long as the leaders of an organization do not deal with such problems severely, it is difficult for ethics to permeate to the very ends of the organization. The magnitude of the problem of repeating scandals is raising major questions by PR practitioners.

With regards to these repeating problems, in September 2002, the new chairman of Nippon Keidanren (the Japan Business Federation; formed from the merger in the same year of Keidanren and the Nikkeiren) former Toyota Chairman Hiroshi Okuda, appealed to company managers about the importance of corporate governance and corporate ethics.

While this shows a high level of interest in PR and communications, there are still only an extremely small number of practitioners specializing in public relations in Japan. Although the majority of companies listed on the Tokyo Stock Exchange (TSE) have a public relations and communications department, it is estimated that there are only somewhere between 12,000 to 14,000 practitioners, even including those in non-listed companies and foreign-affiliated companies. Moreover, the reality is that many of them are inexperienced in this work. Figure 3.3 shows the evolution of public relations in Japan and its problems (Inoue, 2003, p. 76).

## Social movements in Japan

In Japan at the end of the 19th century, labor disputes occurred frequently due to the excessive workloads imposed on coal miners and female workers in textile factories, and several labor unions were formed. But the fully fledged labor movement did not begin until around 1920, with the formation of the Japanese Confederation of Labor Unions, the Japan Farmers' Union, and Zenkoku Suiheisha (a movement for the liberation from discrimination of the Burakumin ethnic group), which unified workers and farmers. These organizations were considerably influenced by the 1917 Russian Revolution. While these labor movements were suppressed before and during World War II, after the war, under the democratization policy of General MacArthur, new labor unions were formed. Then during the Cold War between the East and West, the labor unions added ideological arguments to their positions and at times, they implemented nationwide strikes. During the period of high growth in the 1960s and 1970s, every spring fierce disputes would develop between labor and management over wage increases. But after 1990, at which time wages per capita in Japan had reached the highest level in the

| | Characteristics | Objectives | Problems |
|---|---|---|---|
| 1925–1945 Early Show era End of World War II Dawn of public relations | Propaganda to build up national wealth and military strength | Manipulate the masses | Suppressed free speech and manipulated public opinion |
| 1947–1952 Introduction period of public relations in government by the GHQ | Public information (one-way communication) | To assist GHQ in the implementation of occupation policies | Misunderstanding of the concept and functions of actual public relations. In addition, public relations was mixed up with public information |
| 1950–1963 Educational period on American-style public relations | Advertorial and publicity type (one-way communication) | To assist companies in obtaining social approval | Advertising and public relations became indistinguishable. Focus on advertorials |
| Latter half of the 1950s–1990 Public relations during the high-growth period | Publicity type (one-way communication at the international level) | Sales promotion for creating a mass production and mass consumption cycle | Excessive focus on marketing public relations and lack of introduction of skills for practicing public relations. Worldwide negative image of Japan developed in the 1970s. |
| 1991–2010 Public relations after collapse of the bubble economy | Corporate communication (two-way communication) | Developing a sense of social accountability within the corporate world | Multiple scandals and immature two-way communication |
| 2011–Present A new PR model is required for Japan after the Great East Japan Earthquake and for the world that is developing from a bipolar, through a unipolar, to a multipolar structure | Global communication type (two-way communication | Aiming to create shared value (CSV) from a global perspective | Within globalization, PR that will serve as the foundations has still not fully matured and in addition, there are still no foundations for accepting, for example, diversity |

**FIGURE 3.3** Evolution of public relations in Japan and problems

*Source: Takashi Inoue (2003)*, "An Overview of Public Relations in Japan and the Self-Correction Concept." In K. Sriramesh, & D. Vercic (Eds.), *The Global Public Relations Handbook: Theory, Research, and Practice*, pp. 68–85. partially amended

world, Japan's workers were hit by the storm of the collapse of the bubble economy, the recession, and restructuring. Suddenly labor-management negotiations became more cooperative (Masamura & Yamada, 2002). In the post-war period, labor unions also exercised strong influence on politics through the party they decided to support, but the influence of union members on elections has declined rapidly in recent years.

Conversely, the consumer activism that began in the 1950s in the United States also spread to Japan, strengthening the opposition to established authority. There was an upswell of consumer movements and civil movements in Japan in response to problems that occurred frequently from the second half of the 1950s; like pollution, the harmful effects of drugs, defective vehicles, and other product-related problems. On entering the 1990s, these movements were continued in the form of movements whose goals were to respond to issues like environmental pollution, support for developing countries, international contribution, and measures to address an aging society. In this context NPOs and NGOs rose to the forefront. The NPO Act was passed by the Diet in 1998 and currently 51,728 NPOs are registered as specified non-profit corporations (Cabinet Office, 2014), and the activities of many of these organizations are linked to an international organization. They have attracted the attention of every type of institution and an increasing number of companies are cooperating and forming partnerships with these groups within their social contribution activities. Compared to activists in the past, they are skilled in communication and are passionate about communicating the contents and results of their activities to internal and external audiences. Companies and governments can be expected to implement more effective public relations programs through partnering with these organizations.

## 7. Public relations and the media

Media relations is important to almost all organizations, but is of particular importance for public relations firms, where it is a core competency. As a narrow island nation with a high GDP, Japan has a wide range of media that extensively covers the entire country. A critical problem in Japan is deepening an understanding of the media and building good relations with it, because it has become important as a PR solution in the increasingly complex 21st century society.

### *Japan's media*

Broadcasting in Japan began with radio broadcasting by NHK (Japan Broadcasting Corporation) as a public broadcasting station network in 1925, while commercial radio stations started broadcasting in 1951. NHK started TV broadcasting in 1953 and commercial TV stations began broadcasting in the same year. Currently, as of 2016 NHK has 4,399 TV broadcasting stations (general: 2,214, education: 2,185), 390 radio broadcasting stations, and 532 FM broadcasting stations (NHK, 2016) covering the entire nation. There are also more than 130 commercial broadcasting TV stations (of which, seven are satellite broadcasting stations), including the five key Tokyo stations. Moreover, as of 2017, 206 companies were members of the Japan Commercial Broadcasters Association (JBA).

With regards to newspapers, since the publication in 1871 of the *Yokohama Main-ichi Shimbun*, which was Japan's first daily newspaper, today the combined circulation of the five national newspapers (*Asahi Shimbun, Yomiuri Shimbun, Mainichi Shimbun,*

*Nihon Keizai Shimbun*, and *Sankei Shimbun*) has climbed to 25.3 million copies even for just their morning editions, and when the evening editions are added, their circulation is around 35 million copies (The Japan Audit Bureau of Circulation, 2014). Japan's national newspapers boast a huge circulation beyond comparison with even the United States (Media Research Center, Inc., 2017). The circulation of the morning edition of the *Yomiuri Shimbun*, the newspaper with the highest circulation, peaked at more than 10 million copies, and even though it subsequently declined, it still exceeds 9.5 million copies. The *Asahi Shimbun* has the second largest circulation of more than 7.4 million copies. In addition, industry and economic newspapers, block newspapers and local newspapers, sports newspapers, and industry and specialist newspapers have a total circulation of approximately 70 million copies, even when excluding the evening editions. The estimated circulation of nationwide newspapers, when counting both morning and evening editions, is over 30 million a day or 10 billion copies annually. In addition, about one billion books are sold each year (Ministry of Internal Affairs and Communications Statistics Bureau, 2012) and the information networks of both the print media and broadcast media precisely cover the whole country of 52 million households. For your reference, Figure 3.4 shows an international comparison of newspaper circulations.

Also, the same as the media in the United States, the commercial broadcasting business in Japan is mainly founded on income from commercials, although NHK does not broadcast commercials and instead collects a licensing fee from viewing households throughout the country. NHK was state owned, but it became a public corporation in accordance with the Broadcasting Law of Japan in 1950. As it remains under the jurisdiction of the government, the influence of the government

| | The main daily newspapers | Circulation |
| --- | --- | --- |
| Japan (morning editions) | Asahi Shimbun | 7,433,577 |
| | Mainichi Newspapers | 3,326,979 |
| | Yomiuri Shimbun | 9,561,503 |
| | Sankei Shimbun | 1,610,822 |
| | Nihon Keizai Shimbun | 2,769,732 |
| The United States | USA Today | 1,083,200 |
| | Wall Street Journal | 1,321,824 |
| | The New York Times | 660,324 |
| The United Kingdom | The Guardian | 202,000 |
| | Financial Times | 197,959 |
| China | People's Daily | 2,810,000 |

**FIGURE 3.4**  International comparison of newspaper circulations

*Source for Japan:* Japan Audit Bureau of Circulations, The Statista Portal. *Source for other than Japan:* Media Data Japan, 2017.

ruling party cannot be completely eradicated, but fundamentally its right to free speech is secured.

In addition, as there are national restrictions on speech in accordance with the Military Secrets Act from before the war and the prohibition on the political intervention of religion (separation of church and state), the media has freedom of speech with regards to companies, the government, religious groups, and other groups, except for some industry and specialized publications that rely entirely on advertising income. The same applies to the editing rights of media owners. Also, some newspapers, magazines, and books are published by political parties or religious groups (for example, the *Red Flag* published by the Japanese Communist Party, the *Komei Shimbun* by the Komeito Party, and *Seikyo Shimbun* by Soka Gakkai, a religious organization).

It can be said that there are hardly any government regulations on communication activities except for regulations on broadcasting ethics. The Japanese Constitution guarantees the freedom of speech, publication, and expression. In order to protect the public interest, the media has established an ethics charter to govern itself, but the legal freedom of journalism in Japan can be said to be extremely high.

The mass media first rose to prominence from the second half of the 1950s based on the post-war concept of democracy, and then emerged as the fourth power in the 1990s following the development of information communication in the 1980s, adding to the powers of the political, bureaucratic, and business worlds. In 1993, the media was influential in the establishment of the Hosokawa Administration following the end of the one party regime of the LDP, which had remained in power for a long period until that time. While the LDP did return to power in 2012, the mass media played a major role in the creation of the DPJ regime in 2009.

There are more than 160 million mobile phones (Telecommunications Carriers Association, 2016). A high-density telecommunications infrastructure has been built in Japan and the information sent from the media, including the online media, is powerful. Also, 100% of children receive a compulsory education in Japan and the illiteracy rate is almost zero. Through these media outlets that have developed networks all across the country, an environment is in place in which information is sent to the people who have the right to know and in which they can freely select information.

## Media access

Many large companies have in-house PR and communications departments and they contact the media as necessary. The PR firms with which these companies have contracts also build relations with the media, but as yet the two-way communication form is still being established and in many cases the communication is one-way; information convenient to the organization is sent, while cut off when the information becomes inconvenient.

Japan's media has historically tried to get direct access to the heads of organizations in order to obtain comments from the actual people they want to interview. At times, the heads of organizations have become too friendly with individual journalists and ignored their PR and communications manager, instead directly contacting the media. At other times their relationship with the media has become difficult when their organization is experiencing a crisis. However, increasingly companies must utilize IR and CSR (corporate social responsibility) to respond to challenges such as globalization, environmental problems, and the introduction of new corporate accounting standards, so companies' PR and communications departments are being strengthened. In particular, during one of the frequently occurring scandals, these PR and communications departments and PR firms function as a liaison, providing higher-level and faster responses during times of emergencies and making it possible for the media to obtain accurate information. So while recognizing that reporting would be difficult without them, at the same time the media are starting to feel the convenience of utilizing PR practitioners. However, among these practitioners within organizations, there are still only a few experts with an abundance of experience, and so when a scandal occurs, they are often unable to respond appropriately and rapidly, which in many cases exacerbates the problem. In addition, frequently media journalists in Japan's newspapers are rotated between departments every two to three years, which makes media relations difficult as relations with the media have to be constantly rebuilt. This is unquestionably a major challenge for media relations.

As was described in the preceding chapter, in Japan there exist journalist (kisha) clubs, which began with the opening of the first session of the Diet in 1890. Journalist clubs rent offices within the facilities of central government ministries and agencies, major political party headquarters, local governments, in various industry groups, and in the main economic organizations. As already mentioned, there are journalist clubs nationwide in more than 200 locations, even when only counting the main ones. These organizations are strongly exclusionary and they tend to be allied to organizations like major newspaper companies, the main regional media, TV stations, or news agencies, and they practically exclusively receive information from the organization in which they are situated and write articles based on that information. While on the one hand the journalist clubs established in government agencies and within local government obtain information exclusively and quickly, on the other hand there is the danger that they will be controlled by the information sender.

But for the media, journalist clubs essentially only function as liaison entry points for the specific target of coverage, and Japan's media is open to a significant degree for many of the organizations and groups that want to access it. Japan is an environment in which the media can also be accessed at any time by activists and pressure groups if necessary.

## References

Cabinet Office [of Japan] (2014). "Home Page (*Naikakufu no NPO homupeji*)." *NPO*. [Online] Available at: http://www.npo-homepage.go.jp [Accessed November 14, 2017; NPO total is as of September 30, 2017]

Cabinet Secretariat Public Relations (*naikaku kanbou kouhou*) (1990). "30 Year History of Government Public Information (*seifu kouhou 30 nenshi*)." Tokyo: Cabinet Secretariat Public Relations.

Dentsu Advertising Co., Ltd. (Ed.) (1956). *Dentsu kokoku nenkan [Dentsu AD Annual 1956]*. Tokyo: Dentsu Advertising Co., Ltd.

Edwards, L. & Hodges, C. E. M. (2011). *Public Relations, Society & Culture*. London: Routledge.

Goldman, E. F. (1965). *Public Relations and the Progressive Surge, 1898–1917*. New York: Institute for Public Relations.

Grunig, J. E. (1992). *Excellence in Public Relations and Communication Management*. New Jersey: Lawrence Erlbaum.

Hall, E. T. (1976). *Beyond Culture*. New York: Doubleday.

Harlow, R. F. (1976). "Building a Public Relations Definition." *Public Relations Review*, 2(4) Issue Winter, pp. 34–42.

Heath, R. & Toth, E. L. (2009). *Rhetorical and Critical Approaches to Public Relations II*. New York: Routledge.

Hikami, R. (1952). *Jichitai ko-ho no riron to gijutsu [Theory and Techniques of Public Relations in Local Governments]*. Tokyo: Sekaishoin.

Holmes Report (2016). "The Holmes Report." [Online] Available at: https://www.holmesreport.com/ranking-and-data/global-communications-report/2016-pr-agency-rankings/top-250 [Accessed July 24, 2017]

Ikari, S. (1998). *Kigyo no hatten to ko-ho sen-ryaku-50nen no ayumi no tenbo [Corporate Development and Strategy of Public Relations – a 50 Year History and Perspective]*. Tokyo: Nikkei BP-Kikaku.

Ikeda, K. (1997). *Shanaiho-hyakunenshi [100 Years of In-house Publications]*. Tokyo: Gendai keikei Kenkyukai.

InfoRefuge (n.d.). "History of Public Relations." [Online] Available at: https://www.inforefuge.com/history-of-public-relations [Accessed November 15, 2017]

Inoue, T. (2002). "The Need for Two-Way Communications and Self-Correction." *IPRA, Frontline*, 4(24), p. 17.

Inoue, T. (2003). "An Overview of Public Relations in Japan and the Self-Correction Concept." In K. Sriramesh & D. Vercic (Eds.), *The Global Public Relations Handbook: Theory, Research, and Practice*. New Jersey: Lawrence Erlbaum.

Inoue, T. (2006). *Public Relations*. 1st ed. Tokyo: Nippon Hyoron Sha.

Inoue, T. (2009). "The Self-Correction Model in Public Relations." *IPRA Frontline Online*. [Online] Available at: http://www.ipra.org/frontlinedetail.asp?articleid=1408 [Accessed July 25, 2017]

Internet Live Stats, 2016. "Internet Users." [Online] Available at: http://www.internetlivestats.com/internet-users/ [Accessed July 25, 2017]

Kent, M. L., & Taylor, M. (2002). "Toward a Dialogic Theory of Public Relations." *Public Relations Review*, 28(1), pp. 21–37.

Masamura, K. & Yamada, S. (2002). *Nihon keizairon [The Japanese Economy]*. Tokyo: Toyo Keizai Shinpo-sha.

Media Research Center, Inc. (2017). "Media Data Japan." Tokyo: Media Research Center, Inc.

Ministry of Internal Affairs and Communications Statistics Bureau (2012). "Survey." Tokyo: Ministry of Internal Affairs.

Ministry of Internal Affairs and Communications Statistics Bureau (2016). "Survey." Tokyo: Ministry of Internal Affairs.

NHK (2016). "Broadcast Technology 2016/2017." [Online] Available at: https://www.nhk.or.jp/corporateinfo/english/publication/pdf/technology_2016_17.pdf.

Ogura, S. (1990). *PR wo kangaeru [All About PR]*. Tokyo: Dentsu.

Ozawa, I. (1993). *Nihon kaizo keikaku [Plans for Japanese Structural Reforms]*. Tokyo: Kodansha.

Public Relations Society of Japan (2017). *PRSJ PR Handbook 2017*. Tokyo: Ark.

Saito, S. (2002). *Introduction to Japan's Economy (Nihon keizai nyumon)*. Tokyo: Diamond-sha.

Shiba, R. (1996). *Kono kuni no katachi [The Shape of Japan, Vol. 6]*. Tokyo: Bungei-Syun-Jyu.

Shibasaki, K. (1984). *Kigyo-joho-sanbogaku [Corporate Policy Maker]*. Tokyo: Diamond-sha.

Special Project for Corporate Communications Study (2001). "Survey of Corporate Communication Today." Tokyo: Japan Society for Corporate Communication Studies.

Sriramesh, K. & Takasaki, M. (1999). "The Impact of Culture on Japanese Public Relations." *Journal of Communication Management*, 3(4), pp. 337–352.

Telecommunications Carriers Association (2016). "Number of Subscribers by Carriers." *Telecommunications Carriers Association*. [Online] Available at: http://www.tca.or.jp/english/database/index.html [Accessed July 25, 2017]

The Japan Audit Bureau of Circulation (2017). "Newspaper Circulation in Japan: Still High but Steadily Falling." *Nippon*. [Online] Available at: http://www.nippon.com/en/features/h00084/ [Accessed July 25, 2017]

Tokyo Metropolitan Government (1995). *Senjika tocho no ko-ho katsudo [Public Relations Activities of the Tokyo Metropolitan Office During World War II]*. Tokyo: Tokyo Metropolitan Archives.

U.S. Department of Labor (2014). "Public Relations Specialists." *Bureau of Labor Statistics, US Department of Labor*. [Online] Available at: https://www.bls.gov/ooh/media-and-communication/public-relations-specialists.htm [Accessed July 24, 2017]

Vogel, E. (1979). *Japan as Number One*. New York: Harper Colophon Books.

# 4

# STANDING OUT IN THE GLOBALIZED CROWD

## Brands, reputation, and public relations

### 1 Competing globally through brands and reputation

Just before the official release of the latest iPhone model, lines start to form in front of the Apple Stores around the world, where customers wait through the night and for days on end to be the first to own the newest smartphone – although it is not all that different from the one they already have, and which they could have ordered online and had delivered to their homes. Apple, with its iPhone, its iPad, its Mac computers, does not just have customers it has fans, for such is the power of a great global brand.

Brands are about how your customers and other stakeholders understand the value of what you produce. Reputation is about how they understand the value of who you are as an organization. For companies competing globally the combination of brand and reputation have an enormous influence on global stakeholder relationships. The two are dynamically linked, and together determine an organization's ability to survive and thrive.

When a crisis occurs, because of a product flaw or an external incident, the role of public relations is obvious in limiting damage to both brand and reputation, and to then begin the process of recovery. But, brands and reputation do not just occur, they are built. Customers become fans of a brand, only when a product is designed, engineered, and built with quality that provides great user experience and delivers superior value. And, a company can create highly valued brands, because it is able to attract the best employees and, moreover, to inspire them to use their talents to the best potential. Public relations plays a critical role in building brands and reputation through stakeholder relationship management with employees, investors, suppliers, dealers, and customers.

As for reputation, it is not just following ethics as a guiding force to avoid or to respond to a crisis, it is built through implementation of public relations strategies, which in recent years have come to include such things as corporate social responsibility (CSR) and creating shared value (CSV). These public relations strategies build positive images of the organization in the eyes of its various global stakeholders that increasingly are focusing on the issues of Environmental, Social and Governance (ESG) and most recently the Sustainable Development Goals (SDGs) put forward by the United Nations in 2015. Building reputations and brands are illustrated in two case studies in this chapter: the ITO EN case study covers how this Japanese beverage company improved its reputation by following a CSV strategy of reclaiming abandoned farmland that created a win-win for the company and the local farming community, and the Hyundai Motor Company case study shows how the Korean automaker used strategic public relations to reposition its brand from the low-end "economy car" market into the luxury motor market niche.

## 2 Japan that once was no. 1

Japan had ranked first in the "Global Competitiveness Report" issued by the World Economic Forum for 1991–1992, but by 2002 the nation had dropped down to 27th place. In 2013 it had recovered to ninth place and the 2016–2017 report had Japan as the eighth most competitive nation out of 144 (World Economic Forum, 2017). The World Economic Forum is an independent organization with its headquarters in Geneva, Switzerland that sets issues in global, regional, and industry fields, and strives to improve the world through facilitating cooperation between leaders from business, politics, academia, and other areas in society.

A key reason Japan returned to the top rankings has been the high evaluation given for Japanese companies' active investment in research and development. In the World Economic Forum Report, global competitiveness is defined as "the factors that determine the level of productivity of a country" (World Economic Forum, 2017), and scientific and technological development capabilities are essential to improve productivity. Two indicators of the level of scientific and technological development capabilities are the total spending by public and private sectors on research and development and the number of researchers.

A comparison of spending on research and development by the main countries of the world shows Japan at the top. According to the "Comparison of Spending on Research and Development by the Main Countries of the World" published by Japan's Ministry of Education, Culture, Sports, Science, and Technology, the country's research and development spending was second only to the United States, followed by China, Germany, and France. Japan ranked third in the total number of researchers, after the United States and China. However, it ranked first in the number of researchers per 10,000 members of the population, with 66.2 researchers. South Korea was second with 58.0 researchers, followed by the United States, the United Kingdom, and Germany (Ministry of Education, Culture, Sports, and Technology, 2013).

Many of the products that are said to be the best in the world are assembled from parts supplied by Japanese companies. For example, while Apple's iPhone is assembled in China, more than 50% of its main parts, including the liquid crystal display, are made in Japan (Fomalhaut Techno Solutions, 2014). Also, it is said that Japanese companies like Murata Manufacturing, TDK, and Taiyo Yuden have an 80% share of the world market in ceramic capacitors, which is an essential component of mobile phones (Ministry of Education, Culture, Sports, and Technology, 2011).

In automotive parts too, 90% of the small motors incorporated into a vehicle, such as for electric retractable remote-control door mirrors, are made by Mabuchi Motor (The Economist, 2009). Three Japanese companies – Toray, Teijin, and Mitsubishi Rayon – produce 70% of the world's carbon fiber, which is 10 times stronger than iron but only a quarter of its weight (Ohmae, 2008).

Despite the fact that in such ways Japanese industry possesses extremely high-level technological capabilities in various fields, Japan is still stuck with the label of being "a winner in technology, but a loser in business."

The U.S. brand consultant firm, Interbrand, issues a report of the 100 top global brands, and in its "Best Global Brands 2016" Japan has six brands (Toyota, Honda, Canon, Nissan, Sony, and Panasonic) while France has eight, Germany has nine, and the U.S., which is the nation most advanced in public relations, has 52 top global brands (Interbrand, 2016). For Japanese companies and for those of other countries to be "winners at business" they must also learn to use public relations to build brands with global appeal for which customers are willing to pay a premium.

## 3 Differences between corporate PR and marketing PR

The concepts of "marketing public relations" and "corporate public relations" are easily confused. Both are relationship management aimed at achieving objectives and goals through relationships with stakeholders, but the methods of deploying them differ depending on which of the various publics are being targeted.

"Reputation management" and "brand management" are also related to the above-described two methods. While these respective methods are mutually inter-related, in practice they must be managed strictly as separate activities, as their objectives and methods differ.

In contrast to the various relations that are distinguished according to their main "target audience," such as investor relations and government relations, a public relations strategy is set mainly by its "objectives." There are differences between marketing public relations, corporate public relations, and other communication strategies, which need to be understood, using the approaches taken in the United States.

### Marketing PR

In its broader meaning, marketing has come recently to be defined as: a range of activities from the creation of products and services to their purchase by customers, and for goods, through to the point where they are no longer used and must be recycled. But in its narrow meaning, in quite a few cases marketing PR can be understood as signifying "sales-support activities" for products and services. Therefore, we can define marketing PR as relationship management activities with the primary objective of supporting the sales promotions of products and services.

Its methods take many forms, including realizing product publicity through various media, supporting and sponsoring events, such as product exhibitions, seminars, and symposiums, and supporting consumer publications. It is a strategy of widely disseminating product information and at times improving the product brand and image with the aim of increasing sales. The target audiences are mainly consumers and potential consumers, and from among them the target audience is further narrowed down, for example into gender or age groups, to further enhance the communication effects and efficiency.

## Corporate PR

In contrast, the objective of corporate PR is creating a favorable image at the corporate level with stakeholders, through such PR activities as customer relations, investor relations, and government relations. Corporate PR can be defined as those relationship management activities by which stakeholders come to hold favorable images of a company. Although in the U.S. it has basically the same meaning as corporate communication, normally, corporate PR involves the CEO, the COO, the CFO, and CTO (chief technology officer) in relationship management activities with internal and external stakeholders.

Its methods include media relations and corporate institutional advertising by companies and groups, such as advocacy advertising, which is considered to fall within the category of corporate PR. It also includes various types of lecture meetings and speeches at events, and courtesy calls. Not limited to management philosophy, corporate PR can also explicitly convey the initiatives of the management plan and management strategy. In the case of IR and CSR, corporate PR can convey to stakeholders information about how the company is making efforts to improve such things as the environment, welfare, and education. Moreover, it is a type of PR that does not push the message to the forefront and instead cultivates an image.

The potential target audiences of corporate PR cover a wide range and will differ according to the message content and the implementation time period. In cases such as corporate restructuring and mergers, the content will be employee communication, in which the employees are the target audience, because it is needed to make changes in the organizational environment within the company, as seen in the Boeing case study in Chapter 2. Another example would be a publisher of school textbooks that wants to project an image of being passionate about science projects as a means to prepare students for high school. The publisher might choose to narrow the targeted stakeholders from all students and their families to households with elementary school students and children in their early teens.

## Effectively utilizing a corporate strategy

Marketing PR and corporate PR are both strategies implemented to achieve different objectives, but although each is independent of the other, as was previously described, it is not the case that they are completely unrelated. After conducting marketing PR with promoting sales as the objective, such as holding various events to assist with product publicity and forming images of products, a company's corporate image will also be improved through creating a favorable impression of its products. Likewise, a favorable corporate image through corporate PR can lead to consumers wanting to purchase a company's products.

In other words, both strategies have a cooperative relationship and as a result, each respective strategy also generates derivative effects. However, there often occurs a discrepancy between the objectives and the techniques when marketing PR is carried out to improve the corporate image or when corporate PR is conducted to increase product sales. It seems reasonable to think that in the interrelationship between marketing PR and corporate PR the two are inextricably linked. However, although the two can overlap, it does not mean that synergies can always be expected. There can occur a discord between the corporate image and the product image, and also the failure of one strategy can have an adverse impact on the other. So in this sense also, both strategies must be dealt with as having an inseparable relationship.

Here, the improved image of the company and its products are cited as the derivative effects, but we can probably understand from the explanation up to this point that the overlapping portion cannot be collectively managed in only one of either marketing PR or corporate PR. An image will not only affect sales, but will also have positive or negative effects on members of other publics, such as shareholders and investors, in regards to their evaluation of the company through its image. Therefore, it is necessary for the company to manage the various information and images that its publics will use to evaluate it, which are a part of the brand management and reputation management activities of public relations.

## 4 Brand management: standing out by what you make

The concept of brands is complex and difficult to understand and it cannot be explained in just a few words. It is the product name, but it is also the logo and image that differentiate that product. A brand is both the parts and the whole, and is the comprehensive value to satisfy stakeholders tangibly and intangibly. Buying behavior is influenced by brand power, and identical products can be expensive or inexpensive depending on their respective brand powers. In other words, brand value is determined not by the information sender (a company), but by consumers and other stakeholders as the information receivers. In order to improve the value of a corporate brand, it is necessary to constantly take the viewpoint of stakeholders, including clients, investors, and employees, and also take a CSR viewpoint, and analyze and evaluate the corporate brand from each of these respective viewpoints, which will result in an increase in corporate value.

### *Corporate brands*

Corporate branding has been attracting a lot of attention in recent years. One reason for this is that these days corporate mergers and acquisitions on a global scale have become a common occurrence. Enormous companies that previously were a constant presence have disappeared in the blink of an eye through a merger or acquisition and new companies have been created. Brands also affect the share price and are positioned by companies as an important management resource toward generating cash flow, and their implications in terms of their importance for corporate value are greater than ever.

There are two aspects to the perspective on brand equity that can be seen in M&As. The first is that for the price of the acquisition it is common sense that the greater the physical assets, the more the acquiring side must pay. The acquired assets include not only equipment, human resources, and expertise, but also invisible brand equity that the company being acquired has worked to cultivate over many years. The second is to advance into a new business in less time, rather than starting up product development from scratch, by acquiring a brand that is already trusted by consumers. In this way, the acquiring side is able to realize a shortcut to success.

An example of this in Japan was Kao's acquisition of Kanebo in 2005. Kao was founded at the end of the 19th century and is best known for manufacturing household soap products, and today is a leader in beauty care, human health care, fabric and home care products. The company's number one reason for this acquisition was to acquire Kanebo's cosmetics brand. In actuality, Kao already had a cosmetics brand at that time, but its brand power did not compare to that of Kanebo's. So it can be said that this decision makes sense when considering how difficult it is to develop a brand that is accepted by consumers.

However, in 2013 Kao announced that it was integrating Kanebo's products into Kao's cosmetics product line. Research and sales departments would also be integrated. This is considered to be because Kao judged it would not be easy to recover consumer confidence in the Kanebo brand that had fallen from grace after the "vitiligo" issue came to light in 2013. White blotches appeared on the skin of Kanebo cosmetic users, and rather than addressing the problem head-on, Kanebo management simply ignored customer complaints. Kao decided to quickly consolidate Kanebo products into the Kao brand. This case demonstrates how very important brand image is for cosmetics (Business Journal, 2013).

On the other hand, there are also cases such as Japan's Megmilk Snow Brand Co., Ltd. It was a well-established company, that had been called the Snow Brand Milk Products Company, but in July 2000 some 14,000 persons suffered food poisoning from the company's milk. It was such a big scandal that even Japan's Prime Minister Mori was reported to have said: "Not only rank-and-file workers, but also the executives are getting slack on the job. I think the executives should teach all their employees to make products carefully" (The Japan Times, 2000). The company was forced to change its corporate and brand names, because its brand image had collapsed in an instant. While it takes time to build a brand, it is clear that it can be destroyed very quickly, which is why continuous public relations is required.

Interest in brand management has been rapidly increasing, and it is recognized that brand equity (product and corporate brand equity) makes it possible to have (liquid) asset value and create corporate value.

The management of your company's brands entails positioning them in the market against competing brands and this requires information collection and analysis, and also customer relationship management. Given limited management resources, brands are an efficient way to create competitive advantage with a strong brand identity by which customers see the value of your products over those of competitors.

## Theory of branding

According to Professor Jean-Noël Kapferer of the HEC Business School in France, brand management is broadly divided into the "model of appropriation of the product" and the "loyalty model" (Kapferer, 2001, pp. 3–8). The former, the product appropriation model, is frequently seen in Western companies and corresponds to the brand management of companies like P&G that has product brands including "Max Factor" and "Joy," and Unilever with product brands like "Lipton" and "LUX," and involves adopting a strategy of subdividing the brand. In contrast, the latter, the loyalty model, can be seen in many Japanese companies, and apart from some industries, like automotive, cosmetics, and apparel, it is a model in which trust is built for only one name (company name) and one brand.

But in recent years, while on the one hand companies in the West have been rediscovering the corporate brand, companies in the East have been progressing the subdivision of product brands and brand portfolios (groups of product that meet the need of different customers through diversification in the same product field).

On reflection, when seen from the viewpoint of crisis management that affects a company, while the company name would seem to be the most suitable brand name in order to embody that company's power, continuity, and position, it can also be said that risk is increased when the brand name is the same as the company name.

Conversely, Professor Emeritus David Aaker of UCLA in the United States, who is one of the leading figures in branding theory created the "brand relationship spectrum" that divides brand strategies into the following four categories: (1) House of Brands, in which there are separate standalone brands, for example the large number of individual P&G brands, (2) Sub-Brands, such as Dell's Inspiron laptop computer, (3) Endorsed Brands are new brands that are "endorsed" by a master brand that guarantees reliability and substance to the sub-brand, such as McDonald's "McMuffin," and (4) Branded House, where a single master brand is used with only slightly differing sub-brands, such as Sony and BMW (Aaker & Joachimsthaler, 2009, pp. 104–119).

In each of the four basic categories described above different strategies and programs are implemented, depending on the degree of growth and development of the company and product. For the strategies positioned at the two extremes, (1) House of Brands and (4) Branded House, although there are differences in the terms used, the basic concepts have many points in common with the model classifications of Professor Kapferer.

In a specific brand management plan and its implementation, Professor Kevin Keller (the Tuck School of Business, Dartmouth College) introduced the following four main steps in the strategic brand management process in his *Strategic Brand Management* (2013):

(1) Identify and establish brand positioning and values: Starting from the meaning of the brand and the positions of competitive brands, the company designs the products it provides and their images in order to cultivate a recognition of the superiority of its brand among the consumers and clients who are the target audiences.
(2) Plan and implement a brand marketing program: To build brand equity, planning and implementation is carried out in order to cultivate a strong, favorable, and unique brand association among consumers.
(3) Measure and interpret brand performance: The measurement of the cost-effectiveness of a brand-related marketing program is kept to two items: a tracking survey and a brand equity management system.
(4) Grow and sustain brand equity: By designing and implementing an excellent marketing program, a rock solid brand position can be built and strong brand leadership acquired. However, it is necessary to anticipate and respond to external changes in the marketing environment and internal changes in a company's marketing program through measures taken from a long-term viewpoint (Keller, 2013, pp. 58–59).

When putting into practice these four steps, what is important from a public relations perspective is that if the objective is to increase brand value, then a PR program to achieve this objective must be created. As stated by Keller, it is necessary to go beyond geographical boundaries, cultures, and market segments, or in other words, to practice global brand equity management.

Brand equity is said to be a highly liquid asset, but regardless of how a brand is created, its long-term future is not guaranteed, as it is affected by external and internal environmental changes. Therefore, continual responses to these changes are required by public relations to support brand equity.

Even if a distinction between the company and the brand is necessary at the management level, it still might not be clear at the level of the general public. For the general public, a brand is made up of the accumulation of the various impressions (images) that they have collected and this includes images of the company. Therefore, when they feel critically toward the company, this will have an impact on the brand image as a whole. For this reason, long-term strategic measures are also required, and this forms a counterpart to crisis management that will have a very serious impact on the company's activities.

Japanese companies have conventionally viewed branding as merely one marketing method, and related to this, there has been a tendency among their top management to downplay the importance of brands. But in recent years, even in Japan the importance of the corporate brand has come to be advocated and the awareness has increased that top management must be directly involved in the formation and management of the corporate brand.

Corporate branding is mainly conducted through PR, but in order to carry out product-focused brand communication, cooperation between advertising and PR (mainly publicity) is essential. However, the tendency to place greater emphasis on PR has been growing stronger recently.

## Advertising vs. public relations

In 2002, Al Ries and Laura Ries wrote *The Fall of Advertising and the Rise of PR* in which they stated: "The advertising era is over. Today clients seldom trust their ad agencies to help them make all-important strategic decisions. What used to be a marketing partnership has degenerated into a client/vendor relationship" (Ries & Ries, 2002, p. 4). They point to a survey conducted at the time of their writing, by the American Advertising Federation in which 1,800 business executives rated the importance of the various functions within their organizations. The average rating given to the importance of advertising was only 10%, compared to 16% for public relations. The only function lower than advertising was legal with a 3% rating.

Of particular importance for branding, was the authors' assertion that creating a new brand is a slow process of building an image, for which PR is better suited than advertising:

> In fact, if you are launching a new brand with a PR program, you have no choice. You have to use a slow buildup, as there is no way you can coordinate media coverage. You start small, often with a mention of the brand in some obscure publication. Then you roll out the program to more important media
>
> *(Ries & Ries, 2002, p. 243).*

This contrasts to advertising's "big bang" approach of trying to create a new brand with a flood of advertisements. Their point is that for creating new brands advertising is expensive and ineffective, as well as short-lived. Whereas, public relations is far less expensive and more effective, and is not a one-shot event, but rather a longer-term strategic activity of brand building.

With regards to this trend, in *Kotler's Marketing Lectures* (2004), marketing Professor Philip Kotler, of the Kellogg School of Management at Northwestern University, gave an extremely interesting answer to the question of which tools are growing in importance in the marketing mix. He noted that "While we are overflowing with advertising, PR (public relations) is still not being sufficiently carried out," and that as its importance grows, demand for PR, even in the most advanced PR nation of the United States, would likely further increase in the future (Kotler, 2004).

## Global listing of top brands

Brands are built from information sent by the mass media, which is to say from the position of a third party. According to ranking of the "Top 100" best global brands in 2016 by U.S. major brand consulting firm Interbrand, Japanese companies ranked: Toyota Motor 5, Honda 21, Canon 42, Nissan 43, Sony 58, and Panasonic 68. This reflects Japan's global presence in automotive and consumer and professional information technology markets. The global market is very dynamic and year-over-year for these Japanese companies, Toyota rose 1, Honda fell 2, Canon fell 2, Nissan rose 6, Panasonic fell 3, while Sony remained unchanged. So in total, these six Japanese companies were among the top 100 companies for 2016 (Interbrand, 2016).

U.S. brands continued in 2016 over 2015 to dominate the top level of best global brands: Apple 1, Google 2, Coca Cola 3, Microsoft 4, IBM 6, and Amazon 8. These top U.S. companies are a mixture of traditional companies and newly emerging companies. But in contrast, all of the Japanese companies on the list are manufacturers with more than 70 years of history since their foundation, and unlike the case of the appearance of the U.S. emerging companies on that list, there are still no emerging Japanese companies on the list.

Chinese communication equipment maker Huawei Technologies was ranked 72, and PC maker Lenovo 99. One expects to see more Chinese companies making the list in the coming years. Looking at this ranking, starting with Japan's Toyota and also the leading companies of Apple, Google, Coca Cola, IBM, and Microsoft, we see many companies have adopted what David Aaker labeled as the "endorsed brands" (brands guaranteed under the parent brand) branding strategy.

In the survey by Interbrand, brand equity is converted into monetary totals and ranked through a financial analysis and an evaluation that includes the effects of brands on consumers' purchasing trends. In Japan, the ranking is published every year by *Business Week* magazine and it has become a well-known data source for brand value (Interbrand, 2016).

When considering brand management from a public relations perspective, the type of public relations to be applied will change depending on whether the corporate brand or the product brand is the object. Both affect the stock price, but corporate brand management can be said to be positioned extremely close to "reputation management."

Brands give us a sense of familiarity. Not limited to the millions of trademarks that have been registered throughout the world, we must not forget that all proper nouns, including each and every one of the many product and company names are brands.

### Role of top management's storytelling skills in corporate brand creation

A vital quality required for leaders to be able to give their organizations competitive strength in the world of hyper-globalization is their ability to use "storytelling" skills to effectively communicate to the world the corporate image and the vision of top management. For global businesses, public relations is the foundation for this. This is because in a global society in which information is circulating around the world in real-time, it is necessary to be able to immediately read changes to the external environment and instantaneously and comprehensively analyze information in order to effectively build relations with various stakeholders.

To improve the levels of name recognition and trust in a company and to carry out branding in those countries into which it has advanced, at the point in time a company advances into a local region, it will first communicate a self-introduction and greetings to the stakeholders, including local communities, consumers, government, and business partners, via the media. Specifically, it will tell them: "This is who we are and going forward, we will be conducting this sort of business in your area. We look forward to doing business with you." The questions it will answer include "Why did we come to this area (country)?" and also one's own feelings, "Why will local consumers be happy with our company's products?," "What are the advantages of our company's product and services (including taste, quality, price, services, support, and differences with the alternatives)?," and "What are our targets for the future (leading to the recruitment of excellent local staff)?"

It is necessary to appeal to stakeholders through this sort of storytelling. By top management itself constantly sending out information, it becomes possible for a company to build a high-quality brand. However, top management's storytelling needs to be accompanied by a subsequent follow-up, and it does not end with a simple story, it must also show specific solutions. Therefore, it is necessary to strengthen marketing and PR activities, establish sales methods that create high added value, actively open stores such as through exhibitions, and proactively build relationships with local stakeholders.

## 5 Case study: Hyundai Motor Company, "Genesis" luxury car brand

### Background

In the highly competitive and global industry of automobile manufacturing, where the level of capital investment each year is very high, a car company's brand is of critical importance. The Korean company, Hyundai Motor Company, which had long been a brand associated with cars in the "value vehicles" category, made the strategic decision to move into North America's luxury car market segment, which was dominated by the premium brands of BMW, Mercedes, and Lexus. This strategic move was aimed at changing the consumer's perception of the Hyundai brand from that of manufacturer of only low-end economy cars to the brand of a maker of high-end luxury cars, by producing the new "Hyundai Genesis" model.

To successfully introduce this car into North America, the company developed and executed a public relations campaign designed to:

- Build credible third-party endorsements,
- Win the 2009 North American Car and Truck of the Year (NACTOY) award,
- Obtain diverse media coverage that reached far beyond the automotive trades,
- Change brand perceptions and drive purchase considerations.

The NACTOY awards recognize "game-changing" models that make a statement about the industry and its direction. Chevy Corvette, Chrysler 300, and Toyota Prius received this honor in the past, not just because of their quality, but because of what they represented in the categories of iconic American performance, innovative design, and superior fuel economy. The NACTOY jury, made up of 50 of the most seasoned consumer and automotive press professionals, is an acclaimed group of experts in the auto industry and wield great consumer influence. Hyundai PR and its supporting agencies knew that securing this coveted award would drive broad, diverse media coverage, and alter the perception of the Hyundai brand.

The campaign strategy was to distinguish the Genesis from 50+ new entrants in the market in 2008 by ushering in a new era of attainable luxury. First the car needed momentum from credible, third-party media coverage that would put Genesis on the map. Second, NACTOY jurors needed to be engaged with the vehicle – not only driving it, but fully immersed in the "Genesis Experience" to understand the vehicle's significance for consumers and industry competitors.

A PR campaign had to be planned and executed that would focus on driving home the messages of luxury, performance, design, and value to portray the Genesis as a high-end competitor at a more attainable price.

The PR campaign started with research on the factors that most influenced the jurors of the award, which found:

- Jurors respect other media and are often influenced by their peers,
- Jurors are independent,
- Jurors are inclined to vote for "game changing" cars, as opposed to cars that suit their personal tastes and preferences,
- PR campaign messages should be focused on "obtainable luxury" to differentiate it from other entrees.

## Industry insights

- Auto media is historically skeptical of mainstream brands launching luxury divisions,
- Traditional popular consensus is that only BMW, Mercedes, and Lexus could build a luxury car.

## Target audience

- Influential automotive journalists,
- Mainstream consumer media,
- Prospective Hyundai buyers, especially prospective buyers with an openness to "off brands" when seen as connected with brands that demonstrate confidence,
- NACTOY jurors.

## Planning objectives

- Build credible, third-party endorsements of the Genesis through positive automotive and consumer media coverage,
- Win 2009 North American Car of the Year award,

- Leverage the NACTOY award to obtain diverse media coverage reaching far beyond the automotive trades,
- Change Hyundai brand perceptions and drive purchase consideration.

## Strategy

- Position Genesis as a game-changing entrant into the luxury vehicle category and a competitor to pricier luxury brands,
- Drive early momentum for the Genesis by securing respected third-party endorsements of the car and its capabilities,
- Create a "Genesis Experience" by positioning Genesis as a luxury model in all aspects of the launch program:

  - Shape driving experience for all NACTOY jurors so they are impressed with Genesis and its impact on the industry,
  - Control messaging by ensuring one-on-one meetings with jurors at every opportunity.

## Execution and tactics

The PR team developed a series of launch elements to ensure that all jurors were introduced to the vehicle in a controlled environment which became known as the "Genesis Experience."

1) Korea influencer trip "Genesis Experience"

   - May 6–9, the PR team brought a dozen top consumer media (those most revered by the jurors) to Korea for a "VIP" sneak preview of the Genesis. This was the first ever vehicle preview hosted by Hyundai in Korea in an effort to differentiate Genesis from all previous Hyundai-made cars in the minds of journalists.
   - Reporters drove Genesis on a state-of-the-art high-speed track to validate the performance numbers.
   - Media briefings were conducted with the creators of the vehicle to fully understand its engineering and design sophistication.
   - 3 out of the 12 attendees were NACTOY jurors.

2) National media "Genesis Experience"

   - Hyundai introduced Genesis to national media at the luxurious Four Seasons in Santa Barbara, reinforcing the luxury theme, while also offering a track driving experience to highlight performance.
   - Hyundai set the expectation for luxury comparisons immediately by providing a Mercedes Benz E35, Infiniti M35, and BMW 5-Series as competitive benchmarks for the Genesis.

- Surprise musical performance from former member of the Eagles Don Felder enhanced the overall luxury experience.
- Nine NACTOY jurors attended the event.

3) Regional media "Genesis Experience"

- Five regional media events, reiterating the messages of luxury, performance, design, and value both literally and thematically, reaching another 10 NACTOY jurors in intimate meetings.

4) "Genesis Experience Personal Contact Tour"

- NACTOY jurors received additional demo/drive-time with Hyundai executives in a "Genesis Experience Personal Contact Tour" that followed all formal launch events:

  - 28 Jurors were given personal Genesis loaner cars – most hand delivered by a member of the PR team, with accompanying message points to reinforce Genesis' positioning,
  - Special ride-and-drive events were held for jurors where head-to-head comparisons were made with high-end luxury vehicles,
  - Jurors received special Genesis communications, revealing facts about the car that set it apart from competitors,
  - Communications and messaging remained focused on challenging the notion of traditional luxury,
  - Presentations at each event or individual meeting included feature-by-feature and price comparisons to Mercedes, BMW, Lexus, and Infiniti to drive home Genesis' cost advantage.

## *Evaluation of success*

Hyundai Genesis was announced as the North American Car of the Year on January 11, 2009 at a press conference at the North American International Auto Show in Detroit. It was the first time ever for a Korean vehicle. And what followed was an astounding chain reaction led by positive mainstream media coverage that demonstrated an immediate impact on brand perception.

- Efforts to seed early coverage of Genesis resulted in significant coverage in all five major automotive "buff books."
- Nearly 15 pages of positive editorial in Road & Track, Car and Driver, Motor Trend, Automobile, and Autoweek – the publications most read and respected by the NACTOY jurors.
- 100% of NACTOY jurors experienced Genesis in one of the PR team's controlled environments.
- Media coverage of Hyundai Genesis winning 2009 NACTOY exceeded expectations and drove the highest number of stories and impressions of any Hyundai program in history.

- Extended Genesis consumer media reach in outlets such as Wired, NPR, and "Today Show" among others, with 446 clips, 116,493,643 impressions, USD $14,120,379 advertising value equivalency, 98.3% (119) positive vehicle reviews.
- Positive opinion for the brand increased from 33% to 41% in 2008.
- Purchase consideration for the brand increased from 26% to 30% in 2008 (Each percentage point increase in purchase intent translates to 350 additional vehicles sales monthly).

Hyundai Motor America and Machado Garcia-Serra Communications, Ketchum their PR agency were awarded the "2009 Silver Anvil Award of Excellence Winner – Marketing Consumer Products" by the Public Relations Society of America.

## 6 Reputation management: standing out by who you are

Brand management and reputation management are different, but both are important major assets. According to Professor Charles Fombrun: "Reputations are rent-producing assets—they create wealth. In particular, they are a form of capital that goes unrecorded on corporate balance sheets." And he explained: "Ultimately, reputations have economic value to companies because they are difficult to imitate. Rivals simply cannot replicate the unique features and intricate processes that produce those reputations" (Fombrun, 1996, p. 387). While not all organizations have brands, since not all produce and sell products and services like a company, all have a reputation by which it is seen by stakeholders. Like many other valuable assets, reputations need to be created, enhanced, and protected. Organizations succeed through the support of their many stakeholders, but they can quickly lose that support when their reputations become damaged.

Reputation management is carried out within companies and organizations at a high level following strategic communication activities, such as marketing PR and corporate PR. The reason is that corporate reputation is constructed not only from the corporate image and product images, but also by various other intertwining factors, like corporate profit, dividends to shareholders, CSR relations, the storytelling by its CEO, and the company's future potential. Reputation management involves comprehensively ascertaining and managing these necessary factors. In other words, reputation management is supported by various other strategic activities.

Jointly with the Hay Group, *Fortune* magazine began publishing its ranking of the "World's Most Admired Companies" in 1997. For this ranking, it asks 15,000 business leaders and company managers active in various countries throughout the world about the companies they most admire and respect, and based on their answers, publishes a ranking of the top 50 companies. Figure 4.1 shows the nine evaluation criteria used in selecting and ranking winners (Korn Ferry, 2017). Figure 4.2 shows *Fortune* magazine's actual list of the top 50 ranked companies in the 2017 "World's Most Admired Companies" (Fortune Magazine, 2017).

In the all-company ranking, Apple held the top ranking for the tenth consecutive year, with Amazon second and Starbucks third. Toyota is the only Japanese

1. Ability to attract and retain talented people
2. Quality of management
3. Social responsibility to the community and the environment
4. Innovativeness
5. Quality of products or services
6. Wise use of corporate assets
7. Financial soundness
8. Long-term investment value
9. Effectiveness in doing business globally

**FIGURE 4.1** Nine evaluation criteria for "The Most Admired Companies" list

*Source:* Korn Ferry (Hay Group) http://www.haygroup.com/us/best_companies.

company in the top 50, but its ranking declined from 24th in 2015 to 34th in 2017. However, the fact that there was only one Japanese company in the top fifty points to a very poor performance by the nation. In 1997, which was the first year this survey was conducted, there were three Japanese companies – Toyota, Honda, and Sony. The current rankings, in which there is only one Japanese company, might be taken as indicating that Japanese companies have not focused on public relations within the fierce global competition.

Reputation management should be at the very center of an organization's strategy and the responsibility for implementing it must lie with the leader's organizations. It is said that in Western multinational companies, the CEOs themselves devote between 50% to 80% of their time on activities to improve the reputation of their company. The reputation of the CEO directly connects to the reputation of his or her company. In today's media society, it is no exaggeration to say that the actions of CEOs will determine the reputations of their organizations. It is highly likely that the tendency for top managers themselves to be directly involved in various communication activities will only grow stronger in the future.

## CSR (corporate social responsibility)

On entering the 21st century, interest in corporate social responsibility (CSR) has increased more than ever before. Generally, CSR refers to measures that are not only for a company's pursuit of profit, but that are also for fulfilling their social responsibilities in the three fields of the economy, society, and the environment, through activities that protect the global environment and in many different ways make possible the sustainable growth of society as a whole.

The negative consequences of a pure self-interest doctrine, which might be called irresponsible capitalism that many pursued in the 19th and 20th centuries are clearly apparent, such as the amassing of great wealth without a sense of responsibility for helping one's fellow man out of poverty, the disasters of two world wars, and

| RANK | COMPANY | Industry | Country | RANK | COMPANY | Industry | Country |
|---|---|---|---|---|---|---|---|
| 1 | Apple | Computers | US | 26 | USAA | Insurance: Property and Casualty | US |
| 2 | Amazon.com | Internet Services and Retailing | US | 27 | Goldman Sachs Group | Megabanks | US |
| 3 | Starbucks | Food Services | US | 28 | Whole Foods Market | Food and Drug Stores | US |
| 4 | Berkshire Hathaway | Insurance: Property and Casualty | US | 29 | BlackRock | Securities and Asset Management | US |
| 5 | Disney | Entertainment | US | 30 | Boeing | Aerospace and Defense | US |
| 6 | Alphabet | Internet Services and Retailing | US | 31 | Delta Air Lines | Airlines | US |
| 7 | General Electric | Industrial Machinery | US | 32 | Home Depot | Specialty Retailers | US |
| 8 | Southwest Airlines | Airlines | US | 33 | Singapore Airlines | Airlines | Singapore |
| 9 | Facebook | Internet Services and Retailing | US | 34 | Toyota Motor | Motor Vehicles | Japan |
| 10 | Microsoft | Computer Software | US | 35 | UPS | Delivery | US |
| 11 | FedEx | Delivery | US | 36 | Nestle | Consumer Food Products | Switzerland |
| 12 | Nike | Apparel | US | 37 | AT&T | Telecommunications | US |
| 13 | Johnson & Johnson | Pharmaceuticals | US | 38 | Unilever | Soaps and Cosmetics | UK |
| 14 | Netflix | Entertainment | US | 39 | PepsiCo | Consumer Food Products | US |
| 15 | Costco | Specialty Retailers | US | 40 | Exxon Mobil | Petroleum Refining | US |
| 16 | Coca-Cola | Beverages | US | 41 | Accenture | Information Technology Services | Ireland |
| 17 | American Express | Consumer Credit Card and Related Services | US | 42 | Walmart | General Merchandisers | US |
| 18 | Nordstrom | General Merchandisers | US | 43 | St. Jude Medical | Medical Products and Equipment | US |
| 19 | Procter & Gamble | Soaps and Cosmetics | US | 44 | Target | General Merchandisers | US |
| 20 | salesforce.com | Computer Software | US | 45 | CVS Health | Health Care: Pharmacy and Other Services | US |
| 21 | BMW | Motor Vehicles | Germany | 46 | Intel | Semiconductors | US |
| 22 | JPMorgan Chase | Megabanks | US | 47 | Caterpillar | Construction and Farm Machinery | US |
| 23 | 3M | Medical Products and Equipment | US | 48 | McDonald's | Food Services | US |
| 24 | IBM | Information Technology Services | US | 49 | Visa | Consumer Credit Card and Related Services | US |
| 25 | Marriott International | Hotels, Casinos, and Resorts | US | 50 | Deere | Construction and Farm Machinery | US |

FIGURE 4.2  The World's Most Admired Companies ranking (Fortune, 2017)

Source: Fortune Magazine http://fortune.com/worlds-most-admired-companies/list/

the deterioration of the global environment. The enormous corporate groups that have arisen with the advance of globalization have an impact on the environment and society on a worldwide scale. But, with growing public awareness, especially in this Internet era, it is becoming increasingly difficult for companies to continue to conduct business activities without taking the various stakeholders into consideration. As discussed about the meaning of ethics in Chapter 1 of this book, a desire for what is good is a dominant consideration of stakeholders, and they will likely be very vocal about opposing unethical behavior. Therefore, companies should embrace ethics and should actively pursue strategies that enhance their reputations through CSR measures to protect the environment and to improve society.

The origins of CSR can be found in the church-centered movements in Western nations in the 1920s to boycott companies involved in tobacco, alcohol, or weapons, and to suppress investment in them (Peattie, n.d.). In the United States in the 1950s, the laws and regulations that limited the involvement of companies in social activities were abolished, and the trend of establishing an in-house department responsible for social contribution activities became widespread. In the 1960s, the rise of the civil rights movement and citizens' movements to address pollution problems called into question companies' social responsibilities, and these companies became required not only to pursue profit, but also to exist as organizations that had their roots in society. As a result, various programs were implemented by many public relations practitioners.

In the 1970s and 1980s, charitable operations of the corporate patronage of the arts and philanthropic projects became fully fledged. After the Exxon Valdez oil spill off the coast of Alaska in 1989, in which the responsible company's investment in charitable activities did not safeguard the company's reputation, there was subsequently a shift toward charitable activities more closely linked to business activities. On entering the 1990s, AT&T began, for example, conducting charitable activities in accordance with its marketing and technical support programs, and encouraged and supported employee participation in volunteer activities. At the same time it proposed a new model of linking charitable activities to each department within the company and conducting charitable activities that made full use of management resources.

Since 2000, the collapse of a series of major companies due to scandals, including Enron and WorldCom, encouraged a rethinking of corporate ethics. In addition, the terrorist attacks of September 11, 2001, increased people's interest in social problems and raised their expectations for companies' social contributions. According to the 2004 Cone Corporate Citizenship study, 85% of consumers in the United States would change to the product of a company that was tackling social problems, if its price and quality were the same as the product they were currently using, indicating that the movement toward reinforcing measures for CSR is further strengthening in the United States (Cone Inc., 2004).

On the other hand, in Japan in the 1970s, there was an awakening of citizen awareness following the occurrence of pollution problems and corporate scandals. Then in the 1980s, reflecting the prosperity of the bubble economy, activities to support the arts and culture known as corporate patronage became active, but they declined following the collapse of the bubble economy. From the second half of the

1990s, there was a series of corporate scandals and interest in CSR increased in the form of calling into question corporate governance and corporate ethics.

At this point it is useful to introduce several definitions of CSR. We can see how these definitions differ from the corporate patronage and philanthropy conducted in the 20th century that were merely charitable social contribution activities.

In *Corporate Social Responsibility* (2005), Philip Kotler and Nancy Lee defined CSR as: "a commitment to improve community well-being through discretionary business practices and contributions of corporate resources" (Kotler & Lee, 2005). In other words, it is defined as a company utilizing its main business and contributing to society within this framework.

Conversely, the definition of CSR of the NPO BSR (formerly known as Business for Social Responsibility), which has its headquarters in San Francisco, changes the term to "BSR" because "CSR is too-often construed to mean a narrower focus on social issues." Their understanding is that the focus must be on a broader "Business for Social Responsibility" (Olson, 2016).

What these definitions have in common is that the actions are "voluntary." They do not indicate merely behaving ethically and complying with laws and regulations in the short term, but advocate for a more direct linkage of business activities with the overall benefit of society.

Kotler categorized corporate social initiatives into six categories (Figure 4.3) and gave a specificity to CSR, which otherwise tends to become vague over a wide range of possible activities. He clarified the initiatives themselves by dividing them into six effective methods to realize social contribution themes that utilize a company's main business, namely: (1) cause promotions, (2) cause-related marketing, (3) corporate social marketing, (4) corporate philanthropy, (5) community volunteering, and (6) socially responsible business practices.

| The six categories of corporate social initiatives | |
| --- | --- |
| ① | **Cause promotions**<br>Supporting efforts to raise awareness of social problems |
| ② | **Cause-related marketing**<br>Returning to society part of the profits from product sales through contributions and donations |
| ③ | **Corporate social marketing**<br>Supporting efforts to promote changes in the awareness and behavior of individuals |
| ④ | **Corporate philanthropy**<br>The most traditional form of philanthropic activities, such as contributing to charities |
| ⑤ | **Community volunteering**<br>Employees participate in the volunteer activities of groups in the local community |
| ⑥ | **Socially responsible business practices**<br>Projects and investment to support social problems that are useful for improving the local community and for environmental conservation |

**FIGURE 4.3**   Philip Kotler's six categories of corporate social initiatives

*Source:* Takashi Inoue (2015), *Public Relations: Relationship Management*, 2nd Edition, p. 118

U.S. company Dell, which conducts its businesses in more than 190 countries and has in excess of 100,000 employees, established a sustainability business department and developed CSR activities over Kotler's six categories that used the themes of recycling computer products and producing products that were kind to the environment. For example, by promoting recycling in which Dell itself bears the cost and promoting the production of products with a small environmental impact, and at the same time aiming to unify products with those of competitors, such as HP and IBM, and thereby reducing costs, it is realizing a win–win situation for the company, society (stakeholders), and the environment. Dell has made it clear that:

> Every team member at Dell shares this commitment because being a good company is the right thing to do, but it is also right for our business. We're creating real value for our customers, employees, and partners while driving social and environmental good in the community
>
> *(Dell Inc., 2017).*

The CSR concept of socially responsible investing is called SRI, which is a method of investing in companies that are fulfilling their social responsibilities. Currently, SRI refers to investment that, in addition to a financial evaluation, also involves an active evaluation of the extent to which the investment target is contributing to society and to the environment. In the United States, SRI has spread alongside the expansion of 401k (defined contribution pensions), and in terms of market scale, it has been reported that SRI assets under management at the end of 2011, when combined with the IRA (individual retirement account) personal type defined contribution pensions were worth more than USD $6 trillion, with a ratio to individual financial assets of 16.2% (The Japan Securities Research Institute, 2012). SRI funds have also appeared in Japan, although their market scale is still comparatively small at approximately USD $10 billion (Inoue, 2006, p. 111).

As shown in Figure 4.4, CSR initiatives can be divided into three fields and each respective initiative has a range of effects. The effects that can be expected from these initiatives include increasing sales and expanding market share, strengthening brands, improving the corporate image and expanding influence, activating human

| ① | Economic field | Profitability, growth potential |
|---|---|---|
| ② | Social field | Corporate governance, compliance, ethical perspective, relations with stakeholders (protection of human rights, the labor environment, relations with customers and client companies, etc.) |
| ③ | Environmental field | Measures to protect the global environment, etc. |

**FIGURE 4.4** Three CSR fields

resources, reducing costs, and building favorable relations with investors and other financial stakeholders. To realize these effects, it is essential to take the viewpoints of stakeholders through a two-way communication process and to practice CSR that is directly linked to management. Public relations practitioners and CSR managers are expected to play the role of intermediator between the organization and its stakeholders. In other words, in addition to encouraging a dialogue between both parties and feeding back the voice of stakeholders into their organization, they also inform the stakeholders of their organization's initiatives. This must be reflected in CSR activities and used to further evolve and develop them by analyzing the evaluation of stakeholders' feedback into the organization, and using the results of the analysis to make the necessary corrections.

PR researcher James E. Grunig says that public relations practitioners are activists who have the responsibility to the publics that affect their organizations (Grunig & Grunig, 1996), and also, as explained by Edward Bernays during a lecture at Boston University in 1980, "Public relations is the practice of social responsibility" (Bernays, 1980, p. 47). If this is true, then in this sense CSR activities can be said to be public relations itself.

As previously touched on, social contribution activities that were born in the West in the 1920s passed through various transformations to emerge as CSR in the 1990s, and in the future they are likely to change again over the passage of time. So it is possible that companies will increase their corporate value and improve their results by coming to position CSR at the center of management and making contributions that reflect their management strategies.

Corporate patronage initiatives, which were popular in Japan in the 1980s, have proven to be transient and have come to an end. The key for the future of CSR in Japan is how, within a public relations framework, to strategically implement measures without being preoccupied with superficial activities and to have CSR concepts and activities take root in society and companies over the long term.

Toyo Keizai Inc. announces the annual "CSR (corporate social responsibility) Company Ranking" for "trusted companies."

Figure 4.5 shows the ranking for the 11th survey announced in April 2017 with FUJIFILM Holdings ranked first. FUJIFILM Holdings has been ranking at number one for three consecutive years. It was evaluated highly for its active support of NPOs and NGOs, for taking on the challenge of conducting a BOP (base of the pyramid) business, including for the development and sales of low-priced digital cameras in developing countries, and for the high standards it maintains in its behavior. NTT DoCoMo is also a company that has consecutively ranked in the top 10. The company is implementing CSR activities after clarifying the role it should be playing as a mobile phone company. It was evaluated highly for its approach of linking its business activities to CSR activities, including solving problems that have arisen from the use of mobile phones like "bank transfer fraud" and "using the phone while walking." Another remarkable growth has been showcased by KDDI, making it from 15th place in 2015 to 3rd place in 2017 (Toyo Keizai, 2017).

| Rank | Company name | Total points |
|:---:|:---|:---:|
| 1 | FUJIFILM Holdings | 569.7 |
| 2 | Bridgestone Corporation | 567.9 |
| 3 | KDDI Corporation | 565.0 |
| 4 | KOMATSU Ltd. | 563.8 |
| 5 | NTT DOCOMO Inc. | 563.8 |
| 6 | CANON Inc. | 563.8 |
| 7 | FUJI XEROX Co., Ltd. | 561.4 |
| 8 | DENSO Corporation | 561.1 |
| 9 | RICOH Company, Ltd. | 560.6 |
| 10 | KAO Corporation | 560.6 |

**FIGURE 4.5** Toyo Keizai's 2017 Japanese corporate TOP 700 CSR ranking
*Source:* Toyo Keizai Online, 2017.

### From CSR to CSV

Creating shared value (CSV) is a concept mainly proposed by Harvard University Business School Professor Michael E. Porter, who is known as a leading authority on corporate competitive strategy theory, and who proposed CSV in 2011 as a new concept to replace CSR (corporate social responsibility). While Kotler saw CSR as "an extension of the main business," Porter argued that:

> Shared value could reshape capitalism and its relationship to society. It could also drive the next wave of innovation and productivity growth in the global economy as it opens managers' eyes to immense human needs that must be met, large new markets to be served, and the internal costs of social deficits—as well as the competitive advantages available from addressing them
>
> *(Porter & Kramer, 2011).*

Porter sees that the value of CSV can be said to be utilizing the same talent and creative energy that corporations apply to competing for profits in the market place to also solve social problems. CSV can also be thought of as another application of effective stakeholder relationship management, where public relations strives for a win-win for both the organization and stakeholders.

The Porter Prize, which was named after Michel Porter and is awarded by Hitotsubashi University, was founded in July 2001 in order to recognize those Japanese companies that create innovation in products, processes, and management skills to implement strategies that enable them to achieve and maintain a high level of profitability in their industry.

Two winners of the Porter Prize that were particularly good examples illustrating the reasons why companies win this award were ITO EN (2013), which produces and sells tea leaves and beverages, and YKK (2014), which manufactures and sells clothing fasteners (Hitotsubashi University, 2013, 2014). ITO EN was evaluated highly for creating a unique value chain characterized by a broad product line-up of green tea beverages, route sales, and a tea-producing-area development business. Similarly, YKK was evaluated highly for building a position of being the global leader in fasteners through a uniform, local community-based system that runs from production through to sales in 71 countries throughout the world.

The winning companies strongly reflect Professor Porter's concepts of simultaneously realizing both the corporate social value and economic value. On this point, it is interesting to note that the traditional business philosophy of Japanese *Ohmi* merchants of Japan's feudal period – known as *sanpo yoshi* – which strives for the benefit of all three sides of the seller, the buyer, and society relationship, is very close in many points to CSV advocated by Professor Porter. In the future, there seems little room for doubt that these sorts of corporate activities that prioritize benefit for society will become the mainstream.

## 7 Case study: ITO EN, CSV

Japan's leading green tea beverage company, ITO EN, which as mentioned previously was a Porter Prize winner in 2013, also became a winner in "the Fortune Change the World" list of 50 companies that are recognized as "companies that have had a positive social impact through activities that are part of their core business strategy" (Fortune Magazine, 2016). The business magazine list includes those companies that have business strategies and innovations that are both adding to profits and contributing to solving social problems, and doing so in ways that make the activity scalable and sustainable. The evaluation process bases ranking on a company's degree of: (1) social impact, (2) profitable business results, and (3) innovation.

ITO EN is a beverage company that uniquely produces drinks from mostly natural ingredients. The value proposition of its business model is to produce drinks that are healthy, safe, and tasty from tea leaves, as well as from fruit and vegetables. It targets customers that are health-conscious and prefer drinks made from natural ingredients that are sugar-free and that contribute to their health. ITO EN enjoys a 33% share in Japan's green tea drink market (Nihon Keizai Shimbun, 2016). The company is a global business with a subsidiary in North America, as well as operations throughout Asia.

The ITO EN green tea-based business requires a large and dependable supply of quality green tea leaves, but Japanese agriculture has been in a state of rapid decline that has created some 400,000 hectares of abandoned farmland. The company decided to follow a CSV strategy through the Tea-Producing Region Development Project, which seeks to revitalize the struggling farming sector in Japan. Working with local farmers and governments, ITO EN brings technological assistance to re-cultivate abandoned farmland and procurement practices that make farming profitable for the next generation of tea farmers. In this way, ITO EN has succeeded in returning nearly 1,000 hectares of farmland for tea plantations, supplying it with some 3,300 tons or about 40% of its total tea leaf needs. It also innovatively creates about 50 million cardboard boxes for use in its business from its nearly 49,000 tons of tea leaf waste. Through this CSV the company contributes to social improvements, improves its own profitability, allows it to expand sales knowing that it can continue to expand its supply of tea leaves, and obtains a global reputation by making the *Fortune* magazine list.

In addition, ITO EN has also enhanced its global reputation and profitability through business strategy. Through a research and development (R&D) department that focuses on tea blending and manufacturing, as well as on customer needs, it has created several industry firsts, which include the first canned oolong tea, first canned green tea, and the first hot beverages sold in PET bottles. The company enjoys financial returns that far exceed their industry average.

## 8 Special public relations considerations for government and public agencies

Up to this point in this chapter the focus has been on corporations improving global stakeholder relationship management through branding and reputation management strategies, but the public sector must also use public relations to achieve goals and objectives. While in most cases its stakeholders are groups within the boundaries of a single nation, globalization creates an increasing need for nations to build relationships with other nations in ways that are not all that different from branding and reputation management for corporations.

This need for public relations skills for the public sector has been increasing, especially in Asia. This is understandable when one realizes that the GDP of the countries of Asia will become the largest in the world by mid-century. In the past two centuries and in these first decades of the 21st century the great global challenges, such as global trade friction, armed conflict, combating global terror, and sustainability, have been primarily taken up by the U.S. and the countries of Europe. Soon the nations of Asia will need to begin to directly take leadership roles for these challenges, which will require public relations skills as much as diplomatic skills.

## Role of public relations in governments and public agencies

James Madison, the fourth President of the United States famously said: "A popular Government, without popular information, or the means of acquiring it, is but a Prologue to a Farce or a Tragedy; or, perhaps both" (Hunt, 1900–1910). In a very real sense the objectives of public relations by public sector agencies frequently overlap with the objectives of democracy itself. Certainly, for a government to succeed in a democracy, it must maintain relationships with citizens and voters based on mutual understanding and two-way communication. In that sense, perhaps it can be said that the biggest enemy to effective public relations is indifference and ignorance toward members of society.

If citizens do not have sufficient information and do not actively communicate with government, there is the danger that elected and appointed public officials will not be able to grasp the real needs and interests of voters and local residents. As a result, one need may be overestimated and vast amounts of public money spent on addressing it, while other needs that are actually more urgent remain undiscovered and unaddressed. There is also the risk that decision-making will be excessively influenced by special interest groups. If there is a sudden eruption of civil dissatisfaction that has been bubbling under the surface, an excessively simple message may fan the flames in the minds of the people and blow away an attitude of trying to deeply understand the issue.

Inherently, government and public agencies (the public sector) are in contact with the public (the general public) for every aspect of their activities, and all government agencies, whether in national government or local government, have a close association with public relations and rely on it. The point on which many public relations managers in government differ from their counterparts in the private sector is that even while targeting only one segment of the public, they are not permitted to disregard the other parts. For example in the case of an automotive manufacturer, it is able to target only those adults able to buy a vehicle, but in the case of government, it has to target all citizens.

Also, government agencies' PR and public information managers are civil (public) servants and do not simply provide local residents with services, they are also accountable to them. They must notify the public of a large amount of information, including how they are effectively using the taxes paid by local residents to improve their standard of living and to realize an environment that is worth living in.

The various problems in societies of both the developing world and the developed world, especially in this age of the global village, are adding additional expectations and pressure on government agencies. The services required from a national government and local governments are different, and in addition the services provided to individuals are extremely diverse. For example, services include those related to traffic and transportation, financial and fiscal matters, social welfare, the environment, disaster management, maintenance of defense and security, the law, museums and other culture facilities, and the protection of wildlife. Although these services are managed by public officials, inherently they are intended to meet the needs of the general public. Alongside the diversification and increasing complexity of societal needs, government agencies are expanding on every level, and as a result they now form a huge labyrinth of great complexity consisting of various bureaus, offices, departments, and sections, and also of committees, councils, and governing bodies, which churn out an enormous volume of documents and reports. These documents are practically all written using specialist and public sector-related terms and can be difficult for most private citizens to understand. As a result, there is often confusion in their communication with government agencies.

As was previously described, the difficulty the public sector faces when conducting public relations is how to communicate its policies and measures to obtain the understanding of the public who may be indifferent and have different values. Unless PR practitioners and others that send public information use public hearings and other means of obtaining feedback, the public sector will not be able to grasp the current and future needs of the public, nor will they be able to raise a nation's presence within the international community.

For a long time, communication activities in Japan's public sector mainly used newspaper and magazine advertising and TV commercials. But alongside the increase in interest in PR in recent years, there has been a shift from advertising companies to PR firms. "The tourism brand restoration project" in Shizuoka Prefecture, for example, that began in 2005 was a PR and public information program that left behind the traditional overemphasis on advertising and transferred efforts to public relations, and it is still being deployed today, although under a different name. Today, with the progress being made in decentralization, this development is also being recognized and adopted by other local governments. Moreover, in a number of regions, we can see various PR campaigns by local governments that utilize so-called *yuru-chara* (mascot characters), which is a recently developed trend.

In Japan's local governments that are seeking financial autonomy from central government, a sense of independence and an awareness of not relying on the regulations of central government are rapidly increasing. Former Governor of Mie Prefecture Masayasu Kitagawa set 1995 as the year to focus on significant service improvements for citizens and worked on administrative reforms by incorporating the methods of private sector management into government. In response to this, other local governments appointed certified public accountants for their settlement of accounts and introduced the accounting methods used by private-sector companies, and in such ways attempted to proactively cooperate with industry and academia. Also, in order to strengthen relations with stakeholders (taxpayers, consumers, local communities, and organizations and groups which have relationships with government), it is clear that they are adopting an approach that places greater importance on public relations. In a certain sense, it can be said that those local governments experiencing financial difficulties are exposing themselves to competition that could determine their very survival. They are now attempting to shift the center of gravity away from the conventional, announcement-centric public information toward two-way public relations that has an awareness of the market. Also, the practices of former Mie Prefecture Governor, Kitagawa, that placed consumers as the starting point and used public hearings (*kocho*) for policy planning and for *koho* (public information), are relatively similar to the methods of public relations.

As was introduced at the start of Chapter 3, Thomas Jefferson, the third President of the United States, is considered to be the first person to use the term "public relations" during his election campaign (Inoue, 2006, p. 58). In the United States, government public relations activities are called by the terms "public affairs," "public information," and "public communication," and have been developed from the responses of political and government agencies to meeting various organizational objectives. Public relations is one important component making up the administrative system that has the goal of filling in the gap between the people and the administration. It is difficult to accurately ascertain the number of public relations practitioners employed by the United States government, but according to a 2015 *Forbes* article titled "Meet the 2nd Largest PR Firm in the World: The U.S. Government," it was estimated that federal agencies employed around 3,100 public affairs officers, but still found it necessary to also outsource public relations to private sector firms as well (Andrzejewski, 2015). The number would be much higher if all 50 state governments were included.

For Japan, while there are no clear figures on the number of people employed in PR and public information departments in central and local governments, this can be estimated as follows. Including the Cabinet Public Relations Office, practically all of the central government, 10 ministries, 17 agencies, 47 nationwide prefectures, and more than 1,700 municipalities (as of March 2015) that have PR and public information departments and have appointed PR and public information managers, it can be estimated that in total, there are more than 7,000 people who are engaged in PR and public information work in the public sector in Japan. However, many of them are inexperienced in public relations due to the practice of job rotation within ministries, and their awareness of PR and public information is that it is only one job among the many that they will engage in at some point in their careers. In this sense, the disparity between Japan and the United States in the PR field is tremendous.

According to *Effective Public Relations*, the specific objectives of public relations activities in the public sector (government and public agencies) in the United States can generally be summarized into the following seven activities, regardless of government level or type:

(1) Informing constituents about the activities of a government agency.
(2) Ensuring active cooperation in government programs – voting, curbside recycling, as well as compliance with regulatory programs, such as mandatory seatbelt use, antismoking ordinances.
(3) Fostering citizen support for established policies and programs – census participation, neighborhood crime watch programs, personal health awareness campaigns, support for disaster relief efforts.

(4) Serving as the public's advocate to government administrators – conveying public opinion to decision makers, managing public issues within the organization, encouraging public accessibility to administration officials.
(5) Managing information internally – facilitating and advancing management's messages through a variety of communications tools.
(6) Facilitating media relations – maintaining relationships with local media, serving as the organization's conduit for all media inquiries, educating the media on the organization, its practices, and its policies.
(7) Building community and nation – using government-sponsored public-health campaigns and other public-security programs and promoting a variety of social or development programs (Cutlip Center & Broom, 2006, p. 411).

## Media reporting on government

In Japan the news media engages in the difficult task of reporting on the activities of government, while having to deal with the problem of a shortage of journalists. Due to a rise in the awareness among the people of their right to know and, the spread of globalization and the Internet, the width and depth of the government-related news it deals with is expanding, and compared to the past, the policy themes have become incomparably more complex and diversified, including debates on public finance, international issues, environmental issues, energy, the falling birthrate problem, elderly welfare, and medical-related problems. Understanding the unique work of government agencies requires media specialists knowledgeable in the ways of the public sector, but there is a shortage of such human resources in Japan.

## Global public relations by government

The United States government deployed a global PR campaign through the activities of the United States Information Agency (USIA) from 1953 to 1999 as a strategy for the bipolar world of the Cold War. President Eisenhower established this agency in 1953 with the objective of creating a clear image of the United States as an independent agency responsible for foreign affairs within the administrative part of the government and under the direct control of the president. This organization was a continuation of the Committee on Public Information (CPI; also known as the Creel Committee) established by George Creel during World War I, and the Office of War Information (OWI) established by MacArthur under the leadership of Elmer Davis during World War II.

At the peak of the Cold War, the USIA had an annual budget of USD $900 million and a staff of 12,000 people. But following the collapse of the Soviet Union at the start of the 1990s, its role weakened and in 1999 it was integrated into the State Department, except for its broadcasting function that includes the Voice of America (VOA; currently active as an independent federal government agency). But despite its weakened role, even today it aims to coordinate United States' information and education-related activities, ascertain and analyze public opinion overseas, and send feedback to the federal government from its 190 bases in 142 countries throughout the world (Inoue, 2006, pp. 117–118).

Looking at the Japanese government, its foreign public relations and public information activities, have been the responsibility of the Cultural Affairs and Overseas Public Relations Division and the Public Diplomacy Strategy Division in the Ministry of Foreign Affairs, and for both divisions combined, the activities are carried out via 457 diplomatic missions abroad (embassies, consulate generals, consulates, and government representative offices). In addition, PR and public information activities to support economic activities at home and abroad are conducted by the local offices of JETRO, which has 57 offices overseas, and the Japan Foundation, which has 21 offices overseas. Also, in broadcasting, NHK overseas broadcasts are distributed throughout the world, but Japan has no organization like the USIA. Looking at other countries as examples, the United Kingdom has the British Council, France has the Alliance Française, and China has the Confucius Institute. Each plays a role through their activities of spreading the language and culture of their respective nations. Considering the growth of Asia, Japan and other nations of the continent should begin to follow a similar strategy as soon as possible, and should strengthen cooperation with various international organizations, and send information to the world in order to build a national brand for their respective nations.

## Role of public relations in elections

The victory in Japan of the Liberal Democratic Party (LDP) in the House of Representatives election of September 11, 2005, was a result in which voters answered the question about postal privatization. But for the people of Japan who were asking difficult questions about their country at home and abroad, this election can be described as a unique one rarely seen in post-war Japan that called into question the very future of Japan. This election has also been called the manifesto election of the parties, as most of the existing political parties, including the Democratic Party of Japan (DPJ), presented their party's manifesto to the people. The practice of a political party describing its election pledges in a manifesto is considered to have originated in 1834 in the United Kingdom, but manifesto elections in their current form are said to have begun following World War II. In recent years, the manifestos in the United Kingdom of Conservative Party leader Margaret Thatcher in 1979 and Labour Party leader Tony Blair in 1997 have attracted attention. While referring to these general elections in the United Kingdom, Masayasu Kitagawa proposed the use of manifestos in Japan, and since the 2003 general election, their use has become increasingly widespread among Japan's parties. However, the manifestos presented by the various parties in House of Representatives elections have not necessarily functioned as intended, and a situation of trial-and-error has continued for their use.

Manifestos that show responsibility for achieving certain results become the grounds for the people to confirm that the policies pledged by the government are being implemented as promised and as scheduled, and subsequently for demanding corrections be smoothly made if problems are occurring in their implementation. To realize smooth and effective administrative management that incorporates a manifesto, public relations is essential as the wheels are to a vehicle. Through public relations, it becomes possible to fulfill (achieve) the pledges (objectives) that were made to constituents.

On the other hand, the House of Representatives election of 2005 is said to have been a PR election by the LDP and DPJ, which was founded in 1998. Their PR departments participated in various ways in this election, including in planning policy, writing speech manuscripts, overall image management, media relations, and surveys and information analysis. In an election campaign, presentation has an importance proportional to the frequency of exposure in the mass media.

In *Silent Messages* (1971), U.S. psychologist Albert Mehrabian advocated the importance of non-verbal communication of elements other than words, including tone and volume of voice, body language, and external appearance (Mehrabian, 1971). In today's media era that increasingly uses video, this non-verbal communication has been shown to be particularly highly effective in election campaigns, in which the situation can change quickly, and it is one reason that social media, which is rich in non-verbal communications, will become an increasingly more important part of public relations for political campaigns, as well as for government and public agencies.

## 9 Public relations skills: having what it takes

### *Conditions required to practice as a PR specialist*

A strong sense of purpose and high-level qualities and skills are demanded of public relations managers and practitioners, especially as the need for PR specialists by various organizations has both increased and changed with the times. People engaged in public relations work in the past were not supported by, for example, a license system from qualification exams or a proficiency certification system, so the standards they had to meet in order to be considered specialists were extremely unclear.

In terms of a qualification system in Japan, the Public Relations Society of Japan (PRSJ), for which this author serves as a committee member, launched a qualification certification system in fiscal year 2007. According to the 2017 PR Yearbook published by the PRSJ, the PR planner qualification certification exam was held 20 times up to 2016 and taken by a total of 8,804 examinees, of whom 6,592 passed. Of these, 3,153 advanced to the third-stage exam, and of these, 2,239 obtained the PR planner qualification (PRAJ, 2017).

### *Profiles of the 2,239 people who passed the third qualification certification exam (PR planner)*

For the PR planners, the largest group were those from general companies at 1,095 persons (48.9%), followed by PR/PR business-related at 705 persons (31.5%), and together these two groups constituted 80% of all PR planners. According to age group, 441 persons (19.7%) were in their twenties and 1,097 persons (49%) were in their thirties, making them the majority, while 700 persons (31.3%) were forty or over (PRAJ, 2017).

So what are the qualities and skills required of public relations specialists and practitioners who conduct relationship management? In places where PR is practiced, in addition to having basic business knowledge, at the very least practitioners must have the following qualities and skills.

### Ten qualities and skills required of PR professionals

There are ten fundamental qualities and skills required to be considered a PR specialist:

(1) Integration skills,
(2) Judgment,
(3) Communication (presentation) skills accompanied by writing skills,
(4) Knowledge and practical skills related to marketing, particularly research and analytical skills,
(5) Flexible, bright, and open-minded,
(6) Creativity,
(7) Honesty,
(8) Leadership, problem-solving, and counseling skills,
(9) Comprehension and curiosity,
(10) Perseverance.

However, when thinking of the solutions to the fundamental problems currently facing companies and organizations, in addition to these ten, there are five fundamental conditions that are also required. Next, these conditions will be described in more detail and also the methodology for a specialist education to cultivate them.

### Five fundamental conditions for PR professionals

In addition to the ten qualities and skills, PR professionals also need to possess five fundamental conditions: ethical perspective, positive attitude, ability to create scenarios, IT skill proficiency, and English fluency. Figure 4.6 shows these five fundamental conditions as surrounding the ten qualities and skills, to show a structure to the overall abilities of the PR professional.

### 1) Ethics

As described previously, ethics has been defined from the time of the ancient Greek philosophers as the notion of good and evil in human behavior. Yet, in our time it is understood in terms of "utilitarianism" and "deontology." While ethics across the world are grounded in different cultures and religions, the ethics grounded in "utilitarianism" and "deontology" are currently the mainstream in Western advanced nations, and correspond to the definition of ethics used in this book.

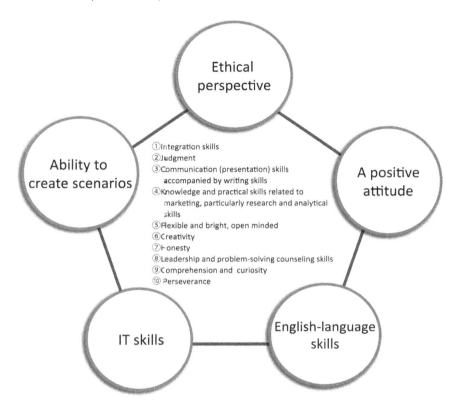

**FIGURE 4.6**   Five fundamental conditions and ten qualities and skills required of public relations professionals

*Source:* Takashi Inoue (2006), *Public Relations*, p. 123

Individuals and groups that are PR professionals have the special skills and abilities to influence society in various ways, but at the same time they also have major responsibilities. This is because society has high expectations for them and in many cases, their words and deeds tend to be trusted unconditionally. To meet the expectations of society and to carry out their work duties appropriately, it is essential that they practice self-governance with an awareness that they must be professionals that possess a strong sense of ethics.

If there are unethical activities in public relations, then there is the danger of public relations falling into the trap of becoming mere "propaganda" in which it sends out information that is advantageous only to the information sender and ultimately is untrustworthy. Conversely, the world is rapidly becoming an advanced information-driven society, in which organizations and individuals both send and receive information in real-time. Society has become very knowledgeable about communications, very aware and sophisticated about paying close attention to the behavior and responses of the individuals and organizations that are sending them information. Therefore, without being grounded in ethics, the publics will not be able to trust public relations messages sent by organizations.

In this way, a high level of ethics is constantly required for public relations. This must be imprinted into the minds of PR practitioners in organizations and PR firms, who must provide honest advice to top management in their own organizations and to clients. Moreover, keeping in mind the lesson that acting ethically will in the long-run result in achieving objectives along the shortest path, when PR professionals see the organization speeding ahead recklessly, they must play the role of applying the brakes.

Ethics can be described as an attitude of respect for the diverse cultures and customs of people from other countries, which in hyper-globalization becomes increasingly important. The International Public Relations Association (IPRA) has a required code of ethics which they call their "Code of Conduct" that all practitioners should adhere to, which is available on its website (IPRA, 2010). In short, when public relations lacks ethics it becomes nothing more than propaganda.

## 2) Positive thinking

Public relations managers and practitioners must think positively. They must constantly have a positive attitude when playing the role of the intermediator with the client or the organization they belong to and also toward the various public relations target audiences. An environment of positive thinking makes it easier to act more flexibly and implement a strategic and creative public relations program with self-correction.

Positive thinking is created from "a spirit of being thankful for everything" and is the acceptance not only of others, but also of oneself, and of viewing the current situation in a positive light. This way of thinking promotes positive and flexible behavior and also forms the basis for self-correction.

Continuously building good relations with various stakeholders in a rapidly changing and complex society requires a wide range of knowledge and experience. Sometimes, there will be issues that cannot be dealt with solely by your individual knowledge and experience. For these issues, it is essential to build relations with people whom you can call on for help. People who think positively naturally attract other people to them, expanding their intellectual network of people who possess diverse knowledge and experiences. It is preferable that this network has both "the depth" of being a group with specialist knowledge, and "the width" that make it possible to accept diversity and to connect to people from a wide range of professions and countries. Obtaining highly specialized cooperation through information gathering and exchanging opinions accelerates the achievement of objectives. Intermediators also have a tremendous impact as a bridge to individuals and organizations.

Conversely, an environment of negative thinking lacks flexibility and the idea of accepting the other party amicably. Therefore, activities in a negative thinking environment tend to be one-way and do not consider the viewpoint of the other party, and this leads to the very great danger of trying to control the other party through propaganda-type actions.

When conducting public relations, first of all the best possible outcomes must be considered. Then, the potential obstacles, issues, and failures are considered so they can be avoided. Also, when implementing public relations activities, there are a number of factors that might become major obstacles, like culture, language, thoughts, beliefs, laws, and systems, and in many cases they can place the public relations program in a difficult situation. However, while the objectives set could easily be scaled down and policies changed, this will not produce desirable results. Even when facing difficulties or a crisis situation, professional PR practitioners must maintain a positive attitude toward achieving the objectives and strive to achieve them completely. Also, the situation can change from moment to moment when implementing a planned program, and when mistakes are discovered during this process, it is necessary to accept the position of the other party and the situation that you find yourself in and then carry out needed self-correction as quickly as possible, so that objectives can be completed along the shortest path.

A positive attitude has two meanings. The first is a positive attitude in order to acquire information and knowledge that will ensure that you keep abreast of the developments in a rapidly changing society and economy. The second is a positive attitude to utilize the information and knowledge you have acquired and to aim to positively face the situation that confronts you.

Public relations activities are relationship management activities with various stakeholders, and when implementing them, managers and practitioners will face a myriad of different issues. There will always be high obstacles that must be cleared, such as culture, language, thought, beliefs, laws, or systems, and frequently practitioners will be required to demonstrate the depth and breadth of their knowledge. At such times, if from the very beginning, before even attempting to clear these obstacles, a person tries to change plans and policies, then this negative attitude indicates that the person does not have the mentality of a PR professional.

Instead, what is required is a positive attitude of asking what is needed to clear these obstacles and what measures can be taken. Then, if any problems with the plans and policies are found when investigating what is required to clear the obstacles, then they can be corrected. But a negative attitude of "this is impossible" from the very start will only lead to failure, rather than a positive attitude of "we can do this" that is a driving force behind resolving problems. In the Nissan/MMC press conference described at the beginning of Chapter 2 the remarks of Carlos Ghosn demonstrated this positive, "a-cup-half-full" attitude. MMC was in the midst of a scandal that seemed to be an almost clear sign of a company that had no future, but Ghosn explained in simple and convincing terms how as a member of the Nissan Alliance, MMC could and would quickly realize both profitability and good governance.

## 3) Scenario creation ability

The ability to analyze an issue or problem and create "what-if" type scenarios of possible future outcomes is absolutely essential for public relations professionals. Even if you are able to clear the obstacles that are clearly visible in front of you, if you cannot also anticipate how future events might develop as you execute your public relations program of action, you will be unable to anticipate pitfalls, and therefore, will be unable to create plans that will achieve your objectives. The methods taken to resolve problems in the current phase will be meaningless, if they will have negative effects in the next phase. Therefore, to reach the best possible outcome for each scenario, practitioners need to be able to also anticipate how the deployment of a certain program of action will lead to various possible results.

## Example of crisis in which a product caused deaths

Consider the following example, in which company S is a pharmaceutical manufacturer that, while knowing a certain pharmaceutical product to have problems, imported it anyway from overseas and conducted sales activities for it. Eventually, many people who took the drug became sick with a life-threatening infection and some people even died, and the media widely reported on this to the extent that it escalated into a social problem. The families of the victims and those infected took company S to court and sued it for liability compensation. An investigation on the suspicion of death and injury due to professional negligence was launched into why the investigation agencies did not take the appropriate action even when knowing there to be a risk of infection. Yet, even as the boycott movement against it peaked, company S continued to insist through the mass media that "We were unaware of the danger" and the situation continued to deteriorate.

Public relations specialist Mr. K was on a business trip in New York, but in a telephone conversation with company S, persuaded the company, advising: "If you honestly tell the complete truth, I will undertake the task of responding to the situation." After confirming that the company admitted to having known the danger of infection and had taken the step of replacing the president, Mr. K created a crisis management program. Because Mr. K had learned enough about the phytotoxicity (drug-induced harmful effects) incidents through the mass media, he was immediately able to create a scenario, which he read over the telephone to the new president of company S.

The underlying idea behind the scenario created by Mr. K was that while it was not possible to provide true relief to the victims of this phytotoxicity problem that had even resulted in people losing their lives, company S must accept responsibility for its actions and fulfill its social responsibilities. The most important issue was providing relief to the families of the victims and those infected, and the compensation necessary for this was a requirement for the survival of company S as a pharmaceutical manufacturer. If company S did not quickly resolve this crisis, it would be severely damaged and the path to rescuing it would become even steeper, and those staff who were completely uninvolved in the sales of the problem pharmaceutical would have their livelihoods robbed from them.

In order to overcome these overlapping problems, Mr. K thought up the following scenario. The new president of Company S would first hold a press conference to take responsibility. Top management would make a full apology that fully conveyed an attitude of sincere remorse, and give a clear explanation about the measures it would take to resolve the problem. The company would explain how the steps to be taken would help wipe away, to the extent that it was possible, the negative image of Company S that the scandal had created, and how that would lead to a de-escalation of the boycott movement against it. As a result, Company S would be able to survive, and it would be able to use profits from its business activities for relief for the victims. Also, those staff who were not directly responsible would not be robbed of their livelihoods, and the company would fulfill its social responsibility to employees and to society.

Company S followed Mr. K's instructions and admitted negligence and apologized at the press conference. Then the company indicated its strong intention to provide relief to the families of the victims and to those infected. Having done this, the media coverage that up to that point had escalated into a storm over several months of continuous coverage, began to subside to a remarkable extent.

The important point to learn from this example is that Mr. K as a professional did not permit himself to consider only the short-term interests of his client or create a scenario that would enable it to evade its responsibilities. It is necessary to calmly see the ultimate societal benefit and not get too emotional with regards to the client. And, as a problem goes from increasingly serious to a full emergency, it becomes time-sensitive, and the ability to create a scenario is critical.

## 4) IT proficiency

The global Internet population currently exceeds 3 billion people (Internet Live Stats, 2016) and so public relations practitioners must have a basic understanding of IT and the technologies to use it.

Public relations managers and practitioners need to have a basic understanding of IT that is evolving on a seemingly daily basis and also be able to consider ways of effectively using it for PR activities. The appearance and spread of the Internet means information is increasingly becoming two-way and real-time, and the ways of communicating are being transformed from the ground up. In the midst of this transformation, while cooperating with technicians who possess professional knowledge, PR practitioners must incorporate new technologies and conduct relationship management that reflects the changing times. The utilization of the Internet and social media makes possible direct, interactive (two-way) communication from point (individual) to point (individual), and this is changing the form in which information is distributed and its qualities, and inevitably is also changing public relations methods.

While this topic is discussed in more detail in Chapter 9, we should note here that PR practitioners need to understand the advantages and disadvantages of the new forms of media that are appearing one after another in fields from blogging to social network services (SNS), such as Twitter, Facebook, Instagram, and LINE. They must understand how to effectively use them for public relations and how to use new digital technologies to effectively give presentations that are appealing audio-visually and with links to video in social media.

In an environment characterized by a flood of information due to the development of the media and the spread of the Internet, the ability to search for and find the information that people want when they need it has become vital. Moreover, PR practitioners must be able to discern which of the information they have obtained is truly important in order to carry out their work duties.

The open nature of the ceaselessly expanding Net society is creating problems that were previously unimaginable. Information on the Arab Spring, which began in Tunisia in North Africa at the end of 2010 and subsequently spread throughout the Arab world, including to Egypt and Libya, was sent around the globe in real-time via Twitter and other SNS, and the once stable governments were shaken to their foundations in the space of just a few months by a series of citizen demonstrations. But as witnessed by the subsequent turmoil, the speed at which information is transmitted on SNS and its real-time quality can plunge an organization into an out-of-control state. In this sort of environment, it is absolutely essential that PR practitioners themselves acquire skills in and knowledge of IT.

### 5) English fluency for PR professionals in non-English speaking countries

English skills (particularly conversational skills) are skills that public relations specialists should absolutely try to master. This is not just in order to conduct business internationally, but because English can also be said to be one of the basic skills needed for accessing the world via the Internet.

Currently, the world's English-speaking population, including those for whom English is either their first or second language, is said to be approximately 1.5 billion people (Statista, 2017), which is the total of those who can read, write, and speak in English. Therefore, learning English signifies opening the door to communication with 1.5 billion potential new friends. The English information that we are able to access is increasing dramatically, adding both breadth and depth to the acquirable information, and at the same time English skills help us to acquire a deeper understanding of the world as a whole by enabling us to come into contact with different cultures through communicating with people from other countries.

However, merely learning a foreign language such as English is insufficient for international public relations practitioners. The ability to speak English or another foreign language is simply one communication tool, and if information is not communicated, or if there is a problem with how to communicate, then that tool cannot be utilized. English fluency for the PR professional is a fundamental condition necessary for acquiring the knowledge necessary for work and having the communication skills needed in a hyper-globalized world.

## 10 PR firms: functions and roles

### Building good relations between organizations and PR firms

In the last few years, it has not only been major companies that have established in-house PR departments, because alongside the changes to the environment in Japan's PR industry, even venture companies and SMEs with unique business models and products and services have been seen to be actively conducting PR activities. The same trends can also be seen in local governments that are calling for decentralization and aiming for reforms, along with the shift of communications from "advertising" to "PR and public information," they are attempting to conduct branding for services more precisely tailored to local residents and that utilize local characteristics.

To put this in perspective, up until the recent past, in many cases PR activities of such organizations were limited to only supporting a small number of individual projects. But this is being transformed to where organizations want PR activities to also include consultation, which is a function PR firms inherently possess.

Originally, an organization accepts the PR firm as a partner and uses it as its brain, facilitating the deployment of more effective public relations by enabling the PR firm staff to demonstrate their true value as specialists who utilize their expertise and personal connections.

There have been quite a few cases in which an organization was unaware of the true value of public relations and this resulted in not only a worsening of its image, but also a major financial loss that jeopardized its very existence. As can be seen in the Snow Brand Milk Product food poisoning incidents and the murky M&A and subsequent resignation of the president of Olympus, there have been several instances in which a passive public relations response that lacked a crisis management function plunged a company into crisis. If we were to compare this to a human body, then it can be described as a dysfunction occurring in the body and it being unable to respond appropriately to external stimuli and changes. If a hospital is the place where people are cured of their illness and have their physical functions restored, then for organizations, this function is played by PR firms.

Just as in a hospital there are specialists in certain fields, such as in cardiac surgery, gastroenterology, or psychiatry, there are PR firms that specialize in, for example, investor relations or media relations. Also, when the cause of the physical dysfunction is unknown, then through a check-up and diagnosis and various types of tests, the specific part of the body that is dysfunctional is identified and corrective measures taken. Similarly, the relations between organizations and PR firms start with a consultation and if the problem can be identified, then the best possible response can be implemented. So there are also PR firms that play a general hospital-type role.

## Functions and roles of PR firms

The basic service provided by PR firms is consultation for overall public relations strategies of their client organizations. The number one objective of this is to effectively utilize the functions of PR firms in order to implement public relations programs that are optimized for each client. Of course, in some cases they only provide advice from the viewpoint of a third party, but in terms of content, they must provide valuable solutions when the leaders of the organizations are making decisions, and this is the real value that PR firms provide.

In the past when a crisis occurred in an organization in Japan, typically it had not concluded a contract with an external specialist able to offer a third-party viewpoint, and there have also frequently been cases where the responses before or after the crisis were slow, or top management took the wrong decision, and the situation has ended up running out of control. Furthermore, there have been occasions where this has developed into a life-or-death management crisis. In order to avoid falling into this sort of situation, companies and organizations must have day-to-day relations with competent PR firms.

Also, in a management environment characterized by speed, when specialists able to provide counseling are asked about a decision that must be taken by clients during an emergency, they have to be able to respond instantaneously. So professionals are constantly required to act in real-time.

In order for PR firms to effectively demonstrate these functions, they utilize a wide range of expertise, successful case studies, and also networks of people, knowledge, and business, including the findings and experiences of their client companies. In this way, they help their clients to achieve their objectives and targets.

For example, the author's firm, Inoue Public Relations, provides public relations consulting based upon the Life-Cycle Model that it has independently developed. The Life-Cycle Model, which is detailed in Chapter 6, is a model of public relations activities that describes the spiraling cycle of public relations activities: first setting the objectives, then setting the business target and communication channels, formulating the strategy, creating the plan, implementing the plan, analyzing and evaluating the results, providing feedback and conducting self-correction, and finally beginning again by setting the next objectives.

Also, PR firms normally have a network of overseas PR firms. They will conduct public relations activities and collect information locally via these overseas bases, but in Japan there are still only a small number of PR firms with this sort of network.

Inoue Public Relations is an independent PR firm, but it is able to provide global public relations services through its cooperative relations with other PR firms with global networks and with the leading local PR firms in various countries.

Public relations and communications are deeply connected to the local culture and language. No matter how wonderful the press release is written in your own local language at the time, it has to be localized and translated for other countries, it needs to be edited not just for the quality of the local language, but also to ensure that the language used is best suited to that locality. Therefore, the basic service provided by PR firms is the local country implementation of messages for a global public relations strategy.

## PR generalists and specialists

PR firms are groups of specialists, and it is useful to understand the differences between generalists and specialists.

The bottom of the triangle in Figure 4.7 represents the field of expertise and the height represents the expertise (the number of years of experience). The people near to the summit of this triangle can be described as specialists in their field. In order to get to near the summit, it is necessary to have considerable practical experience and to have been engaged for a fairly long period in your field of expertise.

In many cases within Japanese organizations, an employee will spend a couple of years in one section before being transferred to a different one, but the same triangle can still be used as an explanation even in the case of transfers between sections. We can see a triangle on the left side adjacent to the original triangle. When the triangles are connected for each transfer, a cone-shaped polyhedron is created. The area at the top of this polyhedron is the area of specialists, but let's see what happens when we remove this part. In the remaining part are generalists who, despite possessing experience in various fields, do not have the same high level of expertise as specialists. The part that has been removed is the group of specialists and can be understood as being groups of specialists in various fields.

Each specialist excels in their particular field, and by forming a group, the organization can also function as generalists. This might be easier to understand if we consider PR firms. Depending on their level of experience as PR practitioners in fields such as semiconductors, automotive, finance, or government agencies, they could be specialists or they could be generalists.

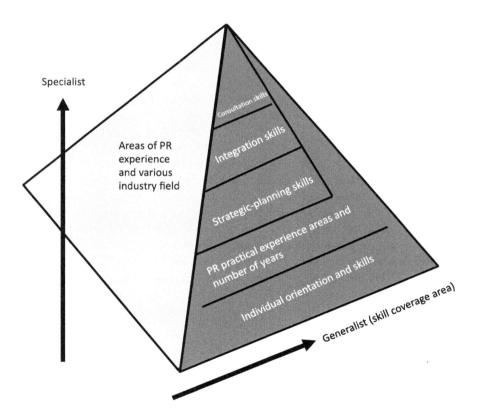

**FIGURE 4.7**    Differences between the PR generalist and PR specialist

*Source:* Takashi Inoue (2006), *Public Relations*, p. 132

## Outsourcing of public relations work by companies and organizations

### 1) Outsourcing and co-sourcing

There are cases when companies and organizations consign a part or all of their public relations work to PR firms that inherently possess high levels of expertise. This is so-called outsourcing. In many cases when the organization does not have a PR manager, such as a foreign company that has only just advanced into the local market, all of the public relations work is outsourced to a PR firm.

Conversely, co-sourcing is when an organization's PR departments carry out the public relations work jointly with PR firms. For example, there are cases when, based on an integrated public relations strategy, an organization's PR departments carry out the work themselves as usual in their home country, but the work is entrusted to a network of PR firms for public relations activities at overseas bases.

Outsourcing is consigning public relations work to external parties, while co-sourcing is an expansion of the public relations function. In terms of human resources in Japan, the number of public relations professionals is overwhelmingly fewer than in other advanced nations, and as it is difficult to train people rapidly in the environment in Japan, outsourcing the work to PR firms that are groups of professionals can be an extremely effective choice. In addition, for Japan's organizations facing high personnel and office costs, outsourcing can also be described as a realistic choice from the perspective of restructuring.

### 2) Outsourcing's cost effects

Outsourcing is premised on the fact that PR firms will carry out public relations work efficiently as a group of specialists. When considering the practice of job rotation, especially in many Japanese organizations, in which a person is transferred to a different section before they have accumulated that much experience, it is also important to consider cost performance by comparing the personnel costs in the PR department with the contract fee that will be paid to the PR firm.

Also, through the participation of PR professionals, it becomes possible to train in-house PR staff in the organization, so educational effects can also be expected from outsourcing. Public relations by specialists gives added value to the performance of organizations in general and contributes to the achievement of PR goals. So when outsourcing, it is also necessary to appropriately evaluate the level of this contribution.

At the stage where PR firms are expected to be active only as the arms and legs of an organization's PR department, it is difficult to draw out the true value of whether to outsource or to co-source.

Premised on information disclosure by their clients, PR firms have a duty of confidentiality for any confidential information they acquire in the course of carrying out their work duties, and this is always included in the contract. Therefore, in principle

PR firms use a "one industry, one client" system, which means not simultaneously having as a client a competitor to a client in the same industry. Rather than a superior-subordinate relationship, outsourcing and co-sourcing are based on a relationship of equality and trust (a partnership) between the client company and the PR firm.

### 3) Key points when concluding an outsourcing contract

There are a number of factors your company should consider when outsourcing (or co-sourcing) its public relations work to a PR firm.

First is the point of whether the PR firm that you are going to conclude the contract with is necessary for your company; specifically, whether or not it possesses relationship management skills, excellent PR-related findings, and a network of contacts that your own staff do not possess. If your company already possesses these attributes, then it should strive to make full use of them, which would reduce the need for outsourcing.

Second is the point of whether the work described in the contract, such as PR counseling, strategy building, problem analysis, and implementation of special projects, is required for a temporary period only or on an ongoing basis. This will also affect the creation of the budget.

The third point is to examine whether the problems your company is currently facing are important enough to demand counseling, an independent analysis, and the viewpoint of PR professionals. If the problems are trivial, then the contract with the PR firm can be postponed, but if their importance is increasing, then it will be necessary to conclude the contract quickly.

The fourth point is that in countries like Japan, where many organizations utilize the seniority system and the top-down approach, it is often difficult to have objective opinions heard by top management, and even if top management does hear them, organizations tend to dismiss the opinions coming from employees below them. It is important to consider whether or not the PR firm will be able to function effectively by submitting its objective opinions to such an organization and providing it with advice on how to correct the path it is taking.

The final point is that when concluding a contract with a PR firm, it is important to ascertain if the results will be different than if your own organization carried out the PR work. If the results will be the same, it makes no economic sense to maintain a contract with a PR firm.

### 4) Approach to the outsourcing budget

After you have considered these various factors and decided to conclude a contract with a PR firm, it would seem appropriate to next think about the contract fee. The contract fee charged by PR firms tends basically to be a retainer fee calculated on a monthly basis and premised on an annual contract. The fee will differ depending on the services provided, but the basic approach is to set time-based fees. For your reference, please refer to Figure 4.8.

Concluding a contract and paying a monthly fee can create a stable relationship between the client and the PR firm. The PR firm's account team, centered on an account executive (AE), will carry out the public relations work.

When concluding a contract with a PR firm, there are a number of methods for determining the annual budget for the public relations work. One method is to charge fees on a retainer basis, where the retainer fees are the fees paid in return for continuous services. Other methods include:

- Determining as a year-on-year increase or decrease,
- Determining as a fixed percentage of sales or profits,
- Determining at the discretion of managers.

Each of these three methods involve simple calculations and are in general adopted by many PR firms. But a problem that remains is that these methods cannot reflect an organization's future policies and needs for PR services.

The basic relationship between PR firms and their clients is an annual contract based on ongoing work with consultations at the core, with the monthly retainer fee set according to the content of this work. The fee conversion is based on time spent multiplied by the hourly fee of the PR firm personnel. The time fee will differ depending on the career, from top-level management down to lower levels of staff. Fees can also be charged on a project basis, where the project fee is applied to work of a specified project, as detailed in the PR contract, rather than by specific work activities performed. It will also be based on time spent and the hourly fee rates.

Another perhaps more preferable method of determining a budget is to calculate it based on a company's medium- to long-term business plan, the setting of PR objectives on a single-year basis in accordance with the business plan, and the PR plan to achieve these objectives.

In the author's experience, as already described in the previous section, "Functions and roles of PR firms," PR firms provide comprehensive public relations

| ① Top level | $500~$800 |
| ② Senior level | $320~$480 |
| ③ Intermediate level | $200~$280 |
| ④ Junior level | $150~$180 |
| ⑤ Staff level | $90~$130 |

Fees rates vary within a level by the AE assigned, due to differences in career experience and the nature of the assignment. Rates shown here are in U.S. dollars.

**FIGURE 4.8** Per-hour fee schedule example

services, especially when founded on something like the PR Life-Cycle Model. Normally, a PR plan is created in accordance with this model, and a budget proposal is submitted to the client. If a client's annual PR budget and the budget proposed by its PR firm are the same, then there is no problem. But in many cases, there is a difference between the two. Even in companies that have an annual budget of hundreds of thousands or even millions of dollars, their budget for PR services can be fairly limited. But in recent years, the shift from advertising to PR has been gathering momentum. Even if the available PR budget is in the range of 10% to 30% of the total communication budget, including for advertising, it becomes easily possible to formulate a diverse PR program and achieve communication effects of several times the budget.

If the budgets of both parties do not match at the final stage of compiling the budget, it will be necessary to make adjustments by reviewing the PR strategy and program based on the criterion of the order of priorities for the objectives and targets.

The contract fee for public relations outsourcing work should not be considered to be an expense that reduces net income, but rather should be thought of as an "investment" in order to create added value from the IR viewpoint of improving the corporate brand (image) thereby increasing earnings. Alternatively it could be seen as an asset that will generate value over several years like a physical asset via, for example, a PR campaign to deregulate a market.

## 11 Urgent need for PR and human relations training in a hyper-globalized world

As was previously described, from the viewpoint of public relations specialists, it is conceivable that the problems associated with the various scandals that have occurred in Japanese society could have been kept to a minimum, if they had been dealt with by practitioners, who had received a specialist education in public relations, particularly one grounded in a sense of ethics. Also, in today's diversifying global society, many problems have emerged that require PR specialists. These are practitioners, who have received a specialist PR education that is wide-ranging academically and practically and who possess depth of knowledge and experience to provide the organization with an ability to defend itself during crisis situations. There is an urgent need for this sort of fundamental, practical PR education in Japan and other countries, and especially the countries of Asia.

Developing human relations skills needs to start as early as possible even from infancy, and is of particular importance for Asian societies like Japan, which have a very group-oriented culture in which group bonding is given priority over development of an individual's own identity. The remainder of this chapter deals with the method for training high-level professionals in public relations and communications and also touches upon measures to address issues in "bonding education" that the author calls "*kizuna* education," which starts in infancy. This is especially important to Asian societies, which are not based on the Western individualism, and are high-context cultures, and therefore, need to learn to communicate effectively to the outside world using low context communications.

The introduction of public relations into society is an urgent issue. When considering specific solutions to the various problems that have been occurring at all levels of society, requires relationship management skills, which are a core skill of public relations, are required. And, it is not just in companies where this is needed, but also in organizations such as educational institutions, including elementary schools, and local communities. The targets of public relations education must be based on the individuals who constitute society. Today, amid the advance of globalization, the question needs to be revisited about the delay in "establishing the identity" of individuals in society, especially Asian society with its inherent possession of a distinctive collectivist mindset compared to people in the West. Indeed, bolstering the establishment of individual identity at an early age from within a group-oriented culture should lead to positive effects spreading throughout the society and then the country's relationship with the international community.

We can think of a variety of educational methods to achieve this, such as educational institutions, or an organization's own in-house education that uses external specialists, or education through industry groups such as public relations associations, or by public relations-related societies. However, in order to realize its fully fledged introduction into society, it is necessary to construct a system in schools with a view to introducing PR education from the compulsory education stage, and even starting from infancy to develop an individual's own identity.

In terms of the educational institutions targeted for this, its starts with "*kizuna* (bonding) education" from kindergartens (nursery schools) to elementary schools. *Kizuna* education in the early childhood period referred to here is education based upon creating human relations. After preliminary education in junior high school and high school, then in higher education, public relations education needs to be taught in junior colleges, four-year course universities, and graduate schools. In other words, it is necessary to build an integrated educational system that can respond organically to this need.

Reflecting its nature, the introduction of public relations into society should be considered on a long-term axis of 10 to 20 years. However, based on the urgent need for PR education, due to hyper-globalization, the first priority must be training PR practitioners by educating teachers in higher educational institutions. These teachers trained in PR would later be expected to become the talented educators that can introduce PR and PR-related education, which is to say training in communication and relationship-building skills, into infant education and compulsory education.

### *Educating PR professionals in higher education*

In order to consider an educational program for higher education, an effective method is to refer to the PR curriculum that has been incorporated into U.S. education in the last 50 years. In the United States, which has experienced the evolution of modern public relations over more than 100 years, the systemization of public relations theory has been extensively completed and its methods have also been standardized. It is necessary to study the curriculum and programs of the United States, where an integrated qualification system has already been established. However, focus needs to be in these four areas: (1) education to train PR specialists, (2) a qualification system, (3) the readiness of organizations to accept these human resources, and (4) training teachers so they can provide instruction within educational institutions.

### *1) Current state of PR education in universities and graduate schools in the United States and its qualification system*

It is not surprising that in the United States, which is very advanced in PR as a nation and is the birthplace of present-day public relations, PR practitioner Edward Bernays gave the first public relations course in 1923 at New York University. Then in 1939, Rex Harlow became the first full-time public relations educator for a course at Stanford University, and in 1947, Boston University became the first to offer a university-level public relations degree in the United States. According to Rex Harlow, Professor of Public Relations at Stanford University, public relations education began from around 1945 and by 1946, 30 universities had launched 47 courses (Inoue, 2006, pp. 148–149).

Currently, there are approximately 400 schools registered in the Higher Education Programs Online Directory of the Public Relations Society of America (PRSA), which tells the story that many universities are providing a vocational PR education in the United States. In terms of its qualification system, various certificates of completion are issued to PR students, who meet the requirements of their individual universities, such as for the specified number of class credits and achieving a certain grade level (Inoue, 2015, p. 285).

### *2) Current state of PR and communication education in Japan's universities and graduate schools*

From September to October 2014, the Japan Public Relations Institute (JPRI), which the author heads, conducted a survey on the status of public relations and *koho* (public information). This covered the May 2013 listing of over 450 universities, excluding four-year colleges, categorized by size. It examined faculties, subjects, and courses. The sources of information on faculties and subjects were each university's homepage, while the courses were searched for from the syllabi. The keywords set for the search were "public relations," "PR," "corporate communications," "*koho*" (public information), "communication," and "media."

According to this survey, as of October 2014 within the *koho* and PR-related classes provided by four-year universities, first with regards to faculties, in two universities, there were 15 subjects and majors, and 41 courses. Other than these universities, there were more than 40 universities providing a PR education in some form (including in conjunction with other faculties), and the number of teachers was also trending upwards alongside the increase in the number of subjects and courses (Inoue, 2015, pp. 149–150).

Recently, public relations and corporate communication (CC) courses have been introduced, of which there are a total of 19 courses – 15 PR courses and 4 CC courses – being provided by 12 universities. In recent years, following the launch of CC courses by Tokyo Keizai University in 1995, courses in PR were launched in the academic year 2004 by Waseda University in undergraduate programs followed by the MBA Graduate School and the Graduate School of Public Management, and from 2012 by the Graduate School of Management, Kyoto University, and Akita International University from 2016, which shows the growing interest in PR in academia.

### 3) Points to remember when introducing PR lectures and courses

When launching a PR program of courses, it is important to prepare the educational environment for: (1) the curriculum, (2) assigned lecturers, (3) the question of the qualification certification, and (4) the readiness of society to accept the students after graduation (including companies and public institutions). Also, universities with a MBA course should incorporate PR courses as part of the overall graduate program.

It is preferable to develop the curriculum and syllabus in collaboration with university research facilities and relevant organizations, such as local public relations associations and societies and also private-sector research facilities.

No matter how well educational institutions train their students to be PR practitioners, if after graduation they are unable to find positions in companies and government organizations as PR professionals, then they will be forced to pursue other careers and the shortage of PR professionals will continue. Therefore, it is necessary for organizations to create positions for PR professionals coming out of universities.

### 4) Creating a social environment that seeks and develops PR graduates

It is important to clarify the social position of PR specialists by making society aware of the concept that PR practitioners are responsible for relationship management – rather than merely for media relations, publicity, and public information – and reminding people that PR is specialist work that requires wide-ranging strategic skills and expertise, and moreover requires individuals with the internationalism needed in the 21st century.

Also, it is important to improve how organizations handle and treat PR specialists. This involves actively creating an environment in which the value and importance of PR and public information specialists is recognized. Companies and other organizations must be encouraged to carry out a sweeping review when recruiting personnel and to establish an executive level PR specialist position within their organization, such as a public relations officer, and in the future, large companies should establish executive vice president or executive director positions. It also involves tireless educational activities and requests to organizations for collaborative programs. If necessary, external practitioners with experience are to be actively recruited, while an essential requirement for a company's top management should be to have PR experience.

## 5) Taking national initiative

Public relations at the country level has to overcome a number of historical and societal obstacles. Moreover, it is finally coming to be understood that one of the fundamental factors behind the scandals and other incidents that have repeatedly occurred, especially in Japan, in the business, political, and bureaucratic worlds is that public relations has not taken root. Previously the understanding was that public relations was only necessary for some organizations, but it can be said that today it has come to be recognized that it is necessary for the wider society. A long-term outlook and imagination will be needed in order to spread the use of public relations widely across society, but a more immediate problem is to have PR students acquire the basic knowledge and a practical education. What is required above all in order to train them to become specialists is to construct an educational system that is able to provide organizations with excellent PR professionals based on effective programs in universities and graduate schools where the necessary educational environment has been established.

The question of how to utilize the graduates who have undertaken and completed such a program relates to creating positions for them within organizations. Knowledge and skills in terms of the level of credits that students acquired in a university or graduate school will not be enough to satisfy the demands of the companies that will receive them. Therefore, in addition to creating demand for such professionals within organizations, it is necessary to create a system to improve the quality of PR graduates once they begin employment.

## "Kizuna" education in childhood

In Japan in 2004, Waseda University started the "Public Relations Theory for the Next Generation of Leaders (Introduction and Advanced Course)" in order to spread the use of public relations – which is not that familiar to the Japanese people – across Japan as this will be necessary in order to become members of global society in the future, and because the training and enhancement of "man power" with an established "identity" is of critical importance.

Today, over ten years after the start of these classes, globalization is proceeding at a breakneck speed, faster than we ever imagined, and a pressing issue is how to, as quickly as possible, introduce and spread the use of public relations, which should be considered to be the foundation of knowledge for people to live in a global society. Therefore, aspects of public relations need to be introduced into education from childhood; that is to say, education only at universities and graduate schools will be too late.

Public relations is "relationship management activities" in order to achieve objectives (targets). In other words, it is not high-context type activities like "heart-to-heart communication and the harmonizing, mentally and physically of two parties engaged in one activity" that are naturally the focus of education in the case of Japan and in other Asian countries from the earliest age. Rather, it is low-context type "relationship-building activities" of "clearly communicating your ideas to the other party," in which there is an awareness of the objectives (targets). In fact "relationship-building activities" is precisely another way of saying "connecting people." The phrase "relationship building" is not well suited to the world of children, so when communicating public relations concepts in kindergartens, elementary schools, and junior high schools, it is better to use the alternate name of "*kizuna* education." Indeed, *kizuna* expresses the essence of public relations itself (Inoue, 2009, p. 5).

# References

Aaker, D. & Joachimsthaler, E. (2009). *Brand Leadership: Building Assets in an Information Economy.* New York: The Free Press.

Andrzejewski, A. (2015). "Meet the 2nd Largest PR Firm in the World: The U.S. Government." *Forbes,* December 14, 2015.

Bernays, E. (1980). "Meeting of Association for Education in Journalism at Boston University." Boston: s.n.

Business Journal (2013). *Business Journal.* [Online] Available at: http://biz-journal.jp/2013/11/post_3280.html [Accessed July 27, 2017].

Cone Inc. (2004). *Cone Corporate Citizenship Study.* Boston, MA: Cone Inc.

Cutlip, S, Center, A., & Broom, G. (2006). *Effective Public Relations.* 9th ed. Upper Saddle River, NJ: Pearson Prentice Hall.

Dell Inc. (2017). "Corporate Social Responsibility." [Online] Available at: http://www.dell.com/learn/us/en/uscorp1/cr?c=us&l=en&s=corp [Accessed August 1, 2017]

Fomalhaut Techno Solutions (2014). *Technology & Market on Parts and Components of Smart Phone.* Tokyo: CMC-sha.

Fombrun, C. J. (1996). *Reputation: Realizing Value from the Corporate Image.* Boston, MA: Harvard Business School Press.

Fortune Magazine (2016). "Change the World: The Top 10." [Online] Available at: http://fortune.com/change-the-world/ [Accessed July 31, 2017]

Fortune Magazine (2017). "The World's Most Admired Companies." [Online] Available at: http://fortune.com/worlds-most-admired-companies/list/ [Accessed July 31, 2017]

Grunig, J.E. & Grunig, L.A. (1996). "Implications of Symmetry for a Theory of Ethics and Social Responsibility in Public Relations." Paper presented to the International Communication Association, Chicago, May 23–27.

Hitotsubashi University (2013, 2014). "Winners of Porter Prize 2013, and 2014." Tokyo: Hitotsubashi University.

Hunt, G. (1900–1910). *The Writings of James Madison*. New York: G.P. Putnam's Sons.

Inoue, T. (2006). *Paburikku rirēshonzu (Public Relations)*. Tokyo: Nihon Hyoron-sha.

Inoue, T. (2009). "'Kizuna' Perspectives: Takashi Inoue's 35 years of PR Innovation in Japan. *PRSA – Public Relations TACTICS*, August.

Inoue, T. (2015). *Paburikku rirēshonzu (Public Relations: Relationship Management)*. 2nd ed. Tokyo: Nihon Hyoron-sha.

Interbrand (2016). "Best Global Brands 2016." s.l.: Interbrand.

Internet Live Stats (2016). "Internet Users." [Online] Available at: http://www.internetlivestats.com/internet-users/ [Accessed July 25, 2017]

IPRA (2010). "Code of Conduct." [Online] Available at: https://www.ipra.org/member-services/code-of-conduct/ [Accessed August 2, 2017]

Kapferer, J.-N. (2001). *Reinventing the Brand: Can Top Brands Survive the New Market Realities?* London: Kogan Page.

Keller, K. L. (2013). *Strategic Brand Management*. Essex: Pearson.

Korn Ferry (Hay Group) (2017). "The Best Companies." [Online] Available at: http://www.haygroup.com/us/best_companies [Accessed August 3, 2017]

Kotler, P. (2004). *Kotler's Marketing Lectures*. Tokyo: Diamond-sha.

Kotler, P. & Lee, N. R. (2005). *Corporate Social Responsibility*. Hoboken, NJ: John Wiley & Sons.

Mehrabian, A. (1971). *Silent Messages*. Belmont, CA: Wadsworth.

Ministry of Education, Culture, Sports, and Technology (2011). *Contributions of Scientific and Technological Progress*. Tokyo: MEXT.

Ministry of Education, Culture, Sports, and Technology (2013). *The Science and Technology Handbook*. Tokyo: MEXT.

Nihon Keizai Shimbun (2016). "Ito-en no konki, nihoncha hatsubai nobi, junrieki 37% zo [Ito-en reaches growth of 37% in net income this term]." *Nihon Keizai Shimbun*, June 2, 2016.

Ohmae, K. (2008). "Source of Japan's Competitiveness (*Nihon no kyōsō-ryoku no gensen*)." *Safety Japan*. [Online] Available at: http://www.nikkeibp.co.jp/sj/2/column/a/145/index5.html [Accessed July 27, 2017]

Olson, E. (2016) "Sustainability and CSR: A Word about Terms." *BSR Blog*. [Online] Available at: https://www.bsr.org/our-insights/blog-view/sustainability-and-csr-a-word-about-terms [Accessed July 31, 2017]

Peattie, K. (n.d.) *History of Corporate Social Responsibility and Sustainability*. s.l.: The Centre for Business Relationships, Accountability Sustainability and Society (BRASS).

Porter, M.E. & Kramer, M. (2011). "Creating Shared Value." *Harvard Business Review*, January–February, pp. 62–77.

PRSJ (2017). *2017 PR Yearbook*. Tokyo: Public Relations Society of Japan.

Ries, A. & Ries, L. (2002). *The Fall of Advertising and the Rise of PR*. New York: HarperCollins.

Statista (2017). "The Most Spoken Languages Worldwide (Speakers and Native Speaker in Millions)." [Online] Available at: https://www.statista.com/statistics/266808/the-most-spoken-languages-worldwide/ [Accessed July 25, 2017]

The Economist (2009). "Japan's Technology Champions: Invisible but Indispensable." *The Economist*, November 7, 2009, pp. 60–62.

The Japan Securities Research Institute (JSRI) (2012) "Outline of the Japan Securities Research Institute (JSRI)." [Online] Available at: http://www.jsri.or.jp/jsri/index_english.html [Accessed November 15, 2017]

The Japan Times (2000). "Snow Brand Faces Criminal Probe Over Tainted Milk." *The Japan Times*, July 13, 2000.

Toyo Keizai Online (2017). *11th TOYO KEIZAI CSR Ranking Top 700*. Tokyo: Toyo Keizai. [Online] Available at: http://toyokeizai.net/articles/-/167266

World Economic Forum (2017). *The Global Competitiveness Index 2016–2017*. Geneva: World Economic Forum.

# 5

# CRISIS MANAGEMENT THROUGH THE EYES OF PUBLIC RELATIONS

## 1 Toshiba's continuing crisis

Toshiba, the global Japanese corporate giant, which played a key role in the "Japanese Economic Miracle," failed to release its April through December 2016 earnings report in February 2017. It then quickly went on to announce a USD $6.2 billion impairment loss for its nuclear power business, and that as of December its liabilities exceeded assets by USD $1.7 billion, with negative shareholder equity of around $5 billion (Nikkei Asian Review, 2017).

This reporting failure and financial loss came on the heels of the 2015 revelation that Toshiba had falsified earnings by some USD $1.2 billion going back to 2007. This overstatement represented about one third of its reported pre-tax profits for the period. By April 11, 2017 Toshiba announced that it could not produce audited financial statements, due to issues between the company and its external auditors, and also stated that "substantial doubt about the company's ability to continue as a going concern exists" (Toshiba Corporation, 2017).

After the 2011 East Japan Earthquake and Nuclear Plant Disaster, the U.S. strengthened their nuclear plant safety requirements, which dramatically increased construction costs. Toshiba's problem was that it had taken on this risk by signing fixed-cost construction contracts with the American utilities that had ordered the plants from Toshiba's subsidiary, Westinghouse. One might simply say that Toshiba was in the wrong industry at the wrong time. Yet, you can also look at this from the eyes of public relations and see it as being caused by a lack of ethics, two-way communications, self-correction, and an insufficient concern for stakeholders.

This chapter is about surviving, and avoiding a crisis. Moreover, it is about succeeding through the discipline of public relations no matter what fate has in store. To understand this, consider the March 14, 2017 press conference held by Toshiba, under the title of "Extension (Further Extension) on the Deadline for Submission of the 178th Third Quarter Securities Report" and "Measures to Rebuild Toshiba" (Toshiba, Investor Relations, 2017).

At that press conference a reporter from *Nikkei Business* asked President Satoshi Tsunakawa: "I remember you used the term 'rebuilding Toshiba' one year ago. You failed and how do you take responsibility?" To which the president calmly replied: "You are correct in saying we are using the term 'rebuilding Toshiba' again. My interpretation is that we went back to the drawing board, due to the incident, so the term connotes a fresh start again, the term is the same, but this time it is meant as a fresh start."

That was all that President Tsunakawa was willing to say. He responded to a question without answering it. The entire Toshiba press conference was like that. Clearly he was not there to communicate and persuade its stakeholders. He was very guarded, and seemed to be there only for the purpose of getting through the press conference without admitting responsibility or wrong-doing. This press conference should have been seen by Toshiba as a critical step on the road to recovery, in which management had to persuasively show that it understood the root causes of the crisis and had concrete and convincing plans to address them, thus enabling it to quickly turn things around. But, Tsunakawa was not in control of this press conference, he was its victim trying to stay alive for another day.

Public relations cannot make a multi-billion dollar loss go away, or help one avoid taking responsibility. It is certainly not magic. But, public relations as described in this book and as detailed in this chapter will help executives, who finds themselves in this same situation as President Tsunakawa, to be able to look past the darkness of a crisis and see through to the light of a future in which the company can be rebuilt. That rebuilding process requires above all enthusiastic support from employees, investors, business partners, associations, government organizations, other stakeholders, and also external auditors, for which public relations as stakeholder relationship management is an essential skill.

## 2 Descending into the darkness of a crisis

In many cases, the first time an organization becomes aware of the importance of crisis management is only after an incident or accident occurs, and then it is not able to respond satisfactorily, bringing it to the edge of an abyss. Often the organization has been sailing at full-steam-ahead without any problems and has made no preparations, such as establishing a system for crisis management. When a problem does occur a company's top managers tend to get caught up in the vortex of media coverage and in a defenseless state, in which the situation descends into one they cannot control. This can even end with them becoming subject to shareholder lawsuits or criminal prosecution. There have been numerous examples of poor responses by organizations to a crisis that has resulted in such things as a consumer boycott of products, a steep decline in share price, which then can destroy the organization's relationship with its bank and even trigger its collapse.

A troubling pattern can be seen from many of Japan's corporate scandals, in which top management, who are ultimately the responsible parties, attempt to evade responsibility. When these managers, after many long years of competition during their career, finally reach the top of their organization, they generally tend to be passive about taking responsibility for a scandal when it occurs, and they do not face the problem or incident head-on by trying to quickly resolve it. This passivity tends to further exacerbate the situation.

## 3 Transcending from crisis to hope

To survive a crisis in the current world of hyper-globalization where instant digital communications – particularly all the different social media applications – have changed the definition of "rapid response" from days to hours to minutes, and where stakeholders have become globalized, it is vital that crisis management and risk management systems be embedded within an organization to avoid and minimize risks, and to respond rapidly and skillfully. Public relations is needed not only for responding to the media in a crisis effectively, but also for relationship management to keep informed and retain the active support of employees, investors, and customers, and many other stakeholders. It is also needed to guide the organization continually in both good times and bad times by the light of ethics and a determination to continuously seek the greater good for all stakeholders.

At the time of the writing of this book, Toshiba is reviewing its options for survival as its management faces very dismal choices. At this same point in time Nissan Motors is well along in its efforts of turning Mitsubishi Motors – which was immersed in a 2016 fuel efficiency reporting scandal – into a successful partner in an alliance that could enable it to reach the level of the world's fourth largest automotive group. However, by July 2017 Nissan had already reached the rank of number one.

Mitsubishi's lack of ethics resulted in a history of scandals, which in turn made it hard to recruit talented engineers, especially those just out of college, resulting in understaffing in critical areas, which in turn put pressure on staff to not act ethically. It also had a culture lacking effective two-way communications between management and its employees, which kept problems from being reported and addressed. Even with good risk management practices, a crisis can happen to even the best, but for the organization with good public relations skills that follows ethics and self-correction, a crisis can be managed successfully, and occasionally even turned into an opportunity. Nissan was able to combine its significant business skills with public relations skills to turn a crisis into an opportunity to do good for Mitsubishi Motors, which was a stakeholder in manufacturing and selling mini-cars, to do good for its many other stakeholders, and also to achieve one of Nissan's own strategic goals of entering the top tier of global automakers.

### *Essential awareness of crisis management*

Unlike marketing activities, it is difficult for an organization to focus on crisis management when an emergency is not occurring, but as many examples have shown lacking an awareness of crisis management can be fatal.

Crisis management involves taking various steps, such as communicating to internal and external audiences the causes of the crisis and the current situation, and entails the two-way exchange of information. For example, an organization's image will be damaged when a defective product is discovered. In particular, when this organization's response to the media and to consumers immediately after the problem arises is poor, its image can be critically damaged. But if it responds rapidly and appropriately, even if there is a temporary loss of sales, the trust in that organization may actually increase. Upon analyzing the various accidents that have occurred in Japan up to the present time, we can see that in many cases, the communication after the accident or incident was poor.

In general, when an incident or accident occurs, a rapid response at the time the events are first set in motion is likely to determine the success or failure of the subsequent crisis management. When building an in-house crisis management system, in order to avoid crises it is essential to take steps to avoid and minimize risk, including extracting the issues in advance and collecting data on risk factors, so that in a crisis you can analyze the situation quickly and calmly. Top management must also demonstrate powerful leadership when a crisis occurs. Depending on the subsequent response to a crisis, it is possible to minimize the direct harmful effects, such as a drop in a company's share price, a product boycott, or employees' increased feelings of distrust in the company.

What is absolutely essential in order to maintain the good image of an organization's reputation, products, and brands is for management and employees to always have an "awareness of crisis management" based on a constant sense of tension about being vigilant, and to also understand that, although risk management will ideally prevent emergencies before they occur, it is impossible to prevent them all and inevitably a crisis will unexpectedly occur.

## 4 Overlapping crisis management concepts

Crisis management is a concept of anticipating the various crises that may occur in the future, formulating and preparing effective measures in response, and when necessary implementing these responses. Unfortunately, in countries like Japan there is only a vague understanding of crisis management, and various related concepts and terms have become jumbled together and have not been arranged coherently.

Crisis management is a complex subject that can best be understood as three separate, but overlapping, concepts of "issue management," "risk management," and "crisis management" (Inoue, 2006, p. 158). Each is used to varying degrees depending on the type of crisis to be responded to. These three concepts are summarized in Figure 5.1.

### *Issue management*

Implementing measures in response to issues that can negatively impact a company is called "issue management." It is a relatively unfamiliar concept that has hardly been introduced in Japan or in many other countries.

Proactively identifying potential new issues, problems, and threats, and then formulating strategies, policies, and processes to implement in response to them, and where possible to gain competitive advantage, is known as **"issue management."**

Extracting risks within a range where it is possible to respond to in normal operations, such as by subscribing to insurance, and thinking of and implementing measures in response is referred to as **"risk management."**

**"Crisis management"** is the activity of responding when events put the organization into crisis, in order to resolve them in ways beneficial to the organization and its various stakeholders, and also to proactively prepare for such possible events.

**FIGURE 5.1**   Crisis management's three overlapping concepts

*Source: Takashi Inoue (2006), Public Relations, 1st edition, p. 158*

Issues include those related to policy, such as for a government's laws and regulations (government relations), and the customs and taboos that companies must take into consideration when conducting a business, regardless of whether domestically or internationally, including marketing in local communities and plant operations. Ignoring issues will certainly trigger a crisis. Compared to crisis management, action orientation is low in issue management, because it is essentially a preventative approach of analyzing issues, formulating solutions, and then trying to influence relevant stakeholders, such as government regulatory agencies, to accept the desired solution before the issue has any negative effects on the company. Under issue management, organizations take a proactive planning stance toward those forces that can put it into a crisis.

Applying public relations in this area is especially useful, because in a major way the "issues" are associated with various stakeholders and therefore a part of relationship management. The concept of issue management began back in 1976 in the U.S. with the work of W. Howard Chase, who saw it as addressing priority issues through a process of analyzing them and then developing and implementing strategies and taking action. The process, according to Chase, was one that "aligns corporate principles, policies and practices to the realities of a politicized economy" (Chase, 1977). By the end of the century others came to more fully define it as: "anticipating, reaching and prioritizing issues; assessing the impact of issues on the organization; recommending policies and strategies to minimize risk and seize opportunities, participating and implementing strategy; evaluating impact" (Tucker *et al.*, 1993, pp. 38–40).

This concept of issue management was initially created in the United States as a method of forestalling government legislation needed to address employment and social problems and was considered to be an effective way of resolving an issue while avoiding major spending. However, today, many companies in the United States have a more in-depth form of issue management that is an essential part of management's strategic planning. In particular, large companies have come to view issue management as a fundamental element for their continued existence. Depending on how an issue is dealt with, on the one hand it might invite an out-of-control crisis, but on the other hand the situation can actually be turned to the company's advantage, if the prevention and resolution measures are successful. In other words, depending on the response, the outcomes can be completely opposite, in terms of profit or loss.

After the now famous incident in 1982 in which capsules of Johnson & Johnson's headache drug Tylenol had been laced with cyanide by some person outside the company was resolved, the broader package safety issue had to be addressed by the entire industry. With its crisis ended, Johnson & Johnson began to take up package safety as part of issue management and proposed new industry standards. Within six months after the crisis, it held a press conference communicating its new tamper resistant package (Berge, 1990). As the first in the industry to adopt the safer packaging, Johnson & Johnson became seen by the public as one the most respected corporations, "and helped the company retain market share of Tylenol" (Cutlip *et al.*, 2005, p. 57).

By effectively utilizing issue management, companies and organizations can expect a number of benefits, such as increased market share, stabilized share price, improved corporate and brand reputations, reduced spending, improved stakeholder relationships, and stabilized management.

For global companies, cultural differences in customs and even basic "common sense" can vary greatly from country to country, and if not properly adjusted can result in business failure. One task for issue management is conducting local surveys to identify such cultural differences and then analyzing the effects these differences have on company activities, and implementing measures in response. However, sometimes a situation arises from the results of the analysis that unexpectedly reveals major obstacles to company activities that then become a subject for risk management.

## Risk management

Risk management is the implementation of measures to avoid risks by being aware of and anticipating them; or in other words, risk management recognizes the possibility and likelihood that organizations will encounter dangers that are either avoidable or unavoidable. In response to unavoidable risks, the organization will decide whether to pass them on to a third party, to protect itself against them by taking out insurance, or to take on the risks itself.

Aon Risk Services is a global risk solutions consulting firm, and Aon produces annually their "Global Risk Management Survey" (Aon Risk Solutions, 2017). From various dealings with Aon Japan, Figure 5.2 was created from the set of six targets of risk management that Aon sees as surrounding an organization: Financial risk (interest rate, exchange rate fluctuations, corporate acquisitions, etc.), Business risk (bankruptcy of a business partner, non-performing debts, etc.), Political risk (war, delays in obtaining approval, consumer movements, etc.), Human-capital risk (loss of employees, labor disputes, fraud by employees or corporate officers, etc.), Natural-disaster risk (earthquake, fire, flooding, drought, etc.), and Legal risk (infringement of patent rights or copyright, liability for environmental pollution, liability of directors and corporate officers, etc.) (Inoue, 2015, pp. 159–160).

Like issue management, risk management is a proactive effort by which the organization anticipates and plans for events that could put it in crisis. One of the products of risk management is the creation of a Business Continuity Plan (BCP) that identifies possible crisis-causing events and provides for a planned and strategic response. Public relations plays an important role in communicating and engaging the organization's various stakeholders, such as employees, customers, distributors, dealers, regulators, and investors with such risk management plans.

## Crisis management

Crisis management refers to the steps taken following the actual occurrence of an incident, accident, or disaster, and these steps will be in accordance with measures determined in advance by risk management, as discussed above. Although, events causing a crisis naturally force an organization into reacting, through sufficient proactive planning done under issue management and risk management an organization will be in a position to more quickly take the needed actions to resolve the situation, and in ways that benefit it and its many stakeholders.

With over 45 years in public relations, the author has personally helped many companies manage their way through a crisis. This included a pharmaceutical company in which its product resulted in some 500 fatalities, a national fast-food restaurant chain with tens of thousands of employees that were subject to severe overworking, and an airline crash with over 250 fatalities. It was from these many experiences, which are frantic times where often it is hard to see past the darkness and to see the light at the end of the crisis, that the three crisis management concepts came to be understood as essential for the ongoing health of an organization.

It is impossible to predict when and what kind of crisis will occur. However, the goal of making preparations with the assumption that crises can occur is to avoid any critical damage in the event of an emergency. The prevention of product-related accidents is the mission of companies that are public in nature, but by anticipating the possibility that some accidents cannot be prevented, crisis management focuses on what measures are to be taken in response and at what cost. On the one hand, this leads to a greater awareness of crisis prevention, and on the other hand this can help save the company's image through the rapid implementation of an appropriate response, when such a crisis actually occurs. Conversely, an incorrect response to a crisis can result in the collapse of the share price or a product boycott movement. A lack of a crisis management function and the absence of a sense of urgency among those responsible for responding to crises can develop into a situation that threatens that company's very existence.

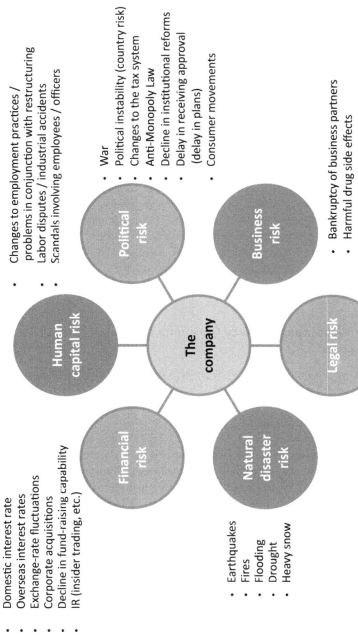

**FIGURE 5.2** Targets of risk management

*Source:* Takashi Inoue (2015), *Public Relations: Relationship Management*, 2nd edition, p. 160

Human capital risk
- Domestic interest rate
- Overseas interest rates
- Exchange-rate fluctuations
- Corporate acquisitions
- Decline in fund-raising capability
- IR (insider trading, etc.)

Political risk
- Changes to employment practices / problems in conjunction with restructuring
- Labor disputes / industrial accidents
- Scandals involving employees / officers

Business risk
- War
- Political instability (country risk)
- Changes to the tax system
- Anti-Monopoly Law
- Decline in institutional reforms
- Delay in receiving approval (delay in plans)
- Consumer movements

- Bankruptcy of business partners
- Harmful drug side effects
- Diversification of IT risk (leakage of confidential information, illegal copying, cyber crime, etc.)
- Delays to / suspension of projects
- Unilateral (one-sided) contracts
- Problems at facilities themselves (fires, etc.)

Natural disaster risk
- Earthquakes
- Fires
- Flooding
- Drought
- Heavy snow

Legal risk
- Location-related lawsuits / officer liability
- Liability for environmental pollution / infringement of the Anti-Monopoly Law
- Infringement of patents / copyrights

Financial risk

The company

Below are some examples of major crises that will damage a company's business:

- Pollution
- Defective products
- Accidents at factories and worksites
- Managers being killed or taken hostage
- Labor disputes
- Computer accidents and cyber crime
- Disputes related to patent infringements, etc.
- Hostile takeovers

Looking back to Figure 5.1 and the three overlapping circles representing the three crisis management concepts, you should now be able to understand how much in common each has and how together they position the organization to best respond to those events that produce a crisis. The issue of preparing for an earthquake, for example, can be identified as part of issue management and risk management, and a BCP document that has been created in advance will be used in crisis management. Another overlapping area, although not shown in Figure 5.1, is how the use of public relations acts as a vital tool in communicating, engaging, collaborating, and coordinating with stakeholders and protecting, rebuilding, and even enhancing the organization's reputation and brand value.

## 5 Case study: West Japan Railway Company train derailment crisis

While it is now over ten years ago, the West Japan Railway Company train derailment accident of April 25, 2005, can still provide many valuable lessons in terms of what not to do when implementing crisis management, as well as lessons for risk management and issue management.

The derailment of a train on the JR Takarazuka Line (Fukuchiyama Line) in Amagasaki, Hyogo Prefecture, was an accident that risk management should have addressed as a very fundamental risk to the railroad business and prevented. The issue of public safety should also have been addressed by issue management. At one level the cause can be said to be the human error of a train engineer driving too fast, but the underlying cause was a corporate failure, and one that cost more than 100 people their lives. Although there are always unavoidable risks, the tragedy is that this fits into the category of an obvious risk, which could and should have been avoided.

Although the direct cause of the accident can be said to be excessive speed that could have been prevented, when we look back over history of similar occurrences one pattern clearly emerges: the lack of the three essential elements that form the foundation of public relations of "ethics," "two-way communication," and a "self-correction function."

### Lack of ethics

According to the newspaper reports, starting in April 2005 the regional director of the Osaka branch of the West Japan Railway Company sent a document to all employees that stated profitability was to be targeted as the top priority and safe transportation was the second target. Within the fierce competition between private railways, the West Japan Railway Company became too conscious of profitability and stuck resolutely to a path of expanding its transportation capacity, such as by increasing speed and having an excessively congested timetable. But, as a result it neglected safety measures, which can be said to have resulted in this catastrophe. It is not possible to glimpse even a hint of ethics in this company at the time, with drivers that were on board the derailed train leaving the site without conducting any rescue activities and staff even holding a banquet on the same day of the accident.

## Lack of two-way communication

Generally, there are two types of feedback from customers: when the customers raise their voices and demand something, and when the service-providing side infers the needs of customers and takes advantage of them for the organization's needs. However, the West Japan Railway Company became too profit-orientated and was not able to understand the most basic and real need of its customers for safety. The need for safety should have been taken up in issue management and should have resulted in the railroad instilling a "safety first" policy as a core principle. But, the lack of understanding of this issue led to the failure of issue management and risk management. Also, the fact that the company had not aggressively pursued a policy of installing the new model of the automatic train stopping system (ATS) equipment and derailment prevention guardrails clearly shows its lack of safety management preparations. It can be said that the tragedy was caused because the company failed to take the viewpoint of the other party and understand what its customers wanted.

Moreover, it is also difficult to see the working of two-way communications in the company, which seems to have been entirely a one-way, top-down style. When a problem occurred, it was apparent that the company's approach was to prioritize placing the blame on individual members of staff, rather than investigating the cause. It seems likely that within this sort of environment, each and every member of staff was forced onto the defensive and lost sight of the perspective of customers. Under conditions of constant and excessive pressure, people are often unable to make appropriate judgments and decisions themselves during a crisis, which seems to have been the case for West Japan Railway Company.

## Lack of a self-correction function

There were many opportunities for the company to analyze the problems that occurred in the past and implement corrections, such as following the May 1991 Shigaraki Kogen Railway accident, or the Ministry of Land, Infrastructure, Transport, and Tourism's recommendations on overrunning, where a train overshoots the platform of the station it is stopping at. Based only on the media reporting, it seems that the West Japan Railway Company missed these opportunities. This clear lack of a self-correction function not only on the management side, but also on the side of the employees in the field in which stories between conductors and drivers were arranged and reports falsified on overrun distances in order for individuals to avoid the blame. It was reported that concealing mistakes and problems had happened every day in the company. This indicates that even if the organization had tried to accurately ascertain the warning signs leading up to the accident and implement corrections, it would likely have failed because a self-correction function was not working.

We can imagine that in the background to this sort of major accident, the company structure, or in other words the corporate culture, was deeply involved. The West Japan Railway Company was founded in April 1987 following the privatization of the government-owned Japan National Railways, but what can be seen from this accident is that its culture, which had been one of a government enterprise, was not substantially changed when it became a private corporation.

First, it was extremely important for this company to view matters objectively from having everything in the open, to perform sufficient analysis and to have discussion that went beyond organizational hierarchies, and to face its problems head-on. Then, it needed to completely review its corporate culture and to foster one that was open and transparent. Furthermore, it was necessary for it to ensure thorough compliance and to implement steps to effectively prevent problem reoccurrence, and to take measures to reconstruct the train-operation systems with safety as the top priority.

Railway companies in Japan are almost monopolistic institutions in which the users are only very rarely given the condition of being able to choose an alternative line. These companies must fully understand this point and their managers and all other staff be strongly aware that safety has to be the top priority. Therefore, it is necessary for these companies to revisit "safety first" as the most basic concept and provide their employees with a thorough education on safety.

After the accident, the new management of the West Japan Railway Company implemented various measures to restore levels of safety, such as installing more ATS equipment and providing safety education to their employees. However, it is necessary for organizations to be prepared for a possible crisis by implementing the three crisis management concepts and also to embed the Self-Correction Model, which is detailed in Chapter 10 and that is based on "ethics," "two-way communication," and "self-correction" at the core of the organization.

## 6 Building-up "image stock" as a protective layer

In a crisis, particularly one involving an accident caused by a product, the company's image and the feelings of trust in the brand will generally worsen, but if it has built up in advance of an incident a substantial positive image, which is called "image stock," then it is more likely to limit reputation damage (Inoue, 2015, pp. 173–174). The term seems to be unique, using the two English words of "image" and "stock" to describe this phenomenon. The concept of image stock is, however, widely recognized in the public relations profession, although not necessarily under this terminology.

Since the media tends to judge incidents involving organizations with a firmly established brand image or involving well-known organizations as being of particular high news value, it will widely report on them. It will adopt a critical tone when a crisis occurs, and if a superficially poor response is made by the organization that does not substantially address causes and solutions, the media will make such poor response the target for a series of critical reports.

But if the organization strives to the greatest possible extent to precisely resolve the crisis, the previous accumulation of a positive image can have the effect of minimizing the negative impact. For example, when the critical tone of the media reporting continues, the readers and listeners may feel sympathy for the organization being subject to "excessively harsh coverage." This is called the "image-stock effect," in which the trust in the organization actually increases, once the situation is brought under control.

However, the image-stock effect only works in cases when an appropriate response and measures are taken, and no matter how wonderful an image the organization has established up to that time, if it has not prepared the measures that must be implemented during a crisis, then its actions will lack consistency, and as it tries to continue to evade responsibility the image stock built up in the past will suffer considerable damage and its effects will be weakened.

Building an image stock requires not only an organization's activities that take into consideration the viewpoint and interests of consumers and CSR activities, but also steady efforts over a long period of time, for example actively cooperating with local community events and clearly demonstrating a positive attitude toward environmental conservation. However, mismanagement arising from a lack of awareness of crisis management can completely wipe out all these efforts, even in the short term. Furthermore, due to the worsening of the organization's image, it may subsequently experience problems in its activities even after the situation has been brought under control, including marketing or in activities to restore the organization's image.

As an example of image stock, some ten years ago Sony was awarded the overall first place in "Brand Japan 2005," a survey of brands by Nikkei BP Consulting. Yet, Sony had continued to experience a slump in its electronics business, which is its main business. Also, looking at the evaluation items in the same survey, we see that the use of Sony products had declined for three consecutive years and in this ranking it had fallen significantly, from 26th place in the previous year to 64th place. So why, despite all these negative factors, did it come first in the overall ranking?

The special edition of *Nikkei Business* on this survey (the April 25 to May 2, 2005 edition) had the extremely interesting headline of "Brand value can achieve 'savings' – Sony is number one even in its slumping main business and its strength is its basic brand." Even though the representation is different, it is obvious that this headline strongly affirms Sony's image-stock effect.

In the "Brand Japan 2014" survey too, in the consumer market (B-to-C), Sony was ranked second only to Disney in the evaluation by general consumers. Below them, the remaining places in the top ten were taken by Studio Ghibli, Amazon,

Uniqlo, Apple, YouTube, Rakuten, HeatTech, and Kirin Brewery, in that order. This strong performance by Sony is further evidence of the working of the image-stock effect (Inoue, 2015, p. 174).

## 7 Responding to a crisis: a public relations approach

### Key elements of crisis management

At the start of a crisis the organization must (1) establish a crisis management team, (2) activate its prepared contact system, and (3) begin public relations focused on media relations to conduct the crisis communications.

What makes this particularly challenging is that "when you are in the middle of a fast-breaking emergency, you may have to do all of these things almost simultaneously and under tremendous pressure" (Saffir, 2000, p. 112). But, crisis management is about surviving, and should be seen as a part of things that could happen to any organization and not as an orderly evacuation of a sinking ship. The positive side of crisis management will likely be the case for those organizations that have prepared and which know how to use public relations to keep stakeholders informed and supportive in anticipation of surviving and then rebuilding.

### Crisis management team

The crisis management team is usually composed of top management, and will include persons from the various departments and divisions with expertise related to the type of crisis. This will sometimes be HR management, when related to employees, or the head of manufacturing, when related to a product defect. In any level of crisis representatives of legal and compliance should be added to the team. For the crisis team to be effective each member and the team as a whole must be removed from the daily running of the organization. A leader for the team must be selected and clearly given the authority for decisions, which will need to be made quickly.

### 1) Appointing external professionals to the team

In addition to members of management various external experts are usually added to the team. The appointment of public relations experts and crisis management experts with an abundance of experience and expertise in responding to crises is essential in order to minimize the damage a crisis inflicts on an organization. Also, it needs to be kept in mind that appointing experts as part of the regular risk and crisis management efforts of the organization will enable them to play an important role in preventing crises before they occur.

Even when all preparations are completed, it is still important not to be complacent by constantly reviewing measures, and outside expertise can help to provide an objective viewpoint. In particular, new factors might need to be considered, which could cause a crisis, or there might be measures currently being focused on that are no longer necessary. Additionally, this type of review is valuable, because it makes it possible to continuously maintain an awareness of crisis management.

## 2) Crisis strategy

The team will need to consider the worst-case scenario of what might happen, and begin to formulate a strategy for handling such a possible outcome. All the while, the team must keep itself in the direction of the ethical sense and try to manage the crisis toward a beneficial outcome, first for the benefit of stakeholders and society, and second to save the organization and its brands and reputation. It must never try to suppress or cover up problems or embarrassing facts. It is of critical importance that problems be dealt with honestly and with a view of learning from them as part of a natural process of self-correction.

## Activating the contact system

Preparing a contact system will enable the organization to accurately and quickly ascertain the state of the emergency and eliminate the concerns of staff and other groups, and also knowing the facts makes it possible for it to quickly and effectively implement precise measures in response. Organizations can expect that preparing a public relations system will enable them to accurately communicate information to the media as quickly as possible, formulate clear response measures, and prevent inaccurate and conjectural reports.

The role for the contact system is not just one of collecting information, it must also be to send out instructional information within the organization to employees. The instructions provided within the organization will be via a two-way communication process so that it can always respond to the situation, such as to collect information or to implement measures. For example, if it is necessary to evacuate local residents in the event of a factory fire, the company will have to give instructions for the deployment of personnel for the evacuations measures, but also for the staff at the actual site to communicate information on the status of the evacuation. Within the scope of not endangering life, it is important to ascertain the actual conditions, including by dispatching staff to the site. Naturally, the relevant authorities must also be contacted without hesitation to mobilize the police, the fire service, or other relevant authorities.

In order to smoothly carry out these tasks, it is essential to firmly construct a contact system during times of non-emergency and to strive to ensure that employees are fully aware of the appropriate actions to take in an emergency situation.

## Crisis communications

In crisis management, crisis communications are very important, because to a large degree the success or failure of managing the crisis depends on them, especially how media relations are handled. Public relations will begin reaching out to all stakeholders. It will begin to identify as many of the facts about the problem as quickly as possible, using information gained from its contact system and from media articles. What must be paid close attention to when conducting crisis communication is that when a crisis occurs, the image of the organization held by consumers and other publics will be most affected by media reporting. Therefore, in addition to establishing a contact system in the event of an emergency, the organization must also fully prepare a public relations system that focuses on media relations.

## 1) Responding precisely and quickly to the media

In addition to contacting the relevant authorities such as the police and fire service, it is also necessary to contact the media. If this contact takes too long, it can lead to negative speculation and the tone of the media is likely to become critical even prior to the causes being identified. The media's ability to collect information can be unexpectedly rapid and it may have actually ascertained more of the facts than the organization. If the organization's initial response to the media is not fast enough, it will appear passive and the media may become suspicious that it "is trying to hide some inconvenient facts" or that it "has not sufficiently realized that an emergency is currently taking place."

Even if the news is inconvenient for the organization, it must not try to hide the facts and needs to have a system in place to quickly respond to requests for interviews and for information so that it can deal with the media appropriately. If the media coverage is intensive, it must demonstrate a proactive approach to providing information, including by actively holding press conferences. It is also important to analyze and evaluate the media coverage after the accident has occurred in order to be able to respond quickly.

Generally, it is said that the initial response to the media (the time taken to provide the media with the first report) must be, generally speaking, within 30 minutes from the start of the crisis, but in this age of social media the organization may be forced to react almost immediately. And, in the aviation industry, a major airline company in the United States has a system in place to respond in seven minutes for an incident anywhere in the world. In the case of a factory fire, for example, people that will be making the decisions in the head office and elsewhere must finish making contact with the relevant authorities, ascertain the status of the fire and the details of the course of events from the actual site, and depending on the situation, implement the necessary measures, including providing evacuation guidance to local residents living nearby. This series of tasks must be done at the same time and in parallel with contacting the media. But in actuality, in many cases the people in the head office and others responsible for making decisions will first find out about the crisis only at the stage when they start receiving inquiries from the media. This shows how difficult it is for an organization to prepare a system to respond to the media in a short period of time.

## 2) *Analysis and evaluation of media coverage after the accident or incident*

It is also essential to analyze and evaluate the content of media coverage in order to respond to the media and to carry out effective two-way communication with other stakeholders in the future.

The sources of practically all of the information that we receive on the economy, politics, society, and culture are the various media outlets, including newspapers, television, magazines, and the Internet, so naturally we are influenced by the media. Therefore, by analyzing and evaluating the content of media reporting as the source of information, it is possible to analyze how readers and viewers (in other words, target audiences like general consumers) evaluate a corporate scandal (or an accident or other incident), which makes it possible to precisely respond to the organization's key stakeholders.

## 3) *Explanations to employees are essential*

In the event of a major accident or incident, it is extremely important that employees do not first find out about it from the media, but are informed of the situation and the sequence of events as much as possible first by the organization and its management in advance.

Most employees will not be in a position to respond to the media, but at times as a "representative" of their organization they will be required to provide an explanation to business partners or to various other stakeholders, and also to friends and acquaintances. Therefore, it is important to build an emergency contact network targeting employees and to prepare a system for the smooth flow of information to them.

Moreover, naturally the leaders of the organization and those responsible for crisis management must provide employees with an explanation that will satisfy them not just during the crisis, but also after the settlement of the crisis. Particularly in the case of an M&A, the employees in the organization being acquired will be concerned about their futures, so it is necessary for the acquiring side and the management of the side being acquired to respond to their concerns with meticulous thoughtfulness.

## 4) *Responding to the press during a crisis*

The response to the media during an emergency will differ depending on the scale of the accident or incident and the extent of the organization's responsibility for it. But fundamentally, whatever the case, it must include the following points:

- Nature of the accident
- Time and place of the accident
- Number of fatalities
- Number of injured

- Details of the locations affected
- Impact on the environment
- Measures to respond to customers
- Acknowledgement by the leaders of the organization of their failures related to the crisis
- Expression of thanks to those involved in restoring normal activities
- Report on the investigation into the causes of the accident
- Explain the safety conditions prior to the accident

Public relations firms provide media training on how to respond to the media, including for media relations during times of non-emergency, responding to the media during a crisis, and making prior preparations and implementing measures. It will likely be effective to have these preparations objectively evaluated by external third parties, such as PR practitioners and crisis management consultants. Figure 5.3 shows the guidelines for holding an emergency press conference.

## 5) Responding on social media

Since compared to conventional media, such as newspapers, magazines, and television, the real-time nature of social media disseminates information far more rapidly, it is necessary for organizations to quickly monitor social media for information that potentially could put the organization at risk, and to continuously respond to it.

Even more than normal times, it is important to monitor information on social media during an emergency, as part of conducting crisis management. It is also necessary to actively utilize external word-of-mouth analysis tools and social listening services that collect information in real-time, and share information among the crisis management team.

It will also be necessary to investigate the authenticity of information on social media, comprehensively analyze information in the general media, such as newspapers and television, and confirm the facts of the problem faced, and determine if there are any mistakes that were made by the organization. It is also necessary for the crisis management team to think of responses. If the organization did make mistakes or is facing problems, it is important that it demonstrates a sincere attitude of regret and acknowledges its failures and provides factual information; and this needs to be done very quickly in this age of instant digital communications of social media. In the event there is concentrated criticism on the organization's official social media account, while it is impossible to respond to every individual, even on its own account the organization will need to respond by providing the facts and details on an occasional basis, including to guide people to its official website where it will have published a statement summarizing its official position and factual information. At the same time, it must also coordinate this information dissemination with the information being sent to the media.

Conversely, when it is clear that the organization was not at fault and is not facing problems, it can adopt a wait-and-see approach and when necessary, provide factual

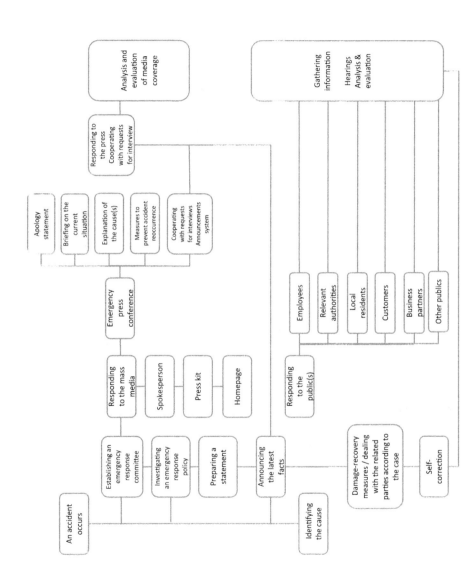

**FIGURE 5.3** Guidelines for holding an emergency press conference

*Source:* Takashi Inoue (2015), *Public Relations: Relationship Management*, 2nd edition, p. 179

information as the basis for rebutting accusations or criticism. When responding on social media also the three essential elements of accuracy, speed, and sincerity must be followed.

## 6) Once the situation is under control, explain with a sincere attitude

Not only when the emergency is ongoing, but even after it has been brought under control, the organization still needs to provide explanations not just to the parties directly involved in the accident or incident, but also to all other related parties, including the local residents living nearby, business partners, and other stakeholders. Even if the organization does not suffer any direct damage, it must still contact stakeholders to inform them of the situation and address any concerns that they may have.

In order to do this, it is good idea to clearly identify in advance the persons responsible for establishing the system. When the managers in-charge and others are to give instructions, it is best to appoint this task to those people in positions of authority who are able to make decisions without hesitation. In particular, to win trust and prevent a deterioration of the organization's image during an emergency, it is vital for managers to act nobly and demonstrate social responsibility, caring first about stakeholders outside the organization, rather than just about limiting damage to the organization.

Because responses must be quick in a crisis, organizations that have come out of a crisis with their reputations either undamaged or even enhanced, typically do not hold even a single meeting when deciding on the steps to take in response to the crisis. Instead, its response starts by activating the contact system that had been prepared in advance of the incident, which allows it to execute predetermined measures without the kind of hesitation that can be fatal in a crisis.

And when such organizations have taken measures that give priority to customers and society, they come out of the crisis with a better image. Such responses actually become an opportunity to make the organization's commitment to ethics more widely known both externally and internally. This is a point that should be understood not just by the responsible managers and public relations managers, but also by every member of the organization.

## 8 Strengthening the organization by opening it up

Surviving and even emerging stronger from a crisis, even more than preparing via risk management, issue management, and crisis management, requires in all cases an organization with functioning two-way communications, a commitment to ethics, and self-correction. For that reason, when carrying out specific internal reforms of the organization, it is first necessary to strengthen the public relations system.

What is most important for an organization is creating an environment to enable internal communication to be carried out smoothly. Even in superior-subordinate relations, the distribution of information must be flat. Particularly in today's organizations, there must be sufficient awareness of the differences in ways of thinking and acting between the generations, and when staff is being organized, it would seem necessary to include younger members among them.

When an accident or incident occurs, the on-site managers tend to hesitate to reveal those facts and also corporate management, when they do learn about them, are passive about making announcements to external audiences. But they must understand that this can exacerbate the problem and collapse their organization. It is vital to create an environment in which mistakes made within the organization are reported honestly to external audiences. A spirit of "hide nothing" is necessary to avoid giving the impression of being a closed and secretive organization.

Moreover, in all cases, openness, fairness, and speed must be thoroughly achieved. This is because if a crisis occurs, these qualities will be critical in determining whether or not the relevant facts can be quickly ascertained, the causes made clear, and appropriate responses made for both internal and external audiences. When the "ventilation" within the organization is poor, reports from on-site tend to include distorted facts and management is provided with incorrect information. Also, during an emergency, various speculation will be flying about within the organization and there is often conflicting information. To avoid confusion it is extremely important to integrate information. Close attention must also be given to not causing confusion, not just within the organization, but also among external audiences, particularly the media, and all audiences must be provided with an accurate view. In order to create an open environment within the organization, it is important to use the Internet so employees can freely obtain an organization's information.

It is of critical importance for leaders of an organization to receive advice from external professionals during an emergency. In the United States, when a major incident occurs it is very rarely the case that the response solely comes from within the organization, and instead organizations will have created an environment in which they can constantly and calmly receive objective advice from external consultants. However, in the case of Japanese organizations, PR managers are generally inexperienced due to the practice of internal job rotation, so it can be argued that the importance of this is even greater in Japan than in the United States.

Time-sensitive crisis management demands professionals with highly specialized experience. When there are multiple difficulties occurring simultaneously, it is essential to receive advice from external PR experts, who have an abundance of experience, in order to be able to respond to this sort of situation within the limited time available.

An organization's culture that has been fostered over many years cannot be changed overnight. Changing a corporate culture requires the strong will of top management; therefore, it is also a good idea to establish a committee of external experts. On establishing a "corporate culture reforms committee," improvements can be expected in the corporate culture and organizational system from the objective advice provided by experts from various fields with an abundance of experience. For the committee members, it will be necessary to appoint a good balance of experts, such as academics, members of the legal profession, journalists, and external company managers. In an organization where a problem has occurred, it is important to confirm that governance and compliance are being maintained within it, and to actively announce through the media the establishment of external oversight committees, and to be open about the process.

As we saw in the Johnson & Johnson case of the successful handling of an emergency that was briefly touched on at the beginning of this chapter, the presence of the three elements of "ethics," "two-way communications," and "self-correction" that constitute the public relations self-correction model are essential for any organization. And, because it is fundamentally strategic as well as ethics-based relationship management, top executives of an organization that can implement public relations will be best able to prepare their organization to both survive and even take advantage of risks and incidents rather than plunging into the darkness of crisis.

## References

Aon Risk Solutions (2017). *Global Risk Management Survey 2017.* s.l.: Aon Risk Solutions.

Berge, D.T. (1990). *The First 24 Hours: A Comprehensive Guide to Successful Crisis Management.* Cambridge, MA: Basil Blackwell.

Chase, W. H. (1977). "Public Issue Management: The New Science." *Public Relations Journal,* October, 33(10), pp. 25–26.

Cutlip, S. M, Center, A. H, & Broom, G. M. (2005). *Effective Public Relations.* 9th ed. Upper Saddle River, NJ: Prentice Hall.

Inoue, T. (2006). *Paburikku rirēshonzu (Public Relations).* 1st ed. Tokyo: Nippon Hyoron Sha.

Inoue, T. (2015). *Paburikku rirēshonzu (Public Relations: Relationship Management).* 2nd ed. Tokyo: Nippon Hyoron Sha.

Nikkei Asian Review (2017). "Where Did Toshiba Go Wrong, and Where Does It Go Now?" *Nikkei Asian Review,* May 15, 2017.

Saffir, L. (2000). *Power Public Relations: How to Master the New PR.* 2nd ed. Lincolnwood, IL: NTC Business Books.

Toshiba Corporation (2017). "Toshiba Investor Relations: Earnings Release – FY2016 Q3." [Online] Available at: https://www.toshiba.co.jp/about/ir/en/finance/er/er2016/q3/ter2016q3e.pdf [Accessed May 23, 2017]

Toshiba, Investor Relations (2017). "Toshiba Investor Relations: News Presentations & Events." [Online] Available at: http://www.c-hotline.net/Viewer/Default/TOSH9c5366 5405ea1f08e1ea3d22fb03951e [Accessed May 22, 2017]

Tucker K., Broom, G, & Caywood, C. (1993). "Managing Issues Acts as Bridge to Strategic Planning." *Public Relations Journal,* 49(11), pp. 38–40.

# 6

# STRATEGIC PUBLIC RELATIONS AND THE PR LIFE-CYCLE MODEL

## 1 Public relations and strategy

In order for public relations to enable a leader to achieve an organization's goals along the shortest path it must be strategic. There are many different interpretations of the word "strategy," but simply stated it is formulating and executing plans to achieve goals with the available resources and within the available time. However, because it is stakeholder relationship management, strategic public relations is focused on "business targets," where the term is used broadly for all organizations to mean those publics that PR is to target to accomplish the organization's goals.

After setting the PR objectives based on the organization's goals, public relations sends information to business targets in order to effectively carry out stakeholder relationship management. This involves building relations of trust between both sides through two-way communication. Moreover, because public relations seeks wide mutual benefit for both the organization and its many stakeholders, based on ethics, PR strategies must be formulated, executed, evaluated, and corrected through a continuous ethics-based self-correction process.

Most readers will already be familiar with strategy as an activity for senior management and their planning and finance departments, and from that point of view the steps within the PR Life-Cycle Model should be familiar. However, public relations strategy has a unique focus on stakeholders. Organizations will still follow strategic planning as they have always done, but realization of organization goals requires doing things by directing, motivating, and inspiring stakeholders, such as employees, customers, dealers, investors, and regulators. Which is to stay, that having decided goals and the associated strategies, the organization should then use public relations as an essential implementation resource, especially for speed, efficiency, and effectiveness.

## Hierarchy of goals and the PR Life-Cycle Model

Large organizations will have many departments and divisions that will need to be directed toward reaching the overall organization goals. This means that there will be a hierarchy of goals, starting with the overall organization objective at the top and followed by underlying supporting "intermediate objectives" that will likely need to engage external stakeholders, for which use of the PR Life-Cycle Model is well suited.

An automaker, for example, may see the emerging market for alternative energy vehicles as an important strategic market segment. To achieve a goal of selling a significant volume of electric vehicles, and doing so at a profit, it will need for various departments and divisions to accomplish specific related "intermediate" objectives. For example, the company's R&D division may need to find technology developed by other organizations for the electric battery. HR may need to help recruit researchers and engineers with needed skills that may be in high demand throughout the industry. The M&A group may be needed to buy existing organizations to obtain required technology. Applying the PR Life-Cycle Model for each of these intermediate objectives will greatly increase the probability of success of the overall organization goal. Thus, this model is applicable to any intermediate goals in any intermediate layer in the organization.

## Not just for businesses

Clients of PR firms are not limited to businesses and can also include various other types of organizations, including nations, government agencies, and in rare cases even individuals. The services provided are not restricted to domestic locations, as they can also take place overseas. This Life-Cycle Model of public relations can be applied to all types of clients, because it is a comprehensive strategic process to achieve goals by influencing the organization's many internal and external stakeholders.

## PR Life-Cycle Model explained

The PR Life-Cycle Model explained in this chapter combines PR strategy with the Self-Correction Model, and in that sense is unique. However, in the 21st century all major PR firms will likely carry out strategic public relations following a model similar to what is described here, but probably without its unique focus on continuous ethical self-correction.

After explaining the model, two real-world examples – Concur case study and the Tenneco case study – are presented involving the various types of public relations, particularly government relations and media relations, required to change regulations in the Japanese market. The PR Life-Cycle Model is more than theory, and was the process by which successful strategic public relations was conducted for both Concur and Tenneco, which were both IPRA award winners.

## 2 PR Life-Cycle

### Model overview

As shown in Figure 6.1, the PR Life-Cycle Model is a model of ongoing strategic activities that form a cycle spiraling up to higher dimensions through the "self-correction" process. The starting point for the model is understanding the organization goals, followed by "research and situation analysis," which provides the current situation of the organization and surrounding environment, and then the "setting the PR objective" takes place. The PR objectives are selected to achieve the organization's goals, but they are different. For example, a company may have a goal of introducing a new innovative product, but the PR objective will be something like "changing current regulations" so that the product can be used, or "convincing consumers of the advantages of the product" to reduce costs and to increase global competitiveness of businesses. In other words, the PR objectives are not the organization's goals, but by achieving those objectives the organization's goals will be achieved.

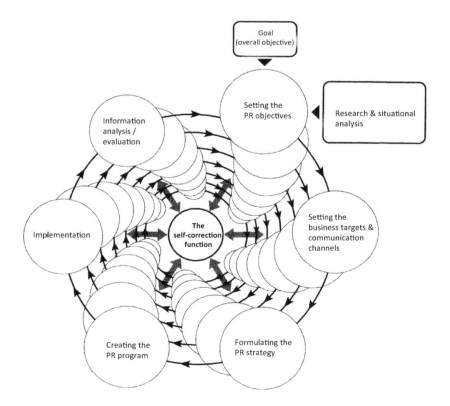

**FIGURE 6.1**   PR Life-Cycle Model

*Source:* Takashi Inoue (2006), *Public Relations*, 1st edition, p. 181

Based on the PR objectives the "business targets" (market) can be set, which in turn allows for setting the "communication channels" that will be used for communicating information to the business target. This also includes selecting influencers, such as the media or opinion leaders, in order to access the business target.

With objectives and business targets set, then begins the "formulating of the PR strategy" to enable the objectives to be achieved given resources, budget, and the limited time frame. This is followed with "creating the PR program" step that involves creating a program on a tactical level in accordance with a strategy that can be practically implemented. Next is the "implementation" of the PR program, and if we consider the steps of the process up to this point to be rehearsal, this step is the actual performance conducted on the stage of public relations.

Concluding this series of steps is the "analysis and evaluation" of the results of the PR activities up to this point in achieving the goals. In this step, the results of the strategic communication activities are fairly analyzed and evaluated to ascertain the kinds of effects and impacts they had on the target audiences and market set in advance, and on wider stakeholder communities. Obtaining feedback on the information that was communicated is useful in order to spiral up to higher dimensions in the PR Life-Cycle Model through the "self-correction function" by which all the other steps may be changed in order to achieve the desired goals efficiently, effectively, economically, and with benefit to stakeholders.

### Research and situation analysis

To begin carrying out strategic public relations activities an understanding of the current situation for your organization is necessary, both domestically and internationally. In particular, collecting and analyzing sufficient data is absolutely essential when building a strategic PR program. Based on this data, you can clarify the position of the organization in the market, including the positive aspects, such as what the competitive advantages are over competitors or what elements differentiate it from them, but conversely the analysis needs to also clarify weak points. In addition, it can confirm the positive and negative perspectives (outlooks), for example by reviewing marketing activities and communication activities or the issues being taken up by the media.

An analytical technique that is frequently used when creating a marketing or corporate strategy is the "SWOT analysis." This evaluates organizations from the four axes of strengths (S), weaknesses (W), opportunities (O), and threats (T), and so is an effective technique for a "situation analysis."

At this stage in the process, the organization itself must conduct an objective analysis to correct an underestimate or overestimate of its own achievements, or to discover factors that have been overlooked. This research and situation analysis prepares the data needed for the "setting of PR objectives" and the "setting of business targets."

The methods of carrying out the research and situation analysis generally include hearing-interviews, media audits, and benchmark surveys.

## 1) Conducting hearings

Depending on the objectives, interviews can include the organization's management team, departments, planning office, PR managers and other managers, general staff, and the main business partners. Interviews are conducted using the consultation method and related methods, and the questions will be on the organization's philosophy, management objectives, market positioning, strengths, weaknesses, opportunities, threats, and how it is differentiated from its competitors and its competitive advantages over them. In addition, data will be collected on marketing strategy and on previous communication activities.

## 2) Media audits (conducting interviews with media organizations)

Media audits are hearing-interviews with members of the media. The interviews are carried out with between five to ten journalists and editors among the media in the industry that the organization belongs to. The points in a media audit are what aspects of the organization the press is interested in, where it feels there are competitive advantages, and furthermore the media's degree of contact with the organization's PR managers. Since the media acts as a mediator between the organization and its targeted stakeholders, it is important to determine any divergence between how the organization recognizes the current situation and the media's perception.

## 3) Benchmark survey

A benchmark survey is carried out in order to statically ascertain positioning in the current situation based on objective facts. A wide scope of sources are used, covering the economy, politics, society, and culture that are obtained from media sources such as newspapers, television, and magazines, as well as from social media. Through their reporting, we come to know about developments not just in our own country, but throughout the world, and we constantly make decisions and act based upon this information. In this way, we are influenced by information – namely, by mass media coverage – whether we like it or not. Therefore, the basic stance of a news analysis survey is analyzing the content of news articles and other reporting to enable an evaluation of the sorts of effects and impacts that this information has on readers and viewers, which is to say on the general consumers and other business targets.

## Setting PR objectives

The setting of PR objectives is carried out based on management and marketing objectives, in addition to being based on the information obtained through the research and situation analysis.

PR objectives and goals are achieved through continuous strategic communication activities from a medium- to long-term viewpoint. While management and marketing objectives, such as increasing annual sales by 10% or achieving one million sales of a new product for example, can be achieved in part by public relations, they are different to the PR objectives discussed here. Public relations aims to influence internal and external stakeholders within the company, the industry, and society in ways that increase the level of recognition and improve the attitude toward it, its business activities, products, and services. Public relations does so through communication-based, comprehensive relationship management. As a result, PR objectives, if successfully realized, will be able to contribute broadly to the achievement of the management objectives and the associated goals.

In addition to "management philosophy" and "management objectives" as the information that should be communicated, the PR objectives will include firmly communicating those points that will differentiate the organization from its competitors and persuade business targets about its competitive advantages.

Naturally, the PR objectives that organizations will need to set will differ depending on their respective situations. For example, in the case of a company newly advancing into a foreign market, the priority objective will likely be increasing the levels of awareness about the company itself and its product and services in the market. In contrast, for a company that is planning an initial public offering (IPO), a vital PR objective will be increasing the awareness of that company among investors and analysts with whom it will have had little contact up to that point. Also, if a company is seen by business targets as being weak in technological development, the PR objective will focus on the company's R&D. Between three to five items is appropriate for the number of objectives. If there are too many, the focus on them may become blurred.

### Setting the business target and communication channels

It is best to understand the setting of PR objectives and setting of business targets to be so closely related as to be inseparable. In a similar way, business targets will determine the specific communication channels. And with that set, then the PR objectives can be communicated to specific audiences in the general public. Of course, this combination of objectives and business targets will then determine the direction taken in the "formulating of a PR strategy" step that follows.

### 1) Business targets

In many cases, business targets are in the layer of the actual purchasers of the products and services that the company provides, and from a PR viewpoint, it can be said that the information to be communicated must be conveyed precisely to the final targets within the public. However, as stated earlier, the term business target is broadly used, so that in the case of PR activities to achieve goals of governmental organizations, "business targets" means targeting citizens and voters.

In terms of an organization practically implementing relationship management with its stakeholders, we can think of some specific examples that will make business targets easier to understand. In the case of companies, first of all they have customers. This should include not only current customers but also potential customers.

In addition, the business targets can be distributors of products and services, such as sales agencies and retailers, and business partners, such as investment firms and venture capital firms, while a company setting a PR objective of receiving financing from the financial securities market will target institutional investors and general investors.

Conversely, private companies not planning an IPO need not include investors in the category of business targets, and moreover distributers cannot be a business target for companies using a direct-sales method. In other words, the business targets will be different depending on each respective company's industry and PR objectives. Also, when setting multiple business targets, it will be necessary to consider in advance their order of priority.

## 2) Communication channels

Communication channels signify the media organizations and the people who are influencers that possess the function of effectively amplifying to a wider range of audiences the transmission of the messages and news sent by the information provider. Within these, the media is an important communication channel, because the news coverage is highly trusted by society and influential in the formation of public opinion. The media, such as newspapers and television stations, are able to reach a large portion of the general public, making media relations very cost effective. And, increasingly, social media (SNS) is also rapidly becoming a major communication channel, and has the advantage of reaching global audiences rather than just the general public of a specific nation.

## Formulating a PR strategy

Once PR objectives and business targets with the communications channels have been set, formulating a PR strategy begins. This provides the framework for the most effective means to achieve the PR objectives through communications with the business targets as part of a specific PR program. The PR strategy takes into consideration the goals, the research, the PR objectives, the business targets and the associated communication channels, the desired completion date, and the budget constraints. It will determine the PR program and the implementation that follows.

## Creating the PR program

The PR program contains the specific techniques and individual activity items to realize the PR strategy. In other words, the PR strategy determines the direction taken by the PR program and there are infinite possibilities for the program content depending on the PR strategy previously formulated. When creating the PR program, close attention must be given to the following six points as shown in Figure 6.2 (Inoue, 2015, p. 192).

The first point is to create a program that is specific and feasible. It is meaningless to create a program if it is unclear what actual activities should be developed and what specifically should be done, because it is impossible to implement

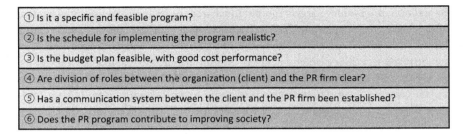

**FIGURE 6.2** Six points to pay attention to when creating a PR program

*Source:* Takashi Inoue (2015), *Public Relations: Relationship Management*, 2nd Edition, p. 192, Amended.

such a program. Also, even if the program is clear and specific about what is to be implemented, if it is impossible or extremely difficult to implement, it cannot be described as a feasible program. So, if attention is not paid to creating a feasible program with clearly defined content, it will not be an effective PR program.

The second point is the PR program's implementation schedule. Generally, the program will be a group of multiple programs in accordance with the PR strategy. In order to obtain the most effective results, it is necessary to consider the order of priority of these programs and make sure to arrange the timing and time periods for their implementation focused on those programs that are high in the order of priorities.

It is better to think of an implementation schedule in terms of units of one year, even when it is based on a medium- to long-term management plan. This is because, although it will not necessarily be clear by what time period the effects of implementing the PR program will be obtained, units of one year can be considered appropriate, including for the measurement of effects, especially when considering that an organization reports financial results on a yearly basis. Selecting units of one year also relates to the budget plan described next.

Third is the budget plan. Assuming there is a budget for the public relations activities as a whole, a PR program must be planned from a viewpoint of obtaining the most effective possible results from within the framework of this budget.

In particular, when an organization (client) obtains consulting services from a PR firm or outsources its PR operations, generally the contract will be for an annual retainer fee. Fundamentally the retainer fee is calculated based on an hourly rate, so the time period in which activities can be carried out is set by the budget framework. Therefore, when obtaining the services of a PR firm, it will be necessary to consider the scope of work (SOW) to understand how much time will be received for the provision of services within the framework of the budget, and also what the quality of the services will be.

Fourth is the division of roles between the client and the PR firm when outsourcing PR operations. Clarifying at the implementation stage who will be responsible for each individual item in the PR program is an essential condition for its smooth implementation. In this instance, an important factor will be the networks of human resources and knowledge possessed by the client and the PR firm respectively. If the division of roles is arranged at the stage of creating the PR program, it becomes possible to prevent omissions and delays in the program at the subsequent implementation stage.

Fifth is establishing a communication system between the client and the PR firm. Alongside the advance of globalization, it is not uncommon for a company's head office function and branch office function to cross country borders. Therefore, when implementing a PR program, it is absolutely essential to clearly establish points-of-contact between the company and the PR firm so that communication between them does not become confused. Within Japan, for example, even for companies with a system of having head offices in both Tokyo and Osaka, it is preferable to establish a point-of-contact focused on one location only. Since communication via email has become common, it is important to determine in advance who to "cc" on the email in accordance with the nature of the information, when emailing the point-of-contact person.

Sixth is to step back and look at the PR program in terms of the requirements of achieving the wider needs of stakeholders by asking if it is contributing to society. When considering the fact that organizations achieve goals through various stakeholders, this step is of critical importance. This will become clearer in the Concur case study, where a PR program was formulated that focused on showing that the proposed regulation change would also benefit competitors, customers, and add to the overall competitiveness of the nation.

## Implementing the PR program

Following the activities, timing, and resources established in the PR program, implementation is carried out. In the case of media relations, for example, various programs will be planned and implemented, including regularly distributing press releases, holding press conferences for announcements with high news value, and arranging press tours, such as for a new development center or factor, to obtain coverage.

The important points for implementation are as follows. First is to assuredly implement the PR program in accordance with the framework of the agreed time schedule and budget. Second is that when the results of the PR program being implemented fall below the expected level of achievement, it is important to address this by immediately analyzing the causes, which could be a change in the business environment – such as currency exchange rate changes or unforeseen government regulations – and then creating a counter plan. For example, in the event that a press conference was held to generate media coverage, but the subsequent coverage in articles and broadcast news coverage fell below what was expected, the PR professionals should make corrections through techniques like arranging individual interviews and providing press briefing material to specific media channels.

## Analyzing and evaluating the results and the self-correction function

The final stage in the PR Life-Cycle Model is analyzing and evaluating the results of activities and information. Fairly analyzing and evaluating the results of PR activities in terms of ascertaining the effects they had on the target audiences that were set in advance, and also on industry and society, makes it possible to realize high-level public relations.

Once the results of the series of PR activities can be verified for each individual process, then it is possible to make needed adjustments and self-correction. In that way, the self-correction function is central, because it allows the problems that were made visible through measuring and analysis to be corrected and makes it possible to assuredly ascend the spiral staircase of the six steps in the PR Life-Cycle Model.

## 3 Case study: Concur, new product requiring change in the law

The average profit margin of Japanese companies is about one-third of that of U.S. companies. One reason is inefficiency and poor management standards for paper-based administrative processes. Rigid government regulations force business and companies in Japan to perform inefficient administrative processes. Companies must keep and manage all business expense-related receipts on paper, a major drain on resources. Concur Japan, which provides cloud-based expense management solutions, undertook in 2014 a public relations campaign to bring about deregulation that would permit electronic expense management using regulator-approved mobile devices.

After conducting research, Concur decided on a creative win-win strategy in which it would invite competitors to participate in fostering a new market by convincing customers and political leaders that regulatory changes would increase the profitability and competitiveness of companies operating in Japan, as well as reducing costs to government.

These stakeholders were identified:

- Liberal Democratic Party of Japan, headed up by Prime Minister Shinzō Abe,
- Japan Image and Information Management Association (JIIMA),
- Japan Association for CFOs (JACFO),
- Japan Association of New Economy (JANE),
- Concur's Japanese competitors.

Concur's public relations objectives were:

- Campaign for bills to be drafted and passed by the Diet to bring about deregulation,
- Regularly supply news and information to mainstream media,
- Hold press conferences,
- Work with professional and industry association influencers to jointly lobby,
- Seek endorsements from Japanese corporations,
- Document the benefits and increased profits expected from deregulation.

Research activities included:

- Interviewing businesses and companies to better understand dissatisfaction with regulations,
- Concur and JACFO jointly identifying issues and potential for deregulation,
- Interviewing business organizations and relevant authorities.

Dialogue with government and business organizations included:

- Presenting numerically backed survey results at over 30 meetings with administration, business organizations, and relevant state authorities on the urgent need for deregulation,
- Following up in an additional 20 meetings on legislation with relevant ministries and organizations, legislators, and industry organizations,
- Repeatedly briefing ranking government officials in various agencies,
- Holding lectures for relevant government entities and providing assistance in drafting guidelines to ensure the desired deregulation outcomes, once the government decided to back deregulation.

Media relations activities included:

- Press release announcing survey results, in order to move public opinion,
- Nihon Keizai Shimbun (The Nikkei) running article on evening edition front page: "Smartphone snaps of your receipts!" (Nihon Keizai Shimbun, 2016)
- Press release: "Concur Joins JANE, to Work for Relaxation of e-Document Laws,"
- Press conference: Deregulation program and product strategy unveiled,
- Nihon Keizai Shimbun front-page feature: "Eliminate ¥1 trillion ($9 billion) in unnecessary costs …" (Nihon Keizai Shimbun, 2016)

Successful results were realized in December 2015, when the Japanese government announced its decision to change regulations to make electronic receipts a valid substitute to original paper documents. This news resulted in Concur receiving 2.5 times more inquiries from interested prospects, and YoY growth that was forecasted to exceed 150%. In 2016 this successful campaign was one of the winners of the IPRA Golden World Awards for public relations excellence that year.

## 4 Case study: Tenneco, PR strategy in Japan-U.S. automotive negotiations

Following a request by the U.S. auto parts manufacturer, Tenneco Automotive Inc. – the current Tenneco Inc. – a series of PR programs were carried out that started with a survey in March 1994 and ran through to May 1996. At that time in October 1994, automotive negotiations between Japan and the United States had heated up in both economic and political levels to the point that it had finally broken down. The rift between them had deepened to the extent that the United States was on the verge of authorizing sanctions against Japan based on Section 301 of the Trade Act. It was the public relations activities in Japan and the United States centered on the Tenneco Report, which had been prepared five months earlier by Inoue Public Relations, that turned around this situation and guided the negotiations to success.

The *Asahi Shimbun* on January 14, 1997 reported on the evaluation by the American Chamber of Commerce in Japan (ACCJ) of the 45 major Japan-U.S. trade agreements between 1980 and 1996. It evaluated 13 to be successful, 18 to be partially successful, four could not be determined, and ten were failures, and cited the settlement achieved in the Japan-U.S. automotive and auto parts discussions in August 1995 as one example of a success (Asahi Shimbun, 1997).

## *Background to the auto repair parts deregulation program*

Tenneco Automotive Japan (TAJ) was established in 1973 as the Japanese subsidiary of Tenneco Automotive, an American auto parts multinational company. Tenneco Automotive had the world's largest brands for mufflers, Monroe, and for shock absorbers, Tenneco, and conducted its businesses in 22 countries across the world. It had established TAJ with the objective of importing and selling auto parts in the Japanese market.

But TAJ had made little progress in the Japanese after-market – which is the auto repair parts market – since its establishment, despite more than 20 years of marketing efforts that had started with the opening up of sales channels and included establishing a technical center within its U.S. head office to develop products compatible with the Japanese market. TAJ suspected that the biggest factor behind its low market share was the exclusivity and closed nature of the after-market in Japan.

In 1994 at that time, the United States trade deficit with Japan had reached USD $60 billion annually, 60% of which was from the automotive-related fields, so this was a problem not just for Tenneco Automotive. Improvements were urgently required to defuse the diplomatic tensions between Japan and the United States. In July 1993, Prime Minister Miyazawa and President Clinton agreed on a framework for comprehensive economic discussions between Japan and the United States, and the auto parts and related fields were positioned as the priority fields within these discussions.

At the government level, surveys by the Department of Commerce in the United States and by the Fair Trade Commission in Japan on the actual state of the exclusivity and closed nature of the Japanese market were carried out, but they only ascertained the actual situation at the macro level and were not intended to clarify the problems in the product field most closely related to the business of TAJ. So the Tenneco head office and TAJ concluded a public relations consultation agreement with Inoue Public Relations and requested that it develop a strategy on the theme of "the deregulation of the after-market and subsequent business development." As the first stage, an independent survey was conducted, and the results of this were summarized in the report to Tenneco.

## Research and situation analysis

A survey over three months, from March to May 1994, was then conducted to ascertain the actual conditions in Japan's after-market. The ultimate objective was to realize government deregulation in Japan's after-market, but this research took the form of verifying hypotheses that predicted the exclusivity and closed nature of the Japanese market to be factors. The issues identified were the regulations in the Road Transport Vehicle Law that defined vehicle safety standards and other standards issued by Japan's Ministry of Transport. The problem related to the motor vehicle weight tax of Japan's Ministry of Finance, and the problem of "*keiretsu*" (Japan's structure of affiliated companies) among Japanese automotive manufacturers. Regulations required "critical parts" to be replaced only by "genuine original equipment parts." Imported parts were not being used for repairs, because imported parts were not recommended by Japanese car manufacturers, and therefore were considered to not be "genuine original equipment parts." Adding to this was the conservative nature of the more than 400,000 nationwide vehicle repair shops that always wanted "genuine original equipment parts" even if not required by regulations, and also the higher price of imported parts due to higher distribution costs.

The research was being done from the hypothesis that the inability of TAJ to successfully expand sales in Japan's after-market was caused by a lack of power of persuasion in media relations and government relations, and by the actual conditions of the legal regulations and the non-tariff barriers – but this had to be verified. Using library materials and other research materials, the PR firm investigated the contents of Japan's Road Transport Vehicle Act and the Enforcement Ordinance No. 74. Also, interviews were conducted either by telephone or in person with a sample size of 50, which included representatives of the nationwide District Land Transport Bureaus that are responsible for car inspections, the representatives of the auto parts industry, sales stores, vehicle repair shops, and various industry experts.

In the three-month survey, many of the points of the hypothesis were verified as being actual problems. Indeed, facts came to light that suggested the hypothesis actually painted a more optimistic picture than the reality. This included the fact that the Japanese after-market was being protected by the double or triple intertwining regulations of the Ministry of Transport, the tax system, and the robust "genuine original equipment myth" that did not allow any room for the inclusion of imported goods.

Based on the results of the survey, the PR firm prepared its Tenneco Report in May 1994, which included recommendations from two viewpoints. The first recommendations were proposals to deregulate the overhaul and structural-changes that are subject to vehicle inspections. Specifically, the recommendations were as follows:

• Exclude minor changes, such as the installation of shock absorbers, from the items subject to inspection in the provisions of the Road Transport Vehicle Act,
• Revise the motor vehicle weight tax re-payment system for structural changes to reduce the economic burden on vehicle users,

- Improve the disadvantages imposed on imported goods during vehicle inspections.

These recommendations prepared the conditions for the expansion of sales of auto parts manufactured overseas, which was the second viewpoint.

The second set of recommendations were as follows:

- Drop the separate "genuine original equipment parts" category and establish a single standard by introducing something along the lines of a "quality certification system,"
- Remove the disadvantages imposed on imported parts in the vehicle inspection system by introducing a shared authentication system for both Japan- and U.S.-made parts,
- The Ministry of Transport and the Ministry of International Trade and Industry should jointly implement a campaign to increase purchases of imports, targeting the auto parts-distribution industry, which has a conservative structure.

By October 1994, automotive negotiations in the parts field between Japan and the United States had become deadlocked and broke down, and the situation was moving toward the United States authorizing sanctions against Japan based on Section 301 of the Trade Act. It was in this environment that the Tenneco Report became an important reference document in the decision-making of the United States government at that time, demonstrating the unfairness of the Japanese market.

## Setting PR objectives from TAJ's corporate goals

The barriers to sales of imported parts in the Japanese auto parts after-market were made clear in the survey in the Tenneco Report. The new facts reported in the report had not been discovered in the earlier survey of Japan's auto parts market carried out by the United States Department of Commerce in the same year, and the relevant parties were shocked by the Tenneco survey's findings. The issue that needed to be prioritized was deregulation and the Tenneco Report was to be used for this. Since TAJ's long-term strategic corporate goal was greatly increasing demand from the providers of car repairs – which included gas stations – using deregulation, and changing customer expectations, the PR objectives to be accomplished over a two-year period were:

- Through government relations utilize the Tenneco Report to realize deregulation,
- Support new sales channels premised on deregulation, such as gas stations,
- Educate consumers about system changes and the benefits of more frequently replacing car parts, etc.

A specific PR strategy would then be formulated in accordance with these three objectives.

## Setting the business targets and communication channels

### 1) Business targets

The PR firm determined that in order to realize deregulation of auto repair parts the PR program would need to separately consider the business targets before and after the regulations were relaxed. Deregulation was a political issue and therefore the main targets to achieve this objective were government agencies in both the United States and Japan. In contrast, the main business targets, after deregulation, were such stakeholders as domestic automotive manufacturers, particularly the responsible executives, department heads, and managers who had the authority to make decisions on new purchases. Other than this group, the business targets were set as vehicle repair shops, auto parts sales distributors, vehicle supplies retailers, such as Autobacs and Yellow Hat, and drivers, particularly auto enthusiasts.

### 2) Communication channels

To reach the business targets, the communication channels were set as influential local newspapers, industry newspapers and magazines related to the automotive and auto parts industries, English-language newspapers, and news agencies, particularly centered on media channels like general newspapers, economic and industry newspapers, and business magazines. Also, in order to effectively use "external pressure" to achieve deregulation, information would need to be actively sent from Japan to overseas audiences. To achieve this, foreign journalists, who were members of the Foreign Correspondents' Club of Japan (FCCJ), and particularly key U.S. media, such as *The New York Times*, *The Washington Post*, *Business Week*, *Newsweek*, and *Associated Press*, were added as the communication channels.

Influencer relations would include the following selected communication channels that had influence among business targets: TV newscasters, freelance journalists, and economic experts and university professors who frequently appeared in the mass media discussing the economic problems between Japan and the United States.

## Formulating the PR strategy and creating the PR program

As with the setting of business targets, the strategy was constructed separately for before and after the relaxation of regulations. Before the regulations were relaxed, government relations, which maximized the use of the Tenneco Report, was the most important element and the main focus of media relations was obtaining the support of the public to encourage the government to carry out deregulation. After the deregulation, the main activity became media relations on the key theme of creating demand through educating consumers. It was decided at an early stage as part of corporate strategy to open up sales channels in anticipation of the timing of the implementation of deregulation, and the PR strategy was created premised on supporting these two key points.

## 1) Pre-deregulation activities

### Setting the key message according to the target audience

The messages formulated for government agencies and the media were that "deregulation would create new business opportunities in Japan's after-market." For consumers, the aim was to educate them to "replace shock absorbers after 40,000 to 50,000 kilometers to maintain safe and comfortable driving."

### PR activities before deregulation were centered on government relations

The key point before deregulation was government relations through lobbying. First, when providing briefings on the Tenneco Report, Tenneco Automotive was responsible for approaching the United States government in Washington, while TAJ and Inoue PR were responsible for approaching the United States Ambassador to Japan and the Japanese government, and a system was established that was able to achieve close communication with these three parties.

In terms of media relations, the timing of the press conference to announce the Tenneco Report before the deregulation was decided on by paying close attention to the developments in the Japan-U.S. negotiations. The press conference for the announcement was attended by the top executives of Tenneco Automotive, one-on-one interviews (individual interviews) were set up for Japan's main media channels, and materials were distributed to the media, such as a feature article on deregulation.

## 2) Post-deregulation activities

After deregulation, the central activities became media relations and educating consumers, and information was disseminated through holding one-on-one interviews particularly with Mr. Kanjiro Shishikura, the TAJ President at that time, since TAJ had become the marketing base in Japan. In addition, TAJ's marketing strategy in response to deregulation and the new sales channels were announced and the message to consumers actively communicated through a mixture of press conferences and press releases.

To educate consumers, the focus was placed on the fact that, while Western car users were accustomed to freely changing auto parts to suit their preferences, hardly any Japanese users were in the habit of doing so due to the regulations that had been enforced for a long period. Therefore the aspects of "safe and comfortable driving" were pushed to the fore and Japanese consumers were educated on the need to "change your shock absorbers after driving 40,000 to 50,000 kilometers."

## Implementing the PR program

In the summer of 1994, as planned, the Tenneco Report was passed from Tenneco Automotive to the trade representatives and the White House via the United States Department of Commerce. On the other hand in Japan, TAJ held briefings for the United States Embassy in Japan, the Ministry of Transport, and the Ministry of International Trade and Industry to deliver them the report. The report was in turn handed to the then United States Ambassador to Japan Walter Mondale and to the Minister of International Trade and Industry, who at the time was Ryutaro Hashimoto.

By the end of September, the automotive and auto parts negotiations between Japan and the United States had broken down and President Clinton wasted no time in announcing that the United States would authorize the application of sanctions for repairs parts based on Section 301 of the Trade Act. It was estimated that the loss that would be incurred by the Japanese automotive industry because of these sanctions would be as much as USD $5.2 billion, and the situation had grown extremely serious. It was at this point that the Tenneco Report was considered to have become influential reference material in the discussions between the governments of Japan and the United States as they tried to find common ground.

At the end of June 1995 in the following year, a compromise was reached in discussions in Geneva between United States Trade Representative Mickey Kantor and Minister of International Trade and Industry Ryutaro Hashimoto, and deregulation was realized as reported in major media at the time as shown in Figure 6.3 (Yomiuri Shimbun, 1995; The Japan Times, 1995; Nihon Keizai Shimbun, 1995).

On the other hand in the media relations, critical changes to the original plan were made. This was because while the plan had been to announce the Tenneco

**FIGURE 6.3**  Japan newspaper articles on the Japan–U.S. auto parts procurement conflict
From left to right Yomiuri Shimbun (October 3, 1994), The Japan Times (June 28,1995), Nihon Keizai Shimbun (July 11, 1995).

Report through a press conference, this report had come to be seen as a critical part of the behind-the-scenes negotiations between the governments of Japan and the United States, and it was necessary to change this plan upon considering the effects it was having. Sensitive to the possible negative impact the report might have with Japan's automotive manufacturers as powerful business partners, Tenneco Automotive head office decided to hold back on the announcement.

In April 1995, for the first time the yen/U.S. dollar exchange rate had reached a high of 79.75 yen to the dollar. With the final trade negotiation deadline set for June 1995, the negotiations between Japan and the United States intensified and were quickly coming to a climax. If these negotiations were to break down, the United States government announced that it would impose sanctions against Japan (equivalent to USD \$5.2 billion). In a situation in which it had not been possible to obtain accurate information up to that time, the media in Japan and the United States continued to wage a war of words condemning the other country. The EU also feared the impact on the world economy from a clash between the two economic superpowers of Japan and the United States and appealed to both countries to deal with the situation calmly. The combined GDP of both countries for 1994 was over USD \$12.2 trillion (Japan 4.9 and U.S. 7.3) or 44% of the world's \$27.7 trillion GDP total (The World Bank, 1994).

In consideration of this situation of rising tensions threatening global economic stability, TAJ and Inoue Public Relations made several requests to Tenneco Automotive head office in America to reconsider its earlier decision not to disclose the Tenneco Report. While the desire to not create further friction by holding back on publishing the report was reasonable, the fact was that tensions were quickly escalating anyway. The cause was that the mass media in Japan, which did not have a detailed understanding of the actual situation as it had only received one-side information from the government and industry, was taking the stance that the U.S. was unfairly attacking Japan. Finally, Tenneco Automotive in the U.S. agreed to allow Inoue Public Relations and TAJ to select major economic newspapers and television channels that were influential in terms of obtaining the understanding and support of the public. They were provided with individual, off-the-record briefings, focusing on the actual situation in the Japanese after-market and the problem points that the media had been unaware of until that time. They were allowed to read the Tenneco Report off-the-record. This succeeded in changing the view of the media from seeing an unfair U.S. attacking a smaller Japan to seeing that Japan's complex set of regulations was at the heart of the problem, and Japan's consumers as well as the important Japan–U.S. relationship would all benefit from deregulation. From this understanding, the media began to correct the public view of the situation. And, ultimately, the media went from being part of the problem to being part of the solution.

Meanwhile, the negotiations were seen to reach a final settlement in the Kantor–Hashimoto talks at the end of June 1995, but prior to this related articles had already appeared in various media channels based on the briefings in conjunction with the developments in the Japan–U.S. negotiations, and this coverage had a major impact on the formation of public opinion, putting pressure on the Japanese government to settle.

In the background to this was the fact that the United States, which was concerned about the growing gap in power between itself and Japan that had been reversed in the automotive industry, openly cited Japan's unfairness and strongly demanded that corrections be made; a demand that was backed by the upward pressure on the yen. Within a situation that had already gone beyond the problems of one company, ultimately the Tenneco Automotive head office prioritized the stabilization of the global economy (public interest) above its own interests (private interest) and the worst-case scenario was avoided.

In addition to the above, Tenneco Automotive increased its level of exposure to the media, including by having its CEO visit Japan and give press conferences and announce reductions in product prices. Also in June 1995, Tenneco Automotive top executives announced that they welcomed the negotiations' agreement.

### Evaluating the results of activities and the self-correction function

On August 23, 1995, the governments of the United States and Japan agreed upon the exchange of letters for the automotive and auto parts discussions. Based on this, the Ministry of Transport removed four items, including shock absorbers, from the list of parts requiring inspections in vehicle overhauls and partially revised the Road Transport Vehicle Act Enforcement Ordinance. This revised ordinance was promulgated and enforced on October 20. In advance of this, on June 29, the Ministry of International Trade and Industry issued a notice to distributors to "not discriminate against foreign-made parts" in order to facilitate the access of foreign-made parts to the after-market. In the same way, the Ministry of Transport required that "foreign-made parts not be discriminated against and vehicle users be provided with the opportunity to select them." This represented the remarkable realization of the two sets of recommendations in the Tenneco Report.

In October, the top management of Tenneco Automotive, including President Snell, once again visited Japan and announced new sales channels in a press conference. The president also announced the start of a sales and replacement service for Tenneco Automotive shock absorbers at the nationwide network of 6,400 JOMO stations, which at that time was the brand name of gas stations owned by Japan Energy.

By April 1996, TAJ's sales in the domestic after-market had increased 150%. In the following May, Tenneco and Japan Energy held a joint press conference as part of the opening ceremony for their new service. This press conference proved to be a major event with both domestic and international media sending over 70 journalists to the venue of a JOMO station in suburban Tokyo (Setagaya Ward). As President Clinton was visiting Japan when this event was held, an informal agreement from the White House had been obtained for the president to attend the opening ceremony, although in the end, unfortunately he was not able to do so.

Other than JOMO stations, which were the gasoline stands affiliated to Japan Energy, TAJ further expanded the opening-up of sales channels to Toyota Motor-affiliated dealers and the stores of major auto supplies seller, Autobacs, which at that time had a nationwide network of around 380 stores.

In the United States, President Clinton, immediately before his visit to Japan in May 1996, in a press conference at the White House in front of a group of journalists from domestic and overseas media, singled out Tenneco for praise, stating that "within the many Japan-U.S. negotiations, the Tenneco negotiations were particularly a success" (Inoue, 2015, p. 203). Based on this great success, the important role played by public relations in this case study can be said to be that Tenneco Automotive calmly analyzed the international situation, utilized the self-correction function, and "prioritized the public interest ahead of private interest."

The Tenneco Report was completed at the end of May 1994 and after only one year and five months from the official start of the lobbying of the Japanese and U.S. governments for deregulation, Japan's Ministry of Transport resolved to deregulate the after-market. The series of public relations programs centered on the Tenneco Report prepared by TAJ and Inoue Public Relations brought about deregulation that was of great significance. as they demonstrated in a practical way that public relations could function to create business opportunities (Figure 6.4).

This series of PR programs was subsequently entered into the IPRA Golden World Awards in 1997 (Congress News, 1997), and from within the 167 entries from 23 countries, it was the first entry from the Asian region to receive the Grand

| The main PR program | Industry developments |
|---|---|
| **March to July 1994**<br>Survey of actual conditions in the domestic auto repair parts market | **October 1994**<br>Breakdown of automotive negotiations between Japan and the United States<br>The U.S. government considers applying Section 301 of the U.S. Trade Act to auto repair parts |
| **June 1994**<br>Start of lobbying | |
| **July 1994**<br>Sending the survey report (the Tenneco Report) to government agencies in the United States and Japan | **April 1995**<br>The yen reaches 79 yen to the dollar<br><br>**June 1995**<br>In the Geneva discussions, an agreement is reached between Minister of International Trade and Industry Hashimoto and U.S. Trade Representative Kantor on the auto repair parts problem |
| **January to May 1995**<br>Off-the-record briefings with key domestic media on the Tenneco Report | |
| **October 1995**<br>• Holding a press conference in conjunction with Tenneco President Snell's visit to Japan<br>• Visiting relevant government agencies and organizations<br>• Holding informal talks with auto manufacturers | **July to November 1995**<br>• Revision of the Road Transport Vehicle Act<br>• Toyota and Nissan greatly increase their adoption of Tenneco products<br>• Japan Energy begins selling Tenneco products at its nationwide chain of gas stations (JOMO)<br>• Sales begin at a major auto retailer (Autobacs) |
| **May 1996**<br>Announcement during the joint Tenneco-Japan Energy press conference for the opening of the first JOMO-GS store | **April 1996**<br>President Clinton praises the role played by Tenneco during a White House press conference prior to his visit to Japan<br><br>**September 1996**<br>In the annual discussions (San Francisco), the progress made on the Japan-U.S. agreement is highly evaluated |

**FIGURE 6.4** Summary of the deregulation PR program and industry developments

*Source:* Takashi Inoue (2015), *Public Relations: Relationship Management*, 2nd Edition, p. 204

Prize for opening a market and creating new business opportunities (Crawford, 1997) within the context of the economic problems between Japan and the United States, which the media tended to cover emotionally. Clearly, for stakeholder relationship management the PR Life-Cycle Model is a proven practical means to implement successful strategic public relations.

## 5 Applying strategic public relations for a nation

Although America has been and still remains the dominant power and economy in the world, it has just elected a president determined to "make America great again." China has become the second largest economy, and while many may expect it to surpass the U.S. in the not so distant future, similar things were said about Japan in the 1980s. China now faces challenges that are very familiar to Japan, which includes an aging population, the gradual loss in its low wage cost advantage, chronic low productivity, and strong competition from the other nations in Asia, such as India, Korea, and Vietnam.

In 2016, the Kingdom of Saudi Arabia issued a document called "Vision 2030" which is a strategic plan that looks at its economic and geopolitical position in time and space, and both its advantages and disadvantages, and then plots out an ambitious path for the near future. It is not just a document aimed at its own citizens. The Kingdom has set up a dedicated webpage to Vision 2030, and in addition to Arabic it has versions in English, Chinese, and Japanese. Reading the document, it is clear that the Kingdom is determined to transform its entire nation from one of a narrow, oil-dependent economy into a broadly diversified economy that is a major global player, which in turn will benefit its citizens, add to the good of humanity, while at the same time retaining traditional values of family, religion, and its Arabic culture.

The 20th century saw Japan and nations of Europe trying to compete globally through world war, giving it the sad distinction of being the bloodiest century. We are now well into the beginning of the 21st century and one hopes that the mistakes of the past do not have to be repeated, but the situation does not look encouraging as more nations acquire nuclear weapons, with the spread of global terrorism, and with millions of refugees and displaced persons. Yet, nations can compete peacefully and constructively by examining their strengths and weaknesses to determine the best way to participate and even lead in those areas that contribute most for themselves and for humanity.

When we talk about public relations, people first think of corporations. However, nations are also a type of organization. A nation needs to accomplish goals like any other organization through stakeholders, only that also includes other nations as its stakeholders. Therefore, nations just like corporations can benefit from the power of public relations to better achieve national goals.

### Conducting a SWOT analysis of Japan

Japan has fallen from second place to third in terms of world GDP, and continues to experience either negative economic growth or very low growth, while other nations, especially developing nations of Asia, are enjoying rapid growth and are moving up quickly. Japan is experiencing regional economic decline, population decline, and an increase in corporate scandals. And, yet as a people and a culture it remains at the top level and can and should play an enormously positive role in making the 21st century far better than the last century. It is long overdue for Japan to step back, examine itself, and to implement strategic thinking about its future.

As a starting point a SWOT analysis, which is an analytical technique frequently used when creating marketing and corporate strategies, is essential, even for a nation, to analyze its strengths (S), weaknesses (W), opportunities (O), and threats (T). Figure 6.5 illustrates some of the components of a SWOT analysis for the Japanese nation, which allows us to read Japan's characteristics. We should also be able to see from this figure the path Japan needs to take to restore its presence in the international community and to reverse decline.

## Creating a new vision for Japan ("Japan model")

As can be seen from the SWOT analysis in Figure 6.5, the various events that Japan has experienced – or will experience in the future – in the economic, political, and social fields, including the Great East Japan Earthquake, have many points in common with the experiences of other countries. As a developed country, Japan is well

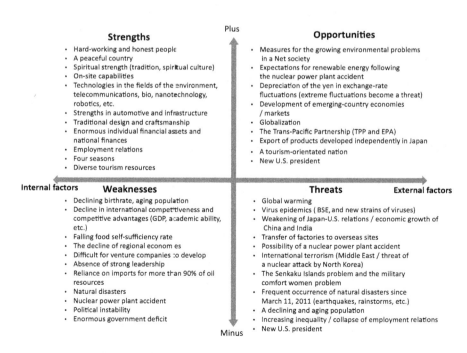

**FIGURE 6.5** A SWOT analysis for the Japanese nation

*Source:* Takashi Inoue (2015), *Public Relations: Relationship Management*, 2nd Edition, p. 214

positioned to act as a model for developing countries and as a source of solutions in terms of both social and technological infrastructure. For this reason the term the "Japan model" is used to describe a new vision for Japan in the coming years of the 21st century.

According to Dr. Hiroshi Komiyama, the former President of the University of Tokyo, Japan is a "problem-saddled developed country" that lacks natural resources and must import all its oil and gas. It also continually experiences natural disasters, as well as the once in a 1,000 year event of the East Japan Earthquake and tsunami. It has already experience and solved the problems of water and air pollution that result from rapid economic development, which now must be addressed by China, India, and other countries throughout Asia. It was through this description of Japan as a "problem-saddled developed country," as well as a personal desire to find a new path for the nation, that led to this author conceiving the idea of Japan as being positioned to follow an "international strategy" of becoming a "problem-solving advanced country" (Inoue, 2011).

Japan has become especially noted for a society experiencing very dramatic and rapid aging of its population. However, the phenomenon of an aging population is a global problem not limited to Japan. According to the United Nations 2015 report on aging: "The world's population is aging: virtually every country in the world is experiencing growth in the number and proportion of older persons in their population." The report goes on to describe the problem as "poised to become one of the most significant social transformations of the twenty-first century" (United Nations, 2015, p. 1). Finding new solutions and developing new technologies to cope with its aging population is something that is well underway in Japan. But, the point of the Japan model, which can be graphically seen in Figure 6.6 (Inoue, 2015, pp. 214–215) is that the nation must see these efforts as a part of its contribution to solving a global problem.

Japan is the only country in the world to have experienced atomic bombing, and the tragedies of Hiroshima and Nagasaki have at least given the whole world reason to avoid a nuclear war. Unlike in the Chernobyl accident, in the recent Fukushima Daiichi nuclear power plant accident it was an earthquake and tsunami that caused the four reactors to become out of control, and the question of how to safely manage this nuclear power plant until it is decommissioned is a challenge that humanity has not experienced up until now. Japan is taking on this challenge. The Japan model includes the nuclear problem as well as those other problems shared with other countries.

After closing its borders to outsiders for 220 years, Japan opened itself up in order to let in aspects of Western civilization. It undertook many bold reforms in order to catch up with, and to even try and overtake, Western powers, but its pursuit of the Western model of imperialism had terrible consequences for its neighboring countries in World War II. From the tragic experience of war, the Japanese learned truly that not everything can be resolved by force, and for that reason any changes to its "peace constitution" that renounced war, remain a highly emotional issue.

Japan's ability to make a tremendous effort when faced with a national crisis can be seen from its post-war prosperity. Japan developed science and technology to

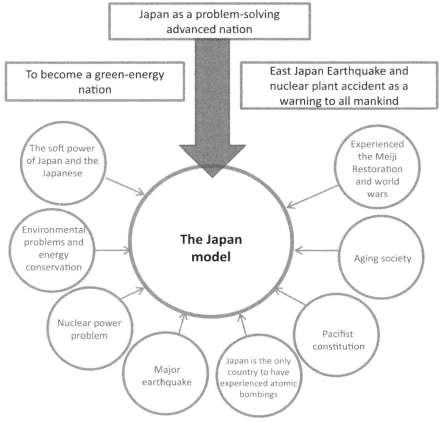

The key factors constituting the Japan model

**FIGURE 6.6** Japan model: Construction of the underlying concept and its background

*Source:* Takashi Inoue (2015), *Public Relations: Relationship Management*, 2nd Edition, p. 215

improve the efficiency of its economy and achieve its objectives. One example of this is nuclear power. It relies on imports for practically 100% of its crude oil, experienced two oil shocks in the 1970s, and therefore decided to actively introduce nuclear power plants. As a result, it constructed 54 nuclear power plants in regions throughout Japan, and prior to the Great East Japan Earthquake it relied on nuclear power for approximately 30% of its total energy needs. This enormous earthquake occurred just when the introduction of nuclear power plants had started to be reconsidered throughout the world as a possible solution to reducing $CO_2$ levels. The leaders of the countries exporting nuclear power plants played the roles of sales men and women as the vanguard of plant exports, and Japan was no exception to this.

The nuclear power plant accident, which has been described as a secondary disaster of the East Japan Great Earthquake and subsequent tsunami, occurred in the context of this increase in concern for the dangers of nuclear power. Why did this sort of major accident occur in Japan, despite the fact that it is the only country to have experienced atomic bombing, and is a country that does not possess nuclear weapons and that will only consider the use of nuclear power for peaceful purposes? Perhaps this is less a matter of coincidence and more a matter of fate, and possibly a warning to the whole human race about its future through Japan and the Japanese people.

The Fukushima nuclear power plant accident is a major problem that Japan needs to resolve, but the problem of reliance on nuclear power and the $CO_2$-emitting energy sources is for all humanity to resolve. Every type of knowledge and expertise must be brought together and efforts focused on developing renewable energy, including solar power, solar thermal power, wind power, biomass, and hydrogen. Japan, which has already started mass production of the world's first commercially viable hydrogen fuel cell car, would do well to transform itself and be reborn as the world's most advanced renewable energy nation, developing alternative energy technology as a "problem-solving advanced country."

The point to be gained from this Japan model is that all nations, not only Japan, have much to gain from using the power of strategic public relations as a tool for contributing more to peace and prosperity for their citizens and for the world.

## References

Asahi Shimbun (1997). "45 major Japan–U.S. trade agreements between 1980 and 1996." *Asahi Shimbun*, 14 January, 1997.

Congress News (1997). "Japanese Agency Won Top Award for Deregulation Programme." s.l.: IPRA.

Crawford, V. (1997). "Public Relations Win Helps Open Auto Parts Market." *The Japan Times,* July 4, 1997.

Inoue, T. (2006). *Paburikku rirēshonzu (Public Relations)*. 1st ed. Tokyo: Nippon Hyoron Sha.

Inoue, T. (2011). "The Japan Model." *IPRA Frontline*.

Inoue, T. (2015). *Paburikku rirēshonzu (Public Relations: Relationship Management)*. 2nd ed. Tokyo: Nippon Hyoron Sha.

Nihon Keizai Shimbun (1995). "Tenneco Shock Aborbers Repair Parts To Be Used by Toyota and Nissan Dealers." *Nihon Keizai Shimbun*, July 7, 1995.

Nihon Keizai Shimbun (2016). "Eliminate ¥1 Trillion ($9 billion) in Unnecessary Costs (Wisdom of the Private Sector in Newly Issued Law). *Nihon Keizai Shimbun,* November 21, 2016.

Nihon Keizai Shimbun (2016). "Smartphone Snaps of Your Receipts!" *Nihon Keizai Shimbun,* November 21, 2016, p. 13.

The Japan Times (1995). "Friendly, Heated Fight Continues (Hashimoto, Kantor Search for Compromise in Car Talks)." *The Japan Times*, July 11, 1995.

The World Bank (1994). "World Bank National Accounts Data, and OECD National Accounts Data Files." [Online] Available at: http://data.worldbank.org/indicator/NY.GDP.MKTP.CD [Accessed August 4, 2017]

United Nations, Department of Economic and Social Affairs, Population Division (2015). *World Population Ageing 2015 (ST/ESA/SER.A/390)*. New York: United Nations.

Yomiuri Shimbun (1995). "Only Vehicle Repair Subject to Section 301 Trade Act Sanction." *Yomiuri Shimbun*, July 11, 1995.

# 7

# MEDIA RELATIONS TRAINING

## Successful executives' competitive career advantage

## 1 Leadership through the power of communications

When asked what makes a global business executive successful, Carlos Ghosn replied:

> If you look at the companies who are struggling, it is not always because the vision is wrong, it is because they have not been able to clearly articulate that vision to motivate and connect to employees, customers, suppliers, and shareholders, and so on. So there is a clear imperative for global leaders to understand, value, and build their public relations skills.

Of course, strategy and technological innovations, for example, are of critical importance, but the point of this book and the point being made by Ghosn is that an organization is a structure that brings various people together; and to succeed as a leader means connecting them to the organization as stakeholders and inspiring them toward the realization of specific goals. As previously mentioned, media relations is a core competence of public relations. And in the new global village of today, media relations skills, both traditional and digital, are vital for global leaders to communicate with stakeholders.

If you search on YouTube for "Masayoshi Son" you will get over 8,900 results. One of the top listings is an interview by Charlie Rose (UnCommon Knowledge/ Charlie Rose, 2016), a famous American journalist and television talk show host, with Mr. Masayoshi Son the charismatic Japanese founder and current chief executive officer of SoftBank. From this interview we can see a fluent English speaker and someone that clearly has the gift of "storytelling" to articulate his vision. Although born in Japan, he went to San Francisco at age 16, attended the University of California, Berkeley at 19, and began his phenomenal business career, while still a student by selling an electronic pocket dictionary to Sharp Electronics. More recently he has demonstrated his speed in spotting global trends and acting quickly, by purchasing Sprint Corporation, being an early investor in Alibaba, and starting a high-tech global investment fund, which attracted a USD $45 billion investment from Saudi Arabia. Understanding the importance of mobile technology, SoftBank acquired for USD $31 billion the British chip designer ARM in 2016, which is considered the leader in mobile processors (Massoudi *et al.*, 2016). Shortly after the election of the new U.S. president in 2016, Son went to Trump Tower where he announced he would be investing USD $50 billion in the American technology sector (Pramuk, 2016). Clearly a person like Son has become very PR savvy and a skillful communicator. That skill should be seen as a powerful force driving his continued success.

Strong leaders are always necessary, but today the ability to also lead through effective communications is particularly critical for leaders to reach out to globalized stakeholders. The Japanese publication *Nikkei Business* made a ranking of the heads of Japanese organizations in terms of their "Power of Communication" (Nihon Keizai Shimbun (Nikkei) Business, 2013). This ranking of Japan's leaders as shown in Figure 7.1 is made up mostly of presidents of global corporations, but also includes the Bank of Japan, which makes the important point that leaders of all organizations, both private and public, need to focus more on communications skill.

Not surprisingly, at the top of the list is SoftBank's Masayoshi Son as number one, followed by Hiroshi Mikitani of Rakuten as fifth. In the global automotive sector the rankings were: Akio Toyoda of Toyota as 4, Carlos Ghosn of Nissan as 7, Takanobu Ito of Honda as 19, and Osamu Suzuki as 20. And, if you were to ask each of these leaders about how they acquired their communications skill you will probably get many different answers, but the points in common with all are likely to be some level of media training, coupled with experience in "storytelling," and they will likely have surrounded themselves with persons schooled in journalism, public relations, and lobbying. They will have learned to speak so that the listeners naturally come to trust and like them, as they speak to them as individuals rather than as a faceless person in a crowd.

## 2 Media training for spokespersons

Media training is extremely important in order to build a high level of trust with the media and it is a core competence for public relations. And these skills for talking to media are transferrable to the many other types of venues in which a successful global executive will talk to groups of stakeholders.

### Objectives of media training

The objectives of media training are to respond appropriately to the media and to effectively communicate a positive image and message, and also to keep a negative image to the absolute minimum. When talking to the media, the objective is not talking to the media, but rather to effectively transmit messages to your

| Rank | Previous ranking | Company name | Top manager | Total points | Mass media score (newspapers, magazines, TV) | Rank | Consumer points (blog) | Rank |
|---|---|---|---|---|---|---|---|---|
| 1 | 1 | SoftBank | Masayoshi Son | 40645 | 4549 | 2 | 36095 | 1 |
| 2 | 3 | Bank of Japan | Masaaki Shirakawa | 11424 | 11000 | 1 | 423 | 27 |
| 3 | 2 | Fast Retailing | Tadashi Yanai | 40624 | 2286 | 9 | 8338 | 2 |
| 4 | 4 | Toyota Motor Corporation | Akio Toyoda | 9088 | 4380 | 3 | 4708 | 5 |
| 5 | 5 | Rakuten | Hiroshi Mikitani | 7766 | 2201 | 11 | 5565 | 4 |
| 6 | 20 | McDonald's Holdings Japan | Eiko Harada | 7372 | 1064 | 25 | 6307 | 3 |
| 7 | 6 | Nissan Motor Corporation | Carlos Ghosn | 6307 | 3433 | 6 | 2874 | 7 |
| 8 | 15 | Nintendo | Satoru Iwata | 4607 | 599 | 51 | 4008 | 6 |
| 9 | 45 | Sony | Kazuo Hirai | 3561 | 2513 | 7 | 1048 | 17 |
| 10 | 8 | KEPCO | Makoto Yagi | 3500 | 3977 | 4 | ▲477 | 100 |
| 11 | 100 | TEPCO | Naomi Hirose | 3429 | 3882 | 5 | ▲453 | 99 |
| 12 | 36 | Sharp | Takashi Okuda | 3030 | 2502 | 8 | 528 | 25 |
| 13 | 28 | Seven & I Holdings | Toshifumi Suzuki | 2966 | 697 | 42 | 2268 | 8 |
| 14 | 27 | Japan Airlines | Yoshiharu Ueki | 2937 | 2205 | 10 | 732 | 20 |
| 15 | 17 | Takeda Pharmaceuticals | Yasuchika Hasegawa | 2877 | 1606 | 15 | 1270 | 13 |
| 16 | 14 | Lawson | Takeshi Niinami | 2792 | 1722 | 14 | 1069 | 16 |
| 17 | 21 | Panasonic | Kazuhiro Tsuga | 2662 | 1940 | 13 | 722 | 21 |
| 18 | 18 | KDDI | Tanaka Takashi | 2469 | 746 | 37 | 1723 | 9 |
| 19 | 9 | Honda | Takanobu Ito | 2427 | 1433 | 17 | 994 | 18 |
| 20 | 7 | Suzuki | Osamu Suzuki | 2354 | 1186 | 23 | 1168 | 14 |
| 21 | 37 | Mitsubishi Chemical Holdings | Yoshimitsu Kobayashi | 2241 | 2019 | 12 | 221 | 49 |
| 22 | | Lifenet Insurance Company | Haruaki Deguchi | 1950 | 291 | 83 | 1659 | 10 |
| 23 | 16 | Mitsubishi Motors | Masuko Osamu | 1940 | 1361 | 19 | 579 | 23 |
| 24 | 38 | GREE | Yoshikazu Tanaka | 1925 | 510 | 62 | 1415 | 12 |
| 25 | 13 | Nidec | Shigenobu Nagamori | 1910 | 483 | 64 | 1427 | 11 |

**FIGURE 7.1** 2013 Global leadership ranking of Japan's corporate presidents

Source: Nihon Keizai Shimbun, Nikkei Business, "Power of Communications." April 29, 2013 – May 6, 2013

organization's stakeholders through it. In other words, besides taking care with your interactions with the media, the successful executive learns how to use these opportunities to fulfill goals of the organization.

Rather than trying to skillfully dodge critical reporting and hiding facts that would be inconvenient for the organization if published, media training conversely aims to eliminate this sort of response and to have you as the spokesperson respond from the perspective of benefiting all of the society of which your organization is a part. This also includes responding to the media in a crisis, which was discussed in the chapter on crisis management. Responding to the media in general is critical for PR activities.

## Three categories of media responses

Responses to the media can broadly be divided into three categories. First is when the organization side actively sends out information based on a PR program, for example through press conferences, press briefings, and one-on-one interviews. Second is when it responds to requests for information from the media side on subjects that they are interested in. Third is responding to telephone calls and requests for interviews during an emergency when the media coverage is concentrated, including the news coverage of an incident or accident involving the organization.

## One-on-one media interviews

In many cases, an organization will give interviews following a request from the media side, and the tendency is for an interview to be held when the organization side agrees to it. But conversely, in a program of media relations, especially when following the strategic PR Life-Cycle, the organization's PR resources will actively arrange interviews, and this type is discussed here.

The following is an example of a media training program, which is basically composed of four parts. Part one is the "basic rules for responding to the media" and focuses on the mental attitude of the spokesperson. Part two is "points to remember during an interview" and describes the specific points to pay attention to in an interview, giving advice on a practical level. Part three is "points to be aware of when holding an interview" and provides advice and identifies points to be aware of when the interview is actually being held. Part four is creating the "checklist for the spokesperson" that enables the entire process to be reviewed.

The training program is carried out by trainers with experience as journalists. Interviews are held using either hypothetical interview content or the expected content of a scheduled interview, and simulated in a realistic setting using prepared recording equipment. The interviews are recorded on video and are reviewed together by the spokespersons undergoing training and the points they need to reflect on are checked.

Recording the simulated interviews has the merit of enabling the interviewees themselves to objectively review their own appearance, attitude, and the impression that they give. For example in a television interview, after actually being interviewed the interviewee is likely to feels regret and disappointment on seeing himself or herself when the interview is played back. This can be avoided to a great extent through the media training program. Most importantly, this type of preparation will enable an executive to respond more effectively during actual interviews.

## 1) Media training program for interviews

### Part one: Basic rules for responding to the media

Part one of the program contains the basic rules for responding to the media. The basic attitude that should be taken by the spokesperson is one of "stating the facts" and never lying and never being deceptive. This is not limited to individual interviews, but is a point in common when responding to the media in all situations.

In the training manual, two types of lies are warned against; "active lies" and "passive lies." The former is when a person deliberately says B when they know the truth to be A, while the latter is when the person knows A, but pretends not to know it. Both are lies and must be avoided as they will be criticized if discovered.

A similar case is when a person accidentally says B while knowing the truth to be A, and care must be taken to avoid this also. Misunderstandings are fundamentally different to lying, but once it is realized that there has been a misunderstanding, it is still necessary to correct it as quickly as possible. Delays in communicating are in actual terms close to being passive lies and communicating nothing might actually be considered to be an active lie. You must also be aware that "anything that is said could possibly end up in print."

In terms of the ordering of the facts you want to communicate, the aim should be to convey the most important facts first in the form of directly answering the questions, and the basic attitude should be to try to actively communicate information.

Also, care must be taken with the use of "no comment." Basically, it is recommended that this phrase not be used. Answering a question with "no comment" indicates that the person does not know the answer to the question, or does know the answer but is unable or unwilling to say it.

Even in the case of the former, rather than giving the interviewer the impression that the interviewee does not actually know the answer, using "no comment" can give the impression that they are unable to give a clear reason for not being able to provide a comment and in the worst case, may actually give the interviewer the impression that the interviewee is untrustworthy. From the start, the interviewee should honestly reply, "I don't know." It is also best to make a quick decision; for example, explaining that you will telephone with the answer after researching it, or will have another person who is more knowledgeable on the question topic promptly provide them with an answer.

In the case of the latter, it is not always bad to use "no comment," but it is necessary to state that, "While I know the answer, I am not able to say it at the present time" and to satisfy the interviewer by explaining the reasons for this, as well as at what point in time you will be able to give an answer.

In addition to the above points, the media training manual provides other advice on the spokesperson's basic attitude, including "how to use specialist terms" and "avoiding speculation."

## Part two: Points to remember during an interview

The following is practical level advice for one-on-one type interviews that can be broadly classified as "points to remember when answering the interviewer's questions" and "advice on improving the impression you give to the interviewer."

When answering the interviewer's questions, in addition to being asked to confirm the basic facts, the spokesperson will be asked questions based on the journalist's approach of finding an opening; which is to stay finding a point from what has been said up to where a natural transition can be made to the main theme of the interview. When this point comes, you can begin to speak about the points that you intend to communicate to your stakeholders through this interview. Keep in mind that a careless answer can make it difficult for the journalist to hear the facts you want to communicate.

Very often in an interview "multiple-choice" and "hypothetical" type questions will be asked. "Multiple-choice" type questions, of course, are when the interviewer limits the choice of answer to A or B, which is intended to elicit an answer of only "A" or "B." However, to convey the facts, you need not stick to only the choices expected by the interviewer, because there will be cases when the answer you want to give is not included in the choices given and so the best answer in order to convey the facts and your message might be C.

"Hypothetical" questions are when the interviewer asks "supposing that …" and are not always premised on the facts. As the answers to such questions can easily tend toward speculation, they can be avoided by answering "I don't want to speculate." But if for whatever reason you have to give an answer, you should begin by first saying something like: "I do not want to speculate, but if I must answer, then I would say …"

Also, if you are asked a hostile or tricky question, you will need to answer based on the approach of "sticking to the facts and not engaging in speculation" and responding, for example, "That is not what I meant. What I want to say is …"

The spokesperson is in a position of representing the company and its corporate image. For this reason alone, if the spokesperson gives a bad impression to the interviewer in terms of their facial expressions or gestures, not only will the spokesperson's image be damaged, but also the image of their company.

So a spokesperson must respond to the interviewer while being aware of this point. For example, an attitude of "responding brightly and clearly," "making eye contact with the journalist," and "listening attentively to their questions" will give a good impression. Conversely, body language like "playing with a pen" and "eyes darting around" can result in a negative image. Moreover, doing things like "shutting your eyes" or "staring at the ceiling" will give the interviewer the impression that you are disinterested. So these sorts of body language should be strictly avoided. Even when a journalist asks a negative question, it is best to as far as possible give a positive answer. In other words, when asked why the glass is "half empty," the appropriate answer would be that it is actually "half full."

## Part three: Key points when holding an interview

Part three of the program contains the most relevant points for interviews, which are divided into the three stages: (1) preparation, (2) during the interview, (3) post interview.

First, in preparation, before the interview begins, the spokesperson must confirm the important elements for the interview in advance and also to a certain extent, get an idea of how the interview will proceed and in what kind of atmosphere it will be held. These important elements will include the name of the journalist conducting the interview, their objectives, the questions they will ask, and when the article or feature will be published or broadcast. After this, it is essential that the spokesperson arranges in their mind the information they particularly want to communicate, but it is important that they do not try to memorize details above what will be needed to answer the question, as excessive information may make the answers sound unnatural.

In addition, in order to respond flexibly to the interview, it is a good idea to prepare in advance several materials and topics that you think will be newsworthy from the viewpoint of the interviewer. Responding flexibly to interviews is itself the practice of two-way communication on the front line of media relations.

Second, during the interview, to give a good impression to the interviewer and have the interview proceed in a friendly atmosphere, it is important to fully understand the previously described "points to remember during an interview" and put them into practice. It will also be necessary to: (1) pay close attention to the questions and to take notes, (2) to avoid refusing to answer a question, (3) to take a few seconds to think when you cannot give a clear answer immediately to avoid redundant answers, (4) to think quickly but talk slowly, (5) and to keep your answers as simple as possible, because complex answers may result in an inaccurate article.

Moreover, in order to demonstrate how much you value the opportunity to communicate with the journalist, it is important to be conscious of using the other person's name, always imagining the audience in the background to the journalist and aiming to send the message to them.

Third, a critically important point to be aware of after the interview is that the spokesperson must not ask to check the content of the article before it is published. This is because at the stage prior to the publication, aspects such as the article's theme, content, and entry point are matters included in the editing rights of the media side and basically are outside of the company side's control. While the desire to check the content of the article is understandable, asking to do so may provoke a hostile reaction from the interviewer and the media organization they belong to.

However, in the event that after the article is published it is apparent that there has been a misunderstanding about important facts, you must point them out without fear. But relations with the media organization will deteriorate if you constantly pester it about whether or not they are going to publish a corrected article. So if the article as a whole was accurate, it is better not to complain about a minor mistake.

## Part four: Interview checklist

Part four of the program is "the checklist for the spokesperson." This involves creating a checklist in the form of simple questions on several of the main points that will enable the interview to be reviewed from the standpoint of the spokesperson. For example:

- Did you communicate the message accurately?
- Did you convey the facts?
- Were you able to give a strong positive image?

For the question "Did you communicate the message accurately?," if it is not possible to clearly answer yes or no, this leads to the reflection that "the interview was conducted with the message still not being clearly established," while if the answer is "no," the reflection will be on which part of the message was not communicated and for what reason, and what needs to be done so that it can be communicated. This results in self-correction toward responding to the media appropriately the next time.

The checklist will be concise and targeted and is to be created not just for one interview, but also for the next time information is sent out, and the awareness of the spokesperson receiving the training is naturally guided back to part one of the program.

Can you answer yes to the following questions?

- ☐ Did you communicate the important message accurately?
- ☐ Did you convey the facts?
- ☐ Did you maintain your composure?
- ☐ Did you anticipate questions intended to trip you?
- ☐ Did you avoid an attitude that would have been distracting to the other person?
- ☐ Did you give a strong positive image?
- ☐ Did you pay close attention to the questions?
- ☐ Were you able to deal well with hostile or off-topic questions?
- ☐ Were you able to ensure reliability?
- ☐ Did you avoid controversial topics?
- ☐ Were you able to clearly communicate technical information in an easy-to-understand manner?
- ☐ Did you avoid causing discomfort to the other person through your appearance or words?
- ☐ Were you able to tell a story? (Particularly in the case of top management)
- ☐ Were you able to use the interview to improve the brand image?

## 2) Importance of non-verbal communication

In the book *Silent Messages*, United States psychologist Albert Mehrabian stressed the importance of non-verbal communication of elements other than "words," for example the impression given by the tone and volume of the voice, body language, and appearance (Mehrabian, 1971, pp. 5–6).

Mehrabian conducted an experiment to clarify what information the other person gives importance to in the specific situation of "conveying feelings, such as friendliness or hostility" when the verbal information, auditory information, and visual information are contradictory. The results were as follows:

- "Verbal information: message content" accounts for 7% of the importance,
- "Auditory information: tone and sound of voice" accounts for 38%,
- "Visual information: body language and appearance" accounts for 55%.

In press conferences, it goes without saying that verbal information is the most important, but the results of Mehrabian's experiment suggest that we must also pay attention to auditory and visual information. The impression given by top management will overlap with their company's image, so naturally these points should be paid attention to, especially in a TV appearance or in front of a large audience.

## References

Ghosn, C. (2017). *Responses to Questionnaire "Public Relations for Hyper-globalization."* Yokohama: s.n.

Massoudi, A., Inagaki, K., Waters, R., & Parker, G. (2016). "Masayoshi Son Arms SoftBank for Internet of Things." *Financial Times.* [Online] Available at: https://www.ft.com/content/a0e0134c-4d08-11e6-88c5-db83e98a590a [Accessed August 4, 2017]

Mehrabian, A. (1971). *Silent Messages.* Belmont, CA: Wadsworth.

Nihon Keizai Shimbun (Nikkei) Business (2013). "Ranking of Presidents' Power of Communication, 2013." *Nikkei Business,* 5.

Pramuk, J. (2016). "Trump Says SoftBank Will Invest $50 billion in the US, Aiming to Create 50,000 jobs." *CNBC,* December 6, 2016. [Online] Available at: https://www.cnbc.com/2016/12/06/trump-says-softbank-will-invest-50-billion-in-the-us-aiming-to-create-50000-jobs.html [Accessed August 5, 2017]

Uncommon Knowledge/Charlie Rose (2016). "Interview with Billionaire Masayoshi Son - Words of Wisdom." *YouTube,* July 30, 2016. [Online] Available at: https://www.youtube.com/watch?v=fEKAJeSOQhw&t=54s [Accessed July 24, 2017]

# 8

# EVALUATING AND MEASURING
# PUBLIC RELATIONS ACTIVITIES

## 1 Necessity of evaluating and measuring public relations activities

In order to practice public relations effectively it is necessary to actively and assuredly implement a program of monitoring, measurement, and analysis. Moreover, it needs to be part of the PR Life-Cycle Model introduced in Chapter 6. Unfortunately, especially in Japan, the reality is that the methods to evaluate and analyze the results of activities and information have generally not been established within most organizations. Even in the West, where PR is more mature, it has only been from the 1990s that evaluating and measuring PR activities began to be widely taken up among practitioners as a topic in seminars and meetings. This is partly due to the difficulty in implementing evaluation of PR activities. But, without a practical way of evaluating results, it is not possible to implement the self-correction function that is a critical part of effective public relations.

### Reasons for lack of evaluation of PR and communications activities

In many cases, PR practitioners cite the "lack of budget and time" as the reason for the lack of evaluation of PR activities. But in actuality, is this the only reason? Since 1980, around every three years, the Keizai Koho Center (Japan Institute for Social and Economic Affairs) has conducted the "Survey of Actual Conditions of Companies' Public Relations Activities" among the managers responsible for public relations and communications in Japanese companies. The 2014 survey of managers responsible for PR and or the simpler "communications" function still found in Japanese organizations, asked them about "the problems you face on a daily basis in a PR and communications department" (Inoue, 2015, p 223). The results in Figure 8.1 show that the number one ranked problem is "the difficulty in measuring the effects of corporate communications activities" (Inoue, 2015). This indicates that a comprehensive method of evaluating and measuring PR activities has still not been established.

| | |
|---|---|
| Difficulty in measuring the effects of PR/communications activities | 72.70% |
| Few PR/communications practitioners | 40.30% |
| Lack of budget for PR/communications | 31.20% |
| Crisis management | 29.40% |
| Lack of understanding among average employees about PR/communications | 29.40% |
| Responding to the mass media | 27.70% |
| Area that PR/communications has to deal with is too wide | 26.80% |
| Responding to social media | 25.50% |
| In-house communications | 23.40% |
| Lack of understanding PR/communications by directors and heads of departments | 22.10% |
| Gap between corporate ethics and common sense in general in society | 14.70% |
| Insufficient authority is granted to the PR/communications department | 14.30% |
| Results are expected immediately | 10.80% |
| Lack of understanding of PR/communications among top management | 6.90% |
| Other (no particular indicators) | 4.80% |

**FIGURE 8.1** Problems faced on a daily basis in PR and communications departments

*Source:* "The 12th Report on the Survey of Awareness and Actual Conditions of Companies' PR and Communications Activities" (2015)

## PR measurement obstacles

The first obstacle for PR activity measurement is PR practitioners' own fear of being measured that makes them shy away from evaluation. Certainly, evaluating the results of PR activities has the aspect of placing psychological pressure on PR practitioners. However, the objective of evaluating and measuring PR activities is not merely to "reflect on past behavior" but also for "creating the next strategic plan" more effectively by following a process of self-correction, which requires a two-way communications process.

PR practitioners need to change the way they think, eliminate their "fears," and adopt an attitude of facing head-on the issues that become visible through the evaluation.

The second obstacle is that clear and measurable PR objectives are not set. If objectives are not set or not set correctly, measuring PR activity results becomes a problem. For example, imagine the PR objective being set as "increasing awareness of our company in the local community as a good corporate citizen." In this instance, it will be necessary to clarify the following before setting the PR objectives:

* What is the current name-awareness of your company in the local community?
* To what extent does the local community feel favorably toward your company?
* What are the physical boundaries of the local community?
* Are you targeting specific target audiences within the local community or all members of it?
* What is the indicator for measuring change?

If these sorts of questions are not answered at the beginning then, for example, even if PR activities have been effective, it will be difficult to measure their extent.

Also, it is essential to be knowledgeable about and have an understanding of communication theory in order to set appropriate PR objectives and to evaluate and measure PR activities. To give an example, can the opinions of people who are strongly opposed or in favor of a certain matter be changed to the opposite opinion through PR activities? According to the hedging and wedging theory, it is considered that even if it is possible to move people with a strong opinion to a neutral position, generally it is extremely difficult to completely change their view to the opposite opinion. If this is not understood and the objective is set of simply reversing the opinions of the people being targeted, rather than more realistically set to changing opinions in a desired direction, then the evaluation method will lose its effectiveness to accurately reflect the full extent and value of the PR activities.

Even if there is sufficient budget and time, if the objectives are vague it will be difficult to carry out specific evaluations and measurements. Also, even if there are numerical objectives, if the values are not set with sufficient consideration to what is viable, then this is likely to lead to disappointing results. In this way, the setting of PR objectives at the start is important in order to derive evaluation and measurement results that will be useful for the subsequent strategic planning.

## 2 Methods of evaluating public relations activities

### Performance measurement indicators survey

In the Keizai Koho Center's twelfth survey (survey period: October to November 2014), among the questions on the evaluation of PR and communication activities, it asked, "Did your company set some sort of objectives for its public relations activities?" Of all respondents (a total of 231 companies, multiple answers possible), 43.3% answered yes. The top five performance measurement indicators selected as displayed in Figure 8.2 were as follows: "The number of lines (column inches)/frequency of appearance in reporting in newspapers, etc." (50.2%), "Measurement from categorizing the reporting into positive/negative/neutral, etc." (26.4%), "The company rankings surveys carried out by various mass media organizations" (23.8%), "The level of attention from mass media organizations (increase/decrease in requests for interviews, etc.)" (24.2%), and "The results of a company image survey regularly carried out by my company" (21.6%) (Keizai Koho Center, 2015, p. 77).

From the results of this survey, we can see that many companies emphasize an evaluation in terms of volume, such as the number of times the company is reported on by the mass media or column inches. These indicators are likely effective if solely looking at the results of PR and communications activities. However, it is difficult to judge the level of importance of these indicators as information premised upon "the planning of strategic PR activities."

### Various evaluation methods and their characteristics

To better understand the evaluation methods currently being used, it is best to look at characteristics of each and then how they are utilized individually and in combination.

| | |
|---|---|
| Column inches (number of characters / lines of text) appearing in newspapers, etc. | 50.20% |
| Measurement by categorizing media coverage as "positive," "negative," or "neutral," etc. | 26.40% |
| Results of a corporate ranking survey conducted by mass media companies | 23.80% |
| Level of attention from each mass-media company | 24.20% |
| Results of a corporate image survey conducted regularly by the company itself | 21.60% |
| Share-price trends | 13.90% |
| Awards, etc., for public relations, communication, and publicity | 6.10% |
| Status of applications from job-seekers anc position in the popularity ranking among students | 7.40% |
| Other (no particular indicators) | 29.80% |

**FIGURE 8.2**    Performance indicators to measure the outcomes of PR and communications activities

*Source:* "The 12th Report on the Survey of Awareness and Actual Conditions of Companies' PR and Communications Activities" (2015)

## 1) Secondary data

This entails implementing a self-evaluation based on the company ranking surveys carried out by the media and research organizations and announced to the general public. The survey data is easy to obtain and is particularly useful if the survey results can be summarized into a file. Aside from the time taken to summarize the survey results into a file and to fill in the data points, no time or money is required. However, as these surveys are not designed by your own company, you will need to take care about aspects such as the methods used to calculate the numerical data that served as the grounds for the rankings.

## 2) Independent surveys

This refers to surveys such as market surveys, customer satisfaction surveys, reader surveys, and media audits or journalist surveys that are independently planned and implemented by the company itself. They are particularly effective for evaluating reputation management. They require spending both time and money, but recently there has been an increase in inexpensive surveys conducted over the Internet.

## 3) Case studies

This method entails utilizing the case studies of other companies as model cases for your own company's strategic planning and is particularly effective for crisis communication. It is also possible to change in advance your own company's responses by referring to the details of past case studies taken up by the media as examples of good or bad corporate practices.

## 4) Media monitoring

Most companies collect print or audio-visual media coverage relating to their own company. However, as the judgment used for the evaluation is usually only the quantity of media coverage without any sort of processing, it treats coverage that is favorable and unfavorable to that company as the same, and also cannot distinguish whether or not the media organization that the coverage appeared in is influential. Moreover, when using this method it is not possible to judge whether the coverage included the message that your company wanted to send. It is essential to check and critically evaluate the content of each and every article.

## 5) Conversion to advertising value equivalents

This is an evaluation method that converts the space for the reporting in the print media, the amount of broadcast time, and exposure on the Internet that relates to your company into advertising value equivalents (AVE). Unlike advertising, which can be completely controlled by your own company, in general the content of reporting can be either very favorable to your company, or can be the exact opposite and be very unfavorable. In addition, sometimes it includes errors or a comparison with your competitors, although recently these sorts of comparisons are also appearing in advertisements.

As is shown in Figure 8.2, a comparatively large number of companies use the "number of lines (column inches)/frequency of appearance in reporting in newspapers" approach. But, when considering the different characteristics of PR and advertising, it seems insufficient to evaluate PR simply by converting it into AVE.

## 6) Media analysis

"Media analysis" is a PR evaluation method that goes beyond the simple media monitoring of the past and is currently the most widely used method among PR practitioners around the world. In particular, in the West a number of research companies are competing by providing ever more sophisticated media analysis services. Compared to an independent survey, media analysis can be implemented faster and at lower cost. While it is not the case that the results of all PR activities can be evaluated through media analysis, based on the reality that PR activities mainly consist of media relations and also the research findings that indicate that the media significantly influences people's thinking and behavior, this analytical method has come to occupy a central position among the various evaluation methods.

As is shown in Figure 8.3, this is the reason why "journalists and related parties" are the most important target audience for PR and communications activities. As an accurate evaluation requires not only the quantitative aspect of column inches but also a consideration of its content, such as whether the message was communicated accurately to the target audiences, this method is therefore an effective tool for creating a PR and communications plan (Keizai Koho Center, 2015, p. 38).

## Automated media analytics

Analysis of media content has evolved dramatically from being primarily a manual process of gathering, reviewing, and rating news clippings from traditional print media to sophisticated software services that include digital media and social media, with its millions of postings per hour. More recently, media analysis has become a

| Journalists and related parties (mass media) | 79.20% |
|---|---|
| Shareholders, investors | 43.70% |
| Employees, employees of group companies | 42.40% |
| Business partners, customers | 41.10% |
| General consumers | 28.60% |
| Local residents, local communities | 22.80% |
| Securities analysts | 10.40% |
| Other | 8.20% |

**FIGURE 8.3** Target audience ranking for PR and communications activities

Source: "The 12th Report on the Survey of Awareness and Actual Conditions of Companies PR and Communications Activities" (2015)

special case of big data analytics that is focused on digital news media, and social media to provide insights about brands, corporate reputation, customer and market trends, as well as the activities of competitors, using the various sources of documents available on the Internet.

## Social media and digital media monitoring

Because of the explosion in volume and importance of social media platforms, sophisticated and automated monitoring software has become an inescapable requirement. As a result, there is now a long list of software, which includes some freeware, such as HootSuite, Google Alerts, Facebook Insights, Klout, Social Mention, as well as fee-based services, such as Brandwatch, Buffer, CustomScoop, Gorkana, LexisNexis, Meltwater, and Sysomos to name just a small sample of what is available.

These analytic software tools provide a variety of benefits that go beyond just evaluating the success of a particular campaign of public relations activities. Gorkana for example, in addition to providing media monitoring provides journalist profiles and contact information to improve media relations activities of public relations. HootSuite provides audience identification tools. Klout helps you find those all-important "influencers." Buffer helps with managing and monitoring Twitter, Facebook, and LinkedIn accounts. Meltwater provides media monitoring, social media engagement tools, helps with marketing campaigns, supports building brand relationships, and provides a big data search engine for insights into customers, competition, market trends, and other information required for strategic planning.

## Media monitoring with CARMA

The CARMA (Computer Aided Research and Media Analysis) automated media analytics service was one of the first to successfully apply automation in the mid-1980s and is worth highlighting in depth, because of its focus as a public relations measurement tool.

Most people will never directly meet Japan's Prime Minister Abe or President Trump, but in general they will still be very familiar with them, and not just in terms of their appearance, but also in terms of the way they think and act. This is clearly because people are influenced by the media coverage of these two leaders, and come into contact with them via media coverage on a daily basis. By analyzing and evaluating the content of media coverage, it is possible to ascertain how media coverage influences readers and viewers. CARMA is a systemized survey method using computers that is based on this idea.

The analytical method is an example of the automation of "media monitoring, analysis, and databases services across all types of media, including print, online, social, TV, and radio" used by PR and communications professionals (CARMA, 2017). CARMA began in 1984, when PR consultant Albert J. Barr developed a system to evaluate PR activities through media analysis utilizing computers.

This media analysis was used in the 1992 United States presidential election between Clinton, Bush, and Perot. It was able to ascertain the change pattern in the support for candidate Bush with a degree of accuracy comparable to the Gallup public opinion poll (Figure 8.4). From this success, CARMA came to be adopted by many leading companies and organizations, and understanding it is important today for PR practitioners (Inoue, 2006, pp. 215–216).

## 1) Steps in the CARMA media analysis

### Preparing the list of survey items

At the planning stage, three types of lists are prepared, which correspond to the survey questionnaire in marketing research. The task of creating these lists while also

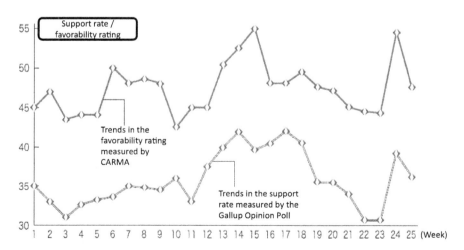

**FIGURE 8.4**   Comparison between CARMA and the Gallup Opinion Poll in the 1992 U.S. presidential election

*Source:* CARMA

confirming the PR objectives will influence the extent to which the results of the analysis can be strategically utilized. In many cases, this task is carried out jointly by the client and the team of the service provider.

**a) Setting the list of issues**    Based on the PR objectives, the PR-related issues and problems are extracted and the list of issues prepared. There are occasions when every type of PR issue and problem will be the target of the survey, but other occasions when the focus is narrowed down to specific events and topics. Normally for the list of issues, several PR target areas are defined as the upper concepts and then sub-concepts for each are set. For example, when a food company's upper concept is "contributing to the local community," the sub-concepts may include factory tours, holding cooking classes, and providing its products at sports events.

**b) Setting the list of messages**    The messages that the client wants to communicate through the PR activities are extracted. These will include its management concept and philosophy, its strategic objectives, and the specific measures to achieve them. They will also include special messages aimed at specific objectives, such as a recruitment-related objectives. Both positive and negative messages will be set.

**c) Setting the media list**    This is the selection of the media channels to be surveyed and entails focusing on the key media organizations for your company from among the various types of media, whether newspapers, magazines, radio, television, or online media. Furthermore, it involves determining these media channels according to budget while considering the ease of collecting material and the volume of reporting.

## 2) Implementing the research

The following six items are the main items to be surveyed:

- Media channels (name, number of subscribers – in the case of online media, PV, etc. – sales regions, etc.),
- Issues (including sub-concepts),
- Messages (both positive and negative),
- By-line (the journalist responsible in the case of a signed article),
- Sources (information sources, including spokespersons, external financial analysts, opinion leaders, etc.),
- The favorability rating.

Unlike conventional media monitoring, a characteristic of media analysis is that it considers the good and bad aspects of the reporting content, and in CARMA, this is represented by the "favorability rating." The favorability rating is an indicator of "to what extent the reporting is favorable" toward the organization for which the survey is conducted.

Even for reporting what is written based on a single press release, the entry point for that reporting is selected subjectively by each media organization and journalist, which is one of the media's "editing rights," and therefore the favorability rating of each media organization can diverge to an unexpected degree.

CARMA's favorability rating system is composed of the seven scales shown in Figure 8.5. The initial points for the favorability rating is 50 for each report, which is equivalent to "neutral" and numbers are added to or subtracted from 50 based on the judgment criteria set for each of the seven scales that produce the final favorability rating of a number from 0 to 100. The evaluation criteria are clarified in advance to ensure that they don't include the researchers' individual opinions or biases, while any blurring due to differences in the survey period and between individual researchers is eliminated.

Even when an evaluation method is described as being media analysis, in many cases this simply entails judging whether the reported content is "positive" or "negative" and calculating the percentage of reports that are "positive" from among all the reports. In contrast, a unique feature of CARMA is this method described above of creating the favorability rating indicator.

## 3) Aggregate analysis

The three essential elements for an analysis are "the number of media articles," which is the number of print or online articles, "the impression," and "the favorability rating." The first stage of the evaluation is establishing the extent to which the company or its messages were taken up in media articles and in the news, the second stage is the number of potential readers (impression is calculated as the sum of

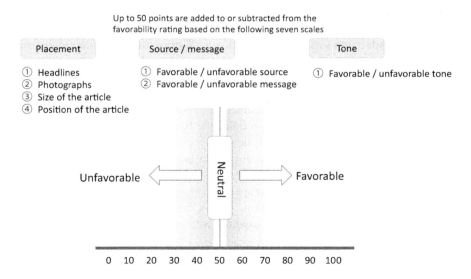

**FIGURE 8.5**    CARMA favorability rating system

*Source:* Takashi Inoue (2015), *Public Relations: Relationship Management*, 2nd Edition, p. 228

the media channel's circulation and the number of households of readers/viewers), and then the third stage is to what extent was the reporting favorable toward the client (favorability rating). With these three points as the pillars, the issues, messages, and media are cross-tabulated.

## Analysis and reporting and a case study of its use

A report is provided to the client as a hard copy or as an online report. For companies implementing a global survey, in an increasing number of cases the approach is to post the report on the Web from where it can be accessed and utilized from anywhere in the world. Also, the CARMA analysis can be used for various aspects of PR activities. The following are the main analysis methods, along with a case study.

**a) Issue management**   Company A had previously calculated the number of reports on it in each media organization, but was unable to categorize these reports according to their respective content. From the results of the CARMA analysis, it is understood that there was a bias in the balance of the contents of media articles, as although both this year and last year a number of media articles appeared on its "products," there were only a few media articles related to its corporate PR activities, such as on its "social contribution" (Figure 8.6).

From this analysis, it was recognized within the company that although the face of the product could be seen, the face of the company itself and of its managers could not be seen. So the company started to focus on corporate issues with strong appeal to the media so that it reported on topics related to its corporate PR activities. The company thereby succeeded in increasing the exposure of management and the company identity.

**b) Comparative analysis with competitors**   Within the same issue setting, an analysis of the reporting is not just on your own company, but also makes clear the difference with competitors, and this makes it possible to construct a strategy after ascertaining the trends for competitors. Figure 8.7 is an example of an analysis of the competing products of five companies. The favorability rating and impression is the highest for Company B, which holds the best position. Company C ranks third for impression, but falls into the negative zone for its favorability rating as its value is below 50, which can be thought of as a potentially fatal position unless it implements some sort of change to address this situation. At this point in time, you can see the composition of these companies is that, in practical terms, Company C has dropped out of the competition, while Company B and Company E, and Company A and Company D, are competing with each other respectively as rivals.

**c) Time-series analysis**   To explain a time-series analysis a fictitious Company S is used in Figure 8.8.

Company S employs more than 20 people in its PR department and evaluates its PR activities through the methods of the hit rate of its press releases and access

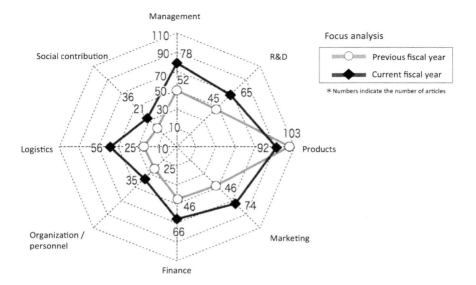

**FIGURE 8.6**   Use in issue management

*Source:* Takashi Inoue (2015), *Public Relations: Relationship Management*, 2nd Edition, p. 230

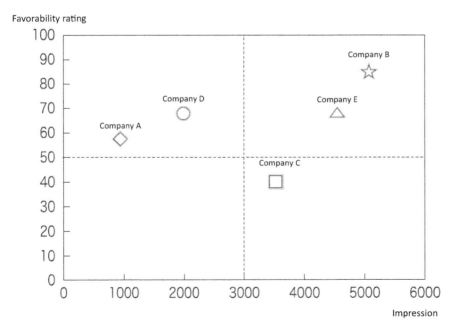

**FIGURE 8.7**   Comparative analysis of competing products by five companies

*Source:* Takashi Inoue (2015), Public Relations: Relationship Management, 2nd Edition, p. 231

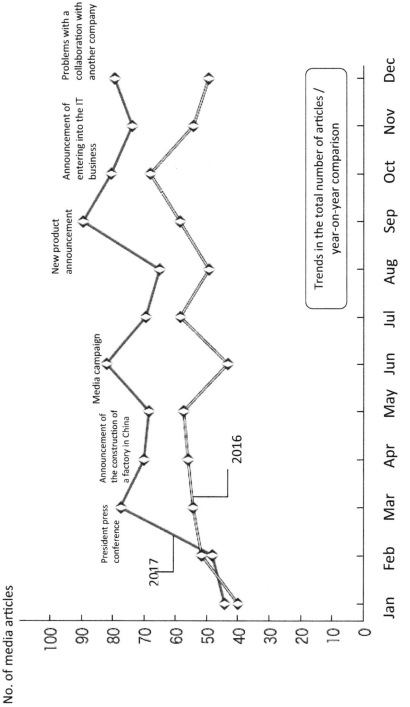

No. of media articles

Problems with a collaboration with another company

Announcement of entering into the IT business

New product announcement

Media campaign

Announcement of the construction of a factory in China

President press conference

2017

2016

Trends in the total number of articles / year-on-year comparison

Jan Feb Mar Apr May Jun Jul Aug Sep Oct Nov Dec

**FIGURE 8.8** Time-series analysis — hypothetical example

rate of its homepage. It carried out a media analysis using CARMA for the first time at the end of 2016, and on reflecting on its PR activities in the past year, two problems came to light.

The first problem was that despite the release of a large volume of press releases for a new product in September, the coverage in terms of the number of media articles on this product had not grown to the extent expected. The second problem was exposure from media reporting in June was extremely low. On researching the causes, it was found that for the former, the announcement of the new product was made around the same time as that of a competitor, and so the announcement was not followed up by interviews with the media. While for the latter, there was a major in-house event in this month and as a result, the efforts to contact the media were weaker than usual as attention was focused elsewhere.

Based on these reflections, in 2017 the company consciously controlled the timing of announcements on important topics and created a plan to implement a media campaign in June. As a result, overall work efficiency improved and this led to a sense of accomplishment in the PR department as a whole.

### d) Favorability rating in media relations
To explain favorability ratings a fictitious Company Y is used. Company Y sent out information centered on topics for business people, but through the media analysis, it became aware that its favorability rating for a particular newspaper was inferior to that of other business publications. It discovered that the cause of this was that it had not provided sufficient briefings for a newly appointed journalist who was responsible for covering it and subsequently, after the company responded fully to this situation, the favorability rating improved.

### e) Source analysis
The company can check the number of appearances of spokespersons and influencers in media reporting and their favorability ratings, and in response, it can investigate and provide the spokesperson with media training and take measures for influencers, who repeatedly make negative statements.

### f) Social media
With the rise of social media, monitoring and social listening have become increasingly important to companies and organizations. CARMA offers multilingual social listening on various social media platforms, such as Facebook, Twitter, and Instagram. Content published on blogs and micro-blogs is also tracked and analyzed in order for companies to get a comprehensive overview of their online image.

### g) Global analysis
United States' hi-tech Company Q left its PR operations up to its local operations in various countries, but upon implementing a media analysis, an issue requiring investigation that had not been apparent up to that time came to light. This was its low favorability rating in Germany (Figure 8.9). Upon investigating the situation locally, it found that there had been claims made by consumers about a product, and that even citizens' groups were participating

in these claims to such an extent that various newspapers had started to report on them. The head office quality control department then was able to query the German operations, and received the immediate feedback that "there was no problem" in addition to a full explanation in response to its inquiry about these claims from local people. Unfortunately, the local PR department had underestimated the situation and neglected to respond to it, and so the controversy escalated to a greater extent than it should have.

This is an example of how the measurement of the favorability rating can unexpectedly play the role of a check function, which is critical in order to implement self-correction.

**h) Crisis management** Media analysis is widely utilized for crisis management, such as by collecting information on a specific theme, collecting information from the media on public opinion when a crisis occurs, and for case studies involving competitors demonstrating what happens when a problem occurs until it is brought under control. As a result, such crisis management analysis can encourage management to be more aware of potential crises, and this can help to prevent them before they occur.

**i) Reports to top management** Reports to top management must be concise and summarize the main points. Other than converting coverage in the media to AVE, Company M's PR department had not previously created briefing materials on the results of PR activities. But after implementing a media analysis, it began preparing reports for top management focused on four points: "The total number of media articles and the favorability rating," "the impression and favorability rating for each main topic," "the company's situation as reported in national newspapers," and "the impression and favorability rating for each spokesperson."

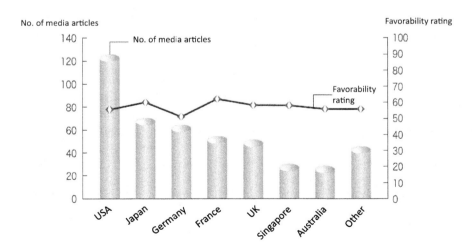

**FIGURE 8.9** Global favorability ratings analysis

*Source:* Takashi Inoue (2015), Public Relations: Relationship Management, 2nd Edition, p. 233

These results clarified the target audiences and succeeded in changing how top management responded to media reporting by taking a more proactive approach compared to its tendency to avoid responding in the past. This is an excellent example of how the feedback from the results of sending information can lead to self-correction in how public relations communicates, and thereby enable more effective dissemination of information.

**j) Stock price and media favorability ratings**   Media intelligence tools can provide insights about many aspects related to an organization. Of particular value is showing the relationship between favorable media coverage and a company's stock price. The tools use a database that includes data collected on a daily basis, including on company names, industry category, the number of media articles favorability rating, names of the various media organizations, report topics, report headlines, and stock prices. Simply by going online and selecting the company name from a pulldown menu, the user will be shown various information in a time-series chart, such as on the favorability rating and the number of media articles. It is also easy to change the display period and add competitors or industry categories as the benchmarks, and the data typically can be downloaded as a spreadsheet file.

In addition, it can also produce a chart showing the relationship between the favorability rating and stock price; one week's worth of reporting headlines are displayed from the point in time you click on the line graph, which enables the relationship between the topics reported on by the media and the stock price to be easily checked.

In the West, the business of public relations was established as a profession, and the methods of evaluating PR activities were mainly introduced by leading companies and organizations. And in Japan also, a major change of direction is taking place in terms of the role of the PR and communications department, from being an administrative point-of-contact for other departments in the company to being "one part of the management function" through planning the strategic deployment of PR. Hopefully in the future, PR practitioners will recognize and implement the evaluation and measurement of PR activities as a strategic PR planning tool, rather than simply relying on experience and intuition for evaluation as they have done in the past.

Also, the launch of Facebook in 2004 and Twitter in 2006 has opened up a new area not only for communication in general, but for public relations also. The spread of mobile devices and the rapid advance of social media is replacing the monopoly of the traditional mass media for the dissemination of information, and an environment has been created where anyone, at any time, and from anywhere can access information. This information is not just sent in one direction, but is being shared by two-way communication, and furthermore, it is proliferating in many directions and expanding its influence. A flow of new information is being created from information on social media that has been introduced from the mass media, or conversely social media information that is flowing into the mass media. In this sense, the analysis of social media has come to occupy an important position in the evaluation and measurement of PR. Also, in order to respond to the new developments in our Internet society, it is necessary when measuring PR effects to further coordinate with IT (information technology), especially in the case of the analysis of big data.

## References

CARMA (2017). "About CARMA." [Online] Available at: https://www.carma.com/about/ [Accessed August 5, 2017]

Inoue, T. (2006). *Paburikku rirēshonzu (Public Relations)*. 1st ed. Tokyo: Nippon Hyoron Sha.

Inoue, T. (2015). *Paburikku rirēshonzu (Public Relations: Relationship Management)*. 2nd ed. Tokyo: Nippon Hyoron Sha.

Keizai Koho Center (2015). *The 12th Report on the Survey of Awareness and Actual Conditions of Companies' PR and Public Information Activities (2015)*. Tokyo: Keizai Koho Center.

# 9

# ESSENTIAL CHANGES IN CORPORATE COMMUNICATION IN A DIGITAL AGE

## 1 Excelling at social media

When in 2016 a non-politician, billionaire businessman and reality-TV host with an "itchy-Twitter-finger" can be elected president of the United States, can there be any doubt that social media has created a new environment in which individuals and organizations must operate? There are over seven billion persons on planet earth and there are now over two billion active Facebook accounts. No one should be surprised as that number approaches three billion. And, here in Japan on a crowded subway car almost everyone is looking at their smartphone, and as people exit the train some will continue to look at their phones as they walk, looking up only to check the color of the street light when they come to the intersection. Even young children being pushed in baby strollers by parents can be seen operating smartphones. This situation is repeated in cities all over the world. The Internet applications of social media and social networks have more than simply added a new channel through which organizations can communicate with stakeholders. In this digital age organizations must excel in their use of social media to promote products, develop products, generate sales leads, build brand awareness and brand affinity, identify and understand new trends, learn about what competitors are doing or planning to do, identify and utilize social media "influencers," learn about actual and potential threats that lead to a crisis, and engage with stakeholders.

This chapter begins by looking at Samsung's successful 2015 launch of a new smartphone through a social media-based public relations program.

## 2 Case study: Samsung, launch of new smartphone

When Samsung, the leader in the smartphone market, was ready to promote their new Galaxy S6 edge smartphone in 2015 to the Indian market, they developed a public relations program around social media. This is particularly relevant given that

Samsung's engineers created new features for the built-in camera of the Galaxy S6 edge, and also given that photo and video content has become such a dominant part of social media.

More than simply introducing a new smartphone, Samsung wanted to bring alive the photographic features of the new phone in ways that would create a buzz of excitement among millennials, who are a critical market segment. With that objective in mind, they created a public relations program, in which they invited key influencers in social media and digital media on a three-day photowalk to the Indian state of Sikkim and covered multiple genres of food, fashion, modern art, and travel. Rather than taking the usual approach of focusing on technical reviews and news, the campaign aimed to create a new paradigm in the way phones are seen.

Armed with the stunning new Samsung Galaxy S6 edge, the selected journalists and influencers were taken on a six-hour drive from Bagdogra to the quaint little town of Pelling, famous for its magnificent views of the snow-capped Kanchenjunga mountain range. This locale provided the perfect opportunity to show off the prowess of the state-of-the-art technology of the camera built into the new Samsung smartphone. The incredibly vivid, bright, and fast front and rear cameras enabled these photography enthusiasts to capture the jaw-dropping views of the Eastern Himalayan Range, Rimbi and Kanchendzonga waterfalls, as well as the Khecheopalri Wishing Lake.

Comments from two participants of the photowalk were:

> The Galaxy S6 is a lovely piece of equipment with an amazing camera. This Photowalk has ensured, the next time I buy a smart phone, I ensure I get a great camera in it. Big Thank you to Samsung for this lovely opportunity & fantastic memories!
>
> *(Mayukh, Deccan Chronicle)*

> The Samsung Photowalk was a really nice initiative. As a reviewer we learned a lot with regards to smart phone cameras & their usage, abilities, etc. It was informative and fun.
>
> *(Anirban, IANS).*

At the center of this type of public relations program is collaboration with those persons that are regularly writing content on various social media and digital media, and who have built up a loyal following among potential buyers. Figure 9.1 shows profiles of those participants on the Samsung photowalk.

The photowalk campaign resulted in 19 published articles, 715 mentions on social media, a total social reach of 538,782, and total impressions of 42,308,081.

Most of the participants used social media as a storytelling platform, where they not only talked about the photowalk hosted by Samsung, but also talked about various features of the Samsung Galaxy S6 edge. They used Twitter and Instagram to showcase the individual stories which focused on various features of the camera.

| Participant | Facebook Friends | Twitter Followers | Instagram Followers |
|---|---|---|---|
| S. Aadeetya | 368 | 143 | |
| Siddhartha Sharma | 1926 | 2291 | 531 |
| Anirban Ghoshal | 171 | 47 | |
| Kunal Khullar | 596 | 393 | 326 |
| Ankit Gupta | 673 | 139 | |
| Pranay Parab | 340 | 412 | |
| Ankit Tuteja | 352 | 739 | 115 |
| Mayukh Mukherjee | 731 | 47 | |
| Ashwin Rajagapalan | 1650 | 372 | 558 |
| Aditya Nair | 433 | 116 | 411 |
| Ankur Sharma | 729 | 5342 | 228 |
| Saurabh Saggi | 562 | 5816 | |

**FIGURE 9.1**  Social media results for Galaxy S6 Smartphone campaign by participant

And, Facebook was used as a storytelling platform, where journalists shared their experiences of the photowalk and the entire journey.

Through the Facebook platform a total reach of 71,649 was obtained, which resulted in impressions of 932,894. In the case of Twitter, tweets from all photowalk participants resulted in 1,428,342 impressions. Instagram was used as a tool to showcase individual stories, resulting in a reach of 23,355, which generated 496,290 impressions.

Samsung's public relations program, using digital media and social media, created engagement with target customers as detailed in Figure 9.2, and resulted in record breaking sales for the company and changed the way smartphone devices were talked about in India. For this innovative campaign, IPRA (International Public Relations Association) gave the 2016 Golden World Award in the category for Digital Media Relations – Agency (Shandwick, Samsung and the PR Agency of Weber, n.d.).

## 3  Net Relations: twin axes of communications and technology

It is growing increasingly important to build a PR strategy on the twin axes of communication and the various new technologies, especially social media. In fact, this is so important that the practice of public relations through the technology of the Internet has come to be known as "Net Relations." It seems no exaggeration to say as Shel Holtz has put it: "the internet represents one of the most significant tools ever employed in the practice of public relations" (Holtz, 2002, p. ix). And, since public relations is about relationship management, it is insufficient for an organization to

| Digital Media Reached by Samsung Photo-walk for Galaxy S6 edge Phone | Article Impressions | Average Monthly visits | Key Highlights of Articles and Postings |
|---|---|---|---|
| the quint | 80,370 | 535,800 | 'Nothing illustrates the sheer quality of phone cameras more than the Samsung Galaxy S6 edge' |
| NDTV Gadgets | 5,994,150 | 39,961,000 | 'Today's flagship smartphones can create stunning images' |
| BETA IBN Live | 392,325 | 2,615,500 | 'A lot have been said and written about the Samsung Galaxy S6's camera, but the results should speak for themselves' |
| dna (Digital News Asia) | 1,143,285 | 7,621,900 | 'Samsung's Galaxy S6 edge (and the edge) ticks off some important boxes for a mobile shooter at a time when mobile shooters look set to eclipse the conventional point and shoot camera. Low-light results are impressive while some of the colours are vivid' |
| IANS live | 22,875 | 152,500 | 'The Samsung Galaxy S6 edge's image quality is best among smartphones.' |
| hindustantimes | 1,770,450 | 11,803,000 | 'The technology behind Samsung Galaxy S6 edge's camera is cutting edge.' |
| Business Standard | 981,375 | 6,542,500 | 'The video camera supports 4k video…' |
| The HINDU | 2,340,000 | 15,000,000 | 'The Galaxy S6 edge captures good detail in all light conditions, colour and white balance are reliable and the AF works swiftly.' |
| YAHOO! News India | 14,710,790 | 1,471,079,000 | 'Samsung had touted that it had come up with a camera unit that it was putting into the S6 series that would be second to none. Sounds familiar? Something that every phone company says nowadays with every launch? Well, Samsung was not kidding at all.' |
| zeenews india | 2,093,550 | 13,957,000 | 'The combo of a premium wide-angle 16MP shooter and a front wide-angle 5MP camera makes it a must-have device if the user is a photography or selfie lover.' |
| FIRSTPOST TECH2 | 1,881,150 | 12,541,000 | 'The camera is constantly in stand-by mode, which means it can be launched under a second by double-clicking the home button.' |
| THE NEW INDIAN EXPRESS | 430,380 | 2,869,200 | 'The edge offers a range of filter effects that can be accessed straight from the main screen and are applied to the full-size image.' |
| INDIA TV | 390,795 | 2,605,300 | 'The technology behind the camera is cutting edge. The combo of a premium wide-angle 16MP shooter and a front wide-angle 5MP camera makes it a must-have device if the user is a photography or selfie lover.' |
| THE STATESMAN | 65,790 | 4,380,600 | 'The Galaxy S6 edge performs well across all video modes. Detail, exposure and white balance are good. On the downside, "rolling shutter" effect is noticeable and under artificial light colour casts can occur although down to a near minimum.' |
| NEWSX | 42,270 | 281,800 | 'The Galaxy S6 edge performed well and with a score of 86 points, is the new number one in the DxOMark smartphone rankings, relegating its stable-mate Galaxy Note 4 and the iPhone 6 Plus to the number two and three spots respectively.' |
| EENADU INDIA | 49,005 | 3,260,700 | 'The South Korean handset-maker has also upped the tech behind its front 5MP shooter. The camera has 43 percent larger pixels than the S5 along with real-time HDR and multiframe low light modes.' |
| Tamilnadu | 104,400 | 6,960,000 | 'Samsung had touted…a camera unit…that would be second to none…Well, Samsung was not kidding at all.' |
| newKerala.com | 49,050 | 3,270,000 | 'The Galaxy S6 edge's image quality is best among smartphones. Be it any light condition the F1.9-lens produces sharp images in good detail in bright light.' |
| Sakshipost | 67,995 | 4,530,300 | 'The gallery app is a breath of fresh air. Images can be viewed by albums or date and you can filter to show people images or documents only. There is also a good range of editing options.' |
| | 32,610,005 | 1,609,967,100 | |

**FIGURE 9.2**   Social media results for Galaxy S6 Smartphone campaign by digital media reached

only post information it wants to communicate to its stakeholders via its own website. Net Relations is about using the Internet to engage stakeholders by obtaining their active participation through a company's website and social media. In many cases, people can freely comment on the information posted by an organization on Facebook or Twitter and thereby two-way communication in real-time is created, which dramatically shrinks the distance between an organization and its publics.

But, it is not the case that the rise of social media has caused the importance of company websites to decline. On the contrary, it would seem no exaggeration to say that it has caused them to become even more important. There has been absolutely no change to the fact that for companies, their website is still the basis for sending out information and that they continue to be a place for the comprehensive presentation of information.

Websites do not only communicate facts, such as news and financial information, they are also a venue for brand communication that expresses, for example, a company's corporate culture and values. Considering that in the future the mutually complementary relations between websites, social media sites, and their functions will grow even deeper, we can say that companies will need to implement a myriad of measures to succeed in Net Relations.

## 4 Understanding the Internet in human terms

### The Internet has changed the way people take action

The Internet environment, where people regularly carry around various devices to stay engaged with online content, is causing changes in human behavior in the way people take action.

### 1) From the AIDMA Law to the AISCEAS Law

Previously, the consumer psychological process was considered to follow the steps of the AIDMA process. That is to say, the act of purchasing followed the steps of: (1) Attention, (2) Interest, (3) Desire, (4) Memory, and (5) Action (purchase). However, this model was advocated by Samuel Roland Hall in the 1920s, which is nearly 100 years ago, so to reflect today's Internet society the AISCEAS concept was created which, while inheriting the steps of AIDMA, further develops the model.

### 2) AISCEAS Law

AISCEAS refers to the series of steps until a person makes a purchase, which are: (1) Attention, (2) Interest, (3) Search, (4) Comparison, (5) Examination, (6) Action (purchase), and (7) Share (sharing information). And this process has been accepted, particularly in web marketing (Senden Kaigi, 2005).

Once a present-day consumer becomes interested in a product, they do not remember it (memory in AIDMA), but instead tend to quickly search for it online using a search engine. For example, when their home vacuum cleaner is broken and they have decided to buy a new one, the steps a consumer goes through are as follows:

- The vacuum cleaner I use is broken: Attention
- I want to buy a new vacuum cleaner: Interest

## AIDMA Processes

## AISCEAS Processes

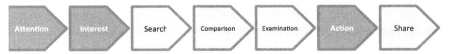

**FIGURE 9.3**   Processes in the AIDMA and AISCEAS consumer purchasing models
*Source:* Created based on "SENDEN KAIGI" May 1, 2005.

- I will search on the Internet for the types of vacuum cleaner available: Search
- I will compare the vacuum cleaners of various manufacturers to see which is the best: Comparison
- From the result of the comparison, I have decided on the vacuum cleaner of Company A: Examination
- I will buy Company A's vacuum cleaner: Action (purchasing behavior)
- After using it, I have found the vacuum cleaner to be very good, so I will share this information with everyone on the Internet: Share (sharing information)

As can be understood from looking at the steps in this AISCEAS sequence shown in Figure 9.3, it can be said that people today have the strong tendency to search for information before they act, whether that be buying a product, eating at a restaurant, or going on holiday, and then, after the action, they share information on their purchasing experience with others.

### Hierarchy of human needs and the rise of social media

The famous American psychologist Abraham Maslow analyzed human needs by dividing them into five hierarchies (Figure 9.4). According to Maslow, human needs start with physiological needs, then move onto the need for physical safety, and finally reach the need for self-actualization: physiological needs, need for safety, need for belonging and love, need for recognition (esteem), need for self-actualization. In other words, the needs rise up from physiological needs to psychological needs. The first basic physiological need is to eat and drink, followed by the need for physical safety, then the need to belong to a community and to be loved, then the need to have one's worth recognized, and finally rising to the need to realize the goal for oneself in the future is to realize one's full potential (Maslow, 1943, pp. 370–396).

Today, using social media, we can share information, connect with people, be recognized, and furthermore utilize these processes toward achieving self-actualization.

**FIGURE 9.4**   Maslow's hierarchy of needs

*Source:* Takashi Inoue (2015), *Public Relations: Relationship Management*, 2nd Edition, p. 246

In other words, we might say that we use social media as an aid toward satisfying our basic human needs.

## Social media networks

The structure of social media is that it connects one individual to other individuals over the Internet and that these connections are developed without limit. So essentially, how do the people who constitute social media connect over the Internet? According to the view of David Easley and Jon Kleinberg of Cornell University (Easley & Kleinberg, 2010, pp. 43–45) within a social network, it is highly likely that two people with a common friend will become friends in the future. This phenomenon of an expanding network of friendship-based relationships on social media is known as "triadic closure."

The first diagram (#1) within Figure 9.5 expresses the connections in a network between person A, person B, person C, up to person G. But, these connections are not static and will increase, as we see in the second diagram (#2) a thick line has been added between person B and person C. This expresses that a new connection has been created between person B and person C, who have person A as a common friend. When the connection is made between person A, person B, and person C, the network structure expands. The term "triadic closure" signifies that an edge is created between person B and person C when B and C connect as friends. With the edge formed between B and C there is triadic closure and a triangle is created. In this way, on the network it is highly likely that person B will be connected to person C via their common friend person A.

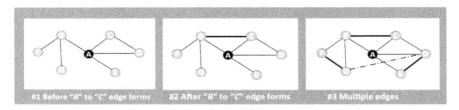

**FIGURE 9.5** Human relations on social media (principle of triadic closure)

However, as more time passes more connections are formed and, as we can see represented in the third diagram (#3) in Figure 9.5, new edges are created. This third diagram shows new edges of a triadic closure have been formed between person G and person F, and between E and D. Moreover, an edge has also been formed between person D and person G, who do not directly have a common acquaintance. In this way, on a social network we see that the network expands in multiple directions based on its members' common friends. So when public relations practitioners are deciding on a Net Relations strategy, they must keep in mind that information connects in this form on social media and is communicated between members who have similar attributes.

### *"Texture of a life lived": social media and the brain*

To further understand the phenomenal rise of social media and social networks, and moreover, to understand its continuous evolution, it helps to look at it in terms of how the brain works. Dr. Daniel Siegel, a clinical professor of psychiatry at the UCLA School of Medicine and Executive Director of the Mindsight Institute (Siegel, 2015), explains that man as a social creature needs to interact socially and to form deep relationships and does so primarily through the right side of the brain, which is the part of the brain that controls emotions.

When we interact socially the brain is presented with a combination of verbal and non-verbal signals. The left hemisphere processes verbal signals, while the right hemisphere processes the non-verbal signals and it is the right side of the brain that controls our physical emotions. He has categorized the non-verbal information that is communicated in face-to-face interactions between people into seven signals:

- Eye contact,
- Facial expressions,
- Body gestures,
- Tone of voice,
- Posture,
- Timing of what is done,
- Intensity in which it is done.

Dr. Siegel explains that the problem with things like emails and written content on a website or in a blog is that they lack non-verbal signals. In contrast, social media contains pictures and videos which give us some of that missing non-verbal information that as humans we hunger for, and it is those non-verbal signals that give us, as Dr. Siegel describes so well, a sense of "the texture of a life lived."

Although social media lacks the fullness of non-verbal signals that come from face-to-face communication with people, and although the number of social media contacts a person has may reach hundreds, and the number of followers can reach from tens of thousands to millions, it is no substitute for real friendship, although in a digitally connected world social media can be said to be the next best thing. As a result, we can expect to see the content of social media increasingly becoming dominated by pictures and video, which are rich in non-verbal and right-hemisphere, brain-processing signals. And, not surprising, video streaming is becoming the new norm, with "Facebook Live" starting in 2016 and "YouTube TV" starting in 2017.

## 5  Engaging stakeholders through social media

Since the brain is the main social organ of the human body that allows us to participate in culture and social interaction with other people, and since it is designed for engagement with the world outside of the body, we hunger for that engagement. Part of social media's phenomenal popularity comes from how it engages us. Social media succeeds by being the best at engaging people in the digital world of the Internet. Since public relations involves engaging stakeholders through two-way communications, social media is becoming a primary tool of public relations as illustrated in the case study showing the successful introduction of the Samsung Galaxy S6 edge via a social media campaign.

### *Engaging customers in brand management*

While companies have used social media accounts to bring product messages to the general public for a long time, a new trend is for companies to engage customers in their brands by getting customers, especially fans, to post their own content showing and talking about the company's products. Lego, the toy maker, has a Twitter account with over 400,000 followers, where customers are encouraged to upload photo and video content showing their own Lego creations. Mymuesli, which is a German cereal company that follows a mass customization model that allows customers to order their own unique mix of organic muesli from over 80 different ingredients, is using Twitter, Facebook, YouTube, and Instagram accounts to allow customers, who are also enthusiastic fans of the company's brand, to share content about their own special mix of flavors, explain how they cook with it, and even about how the empty package containers can be used for arts-and-crafts projects. Another example is the U.S. clothing company for young fashion-conscious women called Free People, which uses Facebook, Twitter, Flickr, YouTube, Vimeo, Pinterest, Tumblr, Rdio, and Google+ to engage customer/fans. Free People's YouTube channel at the beginning of 2017 had over 49,000 subscribers and 4.9 million views. They sell to customers in over 100 countries via the Internet. The clothing retailer engages customers by getting them to upload pictures of themselves wearing their Free People clothing and by encouraging others to rate the uploaded content.

These three cases are examples of companies using social media engagement as a strategy to build brand affinity and brand loyalty, and to leverage the networks of enthusiastic customers. Moreover, these customers/fans provide valuable insight for new product creation, because some individuals post pictures and comments about their use of the product or what they want the product to become, others will rate and comment on that content. This lets customers participate in a company's product development process in a meaningful way.

## Transformation of customer service through social media engagement

Great customer service is needed for successful businesses, and social media "tweets" provide a powerful way to receive and answer customer problems and inquiries without being put "on-hold" or asking them to wait for an email response. Moreover, when a problem is successfully resolved the tweet is public knowledge, which demonstrates to the wider public a company's commitment to helping customers. One city water department in the U.S., for example, uses Twitter to allow residents to quickly tweet about water leaks and problems. The Royal Dutch Airlines (KLM) uses their Twitter account to handle customer service inquiries. On top of their Twitter page the number of minutes that they expect to reply in is prominently displayed and updated every 5 minutes.

## 6 Social media monitoring

To effectively and efficiently monitor social media, it is necessary to use special social media monitoring software tools because of the large number of sites and the billions of social media participants. Social media monitoring tools are used for the following kinds of needs and activities:

- Automated posting of content,
- Deliver easy-to-read results in one page or dashboard,
- Find and monitor influencers,
- Identify audiences,
- Engage in conversations with most engaged customers about your product,
- Keyword search/monitoring,
- Rank content and trends,
- Campaign tracking,
- Collect relevant conversations,
- Market research,
- Engage your detractors and evangelists,

- Boosting brand advocacy,
- Traditional and digital media coverage,
- Media monitoring,
- Monitor results of PR,
- Track media coverage,
- Automated daily reports,
- Benchmark against competitors.

## 7 Strategic PR and Net Relations

Just as with traditional media activities, public relations via the Internet is fundamentally strategic in nature. Given the nature of social media in terms of instant communications, big data size volumes of messages and ease of access by anyone, everyone, and anywhere, it is easy for corporations to get caught up in ad-hoc responses. But, to be effective PR must be strategic. If a strategy is not clearly formulated in Net Relations, then contradictions will occur with activities carried out in real-time and the message may not be communicated to the target audiences or may be misunderstood. Based on this characteristic, above all, speed is first required for Net Relations. Indeed, this acceleration of communications created by the Internet is a leading characteristic of hyper-globalization. And, for that reason upon establishing a PR strategy, selecting an effective action plan based on this strategy is demanded more than in other fields.

### *Importance of storytelling in social media*

Content is most important to build good relationships with stakeholders on the web and on social media. As information on the Net has expanded in recent years, search engine optimization (SEO) has become important to displaying an organization's content at the top of the results by a user's browser. But, while these sorts of techniques are important, what is more important is the content itself.

It is essential that the content does not simply list information about the product, but that it tells a story. In other words, it is important to tell a story that enables the consumer to clearly imagine how their lives will improve once they acquire and use this product. This is because the information-receiver side finds it is easier to accept and to listen to information sent in the form of a story.

According to a survey by the National Center for Biotechnology Information in the United States, the average number of seconds for our psychological attention span fell from 13 seconds in 2000 to eight seconds in 2013. As the attention span of a goldfish is nine seconds, people living in the present day have a shorter attention span than goldfish. The average time spent watching a video on the Internet is 2.7 minutes. Slightly less than 20% of website visitors leave that website within four seconds and only 4% stay on a website for ten minutes or more (National Center for Biotechnology Information; U.S. National Library of Medicine, 2016). In the context of this acceleration of the reduction in the time people spend on gathering information, the importance of content is rising more than ever.

Content that uses storytelling can be expected to attract the interest of the web-page visitor and to greatly increase the time they spend on that webpage. Of course the content presented in websites needs to tell stories to be effective by keeping the attention of those accessing the site, but storytelling also needs to be made in the more traditional sense of the word, where someone is vocally telling a story. Steve Jobs of Apple had that gift as well as many of the other more successful global leaders. And, although some people seem to have that skill as a natural talent, it can be learned. In response to a question about the advice to be given to a promising executive about learning public relations and stakeholder relationship management, Carlos Ghosn responded as follows:

> I would say this: You are not born with the skill to connect with people. You develop it, through training and experience. You are going to start very low. When I was young and starting in my career, I gave boring speeches. How did I know? Because people were sleeping!
>
> If you want to connect with people, you need to work on it. You need to recognize when you are boring, or when you're not making sense. If you hide from it, or deny it, you will never grow. You have to ask what you can do better, and find role models to learn from. Business experience is the best training.
>
> You also need to speak plainly, using facts and objective data. This is cru-cial because it forces you to stick to reality, and it helps build trust and strengthen performance. Finally, in a complex environment, if you wish to be heard and listened to, you need to seek simplicity, and express your ideas concisely.
>
> *(Ghosn, 2017)*

## Brand journalism

"Brand journalism" was one of the keywords heard at the annual meeting of the Public Relations Society of America held in Washington D.C. in October 2014 (Inoue, 2015, p. 248). A characteristic of brand journalism is to try to win the trust of the general public and consumers by providing fair and unbiased information. Rather than following the usual practice of simply announcing new products and giving a list of facts and product features, in brand journalism companies hire free-lance journalists or build up a planning and editing function to create and distribute journalism-like content that combines objectivity and storytelling.

Moreover, successful brand journalism creates content that tells stories, con-necting a brand to the lives of customers, and communicates a sense that the brand cares about customers in a personal way. A good example can be found on Nissan Motor's website which has a report dated October 26, 2016 that is titled "Gain-ing Customers' Satisfaction and Trust with Quality" (Nissan Motor Corporation, 2016). At the top of this webpage is an embedded video, in which a Japanese executive of Nissan talks about the company's view of quality and protecting the safety of their customers. Below the video is text content in a magazine-like layout that gives the impression of something from news journalism. From this example of Net Relations content, one gets the message that Nissan cares about the safety and enjoyment of its customers, and more than just all customers, the message is that it cares about "you" as an individual. Viewers are also given a chance to engage in the "conversation" by posting their "likes" and "dislikes" and comments. Typical of two-way communications, the company cannot control what is said and not all comments will be favorable, as some will post comments such as "I am disappointed in the quality of your cars" or "I love this car, when will you ship it to Italy so I can buy it here."

In this way, brand journalism is an important part of Net Relations as a means of effective stakeholder relationship management that engages customers. Traditionally, one of the important missions of PR has been to effectively get journalists in the mass media to write articles about client companies, but increasingly in the future brand journalism via the Internet will be used in PR to directly send information to the general public and consumers.

## Access analysis

As Net Relations are mainly carried out online on webpages and social media, using access analysis for the results of the implementation of a PR program makes it possible to conduct a rapid and quantitative analysis. In turn, this enables flexible self-correction to be carried out in response to a rapidly changing external environment. For example, if the PR program results are not what was initially expected, it is possible to respond flexibly by conducting access analysis, objectively ascertaining the preferences of the target users that are obtainable at that point in time, and changing the content and the message to reflect these preferences.

The digital and online nature of the Internet means that user access information can also be analyzed and verified in practically real-time. Therefore, public relations practitioners can respond speedily, while reading which way the tide is turning, and indeed they must have this sort of ability to respond.

What is vital to carry out relationship management in public relations is of course, communication with people. Next, from among the many case studies of companies that built excellent communication with stakeholders by using the Net, we will look at two success case studies, one of which was a positive campaign and one of which was a response to a complaint.

## 8 Case study: United States Subaru, CSR, "Share the Love" campaign

In 2008, Subaru of America, the automotive company, deployed a "Share the Love" campaign (Kotler *et al.*, 2012, pp. 98–101). In this campaign, people who have bought a new car or leased a car from Subaru can select one organization from among many non-profit organizations in the United States, and Subaru donates USD $250 to that organization, with the campaign mainly being carried out at the end of the year.

In 2008, the results of conducting this campaign were that the sales increased during the campaign period at a rate of 16.3% (compared to a sales increase rate of 5.3% for the industry), and furthermore 35% of people who bought a new Subaru car came to recognize that they preferred the Subaru brand, indicating it had a positive effect on purchases and consumers.

In addition, in 2011 and 2012 Subaru started to use Facebook for the same campaign. It held a vote on Facebook for the selection of one group out of four charitable organizations: the American Red Cross, Teach for America, the Make a Wish Foundation, and the Children's Miracle Network. To spread the benefits as much as possible to all the organizations in the vote, Subaru created a mechanism that it would donate 10 cents to the respective organization each time it was voted for in the first 200,000 votes.

In that year, the voters most highly evaluated the charitable activities of the Make a Wish Foundation, which received one third of the total of 133,068 votes, and it received one part of the donation of several million dollars that was collected in the Share the Love campaign.

Because of this campaign, the number of "likes" on Subaru's Facebook page more than doubled, from 79,796 to 181,164. This may be indicating that many more consumers liked Subaru and so clicked the like button, contributing to an improvement in its brand image. Also, unlike conventional media, another advantage of social media is that the response to a campaign is easier to quantify and so the impact of the campaign is easier to evaluate.

It is considered that Subaru could skillfully utilize the features of social media for its CSR and externally build excellent relations with its stakeholders, whilst internally helping to improve the level of employee satisfaction (ES).

## 9 Case study: Tirol-Choco Co., Ltd., "Quick and precise handling of a complaint"

At 1 p.m. on June 11, 2013, a Twitter user commented: "I found a caterpillar in my chocolate" and "I can't believe it." The person also uploaded photographs as evidence (Inoue, 2015, pp. 247–248). This was a tweet by a consumer complaining that, when opening up the package of a well-known chocolate brand Hitokuchi Choco (this brand name means in Japanese "one-bite chocolate"), they found an insect inside.

About 30 minutes after the tweet, one after another, customers complained to Tirol-Choco, and furthermore there was an increase in comments posted on Twitter criticizing the company. In an instant, the tweet complaining about finding an insect in the chocolate had been retweeted more than 1,000 times. One hour after the complaint tweet, the photograph of the insect inside the chocolate started to spread across the Internet and the situation was starting to explode.

Meanwhile at Tirol-Choco, the managers attempted to ascertain the current situation and they understood from the photograph of the chocolate that it had been manufactured half a year previously. They requested a specialist analyze the insect, who reached the objective conclusion that it was not possible for this insect to have entered the chocolate during the manufacturing process.

In other words, from the photograph it was judged that, from the size of the insect, it was no more than 30 or 40 days old, but the relevant chocolate had been manufactured six months previously. From this it was understood that the insect had entered the chocolate after it was manufactured and packaged.

Meanwhile, the Chocolate and Cocoa Association of Japan state that insects can easily become affixed to chocolate and that in many cases insects invade chocolate in the period from when it is shipped from the factory until when it is consumed in the home. It assures consumers that they will suffer no direct harm even supposing that they mistakenly eat an insect, but it recommends consulting with a doctor if they are worried.

On the same day, at 4 p.m., Tirol-Choco tweeted as its official opinion the results of its investigation and a link to the webpage of the Chocolate and Cocoa Association of Japan that explained how insects in the home could enter chocolate. This objective and calm tweet by Tirol-Choco succeeded in satisfying customers and dousing the flames of the controversy.

In this case, if the company had made a mistake in how it used social media and how it communicated its message, it might have further fanned the flames of the controversy and caused it to spread to the extent that the story would have been picked up by TV media, which has a greater reach to the general public than social media. However, in around three hours from the time the complaint tweet appeared, the company quickly sent out information on its analysis of the current situation and succeeded in preventing a crisis.

As can be understood from these case studies, the two-way communications impact of social media is extremely strong and immediate to a remarkable degree. Therefore, in Net Relations public relations practitioners must always pay attention to customers and other target audiences and respond rapidly to them.

## References

Easley, D. & Kleinberg, J. (2010). *Networks, Crowds, and Markets: Reasoning about a Highly Connected World.* Cambridge, UK: Cambridge University Press.

Ghosn, C. (2017). *Responses to Questionnaire "Public Relations for Hyper-globalization."* Yokohama: s.n.

Holtz, S. (2002). *Public Relations on the Internet: Winning Strategies to Inform and Influence.* 2nd ed. New York: AMACON.

Inoue, T. (2015). *Public Relations: Relationship Management.* 2nd ed. Tokyo: Nippon Hyoron Sha.

Kotler, P., Hessekiel, D., & Lee, N. (2012). *Good Works!: Marketing and Corporate Initiatives that Build a Better World ... and the Bottom Line.* New York: John Wiley & Sons, Inc.

Maslow, A. (1943). "A Theory of Human Motivation." *Psychological Review,* 50(4), pp. 370–396.

National Center for Biotechnology Information; U.S. National Library of Medicine (2016). "Attention Span Statistics." s.l.: The Associated Press.

Nissan Motor Corporation (2016). "Gaining Customers' Satisfaction and Trust with Quality." [Online] Available at: http://reports.nissan-global.com/EN/?p=17896 [Accessed July 22, 2017]

Senden Kaigi (2005). Issue, May 1, 2005. Tokyo: Sendenkaigi Co. Ltd.

Shandwick, Samsung, and the PR Agency of Weber (n.d.). "Samsung PhotoWalk: Creating a New Paradigm in the Way Mobile Devices are Seen PDF." [Online] Available at: https://www.ipra.org/shop/product/samsung-photowalk-creating-a-new-paradigm-in-the-way-mobile-devices-are-seen-pdf/ [Accessed January 15, 2017]

Siegel, D. D. (2015). "Dr. Daniel Siegel on How Tech Affects Your Brain and Relationships." *YouTube*, April 17, 2015. [Online] Available at: https://www.youtube.com/watch?v=31o_chpzQh8 [Accessed April 2, 2017]

# 10

# BEING ETHICAL AND SUCCESSFUL

## Development of the Self-Correction Model

## 1 Once upon a voyage

In April of the year 1912 the maiden voyage of the then largest steamship ever built carried 2,223 passengers and crew on a journey from the old world of Europe to the New World of America, traveling from Southampton, England to New York City on the White Star Line's newest ship, a ship built as a marvel of the advanced technology of the new 20th century. Millions of Europeans would cross the Atlantic by steamship to come to America filled with adventure and hope of starting a new life in the New World. The horror of World War I was still two years away. Unfortunately, for these hope-filled passengers the name of the ship they traveled on was the RMS Titanic, which would hit an iceberg in the North Atlantic four days into its crossing. Over 1,500 people would die as the ship sank into the freezing waters of the Atlantic Ocean at 2:20 a.m. on April 15.

The sinking of the RMS Titanic has been romanticized in books, movies, and songs. The surrounding facts and myths include such things as the rivets used to assemble the ship being less than top quality, a fire in coal bunker number six continued to burn out of control (Pells, 2008), the crew did not give iceberg warnings to the captain in order to not disturb his sleep, the ship's lookout did not use binoculars that were locked away (Tibbetts, 2007), the ship ran too fast for waters known for icebergs, and lifeboats were only partially filled (Louden-Brown *et al.*, n.d.). Several sources have stated that John Pierpont Morgan, the famous American banker of the period who controlled the holding company that owned the White Star Line, had been booked to ride on the historic maiden voyage of the Titanic (The Editors of Encyclopedia Britannica, n.d.). Although it cannot be confirmed, one account claimed that the banker actually went on board the ship before its departure for New York, but got off when informed of the coal fire, and understanding the seriousness of the fire ordered the ship to sail at top speed in order to put out the fire when reaching New York.

A hundred years have now past since the Titanic sank and it is difficult to sort out fact from fiction about what actually happened, but if only half of the accounts are true, then we can say that the White Star Line might have done a far better job building, testing, outfitting, training the crew, and managing the ship's operation, and might also have delayed the maiden voyage, but management kept to the original departure date. This all occurred at the beginning of the 20th century, and we should stop to remember this historic tragedy and reflect on our own need to build ethics-based self-correction into every aspect of our organizations as we begin our own journey into the 21st century.

## 2 When the obvious becomes invisible

The three concepts of "self-correction," "ethics," and "two-way communications" are in many ways so obvious in meaning and importance that they can easily be overlooked. This is especially true for leaders of any organization, society, or nation too focused on self-interest and materialism. Consequently, companies currently struggling to survive the scandals that surround them are in that sad situation because they showed a lack of true concern for stakeholders, and created or simply failed to correct corporate cultures that lacked an ethical sense and they discouraged two-way communications. In order to have an effective self-correction function you need both the ethical sense and the free flow of two-way communications.

This is particularly tragic, because a self-correction system is a powerful tool by which an organization can succeed, and is not solely a means to avoid or survive a crisis. At the heart of a functioning self-correction system is the ability to direct an organization toward achieving goals and creating new value for the stakeholders it exists to serve. Senior managers of organizations need to understand that to benefit from the power of self-correction they must make it visible and obvious by building it into their organization as an integral and indispensable part of everything it does.

It is not enough to superficially put the word "ethics" in a mission statement, or to just have a code of ethics without embedding it into the activities of the organization. Companies like Toshiba and TEPCO, which were once pillars of Japanese industry, have experienced devastating scandals, but they will only survive, if they can remove their blinders and begin to transform into organizations seeking the greater good of all stakeholders and systematically build into their organizations ethics, the free flow of two-way communications, and self-correction.

## 3 Embedding ethics into the DNA of the organization

This may seem all too academic and all too idealistic. After all, don't companies exist first and foremost to make profits? Well, shareholders are also stakeholders, but for years many Japanese companies have not delivered on the promise of profits, almost as if that was not their major goal. When Carlos Ghosn of Nissan came to Japan to take control of that global automaker, it had very good engineers, world-class factories, and the kind of high quality that makes Japanese companies an example of manufacturing excellence for the world, but it was unprofitable and in desperate need of a turn-around.

The Nissan Revival Plan has now gone down in history as one of those great successes that were achieved not only quickly, but ahead of schedule. Most people are aware of how Carlos Ghosn closed factories in Japan, cut costs, and reorganized the management structure. But, what not enough people understand is that he also made a very determined and successful effort to instill ethics, two-way communications, and self-correction into the entire global enterprise of Nissan. In answer to a question used as part of the research for this book about how to make ethics just as much a part of the DNA of an organization as Nissan's own commitment to quality, Carlos Ghosn responded:

> Quality is a matter of ethics. It's about being true to your customers, employees, and stakeholders, and delivering on your promises as a company. This, as you say, is truly embedded into the very DNA of Nissan.
>
> But you need to make the commitment explicit as well as implicit. When I arrived, we created a global code of conduct that the entire Nissan community could embrace, divided into five mindsets and five actions, called 'The Nissan Way.' All employees are trained on how to reflect this conduct in their daily activities, and they are expected to demonstrate these capabilities as part of how their performance is measured. It starts with good management at the top, and a culture where employees can freely communicate concerns without retribution. And you need to reward those who embody the values of the company (Ghosn, 2017).

For organizations to succeed in this age of hyper-globalization, where stakeholders are becoming more globalized, and also where instantaneous and global communications make a crisis more likely to happen and more difficult to manage, it is essential that ethics, two-way communications, and self-correction be built into a company's DNA. An organization that is truly guided by ethical self-correction will not only be more likely to avoid scandals, and be better prepared to survive a crisis, but will also be more successful in achieving its goals efficiently and quickly through stronger stakeholder relationships with employees, investors, suppliers, and customers.

In the end, perhaps "delivering on your promises as a company" is the best way to explain the Self-Correction Model (SCM) that was developed for public relations, which has been built into the PR Life-Cycle Model, and which is presented here as a general model to inspire and guide you to implement a functioning self-correction system in your own organization.

## 4 Conceptual framework of the Self-Correction Model

### *Self-correction and public relations as a symbiotic model*

In biology the term "symbiotic" explains how two different species can have a long-term close relationship for mutual benefit. A well-known example is that of small pilot fish feeding on parasites living on the sharks that they swim with. In that sense, public relations, which is relationship management, is the recognition of the symbiotic relationship of an organization with stakeholders. This also includes employees that consist of engineers, researchers, designers, marketing, salespeople, and other professionals who have different outlooks and skills, but who need to work in close collaboration. In other words, public relations is the explicit recognition that an organization will only achieve goals by working with others for mutual benefit.

The Self-Correction Model of public relations allows an organization to continually make self-corrections in response to external and internal changes, allowing it to prosper by providing mutual benefit in a symbiotic relationship with stakeholders.

## *Learning from nature*

When we search for the roots of this new Self-Correction Model, we can go all the way back to Walter Bradford Cannon in the 1930s. Cannon was a physiologist at Harvard University in the U.S., where they first introduced the use of X-rays in the medical field. Cannon is also known for advancing the concept of homeostasis, which is the auto-regulation in living organisms. He further noted the relationship between homeostasis in living organisms and in society, and he thought that research on homeostasis in living organisms could be applied to research on stabilization of components of social organizations as well (Cannon, 1932/1959, pp. 213–228).

The concept of homeostasis, which Cannon formulated, opened up a variety of research paths in social sciences in later years, and was researched in many different fields besides physiology, including sociology, economics, and political science. For example, Norbert Wiener, who was a professor of mathematics at MIT, added to Cannon's concept of homeostasis the element of feedback and theorized the concept of self-control in response to changes in the external world. The combination of Cannon's homeostasis model and the inclusion of feedback by Wiener are represented graphically in Figure 10.1. It was this drawing, in which this author put "self-adjustment" in the center surrounded by feedback, that led to the development of the Self-Correction Model (SCM), where "self-adjustment" is replaced with "self-correction." Although this might seem like a minor change, it actually is an important fundamental change. More than simply "adjusting" to external stimuli, human beings have the free-will and ethical sense to make moral judgments about the different possible actions that might be taken.

The public relations scholar, Scott Cutlip, brought the biological concept of dealing with a continually changing environment into public relations, describing it as being PR's essence. In the first edition of *Effective Public Relations* (1952) Cutlip and Center stipulated that "organizations must make adjustments to benefit all interested parties in response to changes," and described this as an essential characteristic of public relations (Cutlip & Center, 1952, p. 19). Learning from advances in biology, Cutlip applied Cannon's concept of homeostasis to a public relations that adjusts in order to adapt to a changing external world.

# External environment

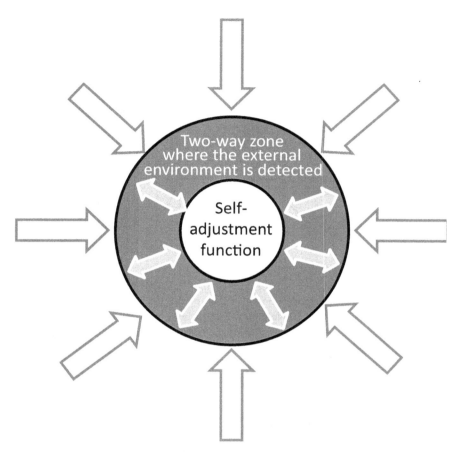

**FIGURE 10.1**   Cannon–Wiener self–adjustment model

*Source:* Takashi Inoue (2015), *Public Relations: Relationship Management*, 2nd edition, p. 259

## *Integration of three elements of the SCM*

The SCM, which was presented for the first time in the academic theory of public relations by the author in English in 2002 (Inoue, 2002, pp. 24–27), integrates the three elements of "ethics," "two-way communications," and "self-correction." In order to implement self-correction it is necessary to constantly work at keeping the "ethical sense" active within individuals and organizations. Also, it is important to then understand your own situation as well as that of other parties. Responses and reactions from the surrounding stakeholders are important in order for individuals and organizations to build effective relations with third parties.

The elements of ethics, two-way communications, and self-correction that form the Self-Correction Model have an interdependent relationship, so that only when these

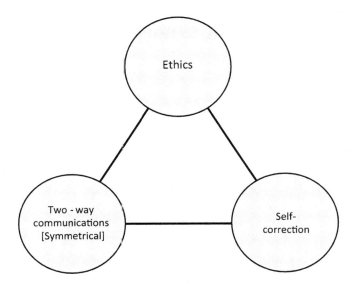

**FIGURE 10.2**  Self-Correction Model's three elements

*Source:* Takashi Inoue (2015), *Public Relations: Relationship Management*, 2nd edition, p. 260

three elements are integrated, as shown in Figure 10.2, do they begin to be effective. No matter how you try to implement self-correction, if you do not have two-way communications with the other party, then you will fall into a relationship where each party is only insisting on their own position. And, corrections that lack ethics can't be directed with complete certainty in a good direction. It is only possible to always move in the correct direction, when using self-correction utilizing ethics as your compass, because only then is it possible to arrive with certainty at your intended destination.

After setting your goals and objectives, feedback from other parties as well as various changes in the external environment can show you where important correction needs to be made. Moreover, from that same feedback an organization may determine that while its goals are fine, it must make fundamental self-corrections in its actions or tactics in order to achieve those goals.

Establishing public relations that possess an ethical sense requires a variety of two-way viewpoints. A global environment demands diversity and requires people that are fully capable of understanding others, while at the same time asserting their own position. The integration of the three SCM elements makes possible a mutual win–win relationship with stakeholders, which is the kind of public relations needed for this 21st century that is ever growing in global complexity.

## 1) Ethics and free-will

The effects of "stimulus and response" from the previously mentioned homeostasis concept of Cannon's belong to the scientific understanding of biological responses to environment changes, but although humans are biological creatures, we must look at self-correction from the perspective that individuals do more than just respond to stimulus. A human being is neither a single cell organism, nor just another creature. A single cell organism has no choice but to respond in a predetermined way to external stimuli. And animals react to their environment without debating the morality of alternative courses of action. Individuals take action based on consideration of many factors and then freely making a decision of their own free-will, rather than reacting automatically without thought, without their own intention. What makes us special among all creation is our ability to make moral judgments about good and evil, which is to say we have a capacity for ethics, and also the freedom to choose.

Two-way communications provides vital information, but we can choose to ignore it. We are also free to choose between doing right or to follow our own self-interest over the common good. In other words, no matter the circumstance under which self-correction occurs, the corrective activity will always reflect one's free-will. In addition, self-correction as we use the term here, is not just an adjustment or change to match changes to external factors outside of ourselves, but is ultimately a deeper, substantial change to one's self. Organizations can successfully encourage their members to choose to act ethically, because it is a fundamental basic human need.

## Using ethics as a guide for keeping on the right course

An ethical sense in a symmetrical two-way communication environment is an important element within the Self-Correction Model, because it is necessary to know one's own position in the overall situation in order to make corrective action that follows a path that is morally good.

A simple way to understand how ethics functions in the model is to use the example where you want to physically travel to a certain destination. Even if you can measure in two-dimensional terms the relative distance to your intended destination, it is not enough, because you need a three-dimensional measure like a global positioning system (GPS) to truly understand where you yourself are (Figure 10.3). In the Self-Correction Model it is the ethical sense that equates to a GPS-like positioning system. Therefore, the ultimate center point or core of the model is the ethical sense, because it is based on solid principles that do not move, and thereby provide the standards needed for deciding the self-correction to achieve goals and objectives.

## 2) Self-correction

### Understanding the importance of "self" in self-correction

Self-correction has been discussed in general terms in economics, biology, education, computer science, and other fields. Norbert Wiener, wrote in his book *Cybernetics* that in order for individuals and organizations to function effectively, they must adjust themselves in a changing environment (Wiener, 1948). This also applies to public relations for achieving objectives through building and maintaining good relations with the public. American public relations experts say that

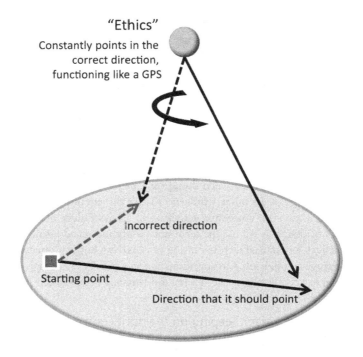

"Ethics"

Constantly points in the
correct direction,
functioning like a GPS

Incorrect direction

Starting point

Direction that it should point

**FIGURE 10.3**   Ethics at the core of self-correction

*Source:* Takashi Inoue (2015), *Public Relations: Relationship Management,* 2nd edition, p. 262

in most cases, where it is thought to be necessary, organizations do "change," "adjust," and "adapt" in response to feedback that results from two-way communications. However, scholars have not discussed in depth about the change and adjustment process, nor about how human free-will is involved. As explained previously, the uniqueness and power of the SCM that is presented in this book comes from adding the essential understanding of human free-will and the need for individuals to make changes to the "self."

Things and processes need to change, but they are changed by people who as human beings have an ethical sense of right and wrong. It should be noted that to make self-correction more accurate and effective requires a self-awareness by individuals that comes from a higher-order of thinking, in a thought process known in philosophy and physiology as "meta-cognition," by which we are able, as it were, to look upon and judge our thoughts from above or outside of ourselves. For things and processes to be corrected in the direction of ethics requires correction to the organization and its individual members, using our ability for meta-cognition. This is the understanding that has been left out by scholars in the past, but which is made a central part of the SCM. While the end result of correction will often be to change a product or service, the starting point is correcting one's self following the ethical sense. Unless the individuals that form an organization are able to make self-correction based on ethics, it is not reasonable to expect the organization to act ethically.

Each of us is an independent individual. First you have individual people, and secondarily relationships are formed between a person and other people. Each of us individually learns uneasiness, feeling peace of mind, and are healed within various interpersonal relationships with others in the external world. In other words, people should not be seen as constant and unchanging, but rather must be understood as changing beings dependent on relationships with others. Even while people exist as individuals, they change and grow within relationships (Nishikawa *et al.*, 1998, pp. 24–25). This way of thinking also applies to organizations.

Let's consider the meaning of one of the keywords in this subject, "self," which is recognized to be "the awareness of others at the same time one is aware of one's self in connection with others" (Wada, 2005, p. 11). The word "self" can be thought to refer to an extremely personal area, but in order for self-awareness to be formed and developed, connections to society, groups, and people play an important role (Nishikawa *et al.*, 1998, pp. 24–25). The *Merriam-Webster Dictionary* defines "correction" as "the act of making something (such as an error or a bad condition) accurate or better: the act of correcting something" (Merriam–Webster Dictionary, n.d.). According to a traditional Japanese dictionary (Kôjien, 1998), the word "correction" is defined as "to repair and correct something that is not good."

## Definition of self-correction for the SCM

For the SCM the term "self-correction" can be defined as a process whereby individuals or organizations freely choose to make internal correction in reaction to their own changing circumstances, using ethics as a guiding standard, in order to maintain stability and growth within an environment of relationships with others.

To "freely choose" means being able to choose or not to choose a given action. A legal requirement, for example, is involuntary change or correction that individuals or entities are simply forced to make, and not freely chosen. "Make internal correction" means changing one's self as a human being following the ethical sense. We define ourselves as an integral part of society "in order to maintain stability and growth within an environment of relationships" as part of our basic human need to be part of something greater than ourselves.

And of course, to make the choices that achieve such self-correction one must have two-way communication and be guided by ethics.

## Clarifying the meaning of self-correction

There are phenomena that are easily mistaken for self-correction. In order for action to be "self-correction" it must have the qualities of: (1) reacting to internal and external changes in the environment, (2) acting freely, and (3) following ethics to do "good" and in consideration of others.

Self-correction occurs when individuals and organizations in a changing environment act of their own free-will to correct what is not good. It is not action made because of being forced to react to outside pressure or threats in response to a crisis or a legal action. Moreover, it is important to keep in mind that even when changes are voluntarily made, but in the absence of ethics, then it is not self-correction, because it is necessary to have ethics in order to know which of many possible alternative actions is the "correct" or "good" action.

For example, it is not self-correction when one makes changes to a strategic plan without being guided by ethics. However, it would become self-correction, if the plan is implemented in order to avoid possible environmental problems, because then the action is guided by ethics in consideration for the benefit of stakeholders in the wider community.

## Need for continuous self-correction

Ordinarily, individuals or organizations are considered to have caused scandals when the scandals themselves are exposed. Crisis management does not occur as long as the scandals remain hidden. When information surfaces, in other words, when it is discovered by being pointed out from within or outside the organization, then the scandal is said to occur for the first time, and a crisis management situation then develops. However, actually, it is necessary to handle potential scandals that have happened when you become aware of them and before they become publicly acknowledged. If a scandal surfaces due to accusations from inside or outside the organization, or due to press reports, before they can be handled by responsible management, then the organization will face a worsening crisis.

Self-correction is a continuous process of making many corrections both small and large throughout the organization, and not just in times of crisis. Just as change for an individual only ends with death, so for an organization self-correction is a never-ending process of sustainable growth. And very successful organizations will use self-correction guided by ethics to adjust to changes in the surrounding environment in order to achieve goals and to improve stakeholder relationships.

## 3) Connecting ethics and two-way communications

There is a connection between the ethical sense and two-way communications. Grunig, who advances the idea of the four models of public relations, states that unilateral, non-symmetrical two-way communications models are ineffective models for managing organizations, and that they are lacking in ethics and do not consider social responsibility (Grunig, 1992, p. 40). In addition he points out that at the same time that symmetrical two-way communications encourage the counterparts to change, one's own side changes. He also explains that symmetrical discussions (communications) based on a good conscience and goodwill make ethical public relations activities possible (Grunig & Grunig, 1996, p. 45). In other words, he makes it clear that the existence of an ethical sense makes it possible to have symmetrical two-way communications. In a similar way, the ethical sense and symmetrical two-way communications are the two sides of the Self-Correction Model.

## 5 Development of the Self-Correction Model

### Evaluation method of the SCM

Because self-correction is often hard to see, the Self-Correction Model has been developed by mapping real-world cases of crisis on an X/Y graph. Events that act as "stimuli" that require "counter corrective action" could then be plotted, thereby making concrete an otherwise almost invisible process. The method for this evaluation is to examine both the corrective "stance" taken when an organization or individual responds to stimuli and the "content of action" taken. Both "stance" and the "content of action" are each then evaluated in terms of two opposite possibilities. "Stance" is evaluated as either "reactive" or "proactive." "Content of action" is evaluated as either "superficial" or "substantial." This results in a combination of four possible evaluation aspects that can then be mapped in the four quadrants of the X/Y graph, Figure 10.4.

### 1) Evaluation of "stance"

The corrective "stance" taken in response to stimuli results in either "reactive stance" or "proactive stance." Reactive stance is adjusting to external stimuli through an extrinsic process of reactive correction. The single cell adjusting to changes to achieve homeostasis with the external environment is a classic example of the

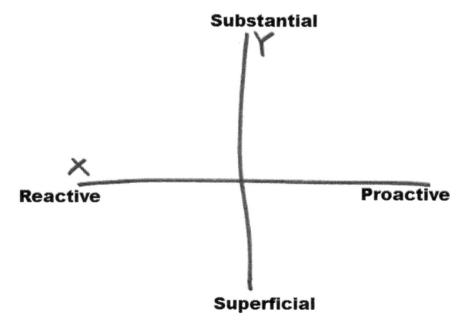

**FIGURE 10.4** Four evaluation areas of self-correction

*Source:* Takashi Inoue (2015), *Public Relations: Relationship Management*, 2nd edition, p. 266

reactive stance. In contrast, proactive stance involves an internal prompting of the self to adjust to changes through an intrinsic process of proactive correction, where the prompting force is the ethical sense. A company putting customer safety and satisfaction above consideration of profit is an example of proactive correction that is prompted by an intrinsic desire for ethical behavior. Both types are correction, but only proactive correction guided by ethics will consistently result in comprehensive transformation that both achieves an organization's objectives and goals and that is good.

These terms "intrinsic" and "extrinsic" are used in such fields as biology and philosophy to distinguish between properties that are an essential part of an object and those that are unessential to the object. Intrinsic properties are independent of the external environment surrounding the object. For example, when we say something is "intrinsically bad," we mean it is evil in and of itself and not a function of factors outside of the object that make it evil. It is like saying "murder is intrinsically evil." In comparison, an "extrinsic" property is determined by external factors. For example, the weight of an object is dependent on the external gravity acting on it, and not a property of the object itself. Something weighing a 100 kilograms on earth would weigh far less on the moon. Therefore, weight is an extrinsic property. Proactive correction is intrinsic, because it is a function of an internal sense of ethics and human free-will that are an essential part of human beings.

Individuals and organizations can take either of these two stances, but it is the strong ethical sense associated with the proactive stance that will lead to truly effective self-correction.

## 2) Evaluation of "content of action"

The action that results from either reactive or proactive stances must be evaluated in terms of the degree of correction that is made. Content of action is either "superficial," resulting in no or very little fundamental correction to a person, organization, or a process, or the content is "substantial" enough to produce fundamental correction.

Let's look at a hypothetical example in which Company X learns of many cases of customers having problems with the company's newly issued cellphones due to a faulty part, and decides to recall the product. Superficial action would be to simply repair the phones with a new part, while substantial action would be to rethink the process for design and development of products. While replacing a faulty part will likely solve the defective product problem, it is superficial in that it does not lead to a substantial correction in how Company X acts as an organization. In contrast, if it rethinks its development process, then it is taking action that leads to significant and long-term correction in how the company functions. As another example, substantial action would be the resignation of top management in order to rebuild the organization, while simply forcing the resignation of a middle manager or an employee to give the appearance of correction, would be superficial correction.

## 3) Four quadrants of the X/Y graph

In terms of the Self-Correction Model, the goal is to embed an ethics-based self-correction function into an organization that allows it to successfully achieve its goals, while also contributing to the wider good of all its stakeholders. An organization, in which self-correction is an intrinsic function, will be able to take a proactive stance to change and respond with substantial actions that allows it to both survive crisis and to take advantage of changes to succeed, where others fail.

The four evaluation aspects of self-correction can be mapped to the four quadrants of the X/Y graph as shown in Figure 10.5, where "Reactive – Superficial" is in the bottom left, "Reactive – Substantial" is in the top left, "Proactive – Superficial" is in the bottom right, and "Proactive – Substantial" is in the top right.

### Simple illustration of SCM mapping

To understand the SCM mapping, let's take a hypothetical case of a baseball team, in which a new ace pitcher, Player A, has recently joined as the great hope of the team. However, after a winning start for the team in the new season, the situation changes and the team's fortunes begin to decline. In this case, we will see the behavior of

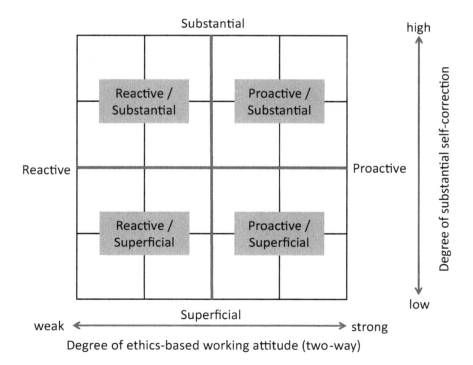

**FIGURE 10.5** Four evaluation aspects of self-correction mapping

*Source:* Takashi Inoue (2015), *Public Relations: Relationship Management*, 2nd edition, p. 269

several different persons, but only the pitcher's "stance" and "content of action" are to be mapped. Five points of "stimuli" and "response" associated with Player A are described and numbered. The five mapping points are then plotted in Figure 10.6.

After winning the first several games in the new season, Player A starts to enjoy the attention being given to him in the media. Player A begins to come late for practice, and repeatedly ignores warnings from the team's coach. A pessimistic atmosphere surrounds the team, morale falls, and the winning streak has changed to a losing streak. So far, even though negative stimuli are starting to appear, Player A has not taken any corrective action, and therefore his actions do not yet appear on the self-correction map.

The coach complains to the team manager, but his words fall on deaf ears. For the manager this all comes at a very difficult time, when he is under great pressure from the team owner, who is disappointed in the team's poor performance. Rather than taking time to listen, the team manager yells at the coach. After this, there is no further communication with the coach on the subject of Player A, and the manager is able to forget about the problem and concentrate on other matters. But, then the coach suddenly asks for a meeting. When the coach walks into his office, the manager can see on his face that the problem has not gone away. The manager gives the coach permission to fire Player A. After the coach leaves and closes the door behind him, the team manager walks over to his office window and looks down at the practice field.

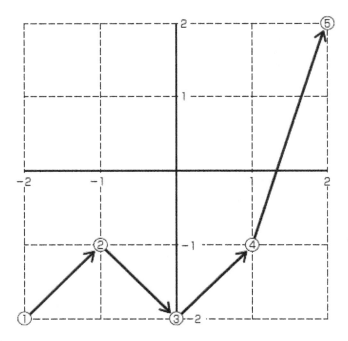

**FIGURE 10.6**   SCM mapping of self-correction journey of "Player A"

*Source:* Takashi Inoue (2015), *Public Relations: Relationship Management*, 2nd edition, p. 272

Player A walks into the coach's office and is shocked, when the coach explains that "things are not working out" and recommends that the pitcher submit his resignation. "After all," explains the coach, "there is always a need for really good pitchers, and the season is just starting." However, if Player A does not resign, he will be fired. Player A asks the coach to give him a few days to make his decision. He leaves the room and starts to try and imagine how he must have made his team mates feel by coming late to practice, and acting as if he were superior to them (mapping point ①).

Player A decides to sit alone way up in the stadium bleacher seats in order to look down at the field and to think. At first he begins to make excuses, telling himself that the team was not as good as he had thought and that he would be much better off playing on another team. After all, he is still an ace pitcher. But, meanwhile another team member, who is also an old friend from his school days, comes up to him. The friend tells the pitcher about his poor attitude. For the first time, since joining the team, Player A begins to feel a sense of regret and shame. He realizes that he has been just fooling himself by making excuses, but now he must take responsibility for his own behavior, which has put him in this situation. Player A tells his friend that he appreciates the honest words of a true friend (mapping point ②).

After his friend leaves, and Player A is alone, he tells himself that he must be honest and realize his pitching recently has not been as good as it should have been, and most likely because of missing practice and not really becoming an equal part of the team. He finally realizes that no matter how well he pitches, games are won by the team not by him, and decides to correct his own attitude (mapping point ③).

Player A walks into the coach's office and apologizes and asks for a second chance. While at this point the easiest thing for the coach would be for Player A to resign, he reflects back on his own failure to talk to Player A and to try to understand him, rather than simply giving warnings. The coach now decides to listen to Player A and to take the time to understand his reasoning and to judge his sincerity. After a long discussion, the coach tells the player he will try to persuade the team manager to allow the player to stay (mapping point ④).

At practice the next day, Player A is the first to appear. As the other players come onto the field he starts to wonder if he made the right decision. The other players seem to be ignoring him, and he becomes aware that the usual chatter between team members at practice has suddenly stopped, and he wonders if the time to admit failure and leave the field has come. He turns toward his old friend to see the reaction on his face. His friend is unexpectedly pointing a finger in the direction of the dugout. Player A turns and sees that standing there alone is the smiling face of the team manager. The silence is broken with the words "play ball!" coming from the coach (mapping point ⑤).

In this hypothetical case of a baseball team we have observed how a player, a coach, and a manager have taken reactive and proactive stances. And, we have seen Player A start by taking only a reactive stance with superficial corrective action. We have seen two-way communications between the coach and manager, the coach and Player A, and the team and Player A, which has allowed an awakening within Player A of his own ethical sense. This environment of two-way communications and a strong ethical sense has enabled Player A to use his own free-will to make self-correction, leading him to take a proactive stance and substantial action that resolves his personal crisis. This is an organization made up of individuals with all the imperfections of human beings, but that is able to succeed where another team might not, because self-correction is embedded in its culture. We can reasonably expect a baseball team that can attract star players and effectively foster their growth as individuals and as members of a team will be able to win championships.

### SCM conceptual diagram

In Figure 10.7 is the conceptual diagram of the Self-Correction Model. The circle on the left is an organization and connected to it is the "ethical filter of self-correction" representing the self-correction process with the four evaluation areas described above. If the organization has self-correction embedded in its culture, then it will be able to take a proactive stance. If not, then it will only be able to take a reactive stance to events, incidents, and significant changing conditions in the surrounding environment.

The circle on the right side represents the organization's various stakeholders. The information flow from two-way communications is illustrated by the two curved arrows circling between organization and its stakeholders. Action and communication taken by the organization and flowing to the stakeholders is shown at the bottom, while the resulting feedback from stakeholders is shown on the top. The corrective actions taken by the organization would include both reactive and proactive stances as well as superficial and substantial content of action.

The rectangle at the bottom represents the environment of internal and external changes with two-way arrows pointing to both the organization and stakeholders.

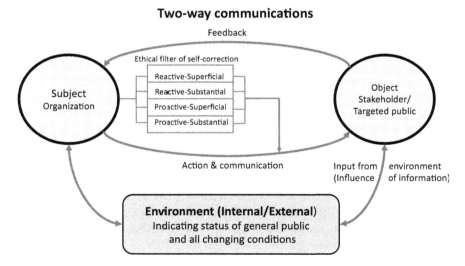

**FIGURE 10.7** Conceptual diagram of the Self-Correction Model

*Source:* Takashi Inoue (2015), *Public Relations: Relationship Management,* 2nd edition, p. 270

While it is usual to show a one-way flow from the environment, the flow shown here is two-way to illustrate the fact that both can influence each other. Examples of changing environmental conditions would be things like the sudden change in a country's foreign exchange rates, the development of significant new technology in an industry, or a major natural disaster that disrupts the global supply chain. In the case of Apple's release of the first iPhone, the company can be said to have changed the environment.

Thinking back on the case of Nissan and Mitsubishi Motors (MMC) described at the beginning of Chapter 2, you can now better understand what happen in that case by using this model (Figure 10.8). While the case began with the MMC falsified fuel efficiency records becoming known publicly, in terms of this model it begins with a change in the external environment, which is the growing concern about $CO_2$ causing climate change that results in a change in customers' desires for more fuel-efficient cars.

Because of this change in the environment, the engineers of MMC come under pressure by management to meet fuel efficiency targets that will show customers that MMC mini-cars burn less fuel and therefore emit less $CO_2$. However, unable to meet such targets, and also afraid to communicate to management the truth of the situation, the engineers continue the 25 year practice of falsifying fuel efficiency reports. MMC management is unaware of the problem, because its culture prevents "two-way communications" and the free flow of feedback.

When its stakeholder, Nissan, brings the matter to senior MMC management's attention, they take a reactive stance. Without an embedded ethics-based self-correction function, MMC management cannot begin to make needed proactive-substantial self-correction. MMC decides to hold a press conference to admit to the public that it had issued fake fuel efficiency numbers. Taking

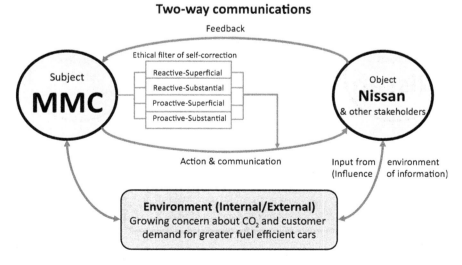

**FIGURE 10.8**  Self-Correction Model for MMC before Nissan purchase

responsibility, MMC's president announces his resignation in the press conference. This action, even though taken from a reactive stance, is substantial correction, because of the president's resignation. But, it still leaves the fate of the survival of the company an open question and the stock price falls dramatically. Looking back at Figure 10.5 ("Four evaluation aspects of self-correction mapping"), we can say that MMC is operating only from the left side of the SCM map, but it needs to move to the right side where the ethical sense is strongest, and then move upward toward the proactive/substantial quadrant. If MMC truly desires to survive, it must embed a self-correction function, and then demonstrate that to its stakeholders.

From Figure 10.9 we can see that Nissan is influenced by the change in the global automotive industry that requires larger and larger economies of scale to justify the cost of developing many new technologies required to survive among growing international competition. While working on the next generation of mini-cars with MMC, Nissan engineers come to realize that reported fuel efficiency could not possibly be correct. Nissan's top management apparently has two-way communication with its engineers, because it quickly learned of the MMC problem.

Nissan depends on MMC to produce its own line of mini-cars, and stands to suffer both in reputation, sales, and profits because of this scandal. However, Nissan has a functioning "Ethical Filter of Self-Correction," which allows it to take a proactive stance and to begin to take substantial corrective actions that lead up to the May 12, 2016 press conference announcing its agreement to purchase a 34% controlling interest in MMC, which faced regulatory fines and customer claims in excess of a billion dollars.

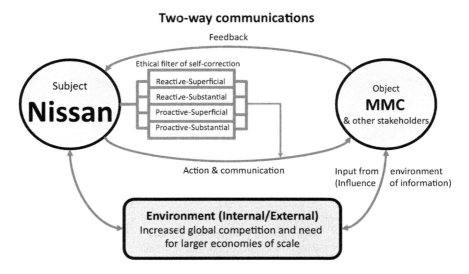

FIGURE 10.9  Self-Correction Model for Nissan before Nissan purchase

Having self-correction as part of its DNA, Nissan is not only able to survive the MMC scandal, but it is able to successfully respond to the environment change by proposing to bring MMC into the Nissan-Renault Alliance. It is also able to purchase controlling interest of MMC at a fraction of the price it would otherwise have had to pay. This was made possible by having a culture of ethical self-correction that allowed it to quickly produce a creditable recovery plan for an organization with great technology and product, but with a very weak ethical sense.

This real-world case illustrates well a central theme of this book, which is that public relations in combination with self-correction allows an organization to more than survive a crisis, but to also thrive. Nissan took the crisis and turned it into an opportunity to greatly expand its alliance into the topmost ranks of the world's auto manufacturers, and to further improve its relationships with stakeholders globally.

## SCM mapping of actual corporate crisis cases

The SCM has been developed from analysis of real-world cases of organizations in the process of managing a crisis. This was done through media analysis of the reporting of each crisis analyzed by taking media clippings from the initial reporting of the event through to final resolution, at which point it stops being a topic for media coverage. The corrective actions taken in each case were then plotted in the four quadrants of the X/Y graph, representing the four possible evaluation aspects associated with each type of stance and type of corrective action.

A particularly interesting finding from this research was that typically a crisis first appears on the SCM map in the lower left quadrant, where "reactive stance" and "superficial action" are recorded. When the incident or scandal is first reported in the press, the organization has no time to think out a final solution, and simply takes the reactive stance. However, in the case of an organization that successfully survives a crisis, the stance early on begins to move toward the lower right quadrant, where the ethical sense is strongest. As the organization reflects and decides to solve the problem it is facing, it will begin to take a "proactive stance." In other words, such an organization will then begin moving upward to the top right quadrant of "proactive stance" and "substantial action." By the time it has successfully brought the crisis to a conclusion the company finds that the very process of self-correction has been a positive and transformative experience (Inoue, 2007).

In contrast, organizations that handle a crisis poorly will remain stuck on the left side of the Y-axis unable to act ethically and accomplish the self-correction needed to learn from mistakes and unable to rebuild relationships with its stakeholders that have been damaged. Lacking an ethical self-correction function, the crisis typically only ends after the organization is either destroyed or so badly damaged that its recovery is in doubt. Without self-correction there is no transformative experience that could lead to a recovery and future growth.

In the following two cases of crisis management, actual media articles published at the time were analyzed in order to judge to what extent self-correction was functioning, and to determine if it was effective. The media articles appear throughout the period of the crisis, allowing the reporting date to be used to provide a chronological picture of the movements through the four self-correction evaluation areas. The first case is an asbestos incident, which is a success story, and the second is a beef mislabeling incident at a food company, which is a story of crisis management failure.

## 1) Case study: successful handling of an "asbestos incident"

This began June 29, 2005, when Company J, a major asbestos manufacturer that made known publicly on its own that 79 factory employees and outside workers had died of pleural mesothelioma cancer since 1978, believed to be due to the handling of asbestos. Even though the cause of the illness and legal responsibility were not confirmed, the company quickly announced that it had decided on its own to take a proactive stance and substantive measures by paying compensation as well as condolence money, and to establish a fund for treatment of workers suffering from asbestos-caused illness.

Due to this proactive stance and substantial self-correction action by the management of Company J, the incident appeared to be largely settled by November of the following year, about 13 months later. Twenty-three articles on the "asbestos incident" from morning and evening editions of newspapers with nationwide distribution from the beginning to the settlement of the crisis were used to plot the company's response to the crisis to show the chronological transition displayed in Figure 10.10.

From this self-correction map, a proactive effort is clearly evident from the beginning in this "asbestos incident." While the final actions take place in the proactive-substantial area, the actions leading up to final resolution move back and forth between the proactive-substantial area and the reactive-superficial area.

## 2) Case study: failure in handling a "beef mislabeling incident"

The first case of BSE (mad cow disease), an infectious disease, was confirmed in Japan on September 10, 2001. In the "beef mislabeling incident" Company X misused the program initiated by Japan's Ministry of Agriculture, Forestry and Fisheries to buy back domestically produced beef as one countermeasure to BSE. The company had their Kansai Meat Center (Itami City, Hyogo Prefecture) mislabel imported Australian beef so that it could be sold to the Ministry as domestic beef, and also sent falsified invoices to the Ministry. This incident was followed by other beef mislabeling incidents by Company Z (a major meat-seller based in Osaka), and Company U, all of which resulted in a loss of trust in food labeling among consumers, creating a general feeling of fear about the safety of meat.

This incident was discovered on January 23, 2002 with the admission by the freezer company, Company T, which had intentionally and fraudulently repacked and mislabeled the beef, and also had manipulated documents at the request of Company X.

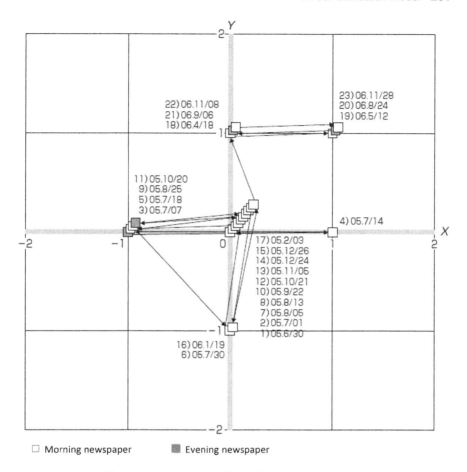

□ Morning newspaper    ■ Evening newspaper

**FIGURE 10.10**    Self-correction mapping of an asbestos incident
*Source:* Takashi Inoue (2015), *Public Relations: Relationship Management*, 2nd edition, p. 274

Beginning on January 23, after holding a press conference, the Hyogo Prefec-
tural police investigated the mislabeling activities for three months to assemble a
case, which developed into a compulsory investigation. Suspicions about Company
X thickened. Under these circumstances the top management of the company took
a purely reactive stance by taking responsibility and resigning. Company X con-
vened an extraordinary meeting of shareholders, continuing to take only a reactive
stance. Three months after the discovery of the fraudulent labeling, Company X,
which was a publicly traded corporation with annual sales of some ¥90 billion
(approximately USD $900 million), took the final "substantive action" of voting to
dissolve the company. At the shareholders meeting on April 26, where the decision
to dissolve the company was formalized, employee shareholders were shouting at
top management to: "Investigate the causes!" And, some even had to be restrained
by officials.

Throughout this crisis, the company's top management appeared to act without much concern for shareholders, employees, and distributors, and was slow to respond, taking only a reactive stance. If the company had a tradition of acting ethically and for the wide benefit of stakeholders, top management of Company X would likely have acted proactively and quickly, knowing that the various stakeholders would be supportive. It then might have survived.

Even though this analysis was made only from media articles, it seem reasonable to assume that Company X had a lack of two-way communications and lack of mutual trust between employees and management. This can be said to have been a major factor pushing the company to dissolution, rather than taking a proactive stance in which self-correction founded on ethics could have led to substantial corrective action and revival. If mutual communications had been good, mutual understanding would have deepened, and it would have been easy to understand the situation within the company, and ethical awareness would have improved. They then might have been able to respond quickly to take the proactive substantial action from inside the company, and thereby might have avoided the closing of the company.

The Figure 10.11 evaluation of articles over approximately three months from January 23, 2002, when the incident was discovered to the dissolution of the company, plots Company X's responses as determined from 11 media articles that focused on this case. These articles provide an indication of the ethical and the chronological progression of self-correction activities by Company X. Chronologically we can see a pattern of self-correction that moves back and forth between the reactive-superficial area and the reactive-substantial area. In this "beef mislabeling incident" we do not see a proactive ethical response on the part of Company X as it approached company dissolution. Nothing was plotted in either the proactive-superficial area or the proactive-substantial area, and the final act resolving the crisis was to close the company. This proved to be a typical example of failure in response to a crisis.

## 6 A final summation

Once you are able to understand this new model of ethical self-correction, then you will be able to embed it into critical processes of your organization. The starting point is to fully appreciate the need for a self-correction process as the key for success of both individuals and organizations. Then you must work to ensure it has, in Ghosn's words: "a culture where employees can freely communicate concerns without retribution." Of course, given human nature that is indeed a challenge, but perhaps for you the most important. Once self-correction and our free-will to choose is fully understood, and with a culture supportive of two-way communications established, then you can make ethical self-correction an intrinsic part of a healthy organization that can make profits for investors, provide jobs and rewarding work for employees, deliver quality products and services that

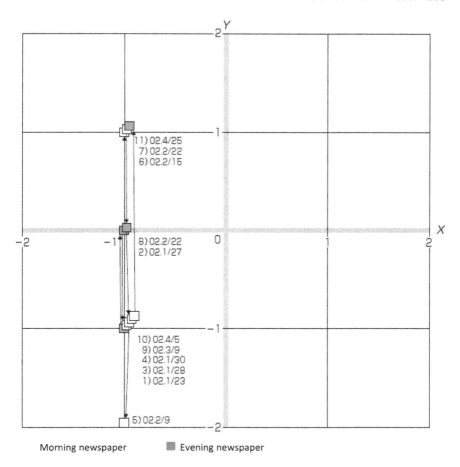

**FIGURE 10.11**   Self-correction mapping of "beef mislabeling"

Source: Takashi Inoue (2015), Public Relations: Relationship Management, 2nd edition, p. 276

improve the lives of customers, and contribute in many other ways to our collective humanity.

Repeatedly in this book the key point has been made that public relations is active and continuous stakeholder relationship management by which organizations achieve goals along the shortest path for the wide benefit of stakeholders globally as the "fifth management resource." Public relations enhances the other four basic resources used by organizations by inspiring employees through employee relations, encouraging investors and shareholders through investor relations, and creating win–win results with many other stakeholders around the globe. It is now time for you to do your part to lead and inspire your organization by applying the power of public relations, and by embedding the Self-Correction Model, so that we can all safely make our way through this turbulent period of hyper-globalization and leave the next generation a better world.

## References

Cannon, W. (1932/1959). *The Wisdom of the Body [Jintai no eichi]*. New York: W. W. Norton & Co. (Tokyo: Sogensha).

Cutlip, S. M. & Center, A. H. (1952). *Effective Public Relations*. Upper Saddle River, NJ: Pearson Prentice Hall.

Ghosn, C. (2017). *Responses to Questionnaire "Public Relations for Hyper-Globalization."* Yokohama: s.n.

Grunig, J. E. (1992). *Excellence in Public Relations and Communication Management*. New Jersey: Lawrence Erlbaum.

Grunig, J. E. & Grunig, L. A. (1996). *Implications of Symmetry for a Theory of Ethics and Social Responsibility in Public Relations*. s.l.: Paper presented at the meeting of the International Communications Association.

Inoue, T. (2002). "The Need for Two-Way Communications and Self-Correction." *Frontline*, 11, pp. 24–27.

Inoue, T. (2007). "Jiko shūsei o seichi ni suru meta ninchi" (Self-Correction Using Meta cognition). *Inoueblog*, April 28, 2007. [Online] Available at: http://www.inoueblog.com/archives/2007/04/ [Accessed 14 August, 2017]

Inoue, T. (2015). *Public Relations: Relationship Management*. 2nd ed. Tokyo: Nippon Hyoron Sha.

Kôjien (1998). *Kôjien*. 5th ed. Tokyo: Iwanami Press.

Louden-Brown, P., Kamuda, E., & Kamuda, K. (n.d.) "Titanic Myths." *Titanic Historical Society*. [Online] Available at: http://www.titanichistoricalsociety.org/articles/titanicmyths.html [Accessed 18 July, 2017]

Merriam-Webster Dictionary (n.d.) "Correction." [Online] Available at: https://www.merriam-webster.com/dictionary/correction [Accessed 18 July, 2017]

Nishikawa, T., Zen. M., & Yoshikawa, S. (1998). *Shin jiko rikai no tame no shinri-gaku – seikaku shinri-gaku nyūmon (The New Self-Understanding of the Nature of Psychology – Introduction to Psychology)*. Tokyo: Fukumura.

Pells, R. (2008). "Titanic Doomed by Fire Raging Below Decks, Says New Theory." *The Independent*, 12 April, 2008.

The Editors of the Encyclopædia Britannica (n.d.). "J.P. Morgan, American Financier." *Britannica.com*. [Online] Available at: https://www.britannica.com/biography/J-P-Morgan [Accessed July 18, 2017]

Tibbetts, G. (2007). "Key That Could Have Saved the Titanic." *The Telegraph*, 29 August, 2007.

Wada, W. (2005). *Jiko no tankyū — jiko to tsukiau to iu koto (Self Exploration – Self-talking)*. Kyoto: Nakanishiya Shuppan.

Wiener, N. (1948). *Cybernetics: Or Control and Communication in the Animal and the Machine*, 2nd ed. Cambridge MA: The M.I.T. Press.

# GLOSSARY

**ABC (Audit Bureau of Circulations)**   A bureau that researches accurate data on the circulations of print media.

**Accountability**   The responsibility of companies and organizations to disclose information on their businesses and activities. In recent years, the responsibility of executives of companies and organizations to clearly explain their businesses and other activities to stakeholders has grown increasingly important.

**Account executive**   The employee of a PR company or advertising agency who manages a client's account.

**Advertorial**   (1) In the print media, advertising in the form of an article. It is generally used in publications for consumers, and used as copy to publicize products and services. (2) Similar to infomercials in the broadcast media.

**Advocacy advertising**   Advertising to advocate the claims and arguments of companies. Used by companies to emphasize their own legitimacy and to obtain the understanding of stakeholders.

**Affiliate**   (1) Radio and television stations that belong to a network, but that are also independent. (2) Partners to PR companies, etc.

**Air time**   The time that radio and television broadcasts start.

**Analyst**   Generally refers to either a securities analyst who does financial analysis for investment purposes, or an industry analyst who analyzes and evaluates industries and specific sectors.

**Anchorman**   The person who presents the news on a television or radio program.

**Angle**   The point that is emphasized in an article or a broadcast.

**Annual report**   A corporate financial report legally required by, for example, the Securities and Exchange Commission (SEC) in the U.S. Frequently written in plain language and summarized for distribution to shareholders and the media.

**A-roll**   The part of the VNR (video news release) containing speech. TV news editors who do not want to edit a VNR use an A-roll. See also: B-roll.

**Associate editor**   An editor-in-chief responsible for the editorial and commentary columns.

**Association relations**   One function of public relations of targeting organizations, such as industry organizations and other associations, and maintaining and improving favorable relations with them.

**Audience**   A collection of people who are the targets of all or part of a PR program. A target group.

**Audit**   As a communications term, it may entail surveying and analyzing opinions among key publics, evaluating imbalances between different parties, or conducting investigations into awareness levels of a company or topic followed by recommendations on how to make improvements.

**Avatar**   An image that moves in three dimensions that embodies the human user in a virtual space, such as on the Internet.

**Back of the book**   Material on a topic published after the main editorial part of a magazine.

**Backgrounder**   Materials prepared for editors and journalists in order to set out or explain the facts on a certain subject and its meaning and background. Used as one part of a press kit.

**Balance sheet (B/S)**   One of the financial statements. A financial report that summarizes the "assets" and "liabilities" held by a company or business entity at a point in time (closing date) and its "capital" as the difference between them.

**Banner**   (1) A large headline on the front page of a newspaper or other publication. Also called streamer. (2) Displayed in the background at a press conference venue by the party holding the conference, showing the name of the company holding the conference, its logo, etc. (3) Advertising inserted into homepages on the Internet.

**Barter**   Paying in goods, such as advertising, instead of a monetary payment. Broadcasting a program with commercials, or broadcasting in airtime without a direct payment to the program, etc.

**BBS (Bulletin Board System)**   An electronic bulletin board.

**BCP (Business Continuity Plan)**   A plan strategically prepared for business continuity during a time of non-emergency so that important operations are not interrupted when a disaster or other risk occurs, or even if business activities are interrupted, to enable important functions to be restarted within the targeted recovery time and to minimize the risk associated with the interrupted operations.

**Beat**   (1) The areas or industries that journalists or people in related positions are responsible for covering. (2) An exclusive article, scoop.

**Benchmark study**   Study conducted before and after the implementation of public relations activities to measure their effects on the target group (to ascertain the current positioning).

**Big data**   A huge data set that allows for analyzing, and is used in "big data analytics."

**Bio**   Abbreviation of biography. Profiles of a company executive, etc., prepared by an organization for the media.

**Blog** Content such as text and images uploaded to a website to express one's own ideas and opinions. It is also possible to include various functions, such as comments and feedback functions.

**Booklet** A booklet is typically of a thickness that can be stapled.

**Boomerang effect** A propaganda term, particularly used for cases that produce results opposite to those intended.

**Bottom line** Generally used to express what are considered to be the most important facts. This meaning is derived from the bottom line of a company's financial report, which shows net profit (net loss).

**Brand equity** A product or a company's brand value. It has become important in marketing in order to raise a brand from being merely a name to having value as an intangible asset, and to maintain and further raise this value.

**Branding** Strategic public relations, advertising, and promotional activities to build a brand. In particular, in addition to product brands, in recent years the key to success in business has been building a corporate brand.

**Brand journalism** Refers to when a company provides content about its products and services in a "journalistic" format. A characteristic of brand journalism is that it attempts to win the trust of the general public and consumers by providing information that is fair and unbiased, compared to some sort of company "announcement."

**Brand management** Managing a corporate or product brand to keep its image at a high level.

**Break** (1) A report that can be announced immediately. (2) The suspension of a broadcast in order to show commercials.

**Bridge** A phrase or sentence that connects two articles or broadcasts.

**Brochure** A brochure can provide an overview of a company, organization, etc. It is typically written in more detail than a booklet.

**B-roll** One side of a video news release (VNR). Of the VNR sent from public relations companies, those without a voice recording in the video material in order for the director to edit them in-house. See also: A-roll.

**BTA (Best Time Available)** A commercial broadcast in the best possible time period.

**Buzz marketing** A marketing method utilizing "word-of-mouth." Buzz was originally used to describe the sound that bees make when they fly. This meaning was appropriated to refer to the "buzzing" of rumors and small talk about a certain topic.

**Byline** The name and title of the journalist who wrote the article.

**Campaign** In advertising or public relations, a series of organized actions or programs to achieve a communications or brand-related goal.

**Candids** Effective photographs that are natural and friendly in which the subject has not been posed.

**CCO (Chief Communication Officer)** The person with the highest authority for their company's communications activities.

**Census** A survey of a nation's people.

**Center spread** An article spread across two center pages.

**Channel**   A television channel. A tool for communication.

**Chat**   An online, real-time conversation.

**CI (corporate identity)**   In its narrow meaning, it is the design to unify logo marks and symbol marks. In its broad meaning, it is a company's image presented through its PR activities.

**Circular**   A single sheet of printed material intended to be widely circulated at practically no cost.

**Circulation**   In print, the number of copies published. In radio and television, the number of listeners or viewers.

**Client**   The company or other organization that receives the public relations services or other services.

**Clip**   (1) In broadcasting, one part extracted from the entire program. (2) In print media, a clipping from an article.

**Clip art**   Previously inserted graphics and illustrations, such as via a computer.

**Clipsheet**   Article selected and sent to the media for use. Printed material of an illustration, etc. prepared so that it will more likely be selected by editors.

**Cluster samples**   Sampling by extracting some people from the group being targeted. Carried out after first dividing them according to respective characteristics or into groups with certain characteristics.

**Coincidental interview**   A public opinion survey by telephone to collect information.

**Cold reading**   A broadcast of the announcer reading the manuscript without a rehearsal.

**Color**   Background or dramatized material used together with factual reporting.

**Combination publication**   A publication distributed by a company or organization to various groups, including employees, external groups, and individuals.

**Comic book**   Pamphlets or magazines that use the methods of comics (such as four-frame series) in order to convey a message or tell a story, often in an entertaining way.

**Commercial online service**   Services that provide a function, such as an online bulletin board, for a fee.

**Communication audit**   See "Audit."

**Community**   Communities include those affected by a company's management policies and production activities and those in an area adjacent to a business site.

**Community relations**   One function of public relations to maintain and improve good relations with local residents and groups within the scope of the organization's activities.

**Competency**   The particular abilities (competencies) possessed by a company or individual, such as ways of thinking or behavior that can differentiate that company or individual from competitors and others.

**Compliance**   Generally, the laws and rules, including the various types of regulations, and the social norms that a company must comply with when carrying out its business activities.

**Conference report**   In companies' and organizations' meetings, a report on the discussions of the various members and on the important points, such as the actions and work assignments.

**Consolidated financial statements**   Generally, consolidated financial statements have been used in Western countries, but non-consolidated financial statements in Japan. However, together with economic globalization, preparing consolidated financial statements based on international accounting standards is becoming a requirement in all countries. It has been required in Japan since 2000.

**Consumerism**   The consumer protection movement. A movement and way of thinking to protect consumers from the viewpoint of purchases of products and services and the safety of products.

**Content analysis**   A research method of objectively describing and analyzing the content of news releases, newspaper articles, speeches, videotapes, film, magazines and other publications.

**Control group**   A group of people who are considered to represent the characteristics and opinions of a population. Often refers to a test group that is not tested and a group showing the same reactions. See also: test group.

**Conversion**   Shifting public opinion from one direction to another for certain issues.

**Co-op advertising**   Splitting the costs of an advertisement between retailers and manufacture. In broadcasting, splitting between national and local.

**Copy desk**   The department in a newspaper, magazine, or radio/television station that edits reports and articles and writes headlines.

**Copyright**   Protection of a work so that it cannot be used without permission.

**Copy-testing**   A method used in advertising for testing in advance on a small group within the target audience before implementing the public relations activities.

**Corporate advertising**   Advertising to raise awareness about a company among the general public to advocate its management policies and corporate philosophy. See also: institutional advertising.

**Corporate brand**   In recent years, greater importance has been placed on the corporate brand rather than on the traditional brand. Improving the corporate brand contributes to business activities and marketing. See also: brand equity.

**Corporate citizen**   A company that behaves ethically as a "citizen" within society is said to be a good corporate citizen. See also: CSR.

**Corporate communications**   (1) Rather than marketing communications, activities to promote the sales of products and services, these are communications activities carried out which are centered upon corporate management. (2) A term that refers to the communications activities as a whole that a company carries out both in-house and externally. In many cases it uses the department name or job title.

**Corporate culture**   The shared values, ways of thinking, and behavior formed among staff through their day-to-day company activities.

**Corporate governance**   Refers to the optimization of management through the controlling function of stakeholders, including companies' internal institutions, shareholders, and creditors.

**Corporate public relations**   Public relations activities centered on corporate management. See also: marketing public relations.

**Correspondent**   Journalists who report from regions outside of their media outlet's home region, often overseas.

**CPM (Cost per thousand)**   (M equals 1,000). The cost of a television segment per 1,000 viewers.

**Crisis management**   In an organization's activities, the management of a crisis when a serious incident occurs that might affect the survival or reputation of that organization. During this emergency, the organization's communications activities to send information to internal and external audiences is called crisis communications.

**Crystallization**   Creating a clear awareness of an obscure or potential attitude in the general public.

**CSR (Corporate Social Responsibility)**   Activities of the organization aimed at contributing to the good of society. Giving financial support to charities has been a traditional type of CSR.

**CSV (Creating Shared Value)**   Management concept proposed by Michael E. Porter of the Harvard Business School, in which a company creates value that can be shared between society and companies that contribute to resolving social issues through corporate activities.

**Customer relations**   Activities to acquire the understanding of consumer behavior, retailers, and distributors through communicating to them information on business content and products and services.

**Delphi method**   A research method for mutual exchanges and to elicit opinions and information between groups of experts to obtain a consensus. Typically, it is conducted by repeating the questions elicited from the previous answer.

**Demographics**   Statistics on readers or viewers. A collection of data on characteristics (attributes), including age, gender, family structure, and economic status.

**Digital divide**   One type of stratification according to literacy in IT (information technology). Generally called the "information gap."

**Digital news release**   Material released to journalists including photographs, videos, and links to related social media.

**Disclosure**   The disclosure of information by a company or organization on its activities, finances, etc., to stakeholders. Generally, information is disclosed to investors.

**Diversity**   Signifies the creation of an environment in which everyone, irrespective of differences in external aspects, such as race, gender, age, and the presence or absence of disabilities. or internal aspects, like values, religion, and lifestyles, or in external appearances, can demonstrate their abilities and contribute to the organization.

**Double-page spread**   An article or advertisement over two pages.

**Due diligence** In the IR field, when investing or conducting a transaction like an M&A, the activities to investigate and conduct research into the targeted company or to investigate an asset, such as real estate or a financial instrument.

**Eco-fund** Investment trust that incorporates the shares of companies that prioritize the protection of the global environment.

**Editorialize** To include individual opinions in a news article.

**Electronic newsletters** Newsletters distributed as digital data, using a computer to send to other computers and electronic devices.

**Embargo** Refers to the time before which the media is prohibited from using a news release, or other written material, in its reporting. It is set by the releasing side.

**Employee relations** One function of public relations, to facilitate good relations between a company and its employees.

**Employee satisfaction** The level of satisfaction among employees.

**Environmental accounting** Converting companies' environmental conservation activities into numerical values and expressing their cost effectiveness.

**Evaluation** Measuring and evaluating the results of planning and activities. A research method to find the answers to two basic questions: were the objectives set at the beginning achieved and to what extent did the activities go well?

**Exclusive** From among the various newspapers, magazines, and radio and television stations, selecting one media outlet only to report on a matter and providing it exclusively with information.

**External publication** A publication issued by a company or an organization intended for an external audience, such as customers, the local community, or the financial world.

**Fact sheet** A document containing the facts that are the basic elements on the relevant issue. It is customarily included in a press kit and normally omits text-based descriptions.

**Feature** Among the various articles in a print media, one that is normally lengthier, more in-depth and is meant to draw the attention of the reader.

**Feedback** Reactions from the target group about PR activities, etc.

**Fill-in stories** Press releases prepared so that the respective necessary information can be filled in. They can be reshaped to meet the needs of editors.

**Financial analyst** An expert in financial matters. Can include analysts within securities companies, banks, institutional investors, etc.

**Financial relations** In its broad meaning, it is the relations with direct and indirect financial stakeholders and includes IR. In its narrow meaning, IR (relations with investors, shareholders, securities companies/analysts) is considered as an independent practice area. See also: investor relations (IR).

**Flack** A slang term for a publicity agent. In a term relating to the arts, it refers to dealing with slander and libel.

**Flagship station** The key station that is the center of the network of broadcasting stations.

**Flyer**   Mail or leaflets prepared to announce and promote a new product, sales, a special offer, or event. Normally one sheet only.

**Focus group**   A test group for extracting the opinions and thinking considered to represent most people for a problem or product (normally less than 20 people).

**Folder**   A folder, often A4, into which printed materials are inserted.

**Freelance**   A journalist or writer who does not belong to a newspaper company or publishing company. They have contracts with media outlets and conduct interviews and provide the media with reports and photographs.

**Freeloading**   The custom among journalists and editors of accepting gifts, entertainment, travel, etc. provided by companies and organizations with the objective of exercising influence over them.

**Free paper**   A newspaper published whose sole funding is from advertising revenues and that is distributed for free.

**Frequency discount**   A discount on fees for large volume advertising.

**Front of the book**   In the editing of a magazine, an article published as the main article.

**Futures research**   Research toward forecasting future events, for example, changes to the political, social, or economic environment.

**Gatekeeper**   A person such as an editor, journalist, or reporter, who is able to sift through information to determine which of it becomes news.

**Ghostwriter**   A person behind the scenes who writes a speech, article, manuscript, etc.

**Goodwill**   Good intentions or a positive attitude directed toward an individual, organization, or group.

**Government relations**   One function of public relations, to develop relationships or resolve problems with government agencies, politicians, etc., and ensure communication with them.

**Grapevine**   An informal method of verbally spreading information and rumors. "I heard it through the grapevine."

**Grassroots**   A grassroots campaign working with or targeting the general public.

**Gross impressions**   The total number of subscribers and audiences in the various media (newspapers, broadcasting, etc.) that report on released information. See also: impressions.

**Handout**   (1) Release used for public information that is distributed widely. (2) Handing out materials.

**Hard sell**   An attempt to forcibly persuade through direct discussions for product advertising, or to press one's opinions.

**Helsinki Charter**   The Helsinki Charter was signed by an alliance of international PR organizations of IPRA, CERP, and ICO, as a protocol they agreed upon to improve the quality of public relations.

**Hold**   To refrain from distributing a news story, etc., until authorized to do so.

**Hold for release**   To refrain from printing or broadcasting a news story until the embargo is lifted.

**Hometown stories** An article written for the local media on an individual, company, or organization who/which participates in certain events or activities in the place where they are from.

**Hotline** Within public relations activities, a free and direct telephone line established by companies and industry organizations to enable them to respond rapidly, particularly to requests for information from the news media.

**Human interest** Articles, etc., designed to appeal to the reader's emotions and empathy.

**HUT (households using television)** The number of households with their televisions turned on during a certain period of time.

**Hype** Effectively using the media, including movie and TV stars, books, and magazines, to conduct promotions. See also: press agentry.

**Hypodermic needle theory** The theory that when people are in a vacuous state, they directly accept the information they receive without being aware of it.

**ICCO** The International Communications Consultancy Organization. An association with its headquarters in London organized of more than 550 public relations companies and which is active in Europe. By country, the associations are Austria (APRVA), Belgium (ABCRP/BGPRC), Czech Republic (APRA), Denmark (BPRV), Finland (VTL), France (Syntec Conseil), Germany (GPRA), Greece (Hellenic PRCA), Ireland (PRCA Ireland), Italy (ASSOREL), Poland (VPRA), Norway (NIR), Portugal (APECOM), Spain (ADECEC), Sweden (PRECIS), Switzerland (BPRA), and the UK (PRCA).

**Image** The potential impression (image) that an individual has about another individual or group. A corporate image is the impression the general public has about a company.

**Image-building** Protecting and enhancing the reputations (images) of individuals, companies, or organizations.

**Impressions** The total number of times released information is reported on by the media (newspapers, broadcast media, etc.) See also: gross impressions.

**Independent station** An independent broadcast station that does not belong to a network.

**Industry relations** One function of public relations. Activities to deal with problems between a company and the industry it belongs to and ensure communication between them.

**Influencer** Also called opinion leaders. People whose opinions are very influential within society in general or an industry. Very often refers to users on YouTube and Instagram with a large number of followers. See also: opinion leader.

**Infomercial** Advertising that communicates its claims via a program on broadcast media. See also: advertorial.

**Insider trading** Securities trading by company insiders, etc., who illegally use inside information on a company that has not been disclosed for trading.

**Institutional advertising** Advertising with the objective of improving a corporate image rather than promoting sales of products or services. See also: corporate advertising.

**Institutional investors**  Refers to large-scale investors such as investment trusts, insurance companies, pension funds, banks, universities, mutual aid associations, agricultural cooperatives, etc.

**Integrated marketing communication (IMC)**  A way of thinking and a strategy for comprehensively understanding communications activities as marketing, such as advertising, public relations (PR), Sales Promotion (SP), and Direct Mail (DM) for the media.

**Intellectual property**  Intended to protect the intangible assets arising from intellectual activities. It covers a broad range of rights, including copyrights, patents, trademarks, and designs.

**Interface**  Connects organizations, individuals, and groups.

**Intermercials**  Video conversations and advertising distributed over the Internet (a maximum of four minutes).

**Internal communications**  Internal communication between the staff and members of companies and organizations.

**Internal publication**  Publication intended for people within a company or organization.

**Interpersonal communication**  Interaction between people in close proximity to each other through conversation and gestures.

**Interviewer bias**  When performing an investigation, the interviewing side causes mistakes, for example by asking questions that protect their own prejudices.

**Investor relations (IR)**  A function of public relations, to deal with issues involving investors and maintaining communication with them. See also: financial relations.

**IoT**  "Internet of things."

**IPRA (International Public Relations Association)**  Established in 1955 with its headquarters in London, it is an international organization of PR practitioners (including academics and researchers) active in more than 70 countries worldwide.

**ISO26000**  Ideas and norms of organizational behavior relating to social responsibility, as well as the international standard that presents the methods of implementing it.

**Issue**  A matter of concern to companies and organizations.

**Issue management**  One type of crisis management. Actions in conjunction with situational analysis planning in order to specify and systematically deal with a problem or opportunity a company or organization is currently facing or may face in the future. See also: risk management, crisis management.

**Junket**  When a company pays the cost of travel for members of the press with the goal of achieving a public information objective. Many members of the media will not accept this sort of payment of travel expenses.

**Knowledge management**  Aiming to improve operations by sharing within the company the various knowledge and experiences of individual members of staff. Rather than simply sharing information, it is the repeated process of collecting, organizing, accumulating, and utilizing rules of thumb and expertise.

**Leaflet**  Printed material typically of four pages

**Leak**   Information deliberately provided (leaked) to certain media before its intended release.

**Libel**   Reporting in print or broadcast media that the courts interpret as damaging the reputation of an individual. See also: slander.

**Line function**   A linear organization for mobilizing a large organization. For example, in a production department, a line of managers and personnel, or in the army, a line of officers and troops. The function of this line is for implementation, rather than for basic planning. See also: staff function.

**Literary agent**   A person who negotiates with a publishing company on behalf of an author.

**Lobbyist**   A person who aims to persuade (lobby) members of political assemblies and other government-related parties on the positions of the companies and organizations they represent. In the United States, lobbyists must be registered.

**Localize**   To tailor something to a local market or audience. For example, for a news article or broadcast distributed widely, to change it so that it touches only on aspects relevant to a certain country or specific region.

**Logotype**   Original typeface, for example for a company name or product name, used to clearly differentiate oneself from competitors.

**Loop**   (1) In audio, a technique for generating a special sound effect. For example, an effect obtained by continuously playing a sound that was recorded in one place on the tape. (2) In order to broadcast a television program nationwide, using videotape to generate effects for kinescope recordings and audio. Enables an online station to pick up the news and programs of local stations. The same image can also be projected repeatedly in a film loop.

**Management buyout (MBO)**   Management acquires the shares in their own company from the shareholders.

**Managing editor**   The chief editor who oversees the editing-related departments.

**Marketing communications**   Communication activities with the objective of promoting sales of products and services. May include public notifications, promotions, and advertising. See also: corporate communications.

**Marketing public relations**   A public relations method to support the advertising of companies and clients and their marketing targets as a whole. See also: corporate public relations.

**Mass publications**   Periodical publications with a large circulation that appeal to a wide range of people.

**Material**   A term used in investor relations to indicate an event that is considered to be significant enough to influence the share price.

**M Bone**   Multiplex broadcast system for transmitting video over the Internet.

**Mecenat (French)**   Activities supporting the arts and culture that are one part of an organization's social contribution activities as a good corporate citizen.

**Media**   As often used in public relations, it is one of the communication channels to reach target audiences. It includes newspapers, social media, online media, magazines, radio, television, etc.

**Media audit**   One benchmark survey method, involving conducting interviews with representatives of the media, usually to get their opinions on companies, products, specific issues, or services.

**Media briefing**   See "press briefing."

**Media monitoring**   Monitoring media reporting or social media posts on the information sent by a company or organization, and also its competitors. See also: press monitoring.

**Media relations**   One function of public relations that aims for two-way communication so a company or organization can disseminate information to, and maintain good relations with, the media.

**Merchandizing**   Promoting products and ideas so they are more appealing and thereby more likely to sell.

**Message entropy**   The tendency for information to become dispersed or disappear as the disseminated message spreads.

**Minority relations**   One function of public relations to address and to communicate with individuals or groups of ethnic minorities.

**Monitor**   (1) To monitor the content of reporting in newspapers and magazines, social media, or by broadcast media. (2) A monitoring device to view television broadcasts, etc.

**Moral hazard**   A state characterized by a loss of order or a lack of ethics.

**Morgue**   A department, similar to a small library, to store materials like published articles and photographs within publishing companies, etc. A reference room.

**Muckrakers**   Journalists who seek out and expose cases of corruption in companies, organizations, and government agencies. Particularly refers to a type of journalist and publication that was active in the United States at the start of the 1900s. Often used in a derogatory sense.

**Mug shot**   A slang term for a photograph of the face taken from the neck-up that appears in newspapers.

**Multiple-channel approach**   A method of using multiple media and communication channels to leave an impression of a concept or theme on the general public.

**Multiplier effect**   An effect by which information sent once prompts the sending of the same information by multiple media outlets.

**Narrow casting**   A broadcast directed toward a specific segment that is interested in a particular problem.

**News conference**   See "press conference."

**Newsletter**   Printed material in letter form published by companies and organizations.

**News release**   An announcement intended to be distributed to newspapers, magazines, broadcast media, etc. See also: press release.

**News tip**   Information for a news article.

**Off-the-record**   The practice of providing not yet publicly disclosed information to journalists with the condition that it is not published (so-called "off-the-record").

**Ombudsman/woman**  A person who investigates complaints from an individual or group about an organization. This system has been introduced not just for administrative agencies, but also for companies.

**Online 2 offline (O2O)**  A term mainly used in the e-commerce field. It refers to policies and activities for companies' and stores' online information and activities to attract customers to and influence their purchasing behavior at real stores (offline).

**Op ed**  A page in a newspaper opposite the editorial page. Currently, it typically includes the opinions of an author who does not belong to the publication.

**Open end**  A space that is kept open by each broadcast station to insert an additional program at the beginning or the end of a broadcast.

**Open house**  When a company or other organization opens its facilities for viewing by the media, employees and their families, dealers, suppliers, or members of the local community. It is one method of community relations.

**Opinion leader**  Also called influencers. See also: influencer.

**Outtake**  Audio or video material that ultimately is not used.

**Over the transom**  Materials provided even though they were not requested by the media.

**Overrun**  The trading practice for printed materials of delivering a maximum of 10% more than was ordered with an additional fee.

**Pamphlet**  Printed material of a few more pages than a leaflet with a cover sheet. Frequently also used as a promotional material.

**Paid public information**  Also called advertorial. Entails purchasing advertising space in a publication such as a newspaper or magazine and submitting an advertisement in the style of an article. It is one part of PR and public information activities.

**Panel**  (1) A group of people who repeatedly provide information, for research and other occasions. (2) A group of people who participate in discussions in a seminar, symposium, etc.

**Parametric tests**  An analysis performed by extracting a group of samples based on different assumptions.

**Pattern speech**  A foundation document written so that by rewriting it just a little, it can be given as a speech by various people in front of different audiences.

**People meter**  A device that calculates how much time one viewer spends watching television.

**Philanthropy**  Companies' social contribution activities. Activities that directly or indirectly contribute to social welfare, etc.

**Pilot test**  Before implementing the public relations activities, testing the message and main points on a group consisting of only a small number of people.

**Pitch**  The selling (pitching) of ideas to the media and other information receivers. A sales pitch to win a new client.

**Planter**  A public information manager who plays the role of delivering news releases to the media and encouraging them to use them as news.

**Planting**  The inclusion in the media of public information material.

**Policy**  An organization's basic doctrines that determine its attitudes and pattern of behavior.

**Poll**   A public opinion survey.

**Positioning**   Creating in the mind of a public (such as customers) the position of your organization and or products relative to other organizations and products.

**Position paper**   A paper that describes in detail the position of a company or organization with regards to an issue of concern to it.

**Power structure**   A dominant structure in society, politics, or the economy.

**PR**   Abbreviation for "public relations."

**PR wires**   Dedicated lines for commercial reception prepared for the media. In public relations, typically refers to a news organization that send out news stories to many newspapers, magazines, and other media.

**Presentation**   An explanation provided at a meeting on planning, services, and various other topics. In many cases, documents, graphic displays, film, and other materials are used.

**Press agentry**   The provision of public information about a certain well-known person that is intended to be of value as news to the media. It is carried out by a press agent.

**Press announcement**   An announcement to the media of important news by a company or organization. See also: press conference.

**Press briefing (or media briefing)**   Different to a press conference for an important announcement, press briefings are to provide the media with an explanation on the background to an announcement, the company's current status, its plans, etc. On occasions, they will include highly newsworthy topics. When conducted over lunch, they are called a press luncheon.

**Press caravan**   Activities in which a company, industry organization, local government, etc., visits each media outlet to explain and to appeal to the press on an important issue, etc.

**Press conference**   Held to provide journalists with information on events and news. The attendees are normally given an opportunity to ask questions.

**Press contact**   Term usually refers to the person within a company or organization who is responsible for providing information to the media.

**Press kit**   A folder, or USB flash drive, distributed to the media that contains news releases, photographs, background information about the client, etc.

**Press luncheon**   Refers to when an organization's leaders and executives have lunch with several media journalists, during which they explain their business and exchange opinions. Rather than announcing news, the aim is to deepen mutual understanding and friendship.

**Press monitoring**   See "media monitoring."

**Press preview**   On the completion and unveiling of an exhibition, event, or facility, inviting only the media for a viewing in advance of the general opening.

**Press release**   See "news release."

**Pressure group**   Organizations that lobby the government, companies, etc., to acquire, retain, and increase their own benefits and rights. They include groups representing professions and industries, consumer groups, etc.

**Prestige**   The fame of an individual, organization, or group.

**Pretesting**   Sampling and testing carried out before the main survey.

**Prime time**   The time band when the viewing rate is at its highest.

**Probability sample**   (1) A sample selected in the expected direction. (2) A sample that can accurately represent the target of the survey. (3) A survey in the form that all the people within the target group have a chance of being asked the questions.

**Product liability**   The PL Law (Product Liability Law) was enacted in 1995, and is the law that stipulates the liabilities of manufacturers for harm suffered by consumers due to product defects.

**Product recall**   A recall from consumers of products discovered to be defective so that they may be repaired or replaced.

**Profit and loss statement (P/L)**   A financial statement for a business entity, etc., showing in detail the calculations of the "revenues" for a certain period (accounting period) and the "costs" necessary to obtain those revenues, and the calculation of the "net profit" (or "net loss").

**Program**   An overview developed when deploying certain activities.

**Promo**   A promotional-use release that is distributed on film, videotape, slides, or some combination of these.

**Promotion**   Special activities carried out to draw attention to a certain person, product, organization, principles, etc.

**Propaganda**   Activities that distort the facts and that are intended to influence the opinions of others. It is an unethical, one-way form of communication.

**Propaganda devices**   Devices used for propaganda to influence people's behavior and opinions. They include speeches, documents, photographs, music, etc.

**Proposal**   A planning and proposal document for certain plans and services. They can be used for a presentation, sent by mail, or distributed.

**PRSA**   The Public Relations Society of America. It was founded in 1949 and has approximately 20,000 members.

**PRSSA**   Public Relations Student Society of America. It was founded in 1968 by the PRSA and has more than 8,500 members.

**Public (plural, "publics")**   The general public or a group of people who public relations professionals attempt to influence. The target public can range from a small group through to company shareholders, employees, customers, local communities, a government, or even an entire nation or the whole world.

**Public affairs**   A term mainly used for the corporate PR activities of government agencies and companies. It aims to realize public acceptance through community relations, consumer relations, etc. Sometimes used with practically the same meaning as public relations.

**Public information**   A term mainly used to refer to the public relations activities of government agencies, social work organizations, universities, etc. Japan's "koho" in its initial period was like this. A one-way type of communication. One method of public relations, focusing on actions within media relations. It is the planning and sending of messages through media outlets selected to promote the interests of the client. No money is paid to the media.

**Public involvement** Reflecting the voice of the people in planning in government. Particularly in regional development, after announcing the plan in advance, it is important to hold sufficient hearing interviews to listen to the opinions of local residents.

**Public opinion** The prevailing consensus among the public.

**Public relations** Generally conducted for the benefit of an individual, group, public or private institution, or company, it refers to the activities or the approach to determine, adjust, or influence the opinions of groups of people (stakeholders), or to guide them in a certain direction. It helps with the coordination between an organization and the groups it is targeting in the general public.

**Publisher** The person at the head of a publishing company, such as a newspaper company or magazine company, who has overall control over all matters, including accounting, technologies, management, and at times the editing and criticism.

**Puffy** Materials used for public information that are exaggerated and not based on the actual situation.

**Punch** A particularly emphasized point within a news article or broadcast program.

**Purposive sampling** Selecting opinion leaders to hear their opinions. Generally carried out when it is considered that the approval of this group is required for the public relations campaign to be a success.

**Quality circle (QC)** In the workplace, a group created to consider improvements, such as to business management methods and work processes.

**Quarterly report** A financial report released by a company showing its results for each quarter (a three-month period).

**Query** A question in writing submitted to an editor or broadcaster about a news report and its treatment.

**Quota sampling** Extracting a group with opinions that reflect the characteristics of the whole population.

**Random sample** An individual or group selected randomly.

**Reach** The number of viewers or households who watched a selected broadcast station's commercials or program during a certain time period.

**Recap** The repetition of the main points of a news article or program.

**Relationship management** Building, maintaining, and developing good relations with various stakeholders and target audiences in order to achieve the public relations targets.

**Relationship marketing** A marketing concept that prioritizes existing customers rather than focusing on the acquisition of new customers. It entails thoroughly surveying existing customers, providing them with products and services that meet their needs, improving the level of customer satisfaction (CS), and building long-term relationships with them.

**Release date** The date when the embargo on a release is lifted. Particularly for the manuscripts of speeches, etc., the embargo is lifted at the time that the speech starts.

**Reporters** News journalists, correspondents.

**Reputation management**   Managing the reputation and prestige of a company.

**Respondent**   A person asked to respond to a public opinion survey, etc.

**Return on assets (ROA)**   Profit divided by total assets (total capital). It is a financial indicator of overall profitability.

**Return on equity (ROE)**   Calculated by dividing the after-tax profits of a company by shareholders' equity. It can be said to be an indicator of profitability as seen from the shareholders' side.

**Review site**   Refers to sites such as Amazon, price.com, and Cookpad. On these sites, users can freely write reviews of products, which other site visitors can refer to as word-of-mouth information when making decisions on purchasing products.

**Risk management**   The management of and preparation for problems relating to the company's continued existence. Positioned between issue management, which is often an investigation in advance of a problem, and crisis management, which are mainly actions taken after the problem occurs.

**Roadshow**   Company briefings for investors. In Western countries, the briefings are held as a series in several locations, not just in one place, and so are generally called a roadshow.

**Round up**   A comprehensive summary in the form of an article.

**Royalty fee**   The fee paid to the writer for each copy of their work sold (normally, 10 to 15% of the retail price). Also, the fee received by the program distributor for the material used in the broadcast.

**Running story or breaking story**   A news story related to an incident that suddenly occurred (broke) and is still ongoing.

**Sample**   Some people selected from the total population to answer questions, such as for a public opinion survey. These opinions are sorted to represent opinions as a whole.

**Sample error**   An error arising from the way of taking the sample.

**Selective attention**   To select a specific item from among many target items in order to focus one's thinking.

**Semantic noise**   The use of words that are incomprehensible to the listening side. For example, the use of specialist economic terms in information for the general public.

**Semantics**   The study of words and their usage and interpretation.

**Sets in use**   Within the surveyed region, the ratio of households listening to the radio in a time period to total households. In the case of television, it is called HUT (households using television).

**Share or share of audience**   Within a certain time frame, the respective ratios (shares) of the total viewers for the programs of each respective station.

**Sidebar**   A subordinate article attached to the main article.

**Situation analysis**   An analysis of the position of a company or organization in its current situation.

**Slander**   Verbal defamation. See also: libel.

**Slant**   A particular emphasis within a news article or program. A tendency or viewpoint.

**Slush pile**  The mountain of unsolicited manuscripts sent to magazines, etc.

**Social contract**  A term generally used with regards to corporate social responsibility.

**Social media**  Refers to media with a strong two-way aspect, such as Twitter, Facebook, and YouTube, where users can create and share content.

**Social networking site/service (SNS)**  Websites that expand their networks through participants encouraging friends and acquaintances to also participate.

**Socially responsible investment (SRI)**  Selective investment in companies with high ethics, for example, on environmental protection or human rights.

**Soft news**  A soft news article is one that is not especially topical as news.

**Source credibility**  To obtain the agreement of the target group, a method that uses the professional knowledge, sincerity, and charisma of the representative.

**Spin**  News or information that has been tweaked or manipulated to express a certain view. People who use spin are called spin doctors.

**Split message**  A method of sending two or three different messages to different target groups to determine which of them is the most effective.

**Split run**  Inclusion of an article, etc., in only part of the total circulation of, for example, a newspaper or magazine.

**Spokesperson**  A person responsible for speaking on behalf of a company or organization, often to the news media.

**Sponsored film**  A movie produced from the funding of a company or organization to send its information or messages. Normally screened free of charge.

**Sponsorship**  The holding of cultural activities, sports events, etc., and the accompanying funding.

**Spread**  A photograph, copy, etc., such as a spread that covers one page without a gutter in the middle. Normally printed using a single printing plate.

**Staff function**  The analysis, planning, and communication carried out at an organization's headquarters, in contrast to the performance of duties by a line or branch.

**Stakeholder**  Investors in a company, shareholders, clients, employees, residents in the community where the company is located, etc.

**Story angle or peg**  The particular content of a story that attracts attention and increases the story's value.

**Straight news**  An article written in a conventional style.

**Stringer**  Journalists relied upon for reporting as required at locations remote from the head office or local bureau.

**Stunt**  An act to attract attention in order to disseminate public information.

**Stylebook**  A handbook for journalists for writing articles, etc. Includes how words are used, abbreviations, etc. Known as the journalists' handbook.

**Survey**  A survey to analyze the thinking of a market or a specific group.

**Sustainability**  In its wider meaning, it is the ability of humans, nations, and societies to sustain their development. In companies, it is developing a business by establishing a clear management philosophy and effectively utilizing internal resources while considering external factors, which wins the support of stakeholders.

**Tabloid**   A newspaper published in a size smaller than usual. Normally, a tabloid version is said to be composed of five columns per page.

**Teleconference**   A meeting held simultaneously at multiple venues with video and audio transmitted via cables or satellite.

**Teletext**   Information displayed on television screens in homes in print form, such as for shopping, share prices, news, etc.

**Telethon**   A program broadcast on television over several hours to raise money. Usually a mixture of calls for donations and entertainment programs.

**Test group**   A group selected to investigate responses to a product or ideas. See also: control group.

**Testing**   Testing of the responses to a product, event, issue, etc., of a limited region or group that have been carefully and skillfully selected.

**Tie-in**   (1) A single event carried out together by two or more organizations or groups. (2) Public information activities carried out in conjunction with an event already planned.

**Tight**   When there is little space or time to add new information in media like newspapers, broadcasts, etc.

**Time classifications**   Fees for broadcast times determined by the viewing rates.

**Tip**   Information leading to a news story.

**Tipping-in**   The work needed to create a printed material that inserts or appends pages that were not originally scheduled to be included. For example, when pages five and six are to be inserted into a ten-page booklet, or when inserting a cut piece of fabric as a sample into a catalogue, etc.

**TOB (takeover bid)**   When aiming to acquire a company, purchasing that company's shares from shareholders in the general public through a public offering. In accordance with the Securities and Exchange Act, the purchase period, the number of shares purchased, and the purchase price must be publicly announced.

**Trade journals**   Magazines and newspapers planned and edited for a certain industry, profession, or vocational group. Industry-specific newspapers and magazines.

**Trademark**   A name, symbol, or other such mark or design attached to a product. Trademarks are officially registered and their use by anyone other than their owner or manufacturer is legally prohibited.

**Trade publications**   Regularly published industry-specific newspapers and magazines. See also: trade journals.

**Traffic**   Department in charge of the production schedule in an advertising company. In broadcasting, the department in charge of all the program broadcasting.

**Transparency**   Management transparency. A company or organization discloses to stakeholders all its business activities without hiding anything. See also: disclosure.

**Update**   Making the information within a news article or other such material up-to-date.

**Video news release (VNR)**   A news release recorded on videotape and distributed to television stations. Some have audio descriptions, others do not.

**Video conference** A private television network that is used to join people together in various types of events, from business meetings taking place at remote locations to entertainment events. Ideally participants will be equipped with all the necessary devices, including large-screen television sets, video cameras, and satellite-relay equipment.

**Vignette** A short video work that can be a humorous or evocative depiction of an event or episode.

**Watermark** A watermark is a mark attached to paper and typically appears when light is cast on it. Today, there are also "digital watermarks."

**White paper** An informational document that explains an often complex issue for an organization.

**Workshop** A briefing session in which the participants can directly experience a company's product, services, etc.

**Wrap-up** A summary, the conclusion of activities, or a final report.

**Yellow journalism** A newspaper headlined by a sensational news story.

# INDEX

When the text is within a figure, the number span is in italic.
Eg, ability to create scenarios 133-*4*
Case studies are listed under that heading, as well as under company names
Eg Samsung 225-7